Future
NATURE

REVISED EDITION

a vision for conservation

W M ADAMS

BANC
CHALLENGING CONSERVATION

EARTHSCAN

Earthscan Publications Limited
London • Sterling, VA

Revised edition first published in the UK and USA in 2003 by
Earthscan Publications Limited

First edition 1996

A catalogue record for this book is available from the British Library

ISBN 1-85383-998-1 (pbk)

Typeset by BookEns Ltd, Royston, Herts/MapSet Ltd, Gateshead
Printed and bound by Creative Print and Design (Wales), Ebbw Vale
Cover design by Danny Gillespie
Cover illustration by Andrew Goldsworthy
Text illustrations by Barry Larking

For a full list of publications please contact:

Earthscan Publications Limited
120 Pentonville Road
London N1 9JN
Tel: +44 (0)20 7278 0433
Fax: +44 (0)20 7278 1142
Email: earthinfo@earthscan.co.uk
Web: www.earthscan.co.uk

22883 Quicksilver Drive, Sterling, VA
20166–2012, USA

Earthscan is an editorially independent subsidiary of Kogan Page Limited
and publishes in association with WWF-UK and the International
Institute for Environment and Development

Contents

Acknowledgements   vii
Foreword: Future Nature Revisited   ix

Introduction to the Revised Edition   xi

Chapter One	Finding Nature	1
Chapter Two	Constructing Conservation	11
Chapter Three	Nature Lost	27
Chapter Four	Conservation and the Global Village	57
Chapter Five	Culture and the Countryside	69
Chapter Six	Making Nature	81
Chapter Seven	Nature and the Wild	99
Chapter Eight	The Conservation Landscape	115
Chapter Nine	Nature, Landscapes, Lives	137
Chapter Ten	Releasing the Wild	159

Postscript   177

Notes and References   211
Further Reading   259
List of Abbreviations   265
Index   267

Acknowledgements

Future Nature was originally written in the mid-1990s for the British Association of Nature Conservationists (BANC) as part of their Conservation Agenda Project. This was sponsored by the World Wide Fund for Nature UK, the Countryside Commission, English Nature and the Department of the Environment for Northern Ireland. Its aims were to provide a critique of ideas and policy for conservation in Scotland, Northern Ireland, Wales and England, and at the same time to explore new thinking about nature (defined broadly to include species, habitats, ecosystems and landscapes) and our relations with it. The views expressed in the book do not represent those of the sponsoring organisations, those working for them, or those on their various governing boards and councils. Nor are the views expressed to be taken as those of BANC itself.

Many people helped me in researching and writing the first edition of *Future Nature*. First thanks must go to Peter Rawcliffe, whose knowledge, insights and support were invaluable. I gained enormously from our numerous and wide-ranging discussions, and from his advice on the project and the manuscript. The book could not have been written without him. I am also grateful to the many people who gave up their valuable time to speak with us and share their ideas and hospitality. I would in particular like to thank David Baldock, Paul Buckley, Adrian Colston, Paul Evans, James Fenton, Alan Holland, Kay Milton, Clive Potter, Adrian Phillips, Derek Ratcliffe and James Robertson, who were members of BANC's advisory group. They, with Mike Harley, Tony Juniper, Philip Lowe, Mark Liniado, Rick Minter and Ken Robertson contributed ideas and gave valuable advice on the first edition, and commented on the manuscript.

In preparing this revised edition of *Future Nature*, I have appreciated advice from some of the same people, and some new ones. I am particularly conscious of learning from John Cameron, Laura Cameron, Adrian Colston, Katherine Hearn, Rob Jarman, Martin Mulligan, Rick Minter,

David Russell and Steve Trudgill. Franc Hughes, Rob Jarman, Rick Minter, Adrian Phillips, James Robertson and David Russell were kind enough to read the new material and comment on it. None of these people bears any responsibility for what I have written: sins of omission and commission are mine alone.

I greatly appreciated Barry Larking's work on the design of the book, and admire greatly his drawings at the head and end of each chapter. I am very grateful to Andy Goldsworthy for providing the image used on the cover of both editions.

Above all I would like to thank Franc, Emily and Tom for their tolerance in the face of too many weekends and evenings of writing, and their wonderful enthusiasm for life.

Cambridge 2003

Foreword: *Future Nature* Revisited

When Bill Adams wrote *Future Nature*, he was arguing for a new approach to nature conservation. The people engaged in this work were "deep in their bunkers", and "entrenched in their own thinking". He appealed for a more confident, outward-looking thrust to conservation, strongly linked to the needs of people and as much about creation as about protection. That was 1995: how does the prescription stand up a few years later?

To me it is clear that the analysis was right then and it is even more relevant now. So, reprinting the bulk of the 1995 text unedited is quite appropriate, and a good way of restating a timely set of messages. But Adams has wrapped around it a new perspective — an Introduction and a Postscript written in the twenty-first century. These show that a lot has happened in a short time: new policy directions, big institutional changes and new conservation initiatives, all against the dramatic background of the upheavals of bovine spongiform encephalopathy (BSE) and foot and mouth. Yet, on the ground — where it matters for nature conservation — progress, if any, has been patchy and setbacks have been many; too often, it seems that "future nature" is dwindling nature.

Perhaps that is why one detects in Adams's new writing less confidence that the corner has been turned. One could believe in the early days of New Labour that transport policies would be fundamentally reshaped, that farming's destructive forces would be tamed, and that "sustainable development" would become more than rhetoric. But the untrammelled forces of consumerism and the lack of high political commitment towards conservation mean that the destruction of wildlife is still with us. It will take more than Biodiversity Action Plans (BAPs) to save tree sparrows, skylarks and dolphins: vested interests must be faced down.

So, where are the grounds for hope? Maybe it is in two ideas that came through strongly in *Future Nature*: the notion that people, not bureaucracies, will save (or destroy) nature; and the potential of large-scale creative conservation.

If you want to see "people power" at work, look at the Scottish island of Eigg. Here, some 60 or 70 people acted to rescue their land from neglectful absentee landlords. Working with the Scottish Wildlife Trust, they are now building a sustainable economy and society based on the protection of the island's superb wildlife and formidable scenic beauty. It can be seen, too, all round Britain in the thousands of local groups — many supported by European, government or lottery money — who are working to improve their own local environment. Such action takes place in villages and towns; it involves young people and ethnic minorities as well as those dwelling in "middle England". Thus, it is bound to be small and local. It does not grab the headlines as do the marches of the Countryside Alliance; but it similarly involves hundreds of thousands of people.

But the most exciting thing about nature conservation today must be the sheer scale of some of the restoration and landscape creation schemes, many of which are discussed in *Future Nature*. The recovery of the Cambridgeshire Fens, the Essex marshes, the heaths of the South and South West and the reedbeds in Wales; the planting of the National Forest in the English Midlands, and the rebuilding of the Caledonian Forests — these and many other projects arise for a bunch of reasons, including the search for alternative land uses and rural economies at a time when some farmland is no longer required for food production; the need for ecologically-based land and water management to deal with the effects of climate change; and the pooling of largish sums of money that were not available for conservation a dozen years ago. Maybe there is even a bit of "millennial" thinking at work here, too. Big projects should bring big benefits for nature; but they also show that there is a place for wildness in our intensively managed land. What better symbol of "future nature" could there be than the Wetlands Centre in Barnes? Surrounded by the metropolis, and over-flown every few minutes by jets bound for Heathrow Airport, it provides thousands of people with access to wild areas of water upon which many species of birds come to feed and breed.

So, this revised edition of Bill Adams's excellent, scholarly, but readable, book is neither a celebration of conservation victory, nor an acknowledgement of its defeat. But we can see now — a little more clearly than we could in 1995 — the scale of the challenge. We will not make much progress towards conservation through the panoply of measures associated with public policy unless we can make nature central to people's lives.

Professor Adrian Phillips, CBE
March 2003

Introduction to the Revised Edition

Feeling the Fens

On damp nights in November, the cold landscape of the East Anglian Fens still seems to reach right into the heart of Cambridge. If, for a moment, you can allow yourself to ignore the intrusive bright lights of high street chain stores, and the acrid grumbling of traffic, you might imagine that the great dark open space of Parker's Piece still carries the whiff of fenland mist. Down by the river there might still be barges at their wharves beneath the green lawns of King's College, and on the rough grass of Stourbridge Common the oyster stalls of the largest town fair in Europe. By day the illusion does not work — the oyster shells are just shards in the grass of the children's playground, and the few warehouses that remain are re-developed as shops and offices. But the shifting, booming, high-tech town of Cambridge lies on the edge of what was once the wetland expanse of the Fens. Sometimes, with a little imagination, you can believe it is still there — a huge expanse of open water, reedbed and seasonal grazing, herons, eels and fen slodgers; out there somewhere, beyond the science park and the torrent of traffic on the A14, is a wild green expanse with a small town at its edge.

It has all gone, of course, long ago. A glance at the map of eastern England shows the sharp diagonal slashes of Cornelius Vermuyden's New and Old Bedford Rivers, dug to carry the waters of the Ouse away to the Wash, and start the long history of draining the Fens to release the fertility of their peat and silt soils. The speculative investment of the Earl of Bedford and the expatriate expertise of Vermuyden and his successors were eventually successful. Wind, steam, diesel and electricity have powered the pumps that have kept the fenland soils dry, desperately keeping pace with the shrinkage of the peat and the fen "blows" that swept the dusty soil away.[1] Some land now lies below sea level, and even house roofs are ominously lower than the river dykes. Apart from the devastating floods of the 1950s, technology has sufficed to keep nature at bay, and the Fens have provided an industrial site for some of Britain's most productive agriculture.

Only here and there did isolated remnants of the old fenland survive, mostly tiny tangled thickets of scrub. They have become famous nature reserves, their names a roll-call of nature saved from the hard drainer's hand: the fens of Chippenham, Wicken, Woodwalton and Holme. Their ecological memory and patches of water and damp soil retain a remarkable diversity of species, and they have been the subject of endless scientific investigation and intricate and painstaking conservation management.[2] For example, Wicken Fen began life as a nature reserve in 1899 when a tiny piece of land (of less than 1 ha in extent) was donated to the National Trust.[3] By its centenary in 1999, it had grown to over 320 ha: a conservation success, although it was still less than one thousandth of the area of undrained wetland that once existed. Its management has involved the re-creation of former economic harvests from the fen — particularly sedge cutting for thatch — now intricately diversified to deal with the impacts of progressive ecological change.

As I described in *Future Nature* in 1995, such places epitomise the energetic science-driven enterprise of conservation in the UK, with prodigious amounts of work being invested to secure and maintain species diversity on small areas of land "saved" from agriculture or urban industrial spoilation. At Wicken, management plans specify distinct regimes of treatment for a mosaic of blocks on the sedge fen, each adapted to optimise conditions for particular species.[4] This furious enterprise has been remarkably successful: over 7000 species have been recorded.[5] At the same time, the fen itself has grown steadily drier, requiring even more extensive attempts to re-wet it by sinking a waterproof outer membrane and pumping in unwanted water from shrinking surrounding farmland. Even this ingenious win–win solution is not unproblematic, since farmland runoff is over-fertilised for the particular ecosystems of the nature reserve.

Places such as Wicken Fen are both the pride and the shame of British conservation: wonderfully managed, artificially maintained and, above all, tiny fragments of habitat.[6] These are, indeed, nature "reserves", plucked from the destructive mainstream of economic life as E.R. Lankester urged way back in 1914 when he wrote about the Society for the Promotion of Nature Reserves, whose founder, Charles Rothschild, presented the first strips of Wicken Fen to the National Trust. For Lankester, nature needed sanctuary from human demands. In announcing the establishment of the Society for the Promotion of Nature Reserves in Nature, he wrote: "It is not too late to rescue here and there larger and smaller areas from this awful and ceaselessly spreading devastation." The solution was: "to secure by purchase or gift the right to preserve from destruction in this country as much and as many as possible of the invaluable surviving haunts of nature."[7] This the conservation movement did through the course of the twentieth century, with remarkable success.

Conservation's century

The rise of conservation as part of the wider Western environmental movement is one of the great stories of the twentieth century. The growth of conservation in the UK, particularly in the period after the end of the Second World War, is described in some detail in Chapters 2 and 3 of this book.[8] The chief measure of the success of that enterprise is the dense network of conservation designations that have flowered across the virtual landscape of planners' maps, and the exotic jungle of acronyms that denote them: National Nature Reserves (NNRs), Sites of Special Scientific Interest (SSSIs), Areas of Outstanding Natural Beauty (AONBs), Special Areas for Conservation (SACs), Special Protection Areas (SPAs) and their many etymologically overweight cousins.[9]

Yet, as *Future Nature* argued, this very success also reflects the profound limitations of the twentieth century's model of conservation; the very forcefulness and industry of conservation's promoters are also their weakness. For, as the diversity and extent of designated land grew, the area of land valued by conservationists shrank. As conservation won mainstream support as a legitimate focus of public concern and expenditure, so it failed to keep pace with the very destruction that fuelled its growth. Conservation seemed locked in an everlasting cycle of lamentation for lost nature, its evangelical zeal continually recharged by its efforts to turn back the rising tide.[10]

For much of the second half of the twentieth century, the dogma of maximising agricultural production was unchallenged in British policy. In debates about the countryside, the Ministry of Agriculture, Fisheries and Food (MAFF) was both church and inquisition, and only conservationists dissented, vainly protesting at the impact of the industrialised methods on the countryside. By the 1980s, conservation in the British countryside had reached crisis point as the very public debates about conservation and agriculture around the passage of the Wildlife and Countryside Act 1981 showed.[11] Through the 1980s there were tentative moves towards adopting a more integrated policy, with — on one side — expensive management agreements to persuade landowners to manage SSSIs in ways that maintained their wildlife interest, and — on the other — innovative agri-environment schemes (such as Environmentally Sensitive Areas – ESAs –

and, eventually, Countryside Stewardship and Tir Cymen) to promote more environmentally-sensitive land use by rewarding landowners who stuck to agreed land management regimes.[12]

By the 1990s, the high cost and limited impacts of this approach to policy were becoming obvious. Furthermore, the post-war consensus about public support for maximising agricultural production had begun to crumble. The vast cost of the Common Agricultural Policy (CAP) and the new international orthodoxy of "free trade" both suggested that time was up for the old regime. The economic and environmental costs of agricultural policy were suddenly more widely clear. Rural communities, stripped of population, employment and services by decades of agricultural intensification, faced real social deprivation, and yet were the subject of unprecedented development pressures from new homes, roads and commercial sites — not least, the rampant parallel universe of consumerism in out-of-town shopping centres. The battle over the Newbury Bypass, with impassioned protestors up trees, and the threatened Desmoulin's whorl snail in the Lambourn Floodplain, was joined and lost.[13]

Despite the apparent policy advances of the preceding decade, wildlife habitats were disappearing at an alarming rate during the 1990s, and conservationists still too often found themselves limited to wailing in complaint over the loss of places, species, landscapes and distinctiveness. The bullish corporate spin of the new national government conservation organisations and the cloning of business thinking in Biodiversity Action Plans brought new flavours to the old recipes for conservation, but — arguably — did little to meet the old challenges.[14] At the same time, there were lots of new ideas in circulation about conservation. One was the challenge of sustainability. The Rio Conference on Environment and Development in 1992 resonated strongly in the UK (see Chapter 9). The government responded with four weighty volumes in 1994 setting out UK policy on sustainable development, biodiversity, climate change and sustainable forestry, and had them signed by every major Minister in government.[15] Local governments were poised to address local sustainability in Local Agenda 21 initiatives.[16] The Environment Act 1995 was finally passed, creating the Environment Agency and the Scottish Environmental Protection Agency, and the long-awaited White Paper "Rural England: a nation committed to a living countryside" was published.[17] Alongside these policy initiatives, there was a growing recognition within conservation circles of the importance of cultural dimensions of human engagement with nature. In the UK, in particular, there was an effort to reach out into the world of the arts. As Martin Spray commented in his editorial in an *Ecos* special issue on "The Art of the Environment", many conservationists are too ready to reject approaches associated with artistic, personal and emotional responses to the world.[18]

Future Nature was therefore published at a time of great self-reflection in British conservation, when debates about conservation, agriculture and the countryside were vigorous and rapidly changing. When I was invited by the British Association of Nature Conservationists' (BANC's) Council to undertake the project that led to the book, they initially envisaged something like a strategic plan for conservation.[19] I think they imagined a new analysis of countryside change and policy opportunities that would set out a vision for the future, complete with targets and policy initiatives. This would have been both very challenging (because many such agendas for action were being produced during the 1990s, most by people much more engaged with the cut and thrust of policy than me); but it would also have been rather formulaic. It could not capture what seemed to me an opportunity to address more profound changes in current conservation debates. There was, at the time, a new mood in conservation, an openness to new ways of thinking allied with a clear dissatisfaction with established ways of doing things.

With the approval of a very engaged advisory committee, and with the support and encouragement of my research assistant and mentor, Peter Rawcliffe, I decided to attempt something different. The book tried to capture some of these new ideas about conservation and to tease out the new thinking about nature, science and society on which they drew. It tried to set these ideas against a background of the evolution of conservation thinking and action throughout the twentieth century. The success of this enterprise can be seen in the chapters that follow, which present the original text of *Future Nature*.

In the book, I tried to link analysis of conservation policy to my own experiences of nature, both past and present. In doing this, I ran the risk of self-indulgence; but I felt that it was important not to pretend that the issues were not personal. Coming back to the text now, eight years later, I recognise the emotional energy that arose from the tension of forging a link between analysis and feeling. I am glad that I made the attempt to ground the book's discussion in place and experience.[20] In preparing the revised edition, I have been inspired and reassured by Kay Milton's book *Loving Nature*, with its careful exposition and defence of emotion in our understanding of nature, and our relation to it.[21]

Since 1995, much, of course, has changed with me as well as with conservation. I have learned a lot, mostly inadvertently. I have discovered that beaches are to be judged as much by their surf as their rock pools, and that mountain huts, and mountain tops, are back within reach. I have become slightly less unaware of views of life through teenage eyes. I have tended to spend more time looking for skateboard ramps and cinemas and less time in local nature reserves than I once did. On the TV, *The Simpsons* and *Robot Wars* have had as much air time in the living room as wildlife documentaries, and the inhabitants of Fanghorn Forest and the Plains of Rohan have become a more common feature of everyday conversation than those of Hayley Wood or the Breckland. None of this has fundamentally changed my understanding of the relations between people and nature. If anything, it has heightened the sense that I had in 1995 that conservation has to be broader (and is, certainly, more fundamental) than it often seemed during the twentieth century, even in those decades when it became an important element in government policy.

In the culture around us, I have watched Sonic the Hedgehog lose out to Tomb Raider and many other virtual realities, and the mobile phone bind everyone into the claustrophobia of the instant. The world wide web has become part of the structure of intellectual life, and the information revolution has so eroded the friction of distance that economic and cultural change seems to transcend geography and homogenise place, nature and culture.[22] These changes are familiar enough, as is their excitement and challenge.[23] Their significance for the way in which we understand and influence non-human nature, and the ways in which we understand and practise conservation, are profound. Many are discussed in the pages that follow, and some of the implications of recent changes are discussed in the Postscript that follows Chapter 10.

What can we say about conservation at the start of the twenty-first century? What has changed since 1995? Certainly, the achievements of the British conservation movement in the twentieth century were considerable, and those who worked and struggled for them may rightly feel proud of their efforts. However, I would still say, as I said in 1995, that these achievements are dwarfed by the challenges at hand. We have rarely managed either bold or joined-up thinking in conservation policy. We have got a long way with compartmentalised approaches, working within the dominant paradigm, albeit sometimes as its conscience and even as a catalyst. At best, we have fought our "corner", accepting that this will be viewed as just one sector of public policy and public life.

But conservation is not something that can be separated from the rest of life. We don't only "do" conservation when we tramp the Cuillin, or enjoy the bluebells in a Bedfordshire woodland — we do it when we drive to work, or cook our Welsh lamb-burgers over our coppice-product charcoal barbecue, or turn on our computers. We do it if we blow our notional carbon budget flying abroad for a conference, or switch on our mobile phone. Mostly, we think of these wider engagements with nature in terms of "environmentalism" or "sustainability", and see them as somewhat removed from the specific task of nature conservation. Without doubt, this is a mistake. As Norman Moore points out in his account of his creation of a nature reserve near his home, *Oaks, Dragonflies and People*, "small things are inextricably mixed with big things".[24] He proposes the concept of "Future Care" politics, to combine the concerns of today with the needs of future generations. There is a link between the naturalist's concern for species with humankind's concern with survival.

Too often, we have offered a thin and dilettante vision of nature, of special things beleaguered in special places. Most people cannot see the significance of such separate nature for their daily lives, or of their lives for conservation.[25] As a result, these connections are all too easily ignored. But we do engage with nature very holistically. We relate to the more-than-human world all the time, not just when we visit nature reserves.[26] We do it through our pleasure in open spaces, clean environments and wildlife; but we also do it by our decisions about the way in which we behave, the way in which we live and the things that we consume and throw away. David Orr recently commented that "something akin to spiritual renewal is the *sine qua non* of the transition to sustainability".[27] Whether or not he is right, there can be no doubt that conservation needs to start at home, in our understanding of ourselves and the rest of nature.

CHAPTER ONE

Finding Nature

This then is what the past offers us for the future. A fine tradition of developing town and countryside as a home, proudly yet modestly decorated. A fine tradition of seizing the opportunities of social and economic change for the creation of new beauties and new possibilities of happiness.
Thomas Sharp[1]

Driving to the sea

On a clear sunny August afternoon last summer, I walked with my family along a beach in North Norfolk. To one side lay the sea, its dark mass picked out by lines of steep white wavecrests, being driven in on the sharp northeasterly wind. To the other side lay the land, a thin green strip of fields and trees, just visible in gaps between the dunes. The beach itself was vast and empty, the wind making sand grains bounce across the surface in a miniature sandstorm, delicate traceries of smoke that prickled bare shins and shotblasted our ankles. The sand was cemented into hard ripples, and in places revealed blocks of ancient saltmarsh muds or was cut by deep channels and pools. Underfoot were flints, lugworm casts, oyster and razor shells and odd fragments of swimmer crabs, presumably abandoned by passing gulls. The only people in sight were a few small groups huddled under the face of the dunes against the wind, some birdwatchers, and in the far distance a line of

1

horse-riders at the sea's edge, horses' legs and riders' bodies impossibly linked by mirage into strange beasts. Above, the sky was blue and clear, a huge bowl stretched from one horizon to the other, from the green strip of land to the brown line of the sea.

The sea itself, when we came to it, was warm and thick with sediment. Along its edge, dancing above the steep wavelets, flew common and sandwich terns, and further out gulls and cormorants patrolled to and fro. As the tide began to turn, small groups of dunlin and the first godwits began to appear, disturbed by the rising waters. The terns were miles from their breeding sites at Scolt Head and Blakeney Point, but much further from their wintering grounds. Soon they would move on their long migration, just as the dunlin had done to reach this coast from the high Arctic. Other birds on passage were there too, although it needed more patience than we had to look for them. Somewhere in the sea-buckthorn and bramble scrub behind the dunes lurked a barred warbler, and with it were many other small birds that had dropped out of the sky onto the comforting vegetation behind the flat, empty beach.

You never know what will turn up on this coast. Anchored to the low fields of East Anglia, the thin strip of shore is at the same time a landmark on flyways that stretch across the earth. The familiar features of the beach have a significance that stretches far beyond the immediate surroundings, over the horizon to other places and through countless networks of links between living things and ecosystems. Walking between the tide's edge and the dunes, with even half an eye for the birds and the beach, there is an amazing sense that you are poised on the edge of the spinning globe, a privileged observer of natural exchange in ecosystems that are linked and that function at a global scale. On that day in August, moving between land and sea and sky, it seemed that nature was all around us, strong and diverse, resilient and rewarding. Wildlife, landscape and people merged in an unbreakable union, unproblematic and accessible.

In Britain we have a love affair with the seaside which shows no sign of ending. It builds on more than a century of fashion and shared experience, combining Victorian beliefs about the salubrious effects of sea bathing and the mass tourism of holiday camps and the private car. The Countryside Commission recently wrote that "we value the coast because it is symbolic for island people with a seafaring history and because for 150 years it has meant holidays".[2] It has certainly always been so for me, for like countless others I have many good memories of holidays on beaches. However my feeling for beaches, particularly wild beaches, goes beyond this unfocused association with pleasures past. These places seem to have a very particular power. This lies in the sense of freedom that beaches offer, their sheer openness, and the diversity and novelty of the life they support.

The notion that wild stretches of coast are in some way precious, and as a result have particular value, is lodged fairly deep in my psyche. If I had to sum these feelings up in a single word, I would say that the thing about beaches that makes them so important to me is their *naturalness*. They are places that literally have a life of their own, where rhythms of tides and seasons set an agenda that seems to stand outside human time. Events like storms or falls of migrants come at moments not of human choosing. Beaches are places where the human frame is dwarfed and where human technology and power are themselves framed. On beaches, it seems as if nature has power, and the human capacity to direct is set in context. Humans are seen to be actors on an open stage.

This sense that nature has both value and power is not, I think, confined to the coast. Through much of my life I have felt very much the same about other places, particularly those that I encountered when I was young. I remember the excitement of finding a bee orchid amidst the richly flowered grassland of the Surrey downs, and the delights of holidays in the open country of Dartmoor. As I got older, our summer holidays were spent camping, and in time the wild places and quiet field corners of North Wales, Yorkshire and Scotland took a valued place in my scrapbook of nature and natural beauty.

As an adult, I have not lost my sense of the value of places such as this. Indeed, I seem to be hard-wired to need them, and to feel concern at the state of their wildlife, landscape and patterns of economic life. Somewhere in my childhood I acquired a kind of instinctive environmentalism, with at its core a sense of the power and the value of nature. This feeling for nature has survived remarkably unchanged through my life. My ideas have grown more complex, and sometimes struggle for air under the welter of fact, theory and conservation activity with which I have tended to burden them, but my basic concerns, I think, have endured. Furthermore, I do not think that my feelings for nature are at all unique, or even very unusual. A similar sense of the power and value of nature lies at the heart of many people's concern for conservation. Behind the political arguments and the advertising, the research and the day-to-day business of conservation organisations, lies a dynamic awareness of nature and naturalness — a sense of the value of wildness.

It is this concern that this book tries to uncover, exploring the links between our ideas about nature and the activities we call conservation. I have chosen the word "nature" to describe the subject of my discourse with care. As will become clear, it is a word that presents a number of elegant and complex problems of definition. These I deal with in later chapters. However, it is the only word that seems to embrace both the utilitarian and scientific concerns of "wildlife conservation", and the pastoral and cultural connotations of "the countryside". It is also the only word I can find whose meaning can grip the sense that I have of the continually renewed vitality of organisms, the dynamism of physical processes and the cultural complexity of landscapes. The turbulence and the wildness of nature is a counterpoint to human

3

creativity and industry. It is the tension between these two, the wild and the human-made, that must surely form the fundamental dynamic of conservation.

Coasts, cars and conservation

The Norfolk coast is the nearest to our home. We go there when we can, to do the things that families do on beaches. We build sandcastles that the sea washes away, we find shells and odd bits of flotsam that the sea provides, we splash in the waves, and we look for birds and beasts. I do pretty much the same things on the beach with my children that I did when my parents took me to the seaside. The beaches are different, but the thrill and the lure are the same. Not much, it seems, has changed in a generation. Indeed, it could be argued that not much has changed in two generations. My mother's parents bought a car as long ago as 1922, and her first experience of family holidays was on the beaches of Cornwall, reached after long and adventurous days on the road. My father bought his first car, a three-wheeled Morgan, in the 1930s, and he was devoted to the joys of motoring and the escape it offered from London to the beckoning countryside.

Living in London as a child, I too came to think that you could escape by driving, to the seaside or to other places. Nature was there, accessible for those willing to rise up early enough. Already, however, things were changing. In the 1960s we drove to visit grandparents on the Sussex coast, bemoaning the traffic. As I grew up I saw the road change, progressively straightened and widened, and the Wealden towns by-passed. It is the same on the road from Cambridge to the sea. To reach the seaside we rush through the Fens and the rolling countryside of Norfolk on roads that are busy but swift, all rebuilt in the last twenty years. The beach we come to has the same appeal, and it looks as "natural" as such beaches ever did. However, the East Anglian countryside through which we travel has been transformed, even since my own childhood. The landscape has been refashioned by industrial farming, its villages and its fields caught up in new economic patterns, and of course it is cut through by new fast roads and the new people and economies they bring. Furthermore, to reach "nature" on the beach, we sit for two hours in a private car, an expensive and ephemeral metal box that consumes resources and leaves behind a cocktail of pollutants. That car both epitomises the economic and cultural changes of the last half-century, and is also the biggest single cause of such change in the countryside.

It is a bizarre paradox that in order to experience the "natural" delights of the seashore I consume resources and endorse the transformation of the countryside in this way. It is not just curious and perhaps embarrassing that I (and the vast majority of "conservationists" in Britain) do this, it also reveals a profound flaw in our understanding of what nature is, and what conservation should be.

The conservation of "nature" cannot be carried out in a vacuum from the rest of life. We care about the countryside and wild species and habitats, but our very lives and lifestyles threaten them in profound and complex ways. Conservation should not be based on strategies that protect "nature" in special places, while it is destroyed or degraded in others. The values of places like the coast are obvious, and cry out for care, but these are not the only ones where "nature" presents itself. The value of special places, like wild beaches, does not mean that other places have no value. The wheat fields of East Anglia, roads and houses and city streets are also places where people can touch the edge of the vastness and complexity of global ecosystems, and where they can be touched by the power and inspiration of nature.

Conserving nature

The coast of the UK seems to be natural and unchanging, but its naturalness and sense of permanence is to a large extent illusory. Not only is it an illusion, it is one deliberately created, a skilful *trompe l'oeil*. The North Norfolk coast is indeed natural in a sense, but it is a naturalness that is closely monitored and maintained through the practice of conservation. This conservation embraces both concern for nature (species and habitats) and for landscapes. It is achieved by a whole battery of legal and administrative measures, particularly the designation of particular areas of land, and is done by a wide range of organisations, including both local and national government bodies and non-governmental organisations (NGOs). Their policies and plans are fostered by grants from diverse sources, and the work of professional staff of many kinds (from boardwalk builders to scientists), and highly committed bands of volunteers. These conservation efforts are supported, to some degree at least, by the general public, in the form of both visitors and local people. They make their contribution to the "naturalness" of the coast by accepting constraints on their freedom of movement and action, for example in following boardwalks to the beach or bans on the use of off-road vehicles.

The North Norfolk Coast is probably the most completely protected landscape in Britain. Almost the whole of the coast is contained within one or more vast Sites of Special Scientific Interest (SSSI),[3] as is a huge area of the Wash to the West. In addition, conservation trusts own long stretches of coast, most prominently the National Trust, the Norfolk Wildlife Trust and the Royal Society for the Protection of Birds (RSPB), and most of the rest is held by private owners who are conservation-minded. Several stretches of the coast (notably Scolt Head Island and Blakeney Point) are designated as

5

National Nature Reserves by English Nature. For good measure, the whole coast around Scolt Head is classified as a Biosphere Reserve (a classification overseen by UNESCO), and the Wash is also a Ramsar Site and a Special Protection Area under the EC Birds Directive. To cap it all, the whole stretch of the coast between Holme-next-the-Sea and Weybourne is designated by the Countryside Commission as a Heritage Coast, and this same stretch and a considerable tract of country inland (an area of some 451 square kilometres) is designated as an Area of Outstanding Natural Beauty (AONB), in recognition of their outstanding landscapes and their need for sensitive management. The North Norfolk coast, with the dunes of Gibraltar Point north of the Wash, are now among the proposed "Special Areas for Conservation", to be listed and protected under the EC Habitats Directive.[4]

This is an astonishing blanket of conservation bureaucracy to be draped over one strip of coast. The range of organisations involved might seem a recipe for disaster, but in fact, whatever the efficiency, or otherwise, of this battery of institutional defences, they appear to have worked. Conservation has not been so successful everywhere in Britain, but there is no doubt that it has allowed the Norfolk coast to retain a large measure of its beauty and biological diversity.

The conservation measures deployed to protect the dunes and marshes of Norfolk mostly date back only fifty years. At the end of the 1940s, conservation became part of a new approach to the manifold problems of town and country, involving the rehabilitation of towns, economic revitalisation of the countryside, planning for leisure and the creation of new national and regional parks and nature reserves. Years of debate in government committees bore fruit in bold new legislation in 1947 and 1949, the centrepiece from the point of view of conservation being the National Parks and Access to the Countryside Act 1949. This established the National Parks Commission and the Nature Conservancy. Conservation had won a recognised place in post-war public life, and had become part of the expanded responsibilities of government. There were lists of candidate National Nature Reserves and National Parks, and government organisations to designate them. The Nature Conservancy had a statutory duty also to manage land. The pattern of postwar conservation began to be established through the designation of protected areas in rural Britain.

The ideas about conservation thrashed out during the 1940s, and the organisations that were then created, have proved tough and mostly fairly serviceable. Without their vision, nature would have met greater destruction long ago. Chapter Two, *Constructing Conservation*, describes the way in which conservation has developed. It looks in particular at the long-running debates about government involvement in National Parks and National Nature Reserves, and explores both what the government bodies have achieved on the ground in the last four and a half decades and the many changes in their organisation and fortunes. It also discusses the rapid growth of the voluntary conservation movement.

Despite this story of successful expansion and growth, the record of conservation achievement since the end of the Second World War has been very poor. This is the subject of Chapter Three, *Nature Lost*. This reviews the now all-too familiar tale of habitat loss and landscape change, looking in detail at the problem of loss of Sites of Special Scientific Interest (SSSIs), as well as problems of pollution and climatic change. It also discusses the prospects for new developments under the EC Habitat Directive and the Biodiversity Action Plan, and the attendant problems.

It is clear that the established approaches to conservation in Britain have limits, and that we are rapidly approaching them. Despite enormous efforts, conservationists have managed to do little but slow or redirect forces that have proved almost universally destructive of wild nature. Whatever aspect one looks upon, nature is in retreat, and the very things about nature that so inspired the passions and the minds of thinkers in the 1940s have been reduced and degraded. Conservation is regarded now as an important factor in planning, and a legitimate land use, yet everywhere conservationists struggle to slow the reduction in the diversity and wildness of natural places, and to turn back the apparently inexorable tide of change. In Chapter Four, *Conservation and the Global Village*, I try to explain this failure, by analysing the forces that have transformed the countryside in the restructuring of the agricultural industry. The analysis goes further, however, to link this restructuring to wider global economic changes, and to link those back to lifestyles, and to conservation itself. Conservation has remained remarkably unchanged in its fundamental approach since the 1940s, but much else has changed.

There is a need now to break the mould of thinking about conservation, and to match conservation practice to the challenges of the late twentieth century. It is commonly remarked that the conservation system in this country needs reform, that new approaches are needed to landowners, to the survival needs of species or to the management of habitat. This is true, but it is not the point. The real problem is not that new powers, or new institutions, are needed (although this also may be true). The real need is for new *ideas* and new ways of thinking. I begin the search for those new ideas in Chapter Five, *Culture and the Countryside*. This considers the fact that while we value the countryside because it seems "natural", in contrast to the city, the distinction is largely in our minds. The chapter discusses ideas about the cultural construction of the countryside, and the pastoral ideal. It concludes that what we value about the countryside is the meanings we attach to it, in art, literature and personal experience. Conservation has a vital role in holding and sustaining these meanings.

Chapter Six, *Making Nature*, explores the way in which nature, too, is to a large extent human-made, both physically and in the sense that we attach values to "wild" creatures or landscapes. Many of the most valued features in the countryside are at least in part the work of human hands. Ecological changes caused by human action blend in complex ways with changes from other causes, and furthermore ideas in ecology about change have themselves begun to shift. The chapter looks at these changing ideas in ecology, and particularly the implications of ideas about disturbance and "non-equilibrium" ecology for conservation. The chapter also discusses the significance of studies of the sociology of science for our understanding of naturalness, and considers the changing role of science in conservation.

Chapter Seven, *Nature and the Wild*, develops the argument that conservation draws deeply on the cultural values attached to both landscape and "wild nature". I focus on the relations between people and nature, and values of nature and naturalness. Nature's cultural value lies both in the histories locked in patterns of species and ecosystems, and also in nature's capacity to stand outside human action and thought. The chapter also addresses the intrinsic value of nature, and emphasises the importance of the essential wildness of nature in providing the dynamic that drives conservation. The chapter discusses utilitarian arguments for conservation, and the use of environmental economics to put a money value on species and landscapes. It argues that these techniques may be useful, but fail to capture the full range of reasons why nature is important. The chapter then goes on to argue that one of conservation's core tasks is to create and maintain links between people and nature, and it outlines opportunities for doing this in urban conservation and in the arts.

In Chapter Eight, *The Conservation Landscape*, I argue that conservation should be developed to embrace the whole landscape. I discuss the problems of the fragmentation of habitats within the landscape, and the problems caused by the isolation of protected areas. I suggest that conservation should move beyond the limits of protected areas to a concern with the whole landscape, and describe various new ideas that are starting to do this. I urge the need for a creative approach to conservation to combat fragmentation in the landscape, describing the need for habitat creation and re-creation, and explaining how this can be done and the problems with it. The chapter explores the potential for such work created by European agricultural surpluses, and the various measures that exist that allow creative approaches to conservation.

These ideas are developed in Chapter Nine, *Nature, Landscapes, Lives*, through a discussion of the place of local communities in conservation, and the needs to link conservation with wider economic patterns. An account of innovations in linking local communities with protected areas leads on to a discussion of the potential for tackling both large-scale conservation objectives and socio-economic renewal in an integrated way, using the example of crofting in Scotland. The discussion is then widened to consider the need to integrate conservation and questions of sustainable development and a green economy, and the possible relevance of the idea of bioregionalism to the UK is considered.

In the final chapter, *Releasing the Wild*, I consider the possibility of developing the ideas of creative conservation (introduced in Chapter Eight) on a large scale, especially the notion of creating large areas of wilderness. I discuss in particular projects to develop large areas of forest in Scotland. Large-scale creative conservation is an exciting possibility, if it can involve both the restoration of nature and the re-invigoration of local communities. However, the most important task for conservation is to address the wildness of nature, and to achieve this it will be necessary to take account of physical and biological processes that work on a large scale and over long time periods. I argue, therefore, that conservation must move from the idea of the conservation of place to the conservation of process, and I explore how this might be done using examples from riverine and coastal environments.

At the end of the book, I offer four simple principles for conservation action that I hope capture the principles and ideas I have discussed. I suggest that we should seek to maintain the diversity of landscapes and ecosystems, particularly through creative conservation; we should build room for nature into economic life, both locally in rural areas and nationally in our choices of how to live; we should try to build connections between people and nature, particularly in cities but also elsewhere; and we should organise our conservation to allow natural processes to function, and create conditions for them to do so.

If there is one central contention in this book, it is that conservation needs to be built on a foundation of individual awareness of and concern for nature. I believe that it is here, on the ground of the relations between people and nature, that conservation must stand if it is to move forwards. It is here that the future of nature lies. Conservation is well-established in the UK; it has a fairly large public following and a reasonable basis for action in existing legislation. What we need now is imagination, combined with a burning sense of the value of nature, its importance to human life and its place in a sustainable economy. Much can be done. It is on our vision, and our energy, that the future of nature depends.

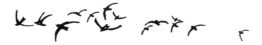

CHAPTER TWO

Constructing Conservation

*There can be few national purposes which, at so modest a cost, offer so large a prospect
of health-giving happiness for the people*
John Dower[1]

Nature and national interest

Recognition of the value and importance of natural places like the north
Norfolk coast dates back a long way.[2] Blakeney Point was given to the
National Trust early in its life, in 1912, and Scolt Head followed it into Trust
hands through a further gift in 1923. Botanical research by F.W. Oliver and
A.G. Tansley had drawn attention to Blakeney Point, and both Blakeney
Point and Scolt Head were on the first lists of proposed nature reserves in
Britain, drawn up by the Society for the Promotion of Nature Reserves in
1915, in an attempt to ward off destruction during the First World War.[3] The
National Trust was also offered Cley Marshes, but they declined to accept
them. The Norfolk Naturalists' Trust was established in 1926 specifically in
order to acquire Cley Marshes as a nature reserve. These places continued to
be among those proposed as nature reserves by a series of non-governmental
organisations through the 1940s.[4] Blakeney Point and Scolt Head were listed
among the 73 National Nature Reserves proposed by the government's Wild

Life Conservation Special Committee for England and Wales, set up by the Minister of Town and Country Planning. By that time, however, concern for small reserves was being set into the context of a much wider debate about conservation and countryside planning.[5]

The argument turned, in the critical years before and during the Second World War, on two closely related questions. How necessary and how urgent was the need for action, for conservation or planning? How should this be achieved? These questions were never addressed singly, but they formed the spine of the debate that spiralled in and out of the corridors of government in the years before, during and after the Second World War.

The driving force behind these debates was concern about change (and particularly the impact of urban development) in the countryside. This was nowhere more acute than on the coast. Authoritative studies of the state of the British coastline were made in the 1940s by Alfred Steers, a physical geographer and subsequently a member of the government's Wild Life Conservation Special Committee. Steers was an established authority on the coastline of England and Wales, but had a particular knowledge of the North Norfolk coast, having published his first paper on Scolt Head in 1926.[6] He had been charged by the new Ministry of Town and Country Planning, with carrying out a survey of the entire coast of England and Wales with a view to advising on its preservation. This he did, with great vigour, calling for urgent action and a national authority to achieve it.[7]

In his work, Alfred Steers addressed both the natural environment and aesthetics. The coast was a place of scientific interest, but also of beauty. He believed that the coast should be regarded as a unit, and its use planned nationally to tackle not only problems of erosion and accretion but also the equally complicated questions of "the proper use of the coast by the country's inhabitants". In 1946, after completing a survey of the Channel coast previously barred to him, he wrote "having seen the whole coast of England and Wales, I cannot emphasise too strongly that if we as a nation wish to preserve one of our finest heritages for the good of the people as a whole, we must act now and act vigorously on a national scale".[8]

By the 1940s the impacts on natural features of rising urban and industrial demands were widely recognised, and had been discussed in a range of governmental and non-governmental committees. There was recognition of the need for a new approach to the countryside and to the problem of unplanned urban growth. National Parks and other protected areas had an important place in this new thinking. Much of it was captured by the word "conservation", which played an important part in the inspired lateral thinking of post-war reconstruction planning. The word "conservation" itself was not at that time widely used outside a small circle of naturalists and planners. Conservation has often been in the headlines in recent decades, but it was not always so. It was not until naturalists marked the 50th anniversary of a walk in the New Forest by Sir Edward Grey and ex-President Theodore Roosevelt that the word "conservation" was used freely by newspapers, television and radio.[9]

The work of the government conservation agencies in Britain, particularly the establishment of National Parks and National Nature Reserves, may make it seem obvious that conservation should be the responsibility of the state, but it was not seen to be so in the first four decades of this century. Conservation, like a concern for public health and public housing, only slowly crept onto the national political agenda, and for some decades was seen to be something best tackled by local and not national government. A Planning Act was passed by Parliament in 1909, and others in 1919 and 1932.[10] These gave powers to local government to try to control urban development, both to make sure that towns provided an adequate living space, and to control their spread. Despite their intentions, these Acts achieved very little. They did not grasp the nettle of limiting developers' rights, and the new powers went largely untried because local governments feared punitive demands for compensation from landowners who were prevented from building. Planned and unplanned suburban development, on estates and on ribbons along major roads, continued apace.[11]

The 1932 Town and Country Planning Act seemed to offer a route to countryside conservation based on co-operative action between local authorities and other parties. However, lack of resources continued to limit the scope and effectiveness of conservation schemes. The limitations of statutory planning by local authorities were demonstrated by the manifold problems of the South Downs through the 1930s, and made public by Parliamentary debate of the South Downs Preservation Bill and the bitter dispute over a proposed motor racing track on Brighton Corporation land at Devil's Dyke.[12] Other areas, such as the Lake District, also demonstrated very clearly that many of the problems of countryside preservation could not be tackled only at a local scale.

An alternative way to promote conservation was for central government to take action. Gradually the idea of National Parks gained ground in the UK. National Parks had already been founded in the USA, Canada, Australia and New Zealand, and within Europe in Switzerland, in the closing decades of the nineteenth century, and at a similar period, state game reserves were established in European colonies in Africa.[13] In Britain, however, there was no equivalent activity at this time. Despite the long agricultural depression that began in the 1870s and ran through to the Second World War, and the massive break-up of the great estates following the First, the power of the landed interest combined with the innate conservatism of government to stifle calls for government action on National Parks.

Outside government, however, there was plenty of action. Societies were formed to preserve open land, notably the Commons Preservation Society (established in 1865) and the National Trust for Places of Historic Interest and Natural Beauty (the National Trust), founded 30 years later.[14] Bills were introduced to Parliament repeatedly between 1884 and 1931 to allow the public access to open country in moorland and mountain.[15] They all failed. Gradually, however, the climate of opinion about rights and uses of the countryside changed. In 1926 the Council for the Preservation of Rural England (CPRE) was formed, closely followed by sister organisations in Wales and Scotland. CPRE was a consortium of 22 different organisations, and it began actively to lobby government. In 1928, a campaign for the purchase of the Cairngorms as a park was launched in the pages of Scots Magazine. Partly as a result of this lobbying, Ramsay MacDonald set up a committee in 1929 under Christopher Addison, Parliamentary Secretary to the Ministry of Agriculture, to enquire into the need for National Parks in Britain. This recommended that a series of National Parks should be established, to be administered by two National Park Authorities, one for Scotland and one for England and Wales.

Government action on conservation would, of course, cost money. Through the 1920s, local authorities concentrated their resources on small urban sites, and initial enthusiasm for a "National Parks Authority" evaporated through the early 1930s as financial problems deepened. However, CPRE and CPRW, with other organisations, maintained pressure, and a Standing Committee on National Parks was established in 1934. Eventually, in 1937, a casual remark by the Chancellor of the Exchequer to the Amenity Group of MPs, about the possibility of a grant to a voluntary body to help establish a National Park, effectively committed the government to some form of support for conservation.[16]

The principle, that conservation was a proper concern for national government, was now established, but debate about how conservation should fit around the emerging system of statutory planning schemes continued. It was eventually overtaken by the outbreak of war. By 1939, the only concrete action beyond purchase of land by voluntary organisations and local authorities was the declaration of two National Forest Parks by the Forestry Commission, in Ardgarten (Argyllshire) and the Forest of Dean.[17]

National Parks

Planning during the Second World War for post-war reconstruction provided a remarkable opportunity for conservation. Proposals for radical reform of land use planning were made early in the war, when Lord Reith became Minister of a newly-created Ministry of Works and Buildings in 1940.[18] Despite determined opposition from other Ministries, the need for government involvement in the planning and management of land use was increasingly widely accepted, both in Whitehall and in public. In 1942 the report of the Committee on Land Utilisation in Rural Areas (chaired by Lord Justice Scott) picked up the recommendations of the Addison Committee, and made specific recommendations that National Parks be established, and that they should be delineated and controlled by a national body under a general Central Planning Authority, or some such organisation.[19]

In 1942 town and country planning powers were centralised in a renamed Ministry of Works and Planning (having previously lain with the Department of Health), and there was further discussion of the need for government support for National Parks to protect scenery and provide for recreation. Pressure upon government came from voluntary organisations promoting National Parks (CPRE and APRS) and from the Standing Committee on National Parks. In 1943 the Ministry of Works and Planning was replaced by a Ministry of Town and Country Planning, and in November of that year the new Minister confirmed that the government had accepted responsibility for preserving the natural beauty of the countryside and for providing facilities for outdoor recreation.[20]

The shape of government thinking about National Parks was greatly influenced by a report to the Minister of Town and Country Planning by John Dower, published in 1945.[21] Dower had a reputation as an advocate of National Parks in the 1930s, and indeed had drafted a model National Parks Bill for the Standing Committee for National Parks in 1939. His report on National Parks arose from his appointment as a member of a survey and research team in Reith's Ministry of Works and Buildings. The report was not intended for publication, but the level of public interest (once it became known that it existed) demanded it. A parallel survey of Scotland was completed between 1943 and 1945, supervised by a Committee chaired by Sir J. Douglas Ramsay, a member of the Scottish Council for National Parks.[22]

Dower regarded it as axiomatic that National Parks should be "in a true and full sense *national* if they are to be worthy of their name and purpose". He argued that they were not for any privileged or otherwise restricted section of the population, but for "all who care to refresh their minds and spirits and to exercise their bodies in a peaceful setting of natural beauty".[23] Dower identified ten possible National Parks in England and Wales, and a further ten as reserves for possible future National Parks. The 1945 Ramsay Committee recommended five National Parks for Scotland.[24] Both reports also proposed the creation of a National Parks Commission as a planning authority to control development. The Forestry Commission, mindful of its Forest Parks and its own interests, opposed the idea of an independent Commission, but the idea took root.

The Minister of Town and Country Planning, hoping for action and not more words, proposed a Preparatory National Parks Commission. Whitehall, however, would not be rushed. The Minister of Agriculture played a key role in blocking moves to establish the Commission, and the Cabinet Reconstruction Committee appointed instead two further committees (one for England and Wales, and one for Scotland) to make detailed recommendations for National Parks, and the National Parks Commission.[25] Their work took a further two years. The National Parks Committee for England and Wales was chaired by Sir Arthur Hobhouse, and it included John Dower as a member. Both committees reported in the Summer of 1947.[26] They supported the conclusions of the 1945 reports that National Parks were needed, and that National Parks Commissions were needed to make national policy. However, these committees did not propose to give these Commissions strong executive powers. The delay of two years while the Hobhouse Committee produced its report had seen the passage of the Town and Country Planning Act 1947. This placed planning powers in the hands of County Councils, and Hobhouse, himself a County Councillor, proposed that they should also control development within National Parks. While the Commission should directly manage land that it itself acquired, its should work elsewhere with other landowners through "assistance, advice and encouragement".

The National Parks and Access to the Countryside Act 1949 duly gave powers to the National Parks Commission in England and Wales in these terms. The Commission was an advisory body, from the start having to learn to work with other organisations and interests to achieve its ends. It had the power to designate National Parks, but they were to be run by committees of one or more County Councils. National Parks could be protected for the nation, although the powers of the National Parks Commission to defend them were slight.[27] Moreover, there were only to be parks in England and Wales. The 1947 Ramsay Committee recommended an independent National Parks Commission in Scotland (with "a considerable measure of independence") but the 1949 Act made no provisions either for such a Commission or for National Parks in Scotland. There were also to be no National Parks in Northern Ireland.

National Nature Reserves

Concern for National Parks had a persistent shadow in calls for National Nature Reserves, and in the various committees that met in the 1940s, these fared rather better.[28] Calls for National Nature Reserves came in particular from the Conference on Nature Preservation in Post-war Reconstruction, the Royal Society for the Protection of Birds (RSPB), the British Ecological Society and from prominent ecologists such as Arthur Tansley. In 1945 Tansley published *Our Heritage of Wild Nature*, a book that was, as its subtitle said, "a plea for organized nature conservation". He argued for a National Nature Reserve Authority that would give "explicit recognition of public obligation to take responsibility for the conservation of wild life — the formal placing of wild life under a State protection".[29]

In his 1945 report, Dower suggested that wildlife conservation and National Nature Reserves should be seen as just part of the work of the National Parks Commission, and he gave them very little space in his report. By 1945, the momentum behind wildlife conservation had grown, and the Hobhouse Committee established a Wild Life Conservation Special Committee to report on a scheme of nature conservation for the whole of England and Wales, chaired by one of its own members, Julian Huxley. In 1946 a similar Scottish Wild Life Conservation Committee was set up under the chairmanship of James Ritchie of Edinburgh University. The Huxley Committee reported in 1947. The lack of preliminary surveys in Scotland delayed the final report of the Ritchie Committee until 1949.[30]

The Wild Life Conservation Committees endorsed the importance of wildlife conservation as a national interest. They proposed 73 National Nature Reserves in England and Wales (covering about 28,000 ha) and 24 in Scotland, plus 4 further reserves within the proposed National Parks (covering almost 45,000 ha). These reserves were envisaged as small in extent, and their designation and even their acquisition by a government body seemed to pose a relatively minor threat to either the interests of private landowners or the emerging system of town and country planning that was in the hands of local government. National Nature Reserves were portrayed not only as a means of protecting wildlife for public benefit, but also as areas that would make a significant contribution to the advancement of science. This gave nature reserves and wildlife conservation a hard edge in the fight for influence that National Parks lacked.

Science had acquired a privileged position in public life during the Second World War, and the Huxley Committee linked wildlife conservation very directly to the advance of science. Huxley himself had argued for the centrality of science to government before the war. In 1943 the British Ecological Society had recommended the creation of an Ecological Research Council, after the manner of the Agricultural and Medical Research Councils. This notion was opposed, particularly by the former, but the idea received support from the Scientific Advisory Committee. The Huxley Committee in particular developed strong arguments that nature reserves should be selected, acquired and managed by a single Biological Service, and that moreover this service should have the research and advisory functions necessary to allow the government to "take a general responsibility for the conservation and control of the flora and fauna of this country and for the protection of features of geological and physiographical interest".[31]

Despite some reluctance from the Ritchie Committee, the idea of a Biological Service, answering to the President of Council and not the Minister of Town and Country Planning, was accepted. The Nature Conservancy was created in 1948, and the following Spring made responsible to a new committee of the Privy Council. It received powers under the National Parks and Access to the Countryside Act 1949 to establish National Nature Reserves and carry out research. Unlike the National Parks Commission, its authority extended throughout Great Britain, although it too had no role in Northern Ireland.

Countryside conservation

The passage through Parliament of the National Parks and Access to the Countryside Act 1949 was a critical turning point in the development of conservation in Great Britain. The new legislation encapsulated years of thinking about conservation, and ended decades of argument about the right means of achieving it. The National Parks Commission and the Nature Conservancy threw themselves with some enthusiasm into their allotted tasks. Their work gave conservation a definite place in the thinking of government and other land users, and, more importantly, they inscribed its pattern on the landscape of Britain through the establishment of protected areas.

Between 1951 and 1957, the National Parks Commission designated 10 National Parks in England and Wales, and followed this over succeeding decades with 38 Areas of Outstanding Natural Beauty and 1500 km of Heritage Coast.[32] The horizons of the Commission were broadened to embrace the whole countryside in 1968, and a new organisation was created to reflect the new agenda, called the Countryside Commission. The Countryside Act 1968 gave the new Commission powers to give grants to landowners or to support projects outside National Parks. In 1974 the Commission moved its Headquarters to Cheltenham, and in 1977 it established a structure of regional offices.

Legislation was passed that promoted conservation in a more general way. Notably, the Countryside Act 1968 placed a duty on every government department to "have regard to the desirability of conserving the natural beauty and amenity of the countryside". While this was rather anodyne (Ann and Malcolm MacEwen describe it as "a verbal genuflection"[33]), it did represent something of the growing realisation of the importance of conservation. Similar clauses have since been included in other pieces of legislation. Worries about the scale and extent of countryside change were expressed in the "Countryside in 1970" Conferences in 1963 and 1965, and surfaced again in the late 1970s, when work began on a new Parliamentary Bill covering all aspects of wildlife and countryside conservation. This became in time the Wildlife and Countryside Act 1981.[34] This introduced a wide range of new provisions relating to access and recreation, and slightly stronger provisions for protection of open moorland.

Despite some difficult periods, the Commission survived, even flourished, through the Thatcher years. It was politically adroit, pragmatic, and above all it was already experienced in the arts of working with other interests to achieve its aims. As "partnerships" became the new buzzword of government, the Commission found itself with experience of action to match the new style.[35] The Commission has launched a series of innovative experiments in combining the interests of agriculture and conservation, for example Countryside Stewardship launched in 1991, and before that the Environmentally Sensitive Areas, which grew out of the Commission's work in the Norfolk Broads. The 1990s saw the first new National Park created in over forty years in the Broads: an area on Dower's reserve list in 1945 and proposed by the Hobhouse Committee in 1947.[36]

The 1949 Act gave no powers to designate National Parks in Scotland, although the Planning Act 1947 allowed the Secretary of State to issue National Park Direction Orders, which required all local authorities to submit planning applications to the Scottish Office within the relevant areas. Despite the long history of calls for National Parks in Scotland, they still have no place in Scottish conservation.[37] Scotland did eventually get a separate countryside agency in 1967, when the Countryside Commission for Scotland was created by Act of Parliament under the Countryside Commission (Scotland) Act 1967. This Commission proposed a series of National Parks in A Park System for Scotland in 1974 (a call repeated since, notably in the 1990 paper The Mountain Areas of Scotland), but without success. Instead, the Countryside Commission for Scotland (CCS) was empowered to declare National Scenic Areas in the areas proposed for National Parks. Some forty National Scenic Areas and four Regional Parks have been created.

Scottish Natural Heritage now has the power to declare National Heritage Areas in places which have "outstanding value to the natural heritage of Scotland", and which are deemed to need special measures for protection.[38] The aim is that they should protect both landscapes and habitats in a single protected area designation, with all affected parties agreeing voluntarily to the designation. Working parties met over two years to discuss the first two areas, the Cairngorms and Loch Lomond and the Trossachs, but came up with rather different proposals. The Cairngorms has been particularly controversial, with proposals for new skiing development in 1980 and 1989, the formation of the "Save the Cairngorms Campaign", and an unsuccessful bid by a conservation consortium to purchase the huge private estate of Mar Lodge in 1992. The estate has now been acquired by the National Trust for Scotland, but will be run as a sporting estate. It has now been agreed that the Cairngorms might be listed by the UK government as a World Heritage Site but here, as elsewhere in Scotland, more specific protection has still to be established.[39] The IUCN Action Plan for Protected Areas in Europe calls for urgent action on parks in Scotland, either to make the Natural Heritage Areas work or to establish an alternative mechanism.[40]

Countryside conservation in Northern Ireland has developed in a way quite distinct from that across the Irish Sea. Although National Parks were proposed in the 1940s by the Amenities Committee of the Planning Advisory Board for Northern Ireland, and powers to designate them have existed since 1965, none have been established. However, the Department of the Environment in Northern Ireland has declared Areas of Outstanding Natural Beauty, and these have slightly more teeth than the equivalent English and Welsh areas. Nine exist, including the Mountains of Mourne, the Antrim Coast and Glens, the Causeway Coast and the Ring of Gullion. Two others have been proposed, both in Fermanagh.[41] Northern Ireland had to wait until 1985 for powers similar to those of the British Countryside Commissions to be vested in the Department of the Environment (Northern Ireland).[42]

Places for wildlife

Provisions for countryside conservation have been accompanied by measures for the protection of wildlife. The Nature Conservancy in its turn began to establish protected areas, the most important of which were National Nature Reserves (NNRs). The first NNR declared was Beinn Eighe in Scotland, and by 1960 no less than 84 NNRs had been declared, covering over 56,000 ha, and the area and number of NNRs continued to grow. Some reserves were purchased by the NCC, others (particularly in Scotland) were either leased or held under a Nature Reserve Agreement with landowners.

The Nature Conservancy also began to designate Sites of Special Scientific Interest (SSSIs). Such sites were originally conceived of by the Huxley Committee, which noted that there were hundreds of small areas scattered throughout England that had biological or other scientific importance, and that could be safeguarded if their owners and "appropriate authorities" knew of their existence. The 1949 Act gave the Nature Conservancy a duty to notify planning authorities of the value of "any area of land of special interest by reason of its flora, fauna, geological or physiographical features",[43] and from this the SSSI system was created. It soon began to acquire increasing importance. County schedules of SSSIs were created rapidly, building on previous lists of important sites drawn up by the regional committees of the Nature Reserves Investigations Committee.[44] By 1962 over 1700 sites had been scheduled, two-thirds of them in England. By 1975 there were over 3000 SSSIs, and the number continued to grow, even though sites were continually being lost. By 1990, the last year of the Nature Conservancy Council's life, there were about 5,500 SSSIs, covering 17,000 km². Almost two-thirds of all SSSIs were in England, with most of the rest (and almost half the total area) in

Scotland. Wales held just 14 per cent of SSSIs, and 11 per cent of the total area.

Despite its energy (or more truthfully because of it) the Nature Conservancy had enemies in Whitehall, and among landowners (particularly in Scotland) who resented its powers to designate NNRs on private land. In December 1955 the Conservancy's proposal to publish a list of proposed NNRs as an appendix to their annual report, the scale of its aspirations in land acquisition, and its interest in land for its general ecological character and its value for science (rather than simply as a home for rare species) caused much disquiet on Conservative back benches, and in the Cabinet.[46] A committee of enquiry was set up, but fortunately its report was favourable, and the Conservancy survived. However, its work remained widely opposed, both inside and outside government. Its pioneering scientific research on the environment, toxic chemicals and wildlife, although very successful and arguably its greatest achievement, was particularly unpopular, especially with the Ministry of Agriculture and the chemical companies.[47]

The Nature Conservancy never acquired the power and strength that those who conceived it had hoped. In 1965 it was placed within the newly-created Natural Environment Research Council (NERC), but the arrangement was not satisfactory, and it was recreated as the Nature Conservancy Council (NCC) in 1973.[48] In the process it lost its scientific research functions, which were kept within NERC as the Institute of Terrestrial Ecology. The NCC survived in its new form through the endless arguments surrounding the Wildlife and Countryside Act, until 1991, when new legislation created a new structure for government conservation. The NCC's role was then taken on by English Nature in England, and new combined agencies for wildlife and countryside in Scotland and Wales, the Countryside Council for Wales and Scottish Natural Heritage.[49]

In what was almost a half century between the creation of the Nature Conservancy and the NCC's demise, there was a succession of new pieces of legislation concerning wildlife conservation. Some sought to protect wild species, notably the Protection of Birds Act 1954, the Conservation of Wild Creatures and Wild Plants Act 1975, and the Wildlife and Countryside Act 1981. In 1991 full protection was afforded to 24 land mammals and 25 sea mammals, all but 35 British birds, a range of other animals and 93 plants.[50]

The "nature" that the Nature Conservancy was charged with conserving embraced not only species and habitats, but also features of geological and geomorphological importance. The Huxley Committee (on which, of course, sat the geographer Alfred Steers) had proposed the notification of Geological Monuments, and the Nature Conservancy included geological sites in its schedules of SSSIs. In 1977 the NCC began the Geological Conservation Review, to provide a systematic basis for geological SSSIs. This identified some 3000 nationally and internationally important geological and geomorphological sites. The first of a prospective 51-volume series of reports (on the Quaternary of Wales) was published in 1989. In 1990 work was begun on the development of a national network of "Regionally Important Geological/ Geomorphological Sites" (RIGS) to complement the SSSI system, and the NCC launched a strategy for earth science conservation.[51]

Although there is no direct equivalent of the Nature Conservancy in Northern Ireland, there are National Nature Reserves. A total of 46 have been declared, although they are small, covering only 0.3 per cent of the land area.[52] The Amenity Lands Act 1965 empowered the Ministry of Development to designate "Areas of Scientific Interest" (ASIs), and it established a Nature Reserves Committee as well as the Ulster Countryside Committee. New legislation in 1985 created a strengthened Conservation Service within the Department of the Environment (Northern Ireland), maintained the Ulster Countryside Committee and created a Committee for Nature Conservation.[53] By 1984, 48 ASIs had been declared under the Amenity Lands (Northern Ireland) Act 1965.[54] These were replaced by Areas of Special Scientific Interest (ASSIs) under the Nature Conservation and Amenity Lands Order 1985.[55]

The ties that bind

The shape of British conservation, and the particular achievements of the government conservation agencies since 1949, stem directly from the two separate agencies created by the National Parks and Access to the Countryside Act. The distinction between "landscape" and "wildlife" conservation has now, of course, been broken down in both Scotland and Wales by the creation of Scottish Natural Heritage and the Countryside Council for Wales.

The artificiality of the separation of landscape and wildlife conservation had long been obvious, but suspicion of government motives and fear of cuts in budget and influence meant that these mergers, and the associated break-up of the NCC, were widely opposed by conservationists. The motive for merger was largely political, a response by the Conservative government to demands (from within the Scottish Office as much as anywhere else) for a devolved conservation agency in Scotland, following the NCC's sustained opposition to the scale of afforestation on the peatlands of the Caithness "Flow Country". The NCC's forthright views on this were highly unpopular locally and among large landowners in Scotland, and led directly to the organisation's dismemberment.[56] Where the Secretary of State for Scotland led, Wales had to follow. The NCC was so small in Wales that it had to be merged with the equally small staff of the Countryside Commission. As a result of that expediency, a new policy of creating unified countryside agencies in Scotland and Wales emerged. The Secretary of State for Environment strongly resisted the idea of a similar merger in England. The resulting agency would have been too powerful, both for the fledgling Scottish and Welsh organisations, and perhaps with respect to the Forestry Commission and the Ministry of Agriculture, Fisheries and Food. English Nature and the Countryside Commission were therefore kept as separate agencies in England, with the Joint Nature Conservation Committee established as something of an afterthought to provide advice to government on UK and international issues, and some scientific co-ordination of work in the new agencies.[57]

The idea of merging English Nature and the Countryside Commission was mooted again in 1994, and again the Secretary of State for the Environment decided against it. Consultants appointed to study the effectiveness of the Scottish and Welsh mergers made it quite clear that such bureaucratic unions were difficult to get right. Scotland enjoyed its own custom-made legislation, while Wales had to make do with a rather crude amalgam of text from existing legislation. Both had worked extremely hard to marry the vastly different sizes of the old agencies, but despite the blizzard of re-labelling and re-organisation that has followed bureaucratic union, the two cultures of the old Nature Conservancy Council and the Countryside Commissions proved difficult to forge into one. The old agencies had quite different traditions, one with executive powers (acquiring reserves, trying to enforce appropriate SSSI management) and the other working through advice and incentive; one with scientific staff relatively thick on the ground and rich in ecological skills, the other with fewer foot soldiers but great strengths and skills in advocacy.[58]

Closing the "great divide" successfully in England, as in Scotland and Wales, would have taken a long time, lots of planning and money.[59] The costs of the new conservation agencies rose subtantially above those of the pre-merger bodies, stimulating a new round of cuts.[60] The experience of Northern Ireland, where there is a single Countryside and Wildlife Branch within the Department of the Environment, suggests that bureaucratic union might not necessarily end compartmentalised thinking. The important question is not how conservation is organised, but whether policies are effectively integrated. The real problem arises if different interests are too differentiated, too tribally divided between nature and landscape. Arguably this has been so at times over the last four decades, but it need not be so now. The challenge for conservation is to build strong and durable bridges across the "great divide", whether it lies between different organisations, or between different parts of the same organisation.

The bridge that in many ways does link the different dimensions of conservation together, and has done so through all the shifts in the identity of government conservation agencies, is the voluntary conservation movement. Since 1949 concern for conservation has extended remarkably from a small number of naturalists and decision-makers to involve very large numbers of people. The achievements of the government conservation agencies have been matched, and to an extent have been enabled, by the fantastic growth of the voluntary conservation movement. This took place at an accelerating pace through the 1960s, 1970s and 1980s, but as we have seen, it had its roots much earlier.

A number of voluntary conservation organisations already existed in the years of war-time planning for conservation, including the Council for the Preservation of Rural England (CPRE) and equivalent organisations in Scotland and Wales, the National Trust and the National Trust for Scotland. The National Parks Commission and the Nature Conservancy were very largely the product of the indefatigable action of the voluntary conservation movement, in the persons of a small number of charismatic and influential individuals. Curiously, their creation appeared to leave no immediately obvious role for further non-governmental action. The Nature Reserves Investigations Committee was disbanded, and at the end of the war the membership of the Royal Society for the Protection of Birds (RSPB) was only 6300 people. In the post-war period, the voluntary nature conservation movement was beset with problems. In 1976 Max Nicholson, a central figure in the story of post-war planning for conservation and who had taken over as Director General of the NC in 1952, said that the voluntary conservation movement suffered low morale, weak leadership, "elderly and largely passenger memberships", and feeble finances.[61]

However, it began to grow. Through the 1940s and 1950s a series of new County Naturalists' Trusts were formed, in Lincolnshire, Yorkshire, West Wales, Leicestershire and Cambridgeshire, and by 1957 the possibility of national federation under the Society for the Promotion of Nature Reserves (SPNR) was being discussed.[62] In 1958 a new body was created to link nature conservation organisations and lobby on their behalf, the Council for Nature. In 1958 the SPNR established a County Naturalists' Trusts Committee, and in 1960 held a national conference for Naturalists' Trusts at Skegness in Lincolnshire. By 1964 there were 36 trusts in existence and the SPNR had changed its name to the Society for the Promotion of Nature Conservation. The number of Wildlife Trusts grew, and so did their combined membership, from 3000 in 1960 to 21,000 in 1965. Membership topped 100,000 in 1975, and in that year Watch, for children, was launched. By the late 1980s, membership lay at about 200,000. The number of Wildlife Trusts has since grown to 48, now including Ulster, London and Avon among others. The SPNC became the Royal Society for Nature Conservation (RSNC), and is now known as "The Wildlife Trusts". In 1988 the Trusts together had an annual income of between £6m and £7m and held and managed over 1700 nature reserves covering about 50,000 ha.[63]

The membership and income of other organisations also blossomed through the 1970s and 1980s. The RSPB had over 10,000 members in 1960, over 30,000 in 1965, and 300,000 by 1975. Membership exceeded half a million in 1980, and (including the Young Ornithologists' Club) was 890,000 in 1994. In that year, the RSPB's total income was over £32 million.[64] Such wildlife conservation organisations represent only part of a much wider environmental movement, which proliferated new bodies as it grew. The World Wildlife Fund (now the Worldwide Fund for Nature) (WWF) was established in 1961, Friends of the Earth (FoE) in 1971 and Greenpeace in 1977. Membership of many of these organisations soared in the 1980s. CPRE membership rose from 30,000 in 1985 to 46,000 in 1993. FoE's UK membership jumped from 18,000 to 230,000 between 1981 and 1993, that of Greenpeace from 30,000 to 408,000 and that of the Worldwide Fund for Nature from 60,000 to 227,000. The membership of the National Trust (the largest conservation organisation) and the National Trust for Scotland doubled over the 1980s, as did the Ramblers Association and (almost) that of the RSPB.[65]

The membership of conservation organisations overlaps, but it probably involves two to three million people in the UK. The conservation movement has prospered mightily, and continues to grow. It is one of the sharper ironies of conservation that this growth has taken place during a period of unprecedented destruction of the countryside and wildlife for which conservationists were coming to care so much. That destruction is the subject of the next chapter.

CHAPTER THREE

Nature Lost

Even in our overcrowded European states there are still lovely bits of forest, marsh-land, and down that man has not yet irretrievably befouled, and from which he has not yet driven by assault nor removed by slaughter the beautiful living things which nature has guided and nurtured in their seclusion
E. Ray Lankester[1]

Losing ground

Behind the story of the growth and success of conservation since the heady days of post-war reconstruction lies another tale. Its plot is rather different, for it is a story of loss and retreat. While conservation, as a movement and as a series of institutions, was being constructed, the countryside and the natural features that the new conservationists cared about were being dismantled. However fast conservation advanced, figuratively in terms of public opinion or literally in terms of site designation, it seemed that nature retreated in the face of massive economic and social forces. The conservation value of places became increasingly well-documented and widely recognised; they were inscribed on lists of special places and drawn on maps that should have diverted development elsewhere, and yet when push came to shove it was repeatedly shown that none of this weighed very heavily in the balance of official decision-making.

Over the last decade and a half, non-governmental organisations (NGOs) in conservation have run series of campaigns, and produced a battery of reports documenting, and lamenting, the loss of landscape and natural habitat in the countryside. For example, Friends of the Earth published *Paradise Lost?* in 1980, *Cash or Crisis* in 1982, and *Gaining Interest* in 1994. In 1985 the RSNC launched the British Wildlife Appeal under the emotive slogan "tomorrow is too late", in 1989 their report *Losing Ground*, and in 1990 *Nature Conservation: the health of the UK*. Wildlife Link, a consortium of conservation NGOs, also produced a range of reports, culminating in a detailed analysis of the shortcomings of the SSSI system in 1991, *SSSIs: a health check*.[2] The titles of this grim litany of outrage and complaint speak for themselves. It seemed that conservation was not working.

The failure of statutory provisions and voluntary pressure to prevent habitat loss and countryside change is nowhere more clear than in the loss of areas of peatland, highlighted in a campaign waged by a consortium of NGOs in the early 1990s. The area of lowland peatlands throughout Great Britain has fallen dramatically since the end of the Second World War due to horticultural peat extraction, reclamation for agriculture and forestry planting. With them has gone their strange and wild landscapes and their increasingly rare fauna and flora. Losses of peatland were most advanced in England. South Cumbria, for example, had 494 ha in 1948, and only 156 ha in 1978; in Lancashire 247 ha had shrunk to only 11 ha.[3] By 1991 there were only 445 ha of lowland peatland in first-class condition in England.

Catherine Caufield has chronicled the drainage and stripping of what was the largest expanse of lowland peat in England, Thorne Moors, the remnant of once vast wetlands at the head of the Humber estuary.[4] Peat has been extracted for many centuries from Thorne Moors, and was cut commercially from the 1880s for animal bedding. At various times in the 1960s and 1970s the Moors were earmarked by local planners as a tip for fly-ash or colliery waste, and as a site for an airport, but never destroyed. However, the pace of peat extraction quickened rapidly in 1963 when Fisons purchased the British Moss Litter Company, and began mechanising. Thorne Moors was steadily bagged up and shipped off to British gardens, and more and more of the moor was drained and excavated. In 1987 Fisons began extraction by surface milling, digging deeper drains and stripping larger areas of moor. This work, like previous threats, was opposed by a local man, William Bunting (to whom Catherine Caufield dedicates her book, describing him as "naturalist, pamphleteer, archivist, rebel, bad-tempered old sod and inspiration"). His doughty campaigns slowly won wider recognition. Eventually Thorne Moors became one of the places at the heart of the national Peatlands Campaign.

The story of Thorne Moors was repeated throughout the British lowlands, and matched by peatland loss in the uplands, particularly through the impact of afforestation, most controversially on the peat bogs of Caithness. The

Peatlands Campaign was launched by voluntary conservation bodies. It spotlighted the largest cause of destruction of peatlands, which was the extraction of peat for horticulture. The picture of species-rich bogs destroyed to make gro-bags for back-garden tomatoes made a neat campaigning message, and consumer pressure on garden centres (plus the availability of benign alternatives to peat) forced the peat companies, led by Fisons, to compromise. They did a deal with the government's conservation agency for England, English Nature, donating 3240 ha of peatland SSSIs in a public deal designed to maximise favourable media coverage. It allowed English Nature to begin habitat restoration on exhausted peatlands, but it did not end peat mining, for it allowed Levington Horticulture Ltd. to continue extraction.[5] Despite the campaign, the area of natural habitat continues to shrink.

Species and habitats

Peatlands are just one example of the much wider problem of habitat loss and landscape change. George Peterken and Francine Hughes, for example, describe the massive and general reduction in the extent of semi-natural habitat that has taken place in the British lowlands.[6] Losses have probably been most acute in grasslands. Robin Fuller calculates that lowland grassland had declined from 7.8 m ha in the 1930s to only 5 m ha in the 1980s, with losses particularly acute in unimproved grasslands, whose area in the 1980s was only 3 per cent of that fifty years before. By the late 1980s, only 4 per cent of British grassland remained unimproved.[7] Much of the habitat that remains in lowland Britain has been degraded through the withdrawal of traditional management, eutrophication and other forms of pollution. There has been a general loss of historical features.

The wider lowland landscape has also been impoverished and eutrophicated, and fast-growing weeds such as nettle, hog weed or cocksfoot have spread at the expense of a much wider variety of slower-growing species. Patches of different kinds of semi-natural habitat have become separated from each other, so that the landscape has become more segregated and different habitats rarely occur alongside each other. Blocks of semi-natural vegetation have become smaller and increasingly isolated from each other, raising the threat of loss of diversity as local extinctions are not compensated for by natural re-introductions. Corridors in the landscape, such as hedges or streams, have progressively been lost or degraded, exacerbating the isolation of what remains. To compensate for this sorry tale of loss, some areas of new habitats have been created, some with a specific eye to conservation (e.g. farm woodlands), some as a side-product of industry (e.g. gravel pits). However, Peterken and Hughes argue that the diversity of these habitats will be limited by the impoverished nature of the landscape around them.[8]

Concern at the loss of habitats is now being swept up into renewed awareness of the need for the protection of particular species. This is one of the oldest themes within the development of conservation in the UK, with legislation dating back to the Seabird Preservation Act of 1869.[9] Vigorous global debate about "biodiversity", following the negotiation of the Convention on Biological Diversity at the "Earth Summit" in Rio in 1992, has provided a context for concern within the UK about the grim scientific statistics of extinction and habitat loss. The Convention was signed at Rio by 152 countries (the United States, which at first refused, did so later), and came into force on 29th December 1993. Ratifications continue, and include those by several European countries. The UK gave vocal support to the Treaty, launched its own "Darwin Initiative", and in January 1994 published *Biodiversity: the UK Action Plan.*

What is biodiversity? The "Biodiversity Convention" defined it as "The variability among living organisms from all sources including *inter alia* terrestrial, marine and other aquatic ecosystems and the ecological complexes of which they are part; this includes diversity within species, between and of ecosystems".[10] Biologists commonly distinguish between genetic diversity (the total amount of genetic information), species diversity (the number and variety of species), and ecosystem diversity (the variety of habitats, communities and processes). In practice, most people think about species, and this will serve for our purposes. The exact number of known species of organisms (all plants, animals and micro-organisms) does not matter very much, although biologists enjoy arguing about it. Edward Wilson estimates it to be 1.4 million.[11]

In some ways, Britain is unremarkable for its biodiversity in a global context. Overall species diversity is quite low in the UK, particularly compared to the tropics, where rainforests epitomise the diversity of life. The UK holds about 32,000 species of plant and 30,000 animals (two-thirds of them insects). This amounts to 3 per cent of the global total of recorded species, although it would be a much smaller proportion if taxonomists were a more common species in the Third World. Some British habitats are of international importance, for example peatlands and the oceanic bryophyte communities of western woodlands, and the UK supports populations of species that are judged to be threatened internationally. Some of these, like the corncrake, are also rare or threatened in Britain. The UK also supports internationally significant numbers of certain species, either breeding (for example the grey seal or the gannet), or passing through (for example the migratory waders and waterfowl that winter on our estuaries). There are relatively few endemic species (i.e. those that occur only in the UK): a report produced by a consortium of non-governmental organisations, *Biodiversity Challenge*, lists 14 lichens, 14 bryophytes (mosses and lichens), 1 fern, 21 higher plants, 16 invertebrates and 1 vertebrate (the Scottish crossbill).[12]

30

Given the scale of the changes imposed on landscapes and habitats, it is perhaps remarkable that so few species have gone extinct in the UK. Of course, bears were gone long ago, and wolves only a little more recently. Since 1900 the UK has lost 1 mammal, 6 birds, 2 fish, 144 invertebrates and 62 plants.[13] Much larger numbers of species are threatened. Some 3500 species are listed in national *Red Data Books*, and the number would be over 5000 if such studies were available for all taxonomic groups. Large numbers of species are declining in numbers or range, including both the obscure and the familiar (or once-familiar), such as the water vole, natterjack toad and grey partridge. A number of species are confined to a very few sites where ecological conditions are suitable. Their vulnerability to ecological change is obviously very acute.[14]

Derek Ratcliffe, Chief Scientist of the Nature Conservancy Council, commented in 1984 that "the culminating effect of a human population of 54 millions on an island measuring only 230,000 km^2 has been to leave very little truly natural vegetation".[15] There have been gains to the British flora, with some new plant species having been introduced, some of which have become aggressive colonisers, such as rhododendron or the Himalayan balsam. However, losses outweigh the gains. Of the 1400 or so native British flowering plant species, one in ten suffered decline of at least 20 per cent between 1930 and 1960, and of the 317 higher plant species listed as nationally rare in 1983, 37 per cent had suffered a decline in distribution of at least a third since 1930.[16]

The human impact

The main human influence on British vegetation has always been the advance of agriculture. For much of the past, agricultural activities, and other forms of rural production, have produced complex and diverse habitats and landscapes, epitomised perhaps by chalk grassland and coppice woodland. In the period since the end of the Second World War the influence has been relentlessly negative.[17] The ploughing of areas of habitat (such as chalk grassland or heathland) for arable, the conversion of flower-rich meadows to grass leys, the reclamation of wetlands, the abandonment of land systems such as water meadows and the impacts of linked ecological change such as the decline of rabbits with myxomatosis in the 1950s, decimated most habitats. The importance of agriculture as the engine of habitat loss was not adequately foreseen in the 1940s. The Committee on Land Utilisation in Rural Areas under Lord Justice Scott reported in 1944.[18] The majority view of that committee was that the traditional mixed character of British farming would continue, and that the agricultural industry would undergo gradual evolution rather than radical change. The key need was for government support to create stability for farming such that land was properly farmed and "maintained in good heart". Scott thought that such support for agriculture would be the cheapest (indeed the only) way of preserving the countryside "in anything like its traditional aspect".

Interestingly, even the otherwise almost visionary thinker John Dower presented a similar argument about the importance of farming to the future of the National Parks. Dower thought that farming provided not only the scenic setting of the parks but also what he called "the drama itself — the rural life and work ... without which the finest of English and Welsh scenery would lack an essential part of its charm and recreational value".[19] He suggested that the interests of agriculture and of landscape beauty both required:

> that bracken, rushes and thorn and bramble scrub should be fought back; that heather should be periodically burned, that waterlogged and derelict fields should be drained and reclaimed; that drains and ditches should be regularly cleared; that hedges should be regularly trimmed; that walls and fences should be kept in repair; and that farm roads and farm buildings should be properly maintained.[20]

In fact, agriculture soon showed itself no friend of conservation in post-war Britain. Far from creating stability, government agricultural support fuelled rapid economic change. Agriculture soon became more capital intensive and vastly more productive. Farms became larger, and farm workers (and farmers) fewer. Mechanisation, pesticides and inorganic fertilisers increased productivity but broke conclusively with the patterns of agriculture that had prevailed in the nineteenth century and through long agricultural depression of the first half of the twentieth.[21] It became clear that land use outside nature reserves and protected areas was becoming increasingly damaging to wildlife and scenery. The impacts of agriculture and other land uses on the wildlife habitat and landscape of the countryside was widely commented upon by the 1960s. They were discussed at the "Countryside in 1970" Conferences, and indeed it was suggested during Parliamentary debate of the Countryside Act 1968 that agriculture should be brought under planning control.

Norman Moore pointed out in 1969 that in thickly populated countries like Britain the land that could be set aside for wildlife was necessarily limited, and so wildlife had to be protected outside reserves, on land whose primary use was for agriculture, forestry or recreation. On such land, "the conservation requirements clash to a greater or lesser degree with the primary land use".[22] That clash almost everywhere led to habitat loss and landscape change. In 1974 the Countryside Commission's *New Agricultural Landscapes* study revealed the dramatic changes in the landscapes of study areas in seven lowland counties in England, although it tried to put an optimistic spin on those changes. A repeat of the "New Agricultural Landscapes" survey in 1983 showed that change in lowland landscapes was continuing, and studies in the uplands and the National Parks revealed similar trends.[23]

Arguments about the destruction wrought by agricultural change were galvanised by the influential broadside by Marion Shoard, *The Theft of the Countryside*, published in 1980. This book was a withering critique of the impacts of intensive agriculture on the countryside, and had an amazing effect on the scope (and the temperature) of debate of the Wildlife and Countryside Bill that was introduced to Parliament shortly afterwards.[24] The need to control landscape change (particularly on moorland, stimulated by controversy over land reclamation for arable on Exmoor) was a major influence on the form of the Wildlife and Countryside Bill.[25] During the debate on that Bill, David Goode, then Assistant Chief Scientist of the Nature Conservancy Council, published an article in *New Scientist* that documented the loss of semi-natural habitat, data confirmed and expanded in *Nature Conservation in Great Britain* three years later.[26]

Measuring landscape change

Norman Moore was based in Dorset as the Nature Conservancy's Regional Officer for South-west England between 1953 and 1960, and there carried out a path-breaking piece of research on the changing extent of semi-natural habitat. Using old maps, he compared the area of heathland in Dorset in 1811, 1896, 1934 and 1960. Only a third of the area of heathland in 1811 had survived to 1960. The change between 1934 and 1960 was particularly dramatic, with 45 per cent of the 1934 area lost, to housing, mineral extraction, forestry and agriculture.[27] The heathland landscape has continued to be fragmented: a repeat survey in 1978 showed that only 6000 ha of heathland survived in Dorset, just 60 per cent of that remaining in 1960, and 20 per cent of the original area.[28]

Norman Moore's 1962 paper was essentially a personal initiative, and not the result of a systematic scientific research effort by the Nature Conservancy. When the NCC came to produce its paper, *Nature Conservation in Great Britain*, in 1984, it found that the database on the impacts of agriculture on habitats and species was remarkably poor, even though no one seriously doubted their severity. That volume contains a summary of the estimated loss of good wildlife habitat, but these are of variable quality and detail. Those for woodlands were particularly good, based upon the NCC's Ancient Woodlands Inventory, while those for other habitats such as grassland were much more fragmentary.[29]

The public and Parliamentary debate about countryside change and habitat loss during the passage of the Wildlife and Countryside Act was loud and rather confused. One source of that confusion was the lack of authoritative and complete data on land-use change. It was only in the aftermath of the debate, in the 1980s, that systematic surveys were begun. Even then, efforts were at first rather muddled. A study as late as 1993 still found that official data on land-use change were "incomplete and misleading".[30] A land use survey had been carried out before the Second World War, in the 1930s, but although this had been repeated in the 1970s (like its predecessor, using schoolchildren as surveyors), the results were not recent enough, or tightly enough defined to be very useful to the burgeoning conservation debate.

In the 1980s a number of government agencies therefore began to commission new surveys, using various mixes of field surveys and remote sensing (air photographs and satellite imagery). They did so independently, and in a sense competitively. The NCC's National Countryside Monitoring Scheme, using air photographs and ground surveys, was designed to provide detailed ecological information on semi-natural habitats, but results have only been published for some counties. The Countryside Commission and the Department of the Environment's "Monitoring Landscape Change" project used satellite data to give a more generalised picture. Neither was entirely satisfactory.

In 1990 the government funded a new land-use change project to record the state of the countryside in 1990, the Countryside Survey 1990.[31] This built on previous land use surveys by the Institute of Terrestrial Ecology (ITE) in 1977, 1978 and 1984. These involved fieldwork in between 256 and 384 one-kilometre squares, carefully selected using the ITE land classification, to produce estimates of landscape change in Britain.[32] The 1990 survey aimed to make quantitative estimates of the extent of different land cover types, landscape features, habitats and species, to establish the nature and direction of changes that had taken place between 1978 and 1990, and to provide a firm baseline against which future changes could be assessed. The 1990 survey combined a complete survey of land cover derived from Thematic Mapper satellite imagery with a sample survey of selected locations using detailed field surveys.[33]

The satellite data show that "semi-natural vegetation" covers about a third of Great Britain, amounting to 57 per cent of Scotland, 39 per cent of Wales and just 17 per cent of England.[34] Between 1984 and 1990 some semi-natural cover types increased in area slightly, although some (e.g. moorland grass) declined slightly. Broadleaved and coniferous woodland increased in area by a few per cent. The most significant shifts between land-use categories were between arable and grassland, but almost 90 per cent of land did not change category. Boundaries did, however, change significantly. The length of hedgerows declined by a quarter and walls and walls with fences by a tenth between 1984 and 1990. The survey also tried to identify more subtle shifts in vegetation, through extensive field surveys using the National Vegetation Classification on sample plots. This showed significant loss of species since 1978 in three kinds of habitat: semi-improved grass, woodland and upland grass.

Pollution and climatic change

Not all the threats to conservation have arisen from physical transformation of landscape and habitat. Industrialisation and urbanisation have had much more widespread and chronic impacts through pollution. Coastal and freshwater pollution from sewage and industrial effluent has been recognised as a serious problem for some decades. Recent studies by the Plymouth Marine Laboratory suggest that land-based pollution is stunting the growth of mussels all along the North Sea coast, particularly in the South. The problem in this case is polycyclic aromatic hydrocarbons emitted by vehicle engines, but heavy metals, sewage and oil spills are all known to be important and damaging, and have been the subject of campaigning by conservation organisations.[35]

As with the sea, the principle that air pollution can affect wildlife and the countryside is familiar, but understanding of the scale and significance of the effects is still growing. One example of this is the problem of acidification, which only surfaced as a major issue for conservation in the 1980s in the wake of wider concerns about acid rain. A study by Plantlife suggests that 54 per cent of mosses, 47 per cent of lichens and 24 per cent of higher plants have suffered regional decline or local extinction due to air pollution, acid deposition or nitrogen deposition.[36] Research by English Nature suggests that 600 SSSIs in England may be at risk from acidification, approximately one in every six.[37] Studies by the World Wide Fund for Nature International suggest that the outlook on acidification is bleak in the UK, along with other countries on the northwest fringe of Europe such as Belgium, The Netherlands, Norway and Sweden. Even after planned reductions in emissions, a significant proportion of protected areas will remain at risk from acidification, and the need for further reductions in emissions is urgent. Acidification is identified as a significant threat to European biodiversity.[38]

There is a further threat to Britain's flora and other species, and that is human-induced climatic change. Although the scale of the impact is not yet fully clear, it may in time prove one of the most profound. Climatic change has always affected ecosystems and species in the UK, of course. Derek Ratcliffe charts the impacts of climatic variations over the last three centuries. Runs of severe winters, or severe summer droughts have measurable impacts on mortality and sometimes distribution of plants at the extreme end of their range in the UK. There has, however, been little sign of a clear trend in climate over this period, and any changes have been masked by the ubiquitous human impact.[39] Recently, however, fears about the "Greenhouse Effect" suggest that human impacts may extend to climate itself. Debate about the evidence for anthropogenic climatic change has been fierce, but the work of the Intergovernmental Panel on Climate Change has established the scientific consensus that it is happening. Conservation organisations have joined the chorus of those concerned about its implications.[40]

It is not easy to predict the impacts of future climatic change on conservation in the UK, because of the level of uncertainty. There is uncertainty about the extent of increases in atmospheric carbon dioxide (partly because we do not know whether policies to reduce CO_2 will work), about the effects of this on temperatures (either averages or extremes), about the implications of temperature rise for other aspects of climate (for example windspeeds, rainfall or seasonality), about impacts of raised global temperatures on sea levels, and about the response of animal and plant species (and human land managers) to changed environmental conditions. The consensus view is that the UK will be warmer and wetter by the middle of the twenty-first century. Temperatures will rise, possibly by 1.5°C in the summer, and by 1.7°C in the North and 1.2°C in the South in winter. There are likely to be fewer winter frosts, earlier springs, and a 5–15 per cent rise in winter rainfall.[41]

It is harder to predict the responses of plants and animals to these temperature changes. Work by the Institute of Terrestrial Ecology using data on the distributions of 251 species listed in *Red Data Books* suggested that 29 per cent of rare plant and animal species might be directly affected in an adverse way by a 2°C rise in mean temperature, and 50 per cent could be affected by changes in the difference between summer and winter temperatures.[42] Some 70 per cent of species could be affected by increases in winter rainfall. Some species (just under a quarter in the ITE study) are widespread and would probably not be affected directly by changed climatic conditions (the corn cockle for example, an arable weed made rare by seed cleaning, herbicides and habitat loss). Others would suffer from increased rainfall (for example the lizard orchid, which might lose out in competition). A group of species with a northwestern distribution might be threatened, including arctic–alpine plants. Other species might gain from warmer conditions, for example butterflies like the reintroduced large blue or the Adonis blue. However, such gains are likely to be prevented by lack of available habitat, and particular problems such as summer drought (which caused the last native population of the large blue butterfly to go extinct in 1976).

The secondary effects of climatic change are even harder to predict. Enhanced levels of carbon dioxide could enhance rates of growth of some species, which will promote ecological change. Farmers are likely to move into new crops, and perhaps new production systems. There may also be changes in the incidence of pest outbreaks or fungal infections. All of these things will have impacts on habitats and landscape. These will depend on local site conditions, for example soil moisture, which will also be affected by changing rainfall patterns. On the coast, impacts on vegetation and landscape are likely to be dominated by the issue of sea-level rise, higher rates of coastal erosion, and flooding.[43] At this stage it is impossible to predict accurately the shape and extent of the impacts of these changes, but their significance is not in doubt.

It is the likely pace of climatic change that is likely to be the greatest problem. Evolutionary processes of speciation and extinction usually happen over periods of 100 or 1000 generations, each of which might last from a few months to a century depending on the kind of organism. The climatic changes expected now will happen within 100 generations for many species. The likely rate of change in temperature will lead to changes in vegetation that are more rapid than those that occurred at the end of the last glacial maximum 10,000 years ago. These temperature changes will take place over periods shorter than the lifespan of individual long-lived species such as trees. The changes will be too rapid for evolution to cope, and extinctions are therefore likely. Organisms with very specialised habitat requirements and those at the southern edge of their range in the UK, will be particularly vulnerable.

The new conditions may support new species, some of them perhaps exotics. The changes will also have relatively slight impacts on those plants and animals that are adapted to disperse readily, for example orchids and flying insects, which may manage to adapt to the changing climate by moving to areas of new habitat. However, the scale of habitat fragmentation means that there may not be enough such areas to move to, particularly in the intensively managed agricultural landscapes of lowland England. Many species sustained within these fragments of land depend on specialised habitats and will be extremely vulnerable to extinction. SSSIs and NNRs are too remote from each other for species to hop easily from one to the next. The protected area system, and indeed conservation as a whole, is ill-adapted to face the new threat of rapid climatic change.

Losing SSSIs

The impacts of change on the countryside as a whole have obviously been serious, but how have the protected areas themselves fared? Have they stood out as a bulwark against change? Sadly they have not. This is most dramatically demonstrated by the threats to Sites of Special Scientific Interest. Passage of the Wildlife and Countryside Act 1981 made the notification of Sites of Special Scientific Interest (SSSIs) the critical central element in government nature conservation policy in Great Britain. The NCC commented in 1984 that "the SSSI device gradually proved to be a more important means of safeguarding important areas than had at first seemed likely".[44] This increasing focus on SSSIs was stimulated by the Wildlife and Countryside Act 1981, which for the first time offered a way beyond simple persuasion to pursue the protection of SSSIs threatened by agricultural and forestry development.

Section 15 of the Countryside Act 1968 allowed the NCC to offer management agreements to owners and occupiers of SSSIs to support conservation management. The 1981 Act made such agreements the lynch-pin of wildlife conservation, by obliging the NCC to offer management agreements to the owners or occupiers of any SSSI whose management of the site threatened its special interest. The NCC had to notify the owner or occupier of each SSSI of the reasons for its importance, and to list the activities that might cause damage. This might include ploughing, planting trees, drainage, grazing above a certain stocking level or fertilisation. If the occupier wanted to carry out these activities, the NCC was obliged to offer a management agreement and pay a sum in compensation for the profit they were forgoing by not doing so. The occupier was supposed not to carry out damaging operations until this had been done. There were some problems initially with what was called the "three-month loophole", because unscrupulous occupiers could in fact legally damage any newly proposed SSSI in the statutory first three months between being told about them and the notification taking effect. This was closed by the Wildlife and Countryside (Amendment) Act 1985.[45]

Unfortunately, the task of notifying and (for existing sites) re-notifying those holding SSSIs proved extremely complex and costly. In the early 1980s, there was great concern in the voluntary conservation movement about the rate at which SSSIs were re-notified (and thus brought under the protection of the new Act), and whether the government would stump up the money to pay for management agreements necessary to give the "voluntary principle" teeth. Early estimates suggested renotification would be complete by 1983, but the date was progressively postponed, and indeed strictly speaking the task is still not complete. By March 1990, 97 per cent of SSSIs in Great Britain had been notified or renotified.[46] Not only was renotification slow, it was expensive, both in direct financial terms and in staff time. The NCC's budget was £10.2m in 1982, but it grew rapidly. By 1987 it was £29m, and in 1989–90, the last year before the demise of the NCC, it was £38.2m. The vast bulk of the increased expenditure was due to the costs of implementing the Wildlife and Countryside Act.

The Nature Conservancy Council finally crawled out from the mountain of work involved in renotification (having fought successfully for more money to do it, and having started to change the culture of its regional staff to be effective deliverers of the package), just in time to be dismembered. By the start of the 1990s, concern was growing that its successor organisations (English Nature, Scottish Natural Heritage and the Countryside Council for Wales) were going slow on the notification of SSSIs, in order to keep the scientific and paper work within bounds, to ensure that they could meet landowners and other parties and deal with their interests and needs in detail, and to limit the cost implications of management agreements. The new agencies were much more aware of the need to have good public relations, both with landowners and with a government whose heart was set on slim organisations and low costs.

Critics of the Wildlife and Countryside Act have consistently argued that management agreements under the 1983 Financial Guidelines (which established the principle that occupiers of SSSIs should be compensated for profits forgone in not damaging a site) were a waste of money (Ann and Malcom MacEwen described them as "hot air balloons which can only be kept aloft by burning money").[47] They have certainly proved expensive. In 1981 there were 70 management agreements under the Countryside Act. They covered about 2000 ha and cost about £25,000. The number of agreements and the area covered (and the cost) grew steadily. By 1986 there were over 1000 agreements, and already they covered more than the NCC's original target of 3000 ha. By 1990 there were over 1700 management agreements covering almost 72,000 ha. They cost almost £7m, plus forward commitments of more than £4m per year. The cost of management agreements of all kinds accounted for 20 per cent of the NCC's expenditure in 1989/90.[48]

The critical question, however, is not whether the SSSI system is expensive, but whether it works. Unfortunately, there is no serious doubt that SSSIs, and ASSIs in Northern Ireland, are being damaged, by agriculture and many other activities. Some of this damage is due to neglect or inappropriate management, some by deliberate acts of development (some indeed with planning permission), some by casual misuse (e.g. motorcycle rough-riding). A great many SSSIs are subject to generalised abuse from airborne pollutants of various kinds. Friends of the Earth carried out a survey of organisations in England and Wales in 1994 that suggested that 723 SSSIs were threatened, 334 of them by acid deposition and 123 by mineral extraction.[49] Threats to SSSIs are not new. By the end of the 1970s almost two-thirds of SSSIs in southeast England had been subject to potentially damaging proposals. In Kent, 4 per cent of SSSIs were being threatened by development proposals every year, and between 1968 and 1979 two out of every three SSSIs in Kent had been reduced in area, and 6 per cent of the total area of the SSSI system in the county had been lost.[50]

Over the last ten years, the statutory agencies have tended to argue that loss and damage is more or less under control, while the NGOs have argued the reverse. The evidence is complex, but fairly clear. Although the 1981 Act had some effect on the loss of SSSIs, loss and damage has continued through the 1980s and 1990s, despite the new and complicated procedures to protect them. Perhaps because of management agreements, losses due to agriculture have become less important, but losses to developments with planning permission or from the activities of statutory undertakers have risen. There is a particular problem with sites in Britain that have very old (but still valid) rights for mineral extraction, such as Carmel Woods SSSI in Wales. The status of the site is literally being undermined by an old Interim Development Order for a limestone quarry.

In 1990 a total of 324 SSSIs were lost or damaged, 6 per cent of the total number. One site was destroyed altogether. This appears to be the worst year on record, and while changes in the recording system may partly explain the rise in problems in that year (especially in the increased recording of short-term damage), there is no doubt that this damage did take place. The vast majority of damage to SSSIs is short-term (97 per cent in 1989–90), and here agriculture was still important, causing three-quarters of this short-term damage, mainly through chronic problems such as overgrazing rather than drastic land-use change. Activities given planning permission were responsible for the SSSI destroyed, and for damage on 31 others. Almost half of this was judged "long-term" or very "serious". Recreation (particularly off-road motor vehicles, horses and walkers) and lack of proper management were other significant problems. In the seven years over which data are available for Great Britain, there have been over 1500 cases of damage to SSSIs. That represents damage to just over one site in four. The conservation interest of seven SSSIs has been completely destroyed.

Terry Rowell found in 1991 that SSSIs were deteriorating faster than had been estimated before the 1981 Act, and that while much of this damage was short term, its aggregate impact was considerable. He also showed that a significant proportion of the problem was caused by third parties (i.e. not the owner or occupier), and that there was little evidence that either consultation with owners or conclusion of management agreements actually stopped SSSIs being damaged.[51]

In Northern Ireland, both declared and candidate ASSIs are also being damaged, although the DoE (NI) does not carry out systematic monitoring, so the size of the problem cannot be properly assessed. Robert Brown reported in 1992 that there was real concern among conservation organisations that sites were being lost or seriously damaged faster than the rate of designation.[52] Progress with declaration of ASSIs under the Nature Conservation and Amenity Lands Order 1985 is very slow. The Department of the Environment for Northern Ireland, the DoE(NI), has a candidate list of about 200 ASSIs, but only 72 had been declared by 1995. The Northern Ireland Environment Service's "Target 2000" programme now aims to put in place a system of ASSIs that matches the system in England, Wales and Scotland and sets in motion an extensive campaign of survey, declaration and site safeguard.[53]

In many ways, the argument about SSSI and ASSI loss generates more heat than light, and the main reason for this is the lack of authoritative data. The Nature Conservancy Council published increasingly detailed information on loss and damage through the 1980s, but in his study for Wildlife Link in 1991, Terry Rowell criticised the ad-hoc methodology. He pointed out the way in which apparent loss and damage levels in adjacent counties in England were very different, and how recorded losses in individual counties changed dramatically from year to year. In Scotland, he said that loss and damage levels were "so low that no effective analysis can be made other than to question their veracity". The official data through the 1980s were not measuring real threats to SSSIs at all, but simply the energy locked up in filling in forms.[54]

The NCC belatedly began regional trials on a new reporting system in 1989-90 that would have produced standardised data across Scotland, England and Wales. Its dismemberment into country agencies prevented standardisation, and no national figures are available after 1990. The Joint Nature Conservation Committee has as yet proved incapable of imposing standard SSSI monitoring procedures, and is not in a position to publish data on the state of the SSSI system across the country.[55] The last Chairman of the Nature Conservancy Council, Sir William Wilkinson, has suggested that the government should "seriously consider instructing the JNCC to carry out a triennial in depth audit of damage to sites and deterioration across the UK, and to publish the results".[56] Without data of this kind it is extremely difficult to work out what is happening to the SSSI system.

Protecting protected areas

The shortcomings of the SSSI system, and the procedures in place to monitor it, are widely recognised. Each of the country agencies is quick to point out that they have the matter in hand. England is probably furthest ahead. The National Audit Office made a specific inquiry into the protection and management of SSSIs in England in 1994, and found that English Nature was giving priority to habitats that are poorly represented in the SSSI system, such as rivers, and that resources were being re-deployed towards managing and conserving existing sites, and "developing better relations with owners and occupiers".[57] English Nature do not consider it cost-effective to monitor SSSIs every year, but aim to visit every three years, while visiting those sites that are "threatened or fragile" more frequently. This pattern varies across the country, partly with the complexion of the 21 local "teams" which have replaced the old regional office structure. New procedures are being planned to provide central data on what is called "site integrity", and this will be linked to a database on visits to the site and exchanges with the owners.

English Nature's search for a slimmer, more open and less unpopular way of dealing with SSSIs seeks to improve the effectiveness with which their important features are maintained, by improving relations with owners and occupiers and making management more positive, and tied directly to the creation of the ecological conditions needed on the SSSI. The Wildlife Enhancement Scheme offers standard payments for positive management of

SSSIs in eight trial areas of England. Management agreements will therefore, English Nature hopes, become increasingly cost-effective; no longer will money be burned in compensating landowners for damaging operations they might not have done anyway; it will be tightly targeted to specific management activities. Far from resenting this "interference", as farmers classically did in the early 1980s, it is hoped that landowners faced with hard times in agriculture will be glad to conclude agreements, and to become "partners" in SSSI management and enhancement. Nor are conservation NGOs forgotten in English Nature's planning, since the new Reserves Enhancement Scheme allows groups (the Wildlife Trusts initially) to apply for money to improve SSSI management, on the basis of standard payments per hectare of different habitats. Some half a million pounds will be devoted to this programme alone in 1994/5.

These new measures to protect SSSIs may well have a good effect, but many conservationists doubt if they go far enough. Wildlife Link called for legislative change to safeguard SSSIs in 1991, as did Friends of the Earth (FoE) in 1994. FoE went so far as to publish the text of a proposed new Wildlife Bill that would extend the powers of the Secretary of State to make Orders to enforce the protection of all SSSIs (rather than just some of them as at present), to extend the conservation agencies' powers to enact by-laws to protect SSSIs (at present only possible on NNRs), to change the financial guidelines for management agreements to achieve positive management (rather than simply compensating owners for profits forgone), and to strengthen obligations on local planning authorities to refuse planning applications on SSSIs except in cases of overriding national importance.[58]

The lack of legislative sticks to back up the carrot of management agreements has been a problem for the SSSI system since the passage of the Wildlife and Countryside Act 1981. In theory such sticks exist. The Secretary of State can protect particularly threatened SSSIs with a Nature Conservation Order under Section 29 of the 1981 Act, and there has always been the possibility of compulsory purchase. However, these powers have rarely been used.[59] The original interpretation of the 1981 Act suggested that NCOs could be made on any SSSI. However, in the mid-1980s, the Secretary of State for the Environment took the view that they could only be used to protect a much smaller group of "elite" sites.[60] The argument was that every site protected by an Order had to be demonstrably of national importance, and that "ordinary" SSSIs were only part of a system, and not of national importance individually. The NCC responded by proposing Orders for only selected sites, and the teeth of the 1981 Act were thereby drawn.[61] As Sir William Wilkinson commented in 1992, "There is a serious and widely held misconception that SSSI designation confers actual protection. In fact it does nothing of the sort. Unless the Secretary of State is prepared to intervene at the end of a negotiating period and ... to authorise compulsory purchase, the site in question is lost".[62]

42

Does the loss of SSSIs matter? Intriguingly, the Department of the Environment sees some flexibility in the question. The Environment White Paper 1990 suggested, surprisingly, that loss and damage to SSSIs has been "more than compensated for by the continued expansion of the SSSI network". This compensation is of course a complete illusion: what matters is the total stock of habitat in the country, and this is shrinking steadily. The creation of new SSSIs just allows us to slide further down the line of declining diversity in the countryside, and further in to the fragmented landscape. Sir William Wilkinson said at the launch of the NCC's last annual report that the mechanisms for the protection of SSSIs were not strong enough. "There needs to be the strongest possible presumption against any development which would involve their damage or destruction".[63] That presumption is no more prevalent now than it was in 1990. Under the present procedures there can be no doubt that erosion of the SSSI system will continue, and with it the inexorable spread of uniformity in the countryside.

The Brussels connection

The long-running debate about SSSIs is now being overtaken by another, involving the implementation of the European Community Habitats and Species Directive, the "Habitats Directive".[64] This provides for the creation of "Special Areas for Conservation" (SACs), which are to form part of a trans-European network of sites, to be called "Natura 2000". Special Protection Areas (SPAs), declared under the Birds Directive, will also be part of this network.[65] The Habitats Directive lists target habitats (Annex I, including heaths, woodlands and raised bogs) and species of special interest for which SACs must be created (Annex II, including species such as the otter, the two horseshoe bats and the great crested newt). The Directive says that SACs should be protected from all development that has a negative ecological impact except in cases of "overriding public interest, including those of a social or economic nature".[66]

The Habitats Directive is potentially a powerful new weapon which conservationists can wield in their defence of wildlife sites. However, inevitably perhaps, there is both controversy and concern about the way the British government will actually implement it. The precedent of the 1979 Birds Directive is not reassuring. The criteria for SPAs are quite clear, based on the international importance of a site in terms of the proportion of European populations present, either breeding, wintering or on passage. A total of 238 SPAs have been identified in the UK, but by April 1991, only 37 complete SPAs had been designated, plus parts of another 10. This is just 20 per cent of the total in ten years. The UK has one of the lowest rates of SPA designation of all EC countries, and the total area protected in this way is very low (less than one per cent of the land area of the UK). The government's performance is particularly poor in Northern Ireland, with only two SPAs designated out of a total of 17 sites.[67]

According to the RSPB, the reasons for the government's backwardness on SPAs include excessive workload on relevant parts of the Department of the Environment, demands for additional survey information, and opposition from other Ministries, particularly the Department of Transport (DoT) and the Department for Trade and Industry (DTI) and the Scottish, Welsh and Northern Ireland Offices, who all feared the potential impact of the designation on opportunities for economic development. A major complicating factor was also that many of the SPAs were on estuaries, reflecting the UK's international importance for migratory waders. Designation as an SPA therefore threatened major infrastructure projects such as estuarine barrages, and also implied constraints on activities such as shellfish dredging that have lain beyond the powers of SSSI/ASSI protection, and therefore present somewhat novel problems for government planners.

SACs are likely to encounter slightly different problems. The government's discussion paper in October 1993, and the Draft Regulations published in 1994, made it clear that there would be no new primary legislation to protect SACs, but that the UK would depend on the provisions of the Wildlife and Countryside Act 1981 to do the job. It is widely understood that there is widespread opposition outside the DoE, particularly in the DoT, DTI and the Welsh Office, to any measures that would increase protection for SSSIs, and perhaps therefore threaten infrastructure development. There is concern that the government appears to believe that the "agri-environment package" (and its provisions for conservation and habitat creation on farmland) will be enough on its own to meet the Habitats Directive's provisions for conservation beyond existing protected areas.

There are real concerns about the extent to which the government will make protection of the SACs effective, and whether what the Directive rather quaintly terms the "favourable status" of the SACs will be maintained. A study list by Derek Ratcliffe for Friends of the Earth found that of 112 possible SACs, 50 were presently poorly protected, and 75 were actively at risk.[68] The protection actually given to SSSIs has been limited by the reluctance of the conservation agencies to go to law to protect them, their inability to press their demands with sufficient urgency on reluctant Secretaries of State, and their unwillingness to extend protection as far as the law allows. Without a new and much more positive attitude throughout government, it is questionable whether site protection under the Habitats Directive will be particularly effective in the UK.

The Habitats Directive may strengthen provisions for the protection of SACs themselves. The government's list of candidate SACs includes 280 sites. However, there may be unfortunate implications for "ordinary" SSSIs and ASSIs. One worry revolves around the question of money. The fear is simple, that because the SACs will be an international and highly visible legal responsibility of government, they will receive the lion's share of resources. Defining and notifying them will cost money, as will paying compensation to owners (for example if minerals planning permission is revoked by local authorities). Unless new money is found, these resources will have to be found by stripping out other programmes, and might suck resources away from ordinary SSSIs. If so, conservationists may yet come to rue their enthusiasm for the Habitats Directive.

Another problem is that all SACs must already be SSSIs. Habitats that are poorly represented in the SSSI series (Scottish lowland raised bogs, for example), and sites with potential for restoration (an important element in the Habitat Directive) may not receive the protection they deserve.[69] Hazel Phillips and Carol Hatton regard the UK's Draft Regulations for the implementation of the Habitats Directive as "a missed opportunity of minimalist and rearguard proposals".[70] The complaint has a sadly familiar ring to it.

Conservation at sea

The EC Habitats Directive for the first time takes the needs of marine conservation seriously. Until recently the marine environment has been a forgotten dimension of conservation in the UK.[71] The Habitats Directive extends the provisions for statutory site protection in marine environments by providing for the designation of Marine SACs. This raises a whole host of thorny technical and legal problems, but at the same time offers an important opportunity.

SSSI and ASSI designation can usually only extend as far from land as the low water mark, which is where local authority jurisdiction ends and that of the Crown Estate Commissioners begins. The 1981 Wildlife and Countryside Act provided for Marine Nature Reserves (MNRs), but gave no legal purchase for SSSIs offshore. However, there are numerous intertidal SSSIs. One review identified 627 SSSIs which extended to the low water mark on ordinary tides.[72] Intertidal ecosystems in the UK are among those of the highest international importance, particularly for migratory birds, and are subject to a number of threats, on all scales. On the largest scale, the construction of barrages, for example in Cardiff Bay (forced through after a long battle), or on the Wash or the Severn, has been highly controversial. More locally, many new yacht marinas threaten habitats, change estuarine hydrodynamics and cause pollution. Commercial shell-fishing and bait-digging have also been shown to have significant environmental impacts, and have also proved controversial, either where stopped by by-laws (e.g. on the salt marshes around Lindisfarne), or where local traditional gatherers find their cockle beds stripped by newcomers with new technologies (e.g. Burry Inlet).

There has been a succession of reports highlighting the threats to the coast, and proposing solutions. The RSPB has been particularly vociferous, publishing *Turning the Tide* in 1990, and subsequently *A Shore Future*, complaining that nothing had been done.[73] The real trouble with the coastal zone is the vast number of government organisations involved in its management, and the fact that their work is uncoordinated. Local planning authority jurisdiction reaches only to the low water mark, Sea Fisheries Committees can establish fisheries by-laws from there to the three-mile limit, and in England and Wales the National Rivers Authority (NRA) can make by-laws to control water quality. In England and Wales the NRA also regulates salmon fishing up to six miles offshore, while outside this the Ministry of Agriculture, Fisheries and Food deals with fishing, and the Department of Energy with oil and gas licenses. Not only is the situation chaotic, but even within the narrow remits of individual organisations, it is clear that marine resources are not managed sustainably, as the debate over the EC's Common Fisheries Policy (and over drift netting) shows.[74]

The only existing statutory basis for the conservation of ecosystems below the low water mark is the Marine Nature Reserve (MNR).[75] MNRs were added into the Wildlife and Countryside Bill during Parliamentary debate and the legislation is not very thorough. They can be declared from the high water mark out to the limit of territorial waters (effectively three nautical miles), around Great Britain (i.e. initially excluding Northern Ireland, Isle of Man and the Channel Islands). The conservation agencies' powers are much more limited than in the case of terrestrial NNRs. The agency can propose an MNR to the relevant Secretary of State, who decides on declaration. Even when designated, the conservation agency can only make by-laws to protect it from a very limited range of human activities. It can control navigation by pleasure boats, for example, but not fishing; it can stop the taking or molestation of any animal or plant, but not if it is fishermen who do it.

The real problem with MNRs is that the measure has proved enormously cumbersome and costly to implement, and very unpopular with fishermen and other economic interests (fish-farm companies for example). Two MNRs have been declared, around Lundy Island in Devon (1986), and the other around Skomer Island and the Marloes Peninsula in Dyfed (1990). The latter proposal lay with the Secretary of State for four years, giving some measure of the controversy surrounding it. Other sites have been proposed for MNRs, including Loch Sween in Argyll, Strangford Lough and Rathlin Island, the Isles of Scilly and the Menai Straits, but progress has been very slow.[76] However, the designation of Strangford Lough at least is being pursued vigorously. A detailed and glossy proposal for a Marine Nature Reserve was published by the Environment Service of the Department of the Environment for Northern Ireland in 1994.[77]

Perhaps because of the complexity of the bureaucratic challenge of effective marine conservation, the British government has opted for a minimal approach in its proposals for implementing the Habitats Directive. It proposes only to place on the Secretary of State for the Environment, the Ministers responsible for agriculture, and the statutory conservation bodies, a duty to "have regard to the requirements of the Directive" in any decisions that might relate to marine SACs. This is a clause much beloved of Parliamentary draughtspeople, and of course provides a vague signal of good intentions without any commitment. It is no solution at all to the wider problems of the conservation of marine ecosystems or resources.

Action for biodiversity

Increasingly, threats to nature in the UK are being described in terms of threats to biodiversity. Edward Wilson argues that "we are in the midst of one of the great extinction spasms of geological history".[78] As this chapter has shown, there are significant threats to nature in the UK as ecosystems are transformed and simplified by human action, and animal and plant ranges shrink.

To a large extent the new language of "biodiversity conservation" simply re-expresses themes that have long been established in British conservation. We have had specific legislation to protect non-game species for well over a century. We have, of course, achieved "biodiversity conservation" by the protection of species and habitats in protected areas of different kinds, and through "ex-situ conservation", in other words the preservation of species outside their natural habitat, in zoos and botanic gardens, and in the non-living storage of genetic material (seeds, sperm, eggs or genes).[79] Yet a new, explicit and targeted concern for biodiversity is now widely thought to be changing the way people think about conservation. In 1993 the Department of the Environment and the Joint Nature Conservation Committee (JNCC) held a meeting at the Royal Geographical Society in London on Action for Biodiversity in the UK. As a result of this and similar meetings the government published Biodiversity: the UK action plan in January 1994, as part of its reponse to the United Nations Conference on Environment and Development at Rio de Janeiro. This plan has become a major focus of new thinking about nature conservation in the UK. Future conservation strategies are likely to be heavily influenced by its ideas and approaches.

The overall goal of Biodiversity: the UK action plan was "to conserve and enhance biological diversity within the UK and to contribute to the conservation of global biodiversity through all available mechanisms". Its underlying principles included the idea of sustainable use of biological resources, the precautionary principle in decision-making, the recognition that the conservation of biodiversity should be "an integral part of Government

47

programmes, policy and action", and the need for a sound knowledge base to guide conservation practice and policy. The objectives of biodiversity conservation were to conserve (and where practicable to enhance) the populations and national ranges of native species, and the quality and range of wildlife habitats and ecosystems. The Plan also aimed to increase public awareness and involvement in conservation and to extend action to the European and global scales.[80]

Fine words, but how do you do it? The government got strongly worded advice on this point from the document written by non-governmental organisations and published late in 1993, *Biodiversity Challenge*.[81] This suggested how to turn words about biodiversity into action. It argued that if you want to achieve biodiversity conservation objectives, you need to have plans, and if you want to know if your plans are working you need targets. *Biodiversity Challenge* made the simple point that these targets should be about biodiversity conservation itself, and not things that might be done to promote it. They should be direct measures of gains or losses in nature (the area of habitats or landscapes left, or the populations of target species), not indirect measures of effort.

The *Biodiversity Challenge* approach is really very simple and logical: carry out an audit of the present status of biodiversity in the UK; agree objectives; set targets for both species and habitats; agree priorities; implement a plan of action to deliver these targets, and finally monitor progress and review actions. Priority species are identified. They include those endemic to the UK or the British Isles, species threatened with global extinction, species where the UK holds a significant proportion of the European population, species in decline, species confined to small areas, and species that had become extinct since 1900. Priority habitats include those on which priority species occur, those that are rapidly declining in area or quality, those for which the UK has international responsibility, and those listed in Annex 1 of the EC Habitats Directive.

Biodiversity Challenge argues that targets for populations of species and the extent of particular habitats should be set, and specific action taken to reach them. The suggested means of doing this was "action plans" or "recovery plans" for both species and habitats. These should be simple, short and sharp, covering objectives, threats, proposed action and provisions for monitoring their effectiveness. *Biodiversity Challenge* suggested that targets should be "realistic, but ambitious", should look ahead about ten years and be quantitative. The 1995 edition included over 100 pages of appendices setting out "targets" for over 600 species and a wide range of habitats, and numerous species and habitat action plans.

In 1994 the Department of the Environment set up a Steering Group to move the Biodiversity Action Plan forwards. It was charged with developing specific costed targets for "key species and habitats" for the years 2000 and

2010 by 1995 (European Nature Conservation Year). Working groups were set up concerned with identifying and setting targets, public involvement and improving data accessibility. *Biodiversity Challenge* argues that new attitudes are needed on the part of government. It suggests that the conservation of biodiversity should be made an integral and effective part of all government programmes, policy and action. Meeting biodiversity conservation targets demands changes across economic sectors, including physical planning, agriculture, forestry, fishing and energy, and strengthened provisions for habitat protection and their extension (for example to intertidal and subtidal areas, and to buffer zones around protected areas).

The current concern for biodiversity in the UK carries both great potential, and some risks. The potential lies in the fact that in signing *Biodiversity: the UK action plan*, all government departments (not just those with a conservation remit) have for the first time committed themselves to taking conservation seriously. This follows successive piecemeal attempts to increase the stringency with which Ministers and government bodies were required to "have regard" for conservation, from the Countryside Act 1968 onwards. This is a small but decisive step. The Action Plan gives conservationists inside and outside government a whole new dimension for applying pressure, and it is one they are firmly committed to exploiting.

The risks, on the other hand, are equally real. One is the mind-boggling effect (on supporters and other government departments) of a strategy for conservation that is organised species by species. Such a strategy, however well organised, is likely to be complex in realisation, and far from simple to comprehend. A second problem is the possibility that a species-by-species strategy will focus resources on species that are rare, but not particularly acutely threatened. Economic, technological and landscape change is sufficiently rapid that there may be significant threats to relatively common species and habitats that demand action (and resources) urgently that are not prioritised in formal action plans.

Biodiversity Challenge takes problems of this sort in its stride, seeing them as relatively straightforward issues of choosing the right targets for action. A more serious difficulty may prove to be the cost of the new action for biodiversity. The action plan is not of itself going to bring any new money for conservation. Money spent on new "biodiversity" initiatives may have to be taken from existing programmes and action. This may not matter if resources are in this way being tightly targeted for maximum effectiveness. But is there redundancy in existing programmes? What would be the effect of slimming them down, or cutting them? There is no obvious intention to carry out a tight economic or financial comparison of the cost-effectiveness of new action for key species and habitats with that of existing activities. Investment in new initiatives might leave holes in established programmes.

It is widely believed that "the best way to protect species is to protect habitats",[82] and it would not be surprising if the "new thinking" about biodiversity were rapidly translated back into "old thinking" about lowland raised bogs, heathland or Caledonian pine forests. If this is the case, there will probably be gains from any new public prominence given to these familiar conservation concerns, and the hope that government can be held more tightly to commitments to protect them. On the other hand, there is a risk that resources targeted on particular habitats will be found by reducing spending on others judged of lesser national importance, or of only regional or local importance. Similarly, enthusiasm for biodiversity might divert spending from other sectors of conservation — for example landscape conservation, urban conservation, or community programmes.

Whatever the outcome of these debates, it is clear that the notion of biodiversity has won an important place in British conservation. In some ways the most remarkable feature of this latest turn of debate about conservation concerns not the details of the action proposed, but the way in which that action is conceived of. *Biodiversity Challenge* is a set-piece of applied business management thinking. In the new language of biodiversity, conservation efforts must be targeted on critical priorities, and locked into a tight programme of activities designed to achieve a specified and agreed output in a predicted time and within a known budget. These ideas match the contemporary rhetoric of public life, and quite fundamental shifts in the way people think — not only about the proper work of government, but also about themselves and the world about them. The next chapter explores the nature and impact of these changes in economy and society, and their implications both for the countryside and for conservation.

CHAPTER FOUR

Conservation and the Global Village

*Britain is now a single interrelated environment from the Highlands of Scotland
to Piccadilly Circus*
Nan Fairbrother, 1970a[1]

New land, new lifestyles

The old Second World War fighter station at Duxford, near Cambridge, is
now part of the Imperial War Museum. Tucked between a hangar full of
aircraft and a vast gun from a naval battery at Gibraltar is a relic of the physical
reconstruction of British cities after the war, a small prefabricated house. It is
an unremarkable box-like structure, not dissimilar in concept or size to the
"starter homes" that appeared like a sudden rash all over the country in the
1980s. The aim, then as now, was principally to get people housed decently
and quickly, although provision then was by the state, and that is no longer in
fashion.

The thing that is remarkable about the little house at Duxford is not its
fabric, but its content. Each room has been furnished with contemporary
household equipment and goods, and with appropriate personal effects. It is,
as the museum planners would hope, a remarkable timewarp, and the
astonishing thing about it is its bareness and the lack of material goods. The
house is self-consciously modern, with a refrigerator and a small cooker, but

51

every room is a foreign country. There are no fitted cupboards, no fitted carpets, no bright fabrics, no electronic goods and no plastics. It is a plain, simple home, but it is a world away from the packed and gleaming interiors of today's many "lifestyle" magazines, or the real homes we make in response to their tutorship of our taste and their grip on our pocket.

The bareness of the post-war house at Duxford is a measure of how far consumer culture has come in the intervening half century for the vast majority of British people. The scope and extent of that change is remarkable. The two decades following the end of the Second World War saw extraordinary economic growth and improving living standards in the UK. It transformed our economy, our patterns of consumption, and our culture. We have products now undreamed of in the 1940s, and they are made of synthesised materials of a range and diversity then unimaginable. We have foods of great variety, and an increasing number of them are pre-processed in a factory, and are brought to us chilled and expensively packaged, and we drive to buy them from vast gleaming emporia quite unlike the shops that served us for so long.

Two generations have gone by since the period of post-war planning. Couples moving into new housing after the war raised the baby-boom generation, who powered the first surge of environmentalist concern in the 1970s. They in turn have raised the present generation, in whose consciousness environmental concerns are being forged anew. Over this time, the pressures on wildlife and the countryside, on nature, have grown inexorably. Support for conservation has grown with those pressures, as has the wider environmental movement. In many ways the most important changes for conservation over this period have not been in the fabric of the countryside, but in economy and society. This chapter describes these changes, and their significance for nature, and for conservation.

It is easy to underestimate the extent of change in lives and lifestyles since the 1940s. Perhaps the most fundamental change is in our use of energy. The mass-produced house of the 1990s is far warmer than its 1940s counterpart, and into it flow enormously increased amounts of energy, both directly in heat and light and power for machines, and indirectly in the form of manufactured products. By 1993 energy consumption in the UK was 220 million tonnes of oil or oil equivalent each year.[2] There have been vast shifts in the form of that energy, with the virtual closure of the deep coal-mining industry and coal use falling by 80 per cent between 1970 and 1993, while the consumption of gas rose 14 times over the same period. Consumption of petroleum products has increased hugely, much of it for road transport.

The decline in manufacturing industry in the UK in the 1970s and 1980s brought a major reduction in industrial energy use (by 40 per cent between 1970 and 1993), but domestic use grew by a fifth over the same period. In 1970 just over a third of British households had central heating. By 1992 the figure was 83 per cent. The modern house is not only warmer but also cleaner, no longer feeding the killing smogs that beset London in the 1950s. However, nuclear power and coal-burning power stations that provide electricity bring their own problems of radiation and acid rain, and even "clean" gas contributes unwanted CO_2 to the atmospheric greenhouse.[3] British consumers merrily make use of the energy bonanza, seemingly unaware of its implications for the environment. For several decades the UK has been floating blithely on the economic bubble of oil and gas from the North Sea, with little real and effective constraint on demand for energy.

Growing appetites have not been confined to energy. In the post-war period, and particularly through the last quarter of the twentieth century, the number and diversity of consumer goods in British homes increased dramatically. This phenomenon is perhaps epitomised by the television. The first regular television broadcasts in the world were begun by the BBC in November 1936. After the war, more and more people began to own and to watch television, the Coronation in 1953 being both a major landmark in the acceptance of the television into ordinary domestic life, and a symbolic event (the first national festivity in which more people participated by proxy, through television screens in living rooms, than in person on the street). By the 1970s, nine out of every ten British households owned a television set. By 1992, 99 per cent of British households owned a television, 96 per cent of them colour.[4]

The television was not alone in its colonisation of living space. Televisions share increasingly electronic living rooms with video recorders, CD players and computers. By 1993, one in every four households had a computer, and by 1994, modems for access to Internet were a top pre-Christmas seller in the high street. The "information super-highway", leading direct from living room to World Wide Web, was starting to move from hype into real life. Kitchens have also felt the impact of new technologies and consumer goods, their appearance and use transformed by refrigerators, washing machines, dishwashers, deep freezes, tumble dryers and microwave ovens.[5] The ultimate consumer good is the motor car. In 1972, half the households in Britain owned a car or van. One in four households now own more than one vehicle. In 1952 there were 2 million cars. By 1992 there were 20 million.

The new technologies that have come to play such an intimate role in our lives have been accompanied by dramatic shifts in the organisation of society. Households have progressively broken away from the post-war mould of the nuclear family. By 1992, a quarter of households consisted of only one person, and over 60 per cent of no more than two. Less than a third of households included children under 15 years old.[6] Furthermore, cultural changes have accompanied changing patterns of consumption. Advertising promoted the consumption of particular goods, and in the process created images that began to affect the way people thought about themselves and their lives. New technologies provided the means for the creation and dissemination of these new consumerist messages, and popular culture began to be defined increasingly by the displays of ideals and styles and products.[7] Television has played a particularly powerful role in this complex process, and continues to do so. On average, people in Britain watch 27 hours of television a week, and it is television that creates the environment in which they understand and live their lives.[8]

Rainforests in the bathroom

In the 1990s, we live in a consumer culture. The economic and political storms of the 1970s and 1980s seem if anything to have heightened enthusiasm for consumption. Both winners and losers in an apparently increasingly divided Britain (where Margaret Thatcher could seriously suggest that there is no such thing as society) have continued to define quality of life, culture, and human worth to a large extent in terms of possessions. Houses increasingly bristle with consumer goods; lifestyles have been transformed to include foreign holidays, people spend long hours watching the television and there is widespread use of private and business cars.[9] These things have not simply been scattered on top of a society that remains unchanged. Like the fruiting bodies of a fungus, consumer goods are the visible parts of much wider and deeper cultural changes. It is not only the countryside that has changed since the war, but we ourselves.

New ideas about fashion, style and design have had serious implications for both the way in which we have impacts on the environment, and on the ways in which we conceive of and organise nature and countryside conservation. Hunger for manufactured products has been insatiable. Consumption draws down stocks of non-renewable resources, uses up renewable resources at an unsustainable rate, and leaves a cocktail of wastes that pollute the environment and ourselves. Some of the demands of consumerism involve direct appropriation of nature, most poignantly perhaps in the use of tropical hardwoods. The search for quality, durability, finish and style has led to a steady demand for hardwood products in the home: tables, window frames, and bathroom fittings. The hardwood toilet seat has come to epitomise the way in which our bizarre tastes and consumer power hack away at nature. Tropical hardwoods fit decor and lifestyles, and they are cheap. From Borneo to bathroom they are sucked across the Earth by the strength of the purchasing power of our industrialised economy.

This linkage between local consumption and distant production has been a significant feature of the world since the end of the Second World War. People have become increasingly distanced (both physically and conceptually) from the source of the products they consume. We have little or no real knowledge of the social or environmental context within which things are grown or manufactured. We have little understanding of how goods are produced, of what (if any) are the costs of their production in the form of chronic pollution or technological hazard, or the condition of life for those who labour to produce them, half a world away, where labour is cheap and environmental and safety regulations may be non-existent.[10]

The UK now enjoys international trade on a scale undreamed of even in the heyday of British imperialism, when the world map was suffused with pink. The British economy has become increasingly tightly linked to others, and as a result, manufactured products and raw materials are drawn into the orbit of our consumption from all over the world. We talk of the "market-place", but this is an inappropriate word to describe the process of extraction, processing, manufacture and exchange that stretches from the rainforests or sweatshops of the Third World to our bathrooms and built-in wardrobes. These links are global, and political economists and pundits of cultural change have in the last decade begun to speak of a process of "globalisation" to describe the tightening connections beyond countries, trading blocs and continents. The UK is ever more closely tied to global capital, transnational corporations and global products.

There has, in the words of David Harvey, been "a sea change in the surface appearance of capitalism" since the 1970s.[11] Both production and marketing of products have increasingly become organised on a world scale. Businesses have become transnational. In their search for maximum returns on capital they invest to overcome the constraints of cultures, of national boundaries and the leaky bags that nation states try to establish as national economies. Capital is now increasingly footloose, moving across the world to locate where production is cheapest, to integrate production in different places, to minimise costs, to minimise delay in reaching markets, and to maximise profits. These represent profound shifts away from the old regimentation of industry, called "Fordism" after the industrial genius and might of Henry Ford and his "Model T". New technology and new institutions have both allowed and, at the same time, driven the globalisation of business. Telecommunications, containerisation and computers have reduced the frictional effects of distance, and allowed complex production processes to be broken down into simple parts that can be tackled by unskilled workers, and allowed different parts to be built far from each other and from intended markets. Computers have displaced workers in manufacturing, and also allowed jobs to be relocated on the other side of the globe.[12]

Global transnational companies compete not only in space, but also in time. They must speed up the rate at which new products are brought onto the market, and minimise the time delay between manufacture and sale. Faster communications have become the necessary ingredient of success in the new global market-place, and what is called "time–space compression" is an important feature of the global economic organisation. Electronic communication cuts the time taken to get new clothes from a Third World factory to a First World boutique, and it also allows money itself to move faster and faster across the flickering screens of stock exchanges in a financial whirlwind that neither waits nor sleeps.[13]

The impact of "time–space compression" is reflected not only in the working of business enterprises, but in people's daily lives in the industrialised world. The telephone, the fax, the internet, and above all perhaps the television, are having a profound influence on society and individual consciousness. The television has become the conduit of ideas and "news" from all over the world, beamed into living rooms, sometimes as it happens. Each of us now is battered by instant "information" of a volume and detail impossible to conceive in the 1940s.

Paradoxically perhaps, globalisation has had a curiously isolating effect on individuals. Globalisation has shifted the location of economic power away from the individuals, local communities and (increasingly) from national governments. The relentless pursuit of efficiency, calculability, predictability and control (nicely captured by the term "McDonaldisation") has drastically reduced the extent to which people can control the economic conditions of their lives, even as the scale at which commerce and industry is organised has expanded.[14] Although it has been an explicit strategy of global enterprise to devise "global products" that can be sold with minimal repackaging right around the world, from hamburgers to rock musicians, the significance of the loss of a sense of "localness" for consumers is not lost on business planners. New technologies allow much greater flexibility in production than was previously possible in unwieldy Fordist production lines. It is possible to identify and meet "niche markets", and to target special products to particular places. Production may be organised globally, and decisions made far away, but products can be devised and sold that are explicitly designed to feel "local", and are packaged and presented as such even if they are sourced half a world away. Globalised business uses "localness" as an explicit part of marketing strategy.

The globalisation of economies, the "eclipse of the local and national", and the scaling-up of business integration and economic interdependence, has been accompanied by an increasingly global culture.[15] Products are sold across the globe through electronic media, and advertisements themselves have become international cultural symbols from which increasing numbers of people (particularly the young) draw their identity. Observers of cultural change have argued that the globalisation of culture, and the exchange of cultural symbols, is creating "a new electronic cultural space, a 'placeless' geography of image and simulation", or a "global hyperspace".[16] It is argued that this goes beyond the marketing strategies of global corporations to comprise a new phenomenon, an age of "postmodernism".[17]

56

"Time–space compression" has transformed both our lives and our understanding of the world. Globalisation of economic production has to some degree at least "dissolved the barriers of distance"[18] and allowed products and ideas to circulate around the world. Some of these products and ideas come from the global periphery (African music or Asian cuisine for example), but they have been captured and are passed around by economic forces that emanate from the industrialised nations of the globe, and particularly the longest-established industrial heartlands in North America and Western Europe.

Restructuring the countryside

Globalisation and economic restructuring have had profound impacts on the countryside.[19] As Nan Fairbrother noted in 1970, "swiftly-changing conditions are part of our impatient new world, and have not only swept away old traditions but leave no chance for new ones to develop".[20] The period since the end of the Second World War has seen fundamental changes in the agri-food industry, and in the organisation of domestic and formal sector labour in the UK.[21] In the home, the foods eaten have changed, and they are prepared, stored and cooked quite differently. Upstream of the kitchen there have been changes in the organisation of food retailing (particularly the rise of supermarkets, their increase in size and their move to the periphery of cities where they are accessible only by car). Upstream of the retail outlet the agricultural system has been extensively restructured, both within the UK and increasingly worldwide.

Fresh produce is now quite conventionally moved across the globe to fill British supermarket shelves, such that, in David Harvey's words, "the whole world's cuisine is now assembled in one place".[22] Furthermore, the products offered there are increasingly manufactured, often to meet specific niche markets, and are standardised in form and quality through the use of chemical additives and ingredients (including colouring, flavouring, preservatives and stabilisers). Fresh food is also packaged, and standardised through the use of agricultural chemicals, and its production and marketing are increasingly controlled by the corporate power of large grocery retail chains.

The post-war transformation in the appearance and ecology of the countryside (discussed in Chapter Three) was wrought by economic change, primarily in the agricultural industry. The basic dimensions of that change are well known. A regime of agricultural support was introduced by the 1947 Agriculture Act that aimed to promote self-sufficiency in food production and to provide a reasonable living for farm proprietors and farm labourers. Prices for agricultural products were fixed, and inputs were subsidised. Two White Papers, *The Development of Agriculture* (1965) and *Food from our Own Resources*

(1975) emphasised the need to drive up productivity, improve technical efficiency and specialise. In an increasingly tight, and arguably incestuous, partnership between industry and government, the agricultural industry was progressively modernised and restructured. Small mixed farms gave way to larger, more mechanised and more specialised farms, traditional organic methods gave way to chemical farming, and the landscape was rationalised to mirror the rationalisation of the industry for which it was the factory floor. Landscape changes were particularly associated with changes of occupancy of farms, for example changes in tenure or area of land farmed, changes in business structure or in key decision-making personnel.[23] As agriculture was industrialised on Fordist principles, so too was the physical fabric of the countryside (species, habitats and landscape), and also its social fabric. Farm workers were shed as the industry modernised, and with them began to go the economic basis of rural communities, schools, shops and social life.[24]

These radical changes in agricultural production and the rural landscape did not take place in isolation, but were part of the reorganisation of the whole agri-food industry. This had implications at all points in the food chain from field to processing factory to supermarket to consumer. David Goodman and Michael Redclift describe the industry's aims, to "standardize product quality and minimize seasonal fluctuations in an effort to approximate conditions of continuous production".[25] With the exception of livestock production and horticulture, the agri-food industry has not yet managed to take the actual process of growing or raising food products beyond the technological and business capacity of the family farmer, or indeed out of the landscape and the influence of ecological processes. However, in the years since the end of the Second World War it has gone a long way towards it. Agriculture still looks traditional, particularly perhaps in the marketing graphics of the big grocery chains who will cheerfully and presumably successfully sell "eggs from speckledy hens", but it is profoundly changed. The pace of such change will quicken. The manifold impacts of biotechnology and genetic engineering have as yet barely begun to be felt.

Entry into the European Community in the 1970s added the Common Agricultural Policy to the portfolio of mechanisms for agricultural support and restructuring, but maintained the general direction of change. The cosy corporatism of farmers' organisations (particularly the National Farmers Union, NFU) and government (Ministry of Agriculture, Fisheries and Food) intensified through the decade.[26] Huge sums of money were fed into the Guarantee Section of the Common Agricultural Policy (CAP) to control produce prices (22 billion ECU in 1985 for example). Structural funds (intended to adjust the economic organisation of agriculture) amount to only 5 per cent of that sum. However, cracks eventually began to appear in what researchers refer to as "the Atlanticist food order" that had dominated since the 1940s.[27] The imposition of milk quotas by the EC in 1984 was the first signal of a farm "crisis" of overproduction and inflated prices. This crisis has dominated debate about agriculture in the UK ever since. The pressure of international debate over the GATT agreement led the European Union towards a policy of reducing price support and pushing more strongly the restructuring of European agriculture: in Clive Potter's words, "agriculture, like other industries, had to be exposed to the rigours of the marketplace. For the first time, the farm problem needed to be solved through means other than farming expansion".[28]

Agricultural restructuring has partly been driven by falling farm prices, and partly by new structural investment. Both environmental and social factors have influenced policy, with the emergence of a "farm survival policy" in the 1980s, aimed at reducing the impacts of restructuring on small and disadvantaged farmers on marginal land, and new measures for environmental improvement. The social and economic impacts of restructuring on British farmers, particularly those working small mixed family farms in the North and West, have been severe. It is no coincidence that the suicide rate among such farmers is so high.

Meanwhile, conservationists have had a field day, trying to devise new schemes to use money available for agricultural support to maintain or recreate landscapes and habitats, including Environmentally Sensitive Areas, Set-aside, and Countryside Stewardship. There has been much discussion of cross-compliance, so that farmers benefiting from structural schemes are also required to deliver public environmental benefits, and about the economic and environmental merits of taking land out of agriculture.[29] However, as Hazel Phillips and Carol Hatton point out, the total spent on agri-environment measures in the UK in 1993/4 was only £107m, 4 per cent of the Common Agricultural Policy budget. The other 96 per cent has tended to have quite the opposite effect. This spending is still of trivial significance compared to the terrific commercial and economic forces behind the industrialisation of agriculture.[30]

These debates about the shape and structure of agriculture have profound implications for local and regional economies, and hence the countryside, the pattern of landscape and the future of habitats and species within them. Change in the countryside has been driven by the restructuring of agriculture, steered rather crudely by government policies. Some of these emanate from Whitehall, more or less repackaged in Cardiff, Edinburgh and Belfast. But increasingly, policy is driven by thinking at a European level, and that in turn is affected by negotiations about international trade. And European farm landscapes are irrevocably linked through the global agri-food industry to producers far away, be they in the American Mid-West or in Senegal.

Compressing the countryside

It is by no means only the restructuring of agriculture that has transformed the countryside. Globalisation and time–space compression have exerted a much wider influence. People in the UK now travel prodigiously, to work, to take weekly leisure, and (above all perhaps) on holiday (between 1982 and 1992, for example, the number of international flights by UK residents doubled). There has also been an enormous increase in travel by car. By 1992, people travelled 366 billion miles by car. Over the same period, the distance travelled by bus fell by half, and by bicycle by three-quarters. People walk, on average, less than 250 miles per year, but they travel almost 5000 miles by car.[31] Official forecasts of traffic growth are controversial, and most would agree deeply flawed, since "demand" is in large part driven by the supply of road space. However, there can be little doubt that traffic growth will increase and that the economic and environmental impacts of the car will grow.

Britain is now amazingly dependent on road transport, and the physical layout of the landscape has evolved to reinforce that dependence, and to isolate those without four wheels.[32] Retail shopping has become increasingly located in town-edge and rural locations, and "superstores" and complexes of retail and leisure facilities have grown in number and influence, while public transport services have atrophied. Over 80 per cent of freight by weight and over 60 per cent of freight miles are carried by road, and the development of newly flexible approaches to manufacture and retail has increased the dependence on "just-in-time" delivery by road as the vehicle effectively becomes a moving warehouse.[33] On top of these economic changes, British society has become more atomised, and individualistic, and we are, of course, deeply obsessed with the car as technology, status symbol and source of personal value and pleasure.

Attitudes of many conservationists to the use of the car have in the past often been rather confused, but have begun to become more critical. A survey of members of the public in 1985 identified the construction of roads as the second biggest cause of change in the countryside over the previous twenty years.[34] My own experience of this is interesting. In 1991 I took over as Chair of the Conservation Committee of my local Wildlife Trust and at my first meeting walked into a sharp debate on a paper on new-road-building prepared by one of the Trust's senior staff. The paper argued that new roads were a very real threat to wildlife, and that we should support those arguing for choice in mobility, and more environmentally benign forms of transport. To my surprise, the view of the meeting, rather strongly expressed, was that road building as such was no business of the Trust unless it directly affected sites of known nature conservation value. We had, after all, driven to the meeting on that cold November evening, and would all trail home again in our cars afterwards. Opposition to roads should be left to other environmental groups like Friends of the Earth or Greenpeace. However, three years later, the committee voted unanimously to endorse a paper from the Wildlife Trust's National Office that made very similar arguments. Times had changed. In the autumn of 1994, the Wildlife Trust magazine listed no less than 21 proposed road schemes that threatened wildlife sites in the three counties of Cambridgeshire, Bedfordshire and Northamptonshire, the M3 motorway was being driven through Twyford Down and there were proposals for multiple-lanes on the A1 and the M25. Wildlife conservationists had begun to have real fears of the destructive power of "the road building juggernaut".[35]

Continuing growth in car ownership and use have profound implications for the countryside. Over half of all motorised traffic is on roads outside built-up areas and motorways. Traffic on rural roads increased by 44 per cent between 1977 and 1987, four times the rate of increase in built-up areas. As facilities available locally have declined (village shops closing for example), rural people have had to travel further, and the shrinkage of bus services has made them increasingly dependent on private cars. Levels of car ownership and use are higher in rural areas.[36] Much of the rural traffic, however, is urban in origin. Where rural enterprises thrive, such as village pubs, they often do so only by attracting customers from a wide area, and often from nearby urban centres, where the image of "the country inn" is a potent attraction. New urban facilities outside urban boundaries create new pressures on rural routes (a problem recognised in 1994 when the Department of the Environment issued new planning guidelines on out-of-town superstores), as do the creation of new enterprises on farms. It is relatively easy to convert a line of pigsties into offices for a computer software company, but the traffic flows that result are very different. Many rural roads have become "rat-runs" as drivers try to avoid trunk-road bottlenecks. There are fears that road-charging on motorways will shift even more traffic onto rural roads.

The impacts of increased traffic on rural roads include pollution, noise, impacts on the landscape and semi-natural habitat. New roads and road improvements (kerbs, lighting, straightening) transform landscape and habitat, and represent major and essentially urban transformations of the countryside. New-road construction also makes demands on the countryside for aggregates. The proposed superquarry on Harris in the Western Isles, which will steadily transform the mountain of Roineabhal into a vast pit, is the result of demands for cheap aggregate for construction projects. It will in turn tend to encourage further road-building by reducing the cost of aggregate supply.[37]

Consuming the countryside

Recreation, leisure, and indeed conservation place new demands on the countryside, and impose new patterns of change.[38] Increasingly, it is the economics of the consumption of the new leisure goods that are forcing the direction and pace of change in the countryside, and not the economics of food production. The *Leisure Landscapes* research team from Lancaster University argue that the government conservation organisations (Countryside Commission and English Nature, Countryside Council for Wales and Scottish Natural Heritage) are increasingly "gravitating towards the need to align themselves with public concern for, and use of, the countryside as a leisure resource". The Forestry Commission, the Rural Development Commission and even the Ministry of Agriculture, Fisheries and Food are doing the same.[39]

The countryside has long been a place for town dwellers to resort to, and conservationists have traditionally deplored the resulting impacts (while, very often, contributing to it themselves). In 1940, Thomas Sharp wrote "it must be recognised that the townsman is more powerful than he was. He is free. If he is not given the freedom of the countryside he will take it, and with strong and damaging hands".[40] In 1965 Michael Dower warned of the "fourth wave" of leisure that was poised to sweep across the face of Britain, in the wake of the growth of industrial towns, the expansion of the railways and "the sprawl of car-based suburbs".[41] The rise of leisure motoring was rapid in the post-war period: by the 1960s, planners had recognised, in the words of Allan Patmore that "urban man has burst from urban confines". Analysts were seriously starting to ask how many people, cars and picnickers the countryside could absorb.[42] The unwillingness of urban families to stray far from their car, and our willingness simply to view the countryside through our cars' windows, was recognised. These habits contained the impact of visitors to the roads and accessible "beauty spots", and it has led to the now-conventional portfolio of ideas about recreation management, including the development of specially designed and tightly managed leisure facilities within the countryside or country parks that seek both to meet recreation needs close to home, and to divert visitors from more "sensitive" places further afield.

There is now an increasing amount of information about who uses the countryside, and why. Not only is the economic importance of leisure widely recognised by government ministers, but the particular role of the countryside in attracting visitors is widely acknowledged, not least in the glossy brochures of the tourist industry. The Day Visits Survey records patterns of visits by adults from home, to eat, drink, partake in sport, shopping or informal outdoor leisure.[43] In 1993, British people made some 2 billion day visits for leisure purposes, of which the vast majority were from home (rather than from a holiday base), and they spent a total of £15 billion. Two-thirds of day visits were to urban destinations, but a third were to the countryside. There were some 185 million visits to forests or woods and 22 million to canals or rivers.

The countryside "leisure resource" is clearly more than a planners' abstraction. People use the countryside extensively, although they may well do so in ways that are very different from the "quiet recreation" that is supposed to dominate in National Parks.[44] Are people at the Glastonbury festival, or an illegal rave, or a stock-car meet using "the countryside"? Clearly the answer is yes, although their use is of a very different kind from those going for a walk, or even those in search of the social and atavistic thrills of a foxhunt.[45] Of course, not everyone in the UK is able to get to "the countryside". The majority of visitors are young, in full-time employment, and in the ABC1 social groups. They tend to have access to a car. Half of all leisure day visits were made by car, and less than one in 20 trips was made by public transport. The countryside is seemingly no place for those too poor to run a car: "ironically it is the unemployed, the prematurely retired and the elderly, among others, who have additional time available for recreation and leisure, yet who precisely don't have the disposable income to buy it in the market place".[46]

That leisure is a product, and the countryside an important place where it is consumed, is beyond doubt. The growing leisure industry has created places and experiences in the countryside that can be sold — even, arguably, made a product of the countryside itself. This process is most marked in the growing concern for "heritage". Interest in place and in the past has grown in Britain, even as modernisation and globalisation have transformed them. "Heritage" has become the label we use to describe the urgent search that took place in the 1980s for cultural reference points in the past. It seems that the more we are locked into consumerist urban lifestyles, dependent on machines in the home and in work, and on the meta-machine of the city for our subsistence and culture, the more we hanker after places and cultures of the past. Howard Newby wrote in 1993 that "the globalisation of economic production and markets has been accompanied by a fragmentation of social identities, norms and values".[47] One result of this has been the acceleration of our urge to reach back to the past, and to conserve it.

Heritage provides some kind of refuge from the traumas of economic and social change, but it has also been linked tightly to "enterprise", forming the twin poles of cultural reconstruction in Thatcher's Britain.[48] Public nostalgia for the past has been both stimulated and served by a booming "heritage industry", supplying public facilities and events, from stately homes to re-enacted battles. Indeed, heritage has become fundamental to many people's conception of leisure in the British countryside, and a mainstay of the national and international tourist industry.[49] Even as we reach back to the past and to seek "roots", we do so through consumption. People want to drive to special places where heritage can be found and to have the past packaged and served up in neat and convenient chunks. There is also a demand for heritage goods, in the form of reproductions of artefacts linked to idealised images of the past, for example in the fashion for cottage kitchens. Heritage is also consumed by proxy, on film and video. The vast success of costume drama on television in recent years is evidence both of a hunger for the past and of the very limited way in which we wish that past to be re-created: in full colour, close-up and fully controlled.

The reworking of the countryside as a product, and the trend towards the privatisation of *de facto* public rights, are strengthening. As landowners "add value" to the countryside by building facilities and attractions, they develop the capacity to charge for access, and landowners' organisations have become increasingly clear in their calls for financial rewards for those who provide public goods. The National Farmers Union and particularly the Country Landowners' Association have argued strongly for a new view of farmers as those best positioned to become providers of new products in the countryside, the niche goods of leisure consumption.[50] In his book *The Culture of Nature*, Alexander Wilson describes the impact of similar pressures in the USA, bringing about "a massive conceptual re-organisation of the landscape", as land was moved from agricultural to recreational use.[51]

Fordism and nature are not easy business partners. Fordist logic demands standardisation, but one of the attractions of the countryside is its diversity, its unique trajectories through time, and its apparent naturalness. Niche marketing can adapt to some of these needs by producing diverse "historical" and "natural" attractions. Alexander Wilson describes how elements of landscape or nature are re-arranged to meet tourist expectations even in apparently wild places in the USA, let alone in the vast rural theme parks like "Dollywood", built in the southern Appalachians. In Britain too, landscapes are adjusted to maximise their appeal, sanitised of discordant images by the removal of "eyesores", perfected in their ecology by skilful habitat management. Visitor attractions like Beatrix Potter's home in the Lake District (owned by the National Trust) are very carefully (and discreetly) managed to attract and please visitors, who in return regard them very often as "theme parks".[52] Images of "the rural" that are created and disseminated in glossy magazines like *Country Living* or in imaginatively designed tourist facilities that are "theatres of rural life" are presented both as cultural icons and as consumer products. Landscapes we visit are transformed, framed by the camera lens and packaged on film or video cassette.

Leisure has become a major theatre of consumption, of both manufactured products and the trappings of popular culture. The leisure industry is now worth £70 billion per year. Even informal countryside recreation, like walking or birdwatching, has become affected by fashion and consumerism. People buy special clothes and equipment from niche-market shops and magazines in order to be equipped technically and in style to go for a walk or watch birds. The North Norfolk coast is a great place to see migrating birds, but no fall of migrants is more fantastic than that of the fully equipped birdwatching brigade at Cley, protected in high-tech jackets of laminated plastics, shod in special footwear and festooned in electronic and optical equipment to capture sights and sounds and take them home. Car parks fill with the machines that brought them here, the town come to the country, closer to "nature". Industry has moved skilfully and fast to meet the boom in rural leisure, supplying the products, from cars to binoculars, that people want. Conservation groups too have embraced the opportunities of "environmental merchandising" with gusto, selling goods through Christmas catalogues and shops, while sometimes at the same time selling environmental ideologies through slogans on T-shirts or coffee mugs.[53]

Globalisation and conservation

The conservation movement has been affected by the processes of globalisation in more profound ways than simply its response to the lure of consumerism. Although wildlife and countryside conservation in the UK has been primarily concerned with the defence of special places (such as SSSIs) locally and nationally, it has also itself become global in its mission and self-image. Television has played a particularly important role in this. It was a major factor in the rise of public awareness of nature and the need for conservation in the UK, and much of its impact came from footage shot outside the UK. In his book *The New Environmental Age*, Max Nicholson rightly praises those television crews who brought images of the immanent beauty and wonder of nature, and environmental impacts of human activities, to our living rooms. Programmes like *Look* and *Survival*, and the films and the books of David Attenborough's *Zoo Quest* were followed by many others such as *The World About Us*. These programmes, and many others, have helped to build a vision of nature and its vulnerability for generations of British people, and they have done so primarily by portraying nature "out there", far beyond British shores.[54]

Of course, there have been many glorious programmes on nature within the UK, but there is no doubt that the power of the film images collected in tropical environments in particular created a highly international vision of nature, and therefore of the need for conservation. In working in this way, television was building on at least a century of British concern for conservation in the tropics, particularly in Africa. The "Society for the Protection of the Fauna of the Empire" was founded as long ago as 1903, and books like Bernard Grzimek's *Serengeti Shall Not Die* (published in 1960) and those in the Survival Series such as *S.O.S. Rhino* (1966) carried on the tradition.[55] Accounts of extinction far away were linked to similar threats at home, and secondly to wider environmentalist concerns, in books such as Robert Arvill's *Man and Environment* (published in 1967), with a global focus but written under a pen name by the Director General of the Nature Conservancy.[56]

By the start of the 1980s, threats to natural habitats and the countryside within the UK had become front-page news. This was largely because conservation organisations put them there, and alongside them they placed broader international issues. Friends of the Earth, for example, launched campaigns on the countryside and on acid rain, and soon began to campaign on threats to tropical rainforests, and in their turn on global warming and the ozone layer. When support for the environmental movement surged in the 1980s, and mainstream politicians surfed the "green wave", much of its energy stemmed from this global dimension.[57] In 1988, for example, the cargo ship *Karin B* roamed European seas with a cargo of toxic waste that had been dumped in the Niger Delta in West Africa, and in the autumn of that year Margaret Thatcher made her famous speech to the Royal Society, stressing the need for global action to combat global environmental problems.[58]

The globalisation of the environmental movement as a whole was mirrored in the more particular concerns of the conservation of nature, and particularly the problem of the extinction of species. Logged and burned rainforests were portrayed as part of a global natural inheritance, the indigenous people in the process as our global neighbours. Direct links were drawn between beef ranching in Amazonia and high street franchises through the "hamburger connection". Rainforests began to be seen as somehow part of our own heritage, and children learned about rainforests, and the rapaciousness of human abuse of nature, in school and on the media. Indeed, so successful has this education been that I suspect that British schoolchildren currently have more appreciation of the problems of the conservation of rainforests than they do of the threats to wildlife and landscape in the UK.

This globalisation of thinking about conservation, epitomised by concern about rainforests, had an odd effect in Britain itself. Jacquelin Burgess and Carolyn Harrison have explored this in studies of the ideas that local people have about nature in the area surrounding Rainham Marshes in Kent. Rainham Marshes is a Site of Special Scientific Interest (SSSI) on the north side of the Thames Estuary. It is not particularly beautiful, and has been treated as waste land for years, with the various trappings of urban fringe dereliction such as fly-tipping and motorcycle rough-riding. However, it supports significant numbers of migratory ducks and waders in addition to insects and plants that are judged rare and worthy of protection. In 1989 a planning application was made by the Music Corporation of America for a £2.4 billion theme park and associated commercial and housing development.

Burgess and Harrison argue that the media reported conservation issues at the end of the 1980s using formulaic words and phrases about threat, disappearance, rarity and danger, thus creating a "discourse of extinction". This was very powerful, but was also very restrictive, and allowed no real breadth of analysis. Local residents used such language to discuss conservation at the global level, but not as a way of talking about the situation on Rainham Marshes. The unattractive and seemingly derelict landscape of the Inner Thames Grazing Marshes SSSI did not match up to the images of nature pre-coded by the "discourse of extinction". To them, Rainham Marshes was a dump, not paradise: conservation was something that needed to happen "out there", in the rainforest. When the issues were really in their own back yard, people became critical of the ideological freight train of conservation rhetoric, as indeed they did of the glossy portfolio of the developers.[59]

To both experts and the general public, conservation has become a global issue, global in the way both the problems and the solutions are conceived. Conservation and environmentalism have themselves become features of an increasingly globalised culture.[60] T-shirts that are fashion items in the British high street proclaim messages about the whale or the rainforest; pop stars walk the rainforest, and high-street cosmetics chains claim to promote "sustainable use" and the interests of rainforest people. The rather tweedy and paternalistic middle-class movement for conservation founded in the 1940s has been transformed by the vigorous and turbulent forces of globalisation. But where, in this maelstrom of economic and social change, should conservation find its place? What implications do these profound changes in economy and society, and in environmentalism, have for the way we understand, and try to conserve, the British countryside? I begin to explore these questions in the next chapter, *Culture and the Countryside*.

CHAPTER FIVE

Culture and the Countryside

Conservation is about negotiating the transition from past to future in such a way as
to secure the transfer of maximum significance
Alan Holland and Kate Rawles[1]

Town and country

About ten miles west of Cambridge lies the National Trust property of
Wimpole Hall. In addition to the house, the estate (unusually for
Cambridgeshire) has both some low hills and a large area of grassland with
cattle and sheep grazing. But its main attraction is the Home Farm, a
magnificently renovated model farm built in the nineteenth century with vast
thatched barns. Here there is a large collection of rare breeds of farm animals,
and a working farm. It is a well-designed and well-run attraction, educational
and (to judge by my family) great fun. There are old tractors to climb on, a
barn full of old implements, and a regular supply of lambs, piglets and other
animals. It is one of the only places around Cambridge where you can see farm
animals close to, and explain to children that meat and milk do not grow in
plastic packets in supermarket chiller cabinets.

Wimpole Home Farm is a great success. The property gets over 120,000
visitors per year, and is advertised widely across southeastern England. On a

69

sunny Sunday the car park overflows into surrounding fields, a vast lagoon of cars, their shiny roofs and windscreens flashing in the sun. It is all astonishingly clean and neat, a sanitised version of the past; strong on old technology and rare breeds, but offering little real insight into social and economic relations. The toil of the farm labourers and their families is assumed, and subsumed, "naturalised as displays of individual resourcefulness and quiet fortitude".[2]

Wimpole Hall, and the many other places like it, offer a version of the countryside as it never was, stripped of poverty and mud alike. Ironically, of course, Wimpole Home Farm itself has always been, in a sense, an imitation, having been built by the Third Earl of Hardwicke at the end of the eighteenth century as a model farm. Like Marie Antoinette's dairy at Fontainebleau, it was created as scenery wherein aristocratic players could enact a tableau of imagined rusticity, and is now revived for a wider but still wealthy clientele (whose daily lives are equally distanced from the world they seek to re-enact), to do the same. Such theatres of heritage are built for town-dwellers, in order to mop up and to contain recreation demand in the countryside. They are as much part of an urban culture as the houses from which their visitors come, as fabricated as the motorways that bring them to the place and as tightly keyed in to advances in urban culture and technology as the sophisticated cars they drive.

Town and country have a place in people's minds today, as they have for so much of the past, as opposites. Urban dwellers have long sought recreation by visiting the countryside. Thomas Sharp caught the need of town for its pastoral antithesis in 1940:

> man cannot without serious loss live always in the highly-wrought highly-organised, highly-tensioned world of the town. He can overtop Nature, but he cannot entirely cast her off. Divorced from contact with her, denied the refreshing contrast between the beauties of natural forms and those of his artificial ones, denied the softening, broadening influences of the myriad-sided life of natural things, the townsman loses much that is essential for his full development.[3]

People come to the countryside seeking something that they perceive to be different; space, peace or "nature". As we saw in Chapter Four, these things are increasingly pre-prepared and packaged, turned into commodities for visitors, as they are (very impressively) on the Wimpole Estate.[4] But does the fact that the "countryside" people go to is deliberately created in this way invalidate the urge to conserve it? Is conservation itself illusory, swept up into the circuit of capital, just another piece of niche-marketed leisure? I will argue in this chapter and the next that it is much more than this.

The conventional distinction between countryside and town has always been somewhat illusory. The dialogue between the two has been repeatedly discussed, notably by Raymond Williams in *The Country and the City*, and recently by authors such as Michael Bunce and John Rennie Short.[5] Thomas Sharp argued that town and country were part of one organism. Developments in communications had broken down barriers and physical distinctions between the two, and forged a new and tight economic integration. Urban life, urban styles and urban manners have spread very rapidly to penetrate most corners of the countryside. The cultural process of urbanisation is far more extensive, and has impacts that are in many ways far more profound, than the mere extension of buildings, tarmac and car parks.

One important source of cultural change has been town-dwellers moving to live in the country. The last ten years has seen an acceleration of the process of "counter-urbanisation", the functional integration of city and surrounding country, as urban people have moved outwards. In a sense this has long happened among the moneyed and leisured classes, but what is new is the extent to which it has taken place and the way in which improved transport and new technologies have allowed urban jobs and urban lifestyles to be carried on in rural locations. The purchase of second homes has become a problem in most National Parks, and metropolitan capital acquired during the 1980s property boom has been invested in rural properties in Dorset or the Welsh Borders, while long-distance commuting to London in particular has expanded. Telecommuting, using computers through modems, has also increased. Sales of microcomputers boomed during the train strikes of 1994.

New people are living in the countryside, and they are living urban lives. These wealthy incomers have a direct impact on rural landscapes. They plant tall cypress hedges and build patios and conservatories. They drive miles to shop in superstores and lunch in specialised pub-restaurants. The pre-war Cotswold villages that Laurie Lee described in *Cider with Rosie* now sprout BMWs behind the hedges. Newcomers also have an impact on local politics, often opposing changes to the appearance of villages while even by their willingness to purchase cottages at high prices they irrevocably alter the social basis of the very village life they have come to emulate. The power of newcomers in opposing housing and job-creating development in their adopted villages (the "NIMBY" syndrome) has been recognised and lamented from Cape Wrath to Cape Cornwall.[6]

The town has invaded the country, but urban popular culture is not only spread by those who move out from towns. The process of globalisation has brought rural as well as urban Britain into its slipstream. In 1970, Nan Fairbrother wrote "every one of us now is a destructive urban influence on the countryside whatever we do and wherever we live".[7] Horizons have widened in the countryside. Many of those who have lived in rural areas for many generations live urban lives, remarkably like those who have fled the city for an imagined rural idyll. *Neighbours* and pizza are as much part of rural British life as they are urban, and they are recent arrivals to both. Nan Fairbrother

71

said in 1970 that as a setting for modern life, the village was "as unreal as a coach-lamp wired for electricity" and she argued that "modern Arcadian comforts are provided by industrial areas, and if the view from our windows is still Arcadian we are living at the expense of someone else's landscape". If what has come to be called the "ecological footprint" of the village were fairly represented in its landscape, it would be surrounded by its own proportion of all the industries and services it lived by. Those fleeing the city hope that these in fact remain locked far away from their new-found rural retreat.[8]

This cultural homogenisation is undoing in a very obvious way the easy distinction once made between urban and rural Britain. The process is very variable in its extent across the country. The cultural resistance to urban, metropolitan or global cultural influences is still great in some areas — the Western Isles or Gwynedd for example — and these places are still culturally very different from say Essex, or the Yorkshire Dales, just as they are different from each other. However, the process of homogenisation is real enough. The country is becoming steadily less distinct from the town culturally, and more tightly linked economically. And yet, paradoxically, recent decades have seen no slackening in enthusiasm for the idea of the *distinctiveness* of the countryside, and its difference from the town. Why does that idea have such power?

Culture and the countryside

The idea of "the countryside" and notions of "natural order (indeed "a *naturalised* order") of rural life are among the foundation stones on which everyday life has been built in the UK, for centuries.[9] The "countryside" does not spring unbidden into human consciousness, however much we might believe that it does. We create it, by the way we think and by what we believe. The various physical and biological elements of the landscape exist, of course, but the way in which we understand them, and the way we describe them is the result of values and ideas that we associate with them, and not their innate properties. The argument is perhaps particularly clear if it is focused on the related issue of landscape. The very word stems from the artistic movement of the seventeenth century, and the representation of actual pieces of terrain. Stephen Daniels and Denis Cosgrove define a landscape as "a cultural image, a pictorial way of representing, structuring or symbolising surroundings".[10] The terrain is transformed into "landscape" by the meanings we attach to it, the images we make (on film, paper or words) and the thoughts and ideas we attach to those images. Many of the arguments we have about the countryside and management are about the values we attach to it. Kay Milton, for example, describes the conflict in Northern Ireland between two competing concepts: "land" and "landscape". "Land" refers to the tangible physical resource that is worked (i.e. farmed) and can be owned, inherited and sold. On the other hand, "landscape" is an intangible resource, one whose characteristics are defined by the way it looks. Kay Milton's landscape is viewed, not worked, and unlike "land" it is conceived of as communal and not private property, by right accessible to all.[11]

Just as meanings are attached to, and read into, landscape, so too it is with the broader entity of the countryside. In his book, *The Country and the City*, Raymond Williams wrote a brief autobiographical sketch, juxtaposing his childhood in a village under the Black Mountains in Wales, his home in a village in Cambridgeshire, "in the flat country, on a headland of boulder clay, towards the edge of the dikes and sluices ... under the high East Anglian skies", and his time in the city. He comments: "The life of the country and city is moving and present: moving in time, through the history of a family and a people; moving in feeling and ideas, through a network of relationships and decisions".[12] The intellectual history of the countryside, the way ideas about it have changed, is matched by the deep roots these ideas have formed in popular culture and individual consciousness.

Williams describes the way in which we have grown to contrast country and city: "on the country has gathered the idea of a natural way of life: of peace, innocence and simple virtue. On the city has gathered the idea of an achieved centre: of learning, communication, light".[13] Our view of the countryside arises from a strong current in England of what historian Martin Weiner calls "anti-urbanism".[14] British culture was already becoming urbanised by the end of the eighteenth century. By the time of the 1851 census, more than half the English population lived in towns. By the start of the twentieth century, Britain was essentially an urban society, and moreover one dominated by a very few urban centres, mostly in England. Both formal and popular culture in Britain had become urban, as indeed it has remained, with metropolitan values assumed as national fashions.

The idea of the countryside is in many ways peculiarly English rather than British, although there are equivalents in both Scotland and Wales built round ideas of Scottish clans and tartans, or the language heartlands of Welsh or Gaelic. The word does not easily translate. In Africa, for example, it is meaningless. People speaking English tend to refer to those areas beyond urban limits as "the bush", another word with strong but very different associations.[15] In Scotland, the Victorian love affair with its scenery owed more to the frisson of perceived wilderness and chaos than the pastoral virtues associated with the calm and controlled landscapes of England. Thomas Gray wrote in 1765, "the Lowlands are worth seeing once, but the mountains are ecstatic and ought to be visited in pilgrimage once a year. None but those monstrous creatures of God know how to join so much beauty with so much horror".[16]

The "armchair countryside" of pastoral tranquility has great cultural resonance, and a long history in English literature, landscape painting and (perhaps most influentially in the present century) in children's books.[17] It is not, however, shared universally in the UK, and the feelings of ethnic minorities in the countryside in particular often reflect unease or dread. This response, and the potent links between landscape, nationalism and race are being increasingly highlighted, for example in the work of photographer Ingrid Pollard.[18] The English landscape has been projected as a symbol of English national identity, and indeed it has been argued that the protection of that landscape itself (for example in the early work of the Council for the Preservation of Rural England) was itself a "symbol of the England, and the Englishness, it was created to preserve and protect".[19]

Myth, change and protest

The countryside is more than a set of places, a set of ecosystems and settlements and units of agricultural production. We load it with ideas about the past, and about its "naturalness". We create what Martin Weiner describes as "the countryside of the mind", a mythic and idyllic place. Visitors who come from all over the world to Beatrix Potter's house in the Lake District village of Sawrey seek just such an idealised English countryside and (such being the effectiveness of the National Trust's conservation efforts) mostly feel they have found it.[20] The power of such idyllic ideas about the countryside derives from the conceptual contrast with the industrial city, and from the overpowering sense of that industrialism penetrating and threatening the idyll itself.

In his classic book, *The Making of the English Landscape* (published in 1955), the historian W.G. Hoskins not only wrote a history of the English landscape itself, but also "made" that history in another sense by interweaving into his story ideas and values about change. These emerge with painful clarity in the final chapter, where he dismisses changes since the end of the nineteenth century, saying that "since that time, and especially since the year 1914, every single change in the English landscape has either uglified it or destroyed its meaning, or both". "What", he asks rhetorically, "has happened to the immemorial landscape of the English countryside?" Hoskins sees the forces of despoliation as legion: the break-up of the big estates, the country houses full of "the atom men", the proliferation of overspill settlements and urban housing, the bulldozers clearing hedges for ranch-farming by the new breed of business-farmers, and the countryside flayed bare for airfields. To Hoskins this is "Barbaric England", created by "the scientists, the military men and the politicians". He laments, "let us turn away and contemplate the past before it is lost to the vandals".[21]

Martin Weiner argues that the aftermath of the explosive growth of industrial cities ("flinging out huge tentacles like those of an octopus"[22]) was a perception in English society of a breakdown in organic unity. Increasingly, cities were seen as chaotic, alienating and uncivilised, in need, indeed, of rediscovery and a new civilising mission that paralleled the enterprise of Empire overseas. These perceptions led the concern at the turn of the century for planning, better housing and public health, and (as we saw in Chapter Two) they were also closely linked to the rise of countryside and wildlife conservation, for example in the foundation of the National Trust. Martin Weiner argues that middle- and upper-class culture in Victorian England was at war with itself, with conflict between opposing symbols, "Machine and Garden, Workshop and Shire".[23] Agricultural depression at the end of the nineteenth century made the countryside less economically important. It was ripe for appropriation as a cultural symbol, "an alternative and complementary set of values, a psychic balance wheel".[24]

The result was that in public consciousness, in literature and in architecture, there developed a series of rural myths. Some embraced the country squire and notions of hierarchy and order, while more egalitarian ideas focused on the doughty peasant fashioning the fabric of the countryside through succeeding centuries, like Rudyard Kipling's Sussex estate worker Hobden.[25] All provided a "protective national shell of rural life", within which England took shelter, harking back to a myth of "Merrie England". The countryside was created, indeed repeatedly recreated in popular culture, as anti-urban, anti-industrial, anti-mechanised and anti-chaotic.

These idealised myths of the rural at the end of the Victorian period proved remarkably persistent. They served to bolster national esteem as British economic power began to slide in the early decades of the present century; they helped mediate the impacts of the First World War and the depression of the inter-war period. They also provided a focus for conceiving of post-war reconstruction in the 1940s. In his reports on the English coastline in the 1940s, for example, Alfred Steers bemoaned alike the devastation wrought by industry (writing for example that "the coalfield coast of Cumberland is a desolation, and the Flintshire side of the Dee estuary is nearly as bad"), and impacts of unplanned housing sprawl ("the ugly and misplaced huts and shacks that sprang up between the two world wars" created because "the drive for seaside holidays has overreached itself").[26]

There is something remarkably familiar about writing from half a century ago decrying the impacts of modernisation and development in the countryside. Typical, perhaps, are the writings of Hugh Massingham, in his book *Through the Wilderness* in 1939. His target was inappropriate house-building on the chalk country of southern England. He wrote that "the things I saw did not encompass the hundredth part of a devastation flung far and wide over England", even the "remoter districts" "peppered with bubukles [sic] and whelks called modern houses and set up, as in the South Cotswolds, on all points of vantage".[27] The consequence of this "foreign invasion" of the "townsman"[28] is to price the "countryman" out of his cottage and disturb the equilibrium of "the manners, the psychology and, what is still more vital, the traditional associations of the rustic with the land of his plough or spade or billhook or milking-stool". The townsman, meanwhile, is "suspended in a vacuum, with little or no commerce with the country itself", oscillating between town and country, "Mr facing-both-ways". Even the new migrants' gardens reveal their lack of "a sense of right values", their wrong education: "compare their gardens with the average cottage garden of the countryman, and you can see at once that they are devoid, ninety per cent of them, of that instinctive rightness and perception that bless a patch often no larger than a cottage kitchen". Massingham's pained and self-critical account (he writes "am I not one of this horde myself?") has a strong contemporary ring to it. He might have been describing the countryside of the 1990s, not the 1930s, and voicing worries about the cultural impact of counter-urbanisation.

This sense that urbanism and industrialisation were despoiling the countryside draws on a tradition of romantic protest that emerged in the late eighteenth century. In her book, *Fantasy, the Bomb and the Greening of Britain*, Meredith Veldman traces the thread of this protest from the poetry of the English Romantic movement (Blake, Keats, Shelley and Wordsworth), through the work of John Ruskin, William Morris and the Arts and Crafts movement into middle-class environmental and anti-war protest in post-Second-World-War Britain. Wordsworth, for example, protested at the "rash assault" of the railway and of organised outings of working people from far-off towns on the Lake District. In his *Guide to the Lakes* he provided both the most influential romantic critique of the impact of uneducated townspeople on the countryside, and indeed presaged the concept of National Parks by speaking of the Lake District as "a sort of national property".[29]

Veldman focuses on the fantasy writing of J.R.R. Tolkein and C.S. Lewis, the work of the Campaign for Nuclear Disarmament (CND) and the early Green movement. She argues that romantic protest was a reaction against the emerging shape of a new society, against industrialisation and empiricism that seemed to be "destroying old boundaries and snapping the bonds of conviction and community". Thus in Narnia and Middle-Earth, Lewis and Tolkein recalled a mythic and lost world of harmony, stability and security; it was a world without industry and technology. In its turn, she suggests that CND's anti-nuclear protest represented a social and cultural critique of technology and society. In the 1960s and 1970s the green movement demanded a radical re-orientation of British society, blending CND's political activism, humanist socialism and principles of non-violence with the medievalism of Tolkein and Lewis, their fear of science and technology, conservatism and religiosity.[30]

Romantic protest in the nineteenth and early twentieth centuries stood against the fragmentation and alienation of industrialisation, the degradation of community life and nature. The protest movements following the Second World War stood against the centralisation, mechanisation and modernisation of Britain, and particularly the production-line thinking of Fordism and "Americanisation", in just the same way, using and building upon the vocabulary and concepts of the romantic tradition.[31] The environmental movement became a major focus for this wider protest against change. Eric Hobsbawm describes the decade of 1970s as "a new era of decomposition, uncertainty and crisis".[32] It was here that environmentalism was forged. The new environmentalists challenged the dominant worldview not only in terms of what they thought about nature, or human use of the environment, but also in their views about the economy, about politics and about society.[33]

Increasingly, it was conservation that captured public concern about rural change and sentiment about the past and channelled them into dreams for the future. As the technological machine of post-war agriculture began to crunch into gear and convert the "fair fields of England" into a factory floor, myths of the rural were again marshalled to provide both a platform for opposition and a bitter battleground for debate. The protest against the damaging impacts of agricultural intensification, led by Marion Shoard's *The Theft of the Countryside* was in large part carried forwards as a conflict between competing myths about the countryside. The argument in the 1980s was at one level technical, about the extent of semi-natural habitat, but at another it was a clash of ideas. One side was the agriculture lobby's myth of the farmer-steward, tweedy and rooted deep in the past, a creator of beauty and value. On the other was a mythic landscape rich in wild creatures that was of great beauty, redolent of freedom and harmony, and that was, above all, "natural". The language used on both sides of the debate, of loss and heritage, of rights and roots, was explicitly designed to evoke images of imagined rural pasts. The power of these myths (and the fact that they were not recognised as such) was one reason why the debate was so intractable.

The image of a rural idyll, untarnished by urbanism or industrialisation, has been a constant feature of opposition to rural change. However, as we peer further back into history the date of this imagined idyll moves back too. Raymond Williams, for example, traces the idea of "organic community" of "Old England" back through the twentieth century and into the nineteenth and then the eighteenth. Always it is "just back, ... over the last hill".[34] This is not simply because of the common human propensity to use the past as a stick with which to beat the present. It is because our longing for the past is highly complex. The values we see in the past and in the countryside change over time and of course they depend on who we are. We create our *own* ideals of the countryside, and from them we build our conception of what conservation is and should be.

Specific changes in the countryside are seen to be (and indeed, as I have argued in Chapter Four, genuinely are) representative of profound changes in economy and society. The historian Samuel Hays argues that, in the USA, support for environmenalism was stimulated, at least in part, by a concern for threats to particular places.[35] In the UK also, the plight of the countryside has seemed to epitomise the wider ills of society. This is still true, as the recent storm of opposition to new-road building demonstrates.

The controversial extension of the M3 through Twyford Down in a huge cutting, in particular, sent shock waves through the conservation movement. The value of the place was obvious: the majesty of the landscape with its sweep of chalk hill, its importance as an open space for the people of Winchester, the fact that it was an Area of Outstanding Natural Beauty, that it was notified as a Site of Special Scientific Interest for its species-rich grassland, and that it was peppered with archaeological features. The Department of Transport's proposals were opposed by the Countryside Commission, English Nature and English Heritage, and a host of environmental NGOs.

Not only were the legislative measures for the protection of designated landscape and natural habitat (and the agencies that wielded them) impotent, but popular protest also failed. The established tools of public debate, thrashed out by NGOs over decades of fighting losing battles, of lobbying, mobilisation and empowerment of public support, of applying pressure through the media, were all unavailing. The protest against Twyford saw the most radical and active protests ever in defence of natural places: not just the familiar peaceful stunts of established radical organisations like Friends of the Earth or Greenpeace, but the arrival of Earth First! and the appearance of monkey-wrenching.[36] The extension of the M11 through houses in the self-styled "Republic of Wanstonia" in Northeast London in 1994 extended the scale and violence of public protest against road-building, and of its repression by police and private security companies, as did protests against the M77 around Glasgow.

The sense of lost nature, and feelings of helplessness in the face of vast forces for change, are powerful stimuli for conservation, which can draw on an inheritance of romanticism that was vigorous, passionate and conservative. Paradoxically, the heroic failures that feature in tales of battles between conservationists and developers, and the stories of the destruction of "pristine" nature or idyllic countryside that accompany them, have won recruits to conservation. Very often these are people who (at first, anyway) do not share the wider environmentalist or green views of the world. Concern at change in particular places, or the destruction of particular individual creatures, can prove radicalising. I can certainly recall one particular event in my own childhood that stands out for its effect on my attitudes to nature, and to the ways people used and abused it.

It happened when I was quite young, and new houses were built in an empty plot opposite my house. Doubtless I idealise the scene, but there was a row of red horse chestnut trees standing above the road behind an old wall, and in my memory they are vast and seemingly immovable. In spring they were resplendent in bright leaves and bold candles of blossom, and at night tawny owls called from their branches. When the old garden in which they stood was sold for housing, the trees were felled. By a terrible coincidence, the work was done in May, when the trees were in full flower. Afterwards, when the chainsaw had stopped and the workmen had gone, there was nothing remaining of the trees at all, except the roadway strewn with red petals. I can still recall my sense of outrage and pain. To do this to trees (*my* trees) was bad enough, but to do it in spring seemed to me a criminal act, an offence to nature and to human decency. To me this was a symbol, a worked example, of humanity at its most outrageous: greedy, selfish, thoughtless and uncaring. Unreasonable as my feelings might have been, they reflected my shock at the impact of normal day-to-day life on nature. The conflict between what seemed the self-evident values of the trees and the casual indifference of those who planned the houses set a chain of thought going. In time this experience, and doubtless many others now lost to mind, turned me from being simply someone who liked birds and bugs into a conservationist.

People who care about nature can often identify similar moments when their feelings crystallised, and they began to understand the effects of industrialised society on wildlife and the countryside. Landscapes have been progressively simplified, and areas of habitat have shrunk and deteriorated. It is the response to this erosion of diversity on the part of ordinary people that empowers and gives life to conservation.

The challenge for conservation

The vast social and economic changes that have taken place since the end of the Second World War offer a profound challenge to conservation. How can the measures put in place in 1949, and adapted piecemeal through the subsequent decades, meet our needs and expectations at the end of the century? They cannot. Bold though the 1940s vision was, it has totally failed to comprehend the scale of change that we have been through. Conservation has been reduced to a grim chess game of land designation and statutory control.

I have tried to argue that the countryside that we care for is very largely a creation of our own minds. It is really there, in the sense that there are hills, hedgerows and silage clamps, but its significance lies not in these things but in what we imagine it to be. The physical fabric of landscape, and its green mantle of ecosystems, changes over time, as do our ideas about it. The impulse for conservation stems primarily from the energy of our uncertainty about these changes. People protest about change in the countryside, particularly when it is their local space or valued place that is under assault, and it is in this concern that the conservation movement has its life and its force. The continual tension between protest at change and the acceptance of that change as something capable of creating new values is of central significance to conservation.

The countryside is a human place, a lived-in patchwork whose form has been worked over time and to which diverse values are attached. Its diversity and its history are essential elements in its value. In 1994, English Nature sponsored an exhibition in Hereford to celebrate the bicentennial of the "Picturesque Movement", an approach to landscape design that stressed "variety, intricacy, irregularity, roughness and ruggedness, the native and the sense of place", in contrast to the smoothed pastoral landscapes favoured by designers like Capability Brown. Landowners like Richard Payne Knight, on whose estate lay what is now Downton Gorge SSSI, created a remarkable amalgam of wild nature and landscaped garden. He created places of beauty and diversity, where the impact of human choice can, in retrospect, be celebrated as having created countryside of great value.[37] The Chairman of Scottish Natural Heritage (SNH), Magnus Magnusson, argues that conservation must give explicit consideration to the question of change. SNH has to address not only what has been inherited from the past, but also what is left to future generations. The conservation task is therefore "to safeguard and enhance that heritage for our successors".[38]

Industry, government and voluntary organisations all share in the creation and dissemination of myths about the countryside. They all, to some extent, invest in the profitable iconography of nature and the past. These myths can serve many different interests, but the making of myths about people and landscape, about people and neighbours, about people and nature, is important. It can be a legitimate part of the task of understanding "how our constructed environment connects to the natural one surrounding it, and to its history".[39] Countryside conservation is, in a fundamental sense, about how to deal with changes in the countryside, about "negotiating the transition from past to the future".[40] Conservation must work with the heavy freight of cultural meanings carried by the countryside. It must address that concern for things past, and so work with them to provide a means of imagining and creating the future.

CHAPTER SIX

Making Nature

*Culture takes bites out of nature every time we can make it function in such a way that
we can repeat and control the function*
Svend Erik Larsen[1]

How natural is nature?

If the countryside is culturally created, and if what really matters about it are
those values that we attach to it, where does that leave "nature" and "nature
conservation"? Alexander Wilson argues that nature too is "part of culture".[2]
It does not spring from the air or the earth as a free-standing and inviolate set
of principles or ideas. He suggests that our experience of the natural world is
"mediated", shaped by photography, television, advertising and aesthetics, and
by institutions like religion and education. If this is so, what does it mean for
nature conservation? On what are all the efforts of British conservationists
since the end of the Second World War founded?

This is dangerous ground. The argument that nature is culturally
constructed seems at first sight to play into the hands of those who would
argue that it is unimportant. The idea is heretical to many conservationists,
and quite rightly so. It is the very naturalness of the countryside that has
seemed to set it apart from the town, the very fact that ecosystems and wild
animals and plants are not made by people, or assembled by industry, that has

81

driven the conservation movement in the UK over the last hundred years. But how "natural" is it?

The naturalness of nature is in one sense inherently self-evident. I recall a walking trip I made some years ago on the high tops of the Cairngorms. For three days we moved through this high country, over the Lairig Ghru from Deeside and back over Cairngorm and Beinn Macdui. Once on the summits, we were alone, but for the occasional figure looming on distant tops. It was early July, and we took a chance on the weather, and slept out on both nights. We were lucky, and I remember lying on my back above Loch Avon, too cold to sleep, looking up at the stars. It seemed above all a hugely natural place.

The vegetation zones change seamlessly with altitude, from heather to bilberry and crowberry heaths on middle slopes and moss heaths on the tops.[3] I had recently read the "New Naturalist" volume on *Mountain Flowers*, and remember still the thrill of finding some of the characteristic plants of the northern mountains. We found cloudberry tucked tightly down into the heath, a living link to the vastness of the arctic. Further up, on the bare tundra of the tops, we found moss campion in flower, small delicate pink flowers on bright rounded cushions of green. In the wet flushes of the mountain-sides there were long-leaved and round-leaved sundew, butterwort and heath spotted orchids, and down on the valley floors were the ancient Scots pine trees, remnants of the Caledonian pine woodlands of the Mar Forest. We saw red deer and golden eagle, and up on the tops ptarmigan and mountain hare. We spoke to no one but each other for three days.[4]

To me, the Cairngorms on that trip without doubt felt "natural", and indeed still do. But what do I mean by this word? They were certainly not free of human influence, for this was clear everywhere, as indeed was the human species itself, in the distance. Some human impacts were very obvious. It seemed that we took hours to tramp up across the ski development of the north slopes of Cairn Gorm. Underfoot the montane heath vegetation of bilberry and bearberry was rudely slashed by the bulldozed smoothness of the ski pistes with their fairways of fertilised lowland grasses, while up overhead hummed the wires and pylons of the ski tows. Quite apart from the ski area, the mountain tops were crisscrossed by paths. Rocks were worn, vegetation trampled, and paths scoured by passing boots. Research has shown the montane ecosystems of Cairngorm to be very susceptible to such wear and tear, and of course our boots added their own impact.[5] Air photographs show more and more footpaths in the Cairngorms in recent years, going (as drovers' and shepherds' paths never did) straight up steep and erosive ridges. These impacts were small compared to the fresh scar of the new road that had been bulldozed across the hillside above Glen Derry, presumably to get deer-shooting clients up to their quarry in the comfort of four-wheel drive.

Other human impacts in the Cairngorms are more subtle. The dwarf shrub vegetation of Cairngorm is zoned by altitude, but the tree line (at 490m) is well below its potential level of 610–685 m. It is kept suppressed by grazing and exposure.[6] Much of that grazing is directed by human action. The arctic flora stimulated some years ago the introduction of a herd of domesticated reindeer from Norway. I have cross-country skied in these hills in winter, and seen reindeer trailing across the snow in a long line just as they do in the mountains of Norway. The reindeer also look "natural", but people brought them there. The other large mammal in the Scottish hills is the red deer, and while strictly "wild", their presence and impact is also controlled by people, the owners of shooting estates. Their natural predators were hunted to extinction centuries ago, and no one has yet introduced wolves to accompany the reindeer. Winter mortality is reduced by artificial feeding, and throughout Scotland deer numbers have been allowed to rise year on year to maximise returns to estates. Deer are now effectively farmed on the Scottish hills, and cropped by rich clients who pay well for the privilege. I remember on that July visit, outside the shooting season, watching them stooging tamely around the valley floor in Glen Derry.

The choices made by those people who own land and manage deer in the highlands have considerable ecological significance. The deer have a particular impact on the Caledonian pine woodland on low ground, to which they retreat in hard weather. Red deer like to eat young pine trees, and lots besides, in the rich ground flora of the Caledonian pine woodland. High deer numbers mean that the woodland does not regenerate; existing trees get older, and are not replaced. This is not a recent phenomenon. Research by Adam Watson on historical records relating to the Mar Forest shows that deer numbers rose in the late eighteenth century, after vigorous action against poachers by the Earl of Fife and the creation of the forerunner of the twentieth century sporting estate. High deer numbers have prevented subsequent regeneration. Most of the trees standing now are 140–200 years old, and the woodland has become a shrunken parkland of mature trees beneath which stately deer stand to serve their turn as sporting game on the open hills above.[7]

This problem of pressure of grazing is now being recognised in all upland areas, from Caithness to Devon.[8] It is a common view among conservationists that many upland ecosystems are severely overgrazed. Arthur Tansley commented in 1945 that most of the vegetation of hill grazings "owes its present condition largely to the continual nibbling of the sheep", and the same is true today. Tansley recognised that the ecology of the apparently wild and natural hills was shaped by the appetites of the herbivores with which they were stocked.[9] The culprit outside Scotland (and widely within it) is the humble baggy sheep. Sheep numbers in the UK as a whole have soared, as hill farmers have chased European Community subsidies. Hill farmers throughout the UK depend on headage payments. Indeed, the upland livestock economy is driven by those payments, which far outweigh the value of carcasses or wool. What matters therefore is to have as many animals on the hill as possible at the relevant time for applying for headage payments, and to spend as little as possible keeping them there. Some farmers run vast flocks on lowland grazing land, and bus them up to the hills at the relevant time. Others run as many sheep as they can on the uplands all through the year. Either way, they have a major impact on upland vegetation, grazing selected areas down, moving and concentrating nutrients.

The vegetation of the British uplands is not, therefore, particularly "natural" if what is meant by that word is that it is free of human influence. It is a creation of the grazing patterns that the agricultural economy has imposed. Human impacts have been long felt. Snowdonia had a grazing system based on transhumance until the nineteenth century, rather like that of the Swiss Alps that still hangs on today. Cattle were brought up in early March and grazed on pastures and fed stored hay until June. They were milked to make butter and cheese, and unused vegetation was cut as hay. Sheep stayed on after the cattle. The introduction of intensive sheep production and all-year grazing began between 1780 and 1820. It transformed the culture and economy of Snowdonia as surely as the slate mines, and it may be presumed that it also had an impact on the ecology of the hills, although there were no ecologists in the field to record it. Overwintering was replaced by summer grazing at the start of the present century. This change in grazing management also had an environmental impact, although it was subtle and complex. Reduced winter grazing by sheep in the present century allowed the relatively unpalatable species within the hill grasslands (mat grass, purple moor grass and soft rush) to expand, producing rather poor pasture.[10]

Whatever the ecological detail of the impacts of changing management, it is obvious that the "naturalness" of the hill pastures is in the eye of the beholder. Like chalk grassland, hill pastures bear the mark of the human hand, whether it has thereby enhanced diversity (as in a chalk grassland) or reduced it (as in a Welsh mountain coated with mat grass). The ecosystems of the "wild" hills are human-made.

Human-made ecosystems

It is no great revelation that the British countryside is so influenced by human action. Arthur Tansley pointed this out very clearly in 1939 in *The British Islands and their Vegetation*, when he described British vegetation as "semi-natural". He later rather nicely described this as vegetation that had "come by itself", but under conditions determined by human agency, in contrast to that which was "entirely natural, unaffected by man", and the sown fields and plantations that were deliberately created.[11] Tansley's distinctions are still found useful: in 1989 the Nature Conservancy Council defined "semi-natural" habitat as "modified by human activity from its original state but with a vegetation composed of native species, similar in structure to natural types, and with native animal species".[12] The only places where human feet, or the feet of livestock, have barely trodden in the UK are some river islands, sea shores, sea cliffs and mountain crags. In these days even these last ring to the click of karabiner and ice hammer, and plants are liable to be "gardened" away by determined rock climbers. Most ecosystems in Britain are influenced by people to a such profound degree that it is reasonable to say that they are *made* by them. As Oliver Rackham has so engagingly taught a generation of British conservationists, the countryside has a history, and so too do the habitats within it. They have a *human* history, for they form a human-crafted landscape.[13]

Many of the fragments of habitat that form the target of so much conservation effort are effectively assembled by human action, rather like biotic *Lego*, piece by piece. Not all the assembly is deliberate, but it all follows from deliberate acts. No one, for example, particularly chose to carpet the floor of the woodlands of West Cambridgeshire with dog's mercury, sedges, bluebells and oxlips, but there they are. Oliver Rackham identifies seven vegetation zones in Hayley Wood, perhaps the best documented of these much-studied woodlands. The distribution of each vegetation zone within the wood is determined by specific ecological requirements and highly complex patterns of soils and water, but their existence depends on the human making of the wood, and on the historical tradition of woodland management. Rackham writes "a well-ordered coppice cycle, uncomplicated by deer, benefits nearly all classes of ground-vegetation plants in turn, and its continuance down the centuries is responsible for much of the richness and variety of ancient woodland vegetation".[14]

The ecology of such "ancient woodlands" is human-influenced to a large degree. The recorded history of Hayley Wood goes back to 1251 when it was mentioned in the Old Croucher Book of Ely. It was continuously managed for its timber and underwood until 1922, when the last commercial coppicing was done. The wood is on heavy clay soils, and is extremely wet underfoot (as present-day winter visitors discover, to their delight or consternation, depending on their age). It was too wet to be ploughed up in the agricultural boom years of the mid-nineteenth century, and indeed farmland was abandoned around it in the depressions of the 1880s and 1920s. In this century the woodland was used for shooting, until purchased by the Cambridge and Isle of Ely Naturalists' Trust after a public appeal for funds in 1962. Coppicing was re-started in 1964.[15]

The square chunk of trees that is Hayley Wood, a tuft of green just under 50 ha in extent, sits marooned now in an ocean of arable land on the border between Cambridgeshire and Bedfordshire. Almost within sight lie other woods, other islands scattered across the clay landscape: Cockayne Hatley, East Hatley, Gamlingay, Waresley and Gransden Woods, and others beyond them. Some of the these have been acquired by the Wildlife Trust, and most are now managed to some extent at least in a way that is sensitive to their biological diversity and their long history of human use. These woods form conserved elements in a wider landscape that is mostly without conservation interest. By contrast with the fields around them, most people would regard them as "natural" parts of the landscape.

George Peterken suggests that "a woodland or any individual component of woodland is 'natural' if its characteristics have not been significantly affected by man". It is important to distinguish between such woods and those recent secondary woodlands that have been wholly and recently created, for example by the tireless efforts of the Forestry Commission and private timber companies, although the boundary between the two inevitably tends to be arbitrary. Peterken also suggests that it is possible to think about distinctions between different kinds of naturalness. Thus forests of the late glacial, before any possible human influence, have "original naturalness". Forests today if people had not had any impact on them would be rather different (because of climatic change for example), and would display "present naturalness". If all human influences were to end at once, forests would be in yet a different state, of "future naturalness". This categorisation of "naturalness" is useful, but the interplay of human and non-human influences is in practice extremely complex to tease out.[16]

Take Hayley Wood again. Rackham believes that it probably became a woodland island in about the ninth century. Isolation would have begun to have ecological effects quite soon. When intensive woodland management began (certainly by the thirteenth century), the ecology of the wood must have changed further. Coppicing would have driven out tree species that either do not like to be coppiced (like Scots pine), or compete poorly after cutting (like small-leafed lime), and would have suppressed ground flora that was maladapted to the cycles of sun and shade created by a regular coppice cycle. Old trees, fallen timber and brash would have disappeared, and with them fungi and other denizens of rotting wood. Pigs rooting up the forest floor must have added their own inimitable ecological signature.

The ecology of the woodland under coppice management might have been rather stable for many centuries, but human impacts changed again with the abandonment of coppicing in the present century. The wood began to lose the mixed age-structure of the underwood (a problem tackled by the re-introduction of coppicing as a conservation management method), and it also enjoyed the arrival of a herd of fallow deer. The abandonment of coppicing in some ways allowed the wood to achieve Peterken's state of "future naturalness", as did the abandonment of a field in the area known as "The Triangle" at the North edge of the wood, where bluebells and dog's mercury are now slowly advancing under thick hawthorn across the humps of old ridge and furrow. Whatever happens, the wood will never go back to its condition before its first isolation, or the first axe-cuts and human fires. That original naturalness is gone, irrecoverable. And yet the woods that we have now, the fragments that survive from what Oliver Rackham memorably refers to as "The Wildwood", are still "natural" to some extent. They are human-made, but not to the same extent as a motor-car or a shopping arcade. To understand the dynamics of this "naturalness" we need to digress a little to consider the way in which ecologists think about ecosystems, and ecosystem change.

Nature and ecological change

A major body of ecological writing, particularly in the UK and the USA, has been deeply influenced by ideas of equilibrium and stability. The work of the American ecologist F.E. Clements in the first decades of this century has been particularly influential. In his book, *Research Methods in Ecology*, Clements proposed a "dynamic ecology" to replace the static descriptive work then current, and he developed ideas about plant succession that have proved, in the words of the historian Robert MacIntosh "remarkably resilient".[17] His was the notion of progressive change towards a "climatic climax", with the vegetation formation like a complex organism "developing" through time, in a way deliberately analogous to the growth of individual organisms. Under this thinking, the pre-clearance woodland would have been a climatic climax, and the human artefact of the coppice wood a "plagioclimax", or sub-climax.

Clements' ideas were soon challenged, both by American ecologists like Cowles and Gleason, and by those in Europe. In the UK, Arthur Tansley argued for a more complex pattern of succession, with soils, physiography and human action all driving succession under different conditions. However the general structure of Clements' thinking about ecology survived in what has been called the "classical paradigm" or the "equilibrium paradigm" in ecology.[18] The features of this included a particular interest in the end-points of ecological processes and a view that ecological systems were closed. It placed great emphasis on the notion that ecosystems were self-regulating and if disturbed would tend to return towards equilibrium. This paradigm fed ideas that there was a "balance of nature", easily upset by inappropriate human action.

When pollen analysis was developed, of course, ecologists began to gain a wholly new picture of just how dynamic vegetation had been over long periods of time. It was clear that in the UK, as everywhere else, natural systems have been disrupted by a vast range of different forces, and that they were far from an "equilibrium" state. Thus ice cleared Cambridgeshire at the end of the last glaciation about 10,000 years ago, probably rather quickly. Birch woodland probably developed rapidly, joined relatively soon by hazel and pine. The climate was warm and temperate between about 9000 and 5000 years ago, and at the end of that period was probably considerably warmer than it is now, with summer temperatures some 2-5°C higher.[19]

Forest carpeted the entire landscape except for local gaps due to fire, soils, poor drainage or tree falls. In England the forest would have been broadleaved, with oak, elm and lime, and beech and hornbeam in the southeast. In most of Scotland, Scots pine and birch were dominant. From 5000 years ago the climate became somewhat colder and wetter. Rainwater stripped out forest nutrients, and soils deteriorated, particularly in the uplands. Extensive upland heaths and blanket bogs developed at this time. There was an intriguing and rather sudden decline in elms throughout the country, possibly as a result of something like the "Dutch Elm Disease" of the 1970s, but Neolithic farmers also appeared in the forest at this time, and the forests began to change and to shrink in response to the axe and fire, the appetite of cattle, sheep, goats and the demands of agriculture. These processes were accelerated by the arrival of the plough and by further climatic decline about 2500 years ago. By the time Julius Caesar's army sighted the British coast, the landscape was widely cleared and farmed.

There has not been time for a "climatic climax" to develop in Britain. Vegetation patterns have changed in complex ways over time. Studies of plant-fossil records of wetland (hydrosere) succession show that ecological change can follow a variety of different pathways, such that specific successional pathways are difficult to predict. Furthermore, not all past vegetation communities have a modern analogue, and some modern plant communities have assembled only recently and have no past precedent.[20] The notion of "climax" vegetation, of ecosystems moving through predictable stages to a stable end-point is not very useful in understanding how ecosystems change.

It is no good looking back into the past to seek an equilibrium state of nature which human action has disturbed. Ecosystems are dynamic, changing continuously in response to climate. Over the Holocene period, the last 10,000 years, ecosystems have been continuously in flux in response to warmer and colder periods. Nature is not an organism, a system balanced at equilibrium. Rather, as Peter Moore argues, "Species, it would seem in these unstable days, are wandering the earth in response to their physiological limitations and their competitive capacities, complicated in some cases by sheer historical accident".[21]

Ecologists increasingly recognise the scientific challenge to old equilibrial ideas, and are turning to consider the instabilities in landscapes, particularly the problem of disturbance, and different scales in space and time. As the historian Donald Worster put it, "nature, we are told now, should be regarded as a landscape of patches of all sizes, textures, and colors, changing continually through time and space, responding to an unceasing barrage of perturbations".[22] There is a new school of thought about ecology abroad, a "nonequilibrium paradigm". This emphasises the openness of natural systems, and the need therefore to understand them in the context of their surroundings, and past events and disturbances that have affected them. Non-equilibrium ecology recognises that the factors that are important in explaining how things change will depend on the length of time and the area over which change is analysed.[23]

Disturbances come in many shapes and sizes, from frost or individual tree falls to gales like the one in October 1987, that caused such consternation in southern England, or widespread disease epidemics. Disturbances tend to occur at a frequency, intensity and scale that is characteristic of particular landscapes, and is determined by climate, weather, topography, geology and the species present. Increasingly, these disturbances involve human influence, from the level of the individual bulldozer through the replanting of woodland to our various uncontrolled experiments with atmospheric chemistry.[24]

Growing interest in the fractal geometry of nature, and the ecology of chaos rather than equilibrium, turns ecologists to exploring the ways in which different processes determine landscape pattern at different scales. This provides a new way of understanding human interactions with natural disturbances. Humans are significant agents of ecological change. Indeed, Robert May argues that the scale and intensity of human activity is such as to transform our understanding of the relations between physical and biological systems. No longer can ecologists assume that terrestrial ecosystems simply respond to climate changes and internal processes of competition. Transformed by human action, ecosystem change can itself potentially drive climatic change. Ecology has to be able to shift scales in pursuit of explanation, to "reach down to the molecular biology of the gene and up to the interplay between biological and physical processes on a global scale".[25]

The ideas that drive the science of ecology are changing, and with them our understanding of nature and ecological change. Landscapes are being seen as "a dynamic mosaic of patches-within-patches" over a wide range of scales. Ecology is undergoing a profound shift from the notion that nature is a well-behaved, deterministic system towards a view in which equilibrium states are "the exception to the rule".[26] Gone are the days when ecologists (and conservationists) could conceive of "nature" in equilibrium, and hence portray human-induced changes in those ecosystems as somehow "unnatural". Nature itself is dynamic and highly variable, its patterns at one particular place and time contingent on preceding events, its trajectory through time is open-ended and not tending to an equilibrial point. Human actions are part of the web of influences on ecological change, not external equilibrium-disturbing impacts.

Science and conservation

The changing scientific understanding of ecosystems has obvious implications for conservation. "Conservation science" has been used (particularly in the UK) to generate technocratic recipes for manipulating nature, predicting the outcomes of management action and reconstructing desired ecological conditions. Used in this way, science provides an instrumentalist approach to nature, with the scientist as external to natural processes, spanner in hand. This approach has been used in conservation both to manage recreation and the scenic aspects of landscape (revegetating the scars of ski pistes for example), and to manage detailed aspects of populations of wildlife species and habitats, such as assessing the relative impacts of parasite infestation and predation on populations of red grouse.[27]

The nature of ecological science is, however, also important to conservation in another way. Ever since the 1940s, wildlife conservation in the UK has leaned heavily on an association, in the official mind, with science. In doing so, it has gained from the privileged status science held in popular culture in post-war Britain. During and after the Second World War, science and scientists were held in esteem both by the general public and by government because of their contribution to the war effort. The argument that conservation was necessary *for science* justified public spending on conservation. Science proved most effective as a justification for conservation action. This became apparent in the debates about conservation during and following the Second World War, discussed in Chapter Two. The British Ecological Society was a major force in the planning for government involvement in nature reserves, and it was the veteran ecologist Arthur Tansley who took over the chairmanship of the "Huxley Committee" when Julian Huxley left to run UNESCO.[28] The importance accorded to National Nature Reserves (NNRs) in both the Huxley Report and the National Parks and Access to the Countryside Act 1949 related to their supposed contribution to scientific research.

Science was also high on the agenda of the fledgling Nature Conservancy. Its first Director-General, Max Nicholson, wrote in 1957, "Nature Reserves are regarded perhaps more than anywhere else as outdoor laboratories where the workings of nature can be studied, in addition to being outdoor living museums or wildernesses in which nature can be preserved as a national heritage".[29] To some, indeed, the Conservancy was not doing enough science. A reviewer of the Nature Conservancy's 1957 report wrote disparagingly that "ecological research is evidently to be merely the handmaiden of conservation, and conservation to be virtually equated with preservation". The Conservancy's role should be ecological research in the national interest, advising on the best allocation and use of land and means of its improvement; indeed "the one thing the Nature Conservancy should not do is conserve".[30]

To guide the management of NNRs, it was necessary to develop new knowledge and skills of environmental management. Although now the basic principles of managing wildlife habitat are widely known and taught, in the 1950s little research had been done except for agricultural grazing or forestry. Neither of those provided a good model for very many of the new tasks of conservation. Max Nicholson believed that effective reserve management demanded "deep scientific knowledge of the conditions governing water levels, evolution of the vegetation and the balance of animal populations". In some cases this would require intrusive forms of management. Nicholson commented: "paradoxically we can ensure the survival of wild places of Britain only by finding out what happens when we interfere with them".[31] The acquisition of that knowledge is an underestimated achievement of British conservation. The resulting enthusiasm for intervention in management and environmental manipulation is arguably its distinguishing feature.[32]

In time, it was SSSIs, Sites of Special *Scientific* Interest, that became one of the most important weapons in the armoury of the Nature Conservancy and its successors. Rubric about the "scientific interest" of nature persists in conservation legislation even to this day. This is, perhaps, somewhat surprising, because ecological science has changed rather more than conservation has. When Tansley was helping to set the principles of post-war conservation, British ecology was highly descriptive, and a complete "set" of natural or semi-natural habitats was indeed vital to scientific advance. It was then reasonable to argue that the comparison of manipulated and "natural" ecosystems was vital to the advance of ecological knowledge and under-standing. A good case could be made that scientists (i.e. ecologists) needed nature reserves and SSSIs for their research. However, as time wore on, ecology became more experimental (and hence interested in highly controlled and artificial ecosystems), more interested in modelling (and abstracted analogue versions of ecosystems locked inside machines) and in reductionist approaches to nature, such as the analysis of energetics or (more recently) molecular biology and genetics. Nature reserves and SSSIs were no longer central to these scientific endeavours.

The famous case of Cow Green Reservoir demonstrated the emerging gap between what scientists actually used, and the places that conservationists wanted to protect on the grounds of their "scientific interest". A major reservoir was proposed on the Upper Tees in the North Pennines in the 1960s, on land that held a remarkable community of arctic–alpine plants. These relics of the last glacial period 10,000 years ago were miles from their nearest relatives and at relatively low altitude. The area was an SSSI, and once alerted by detailed survey, the Nature Conservancy, under its Director General Max Nicholson, fought the proposed reservoir tooth and nail, right up to Parliament, where the Private Bill to allow the reservoir was debated. The story is complex, but the conservation case was basically that the plant communities of Widdybank Fell were unique and of great scientific importance. This argument was defeated by the proponents of the reservoir by the simple expedient of demonstrating that however many scientists signed up to the value of the site, very few had visited it and little research upon it had been published. It was cleverly argued that scientists had not shown enough "scientific interest" in the site until it was threatened, and some of those who stood on their high horse to defend it had not been there. The demonstrable level of "scientific interest" was weighed in the balance against conventional arguments of the need for the development of the site, and found wanting.[33]

This affair has many ironies, not least that money paid by the developers in mitigation has now made Widdybank Fell one of the best-researched upland sites in Britain, with huge efforts put in to study the threatened vegetation, and a large scientific literature devoted to it. The important thing about the case, however, is not that it was lost by the conservation interest (or that the apparently "urgent" need for the reservoir was rather temporary), but that the argument that it was important because of the value of the area for *science* was defeated. Its defenders did not argue that the reservoir was a waste of money, or that it intruded on the landscape, nor did they try to argue that the vegetation of the area had economic value or the landscape "wilderness value", although all of these were arguably true. Nobody even dreamed of talking about "sustainability". Ideas like this have been developed since the 1970s, and have replaced the rather simplistic arguments put forward in defence of the arctic and alpine plants of Widdybank Fell SSSI. They have been needed primarily because over time it has proved impossible to continue to defend nature on the basis of its importance to science.

Not only has the link between science and conservation changed since the late 1940s, but the honoured status of science in public life has also been much eroded. People lost confidence in Harold Wilson's "white heat of technological revolution", partly as a result of fears about nuclear power and nuclear weapons, and the perceived culpability of science and technology in the emerging environmental crises of the 1970s and 1980s.[34] Environmental groups often use science to "speak for nature", but the expert knowledge they invoke about the natural world can sit uneasily with environmentalist opposition to the industrial applications of science.[35] Ecology has served to identify "niches for humans to appropriate"[36] at least as often as it has to suggest ways to conserve nature or minimise the impact of human exploitation. Although science remained a decision-support tool on which conservation land-managers remained dependent, the changed position of science in public life meant that by the 1980s science was no longer a very effective justification for nature conservation.

In some ways, however, this change has been less profound than might be thought, for even the "scientific" basis of conservation has always been

92

accompanied by ideas about nature that are not in any sense scientific. Arthur Tansley said:

> when I am commenting on the merits of a proposed nature reserve, after describing the scientific merits of its flora and fauna, I often find it hard to resist bringing in the scenic beauty of the landscape or the attractiveness of the vegetation, though my allusions to these take on an almost apologetic tone. It is as if I were trying to say 'and, of course, the place is really beautiful as well, though perhaps I ought not to mention the fact!'[37]

The diversity or rarity of wildlife and the beauty of landscapes were clearly seen to be closely linked by many of those who were fighting for conservation through the labyrinth of government committees in the 1940s. Julian Huxley, Chairman of the Wild Life Conservation Special Committee for England and Wales, noted that in the countryside, physical structure, climate, natural and semi-natural vegetation, crops grown and agricultural regime "blend into a whole which often possesses singular beauty and high scientific interest, and the defacement or disappearance of the distinctive characters of such a region involves an irreparable loss which it is hard to overestimate".[38]

SSSIs, too, have always reflected a broader suite of values than the narrowly "scientific". The first SSSIs were chosen rapidly, and without rigid criteria, on the basis of the existing knowledge of natural history societies and a few experts working under contract to the Nature Conservancy. Norman Moore said of the process, "Everyone worked under great pressure against the clock. There was rarely time to survey sites very thoroughly. There is a story that Mr Lousley selected one SSSI in Cornwall from the window of a train. Those of us who knew Mr Lousley well were not surprised when subsequent studies showed that he had chosen well".[39] This rooting of "conservation science" in wider human perception of nature is a great strength. As the criteria used in SSSI selection have been progressively redefined and tightened, they have amply confirmed the intuitive feel for species, habitat and landscape of these pioneers. Review of the SSSI system under new criteria in 1979 confirmed almost all the existing sites. SSSIs were mostly knocked off the list because of better surveys and more knowledge (surveys in new places, or better surveys in known sites), or because they had deteriorated so much in the intervening years.

Science is necessary to select (and manage) SSSIs, but it no longer figures prominently as a *reason* for their selection. SSSIs are places for nature, not for scientists. Ironically, the need to understand and study the ecological impacts of global climate change has in the 1980s created a scientific need for just the kind of national series of open-air laboratories envisaged by Tansley. National Nature Reserves feature prominently in plans for terrestrial parts of the suddenly fashionable and urgent "global environmental change" research. However the justification for conservation has moved on.

For this reason there is now much more common ground between the once-divided interests of "landscape" and "wildlife" conservation. It has always been a ridiculous notion that National Parks are beautiful, and Sites of Special Scientific Interest merely interesting, whether to scientists or others. Nature will not be categorised in this way, and people's experiences of nature have never fitted the old institutional mould of British conservation. Is the dragonfly over the pond or the eagle over the hill only scientifically interesting, while the landscape around it is beautiful? SSSIs can be stunningly beautiful, and enjoyed without any reference to their "scientific interest", or their importance in terms of some abstract notion like "biodiversity". Indeed, the beauty of such fragments of nature can be quite remarkable. In *Our Heritage of Wild Nature*, Tansley set out what he saw as the claims of wild and semi-wild vegetation to a place in plans for the future. His first reason was simply that "all the existing beauty of England depends upon it".[40] "Landscape" and "wildlife" are both part of nature, two ends of the same piece of string.

Science and nature

The association between conservation and science, particularly ecological science, is very important, because not only have the ideas current within that science shifted somewhat (as we have just discussed), but there is increasing awareness of the limitations of the very process of "doing science". A growing body of work on the sociology of science is demonstrating that scientific ideas reflect the society in which they are formed and exchanged. When scientists think they are making impartial observations, and drawing conclusions from them about the way nature really works, they are in fact producing views of nature that are profoundly influenced by social context. The ideas we have about nature reflect the ideas we have about ourselves, and about the society in which we live. This critique of the notion of "value-free" science is by no means specific to the science of ecology and the practice of conservation, but it is highly relevant to it. The arguments are particularly well developed in feminist critiques of science, for example by Donna Haraway.[41]

Haraway writes about changing scientific ideas about primate behaviour, and compares the social context within which successive theories have been generated and published. Ideas, of course, change over time, as scientists find new data and argue with each other. What is important is the way in which she demonstrates that there are links between the competing scientific "stories" told in the academic literature and the contemporary political struggles in which the scientists were involved, particularly over the reproductive social behaviour of women. Ideas about what women were like, and how they ought to behave, were inextricably linked to the conclusions scientists drew (from "the data", of course) about non-human apes. Haraway's analysis suggests that science cannot produce meanings that are free of their context. She argues that we need to "demystify" science, and open up the ways in which scientific ideas are created and used in ordinary life.

Science does not make meanings: people do, and the ideas that emerge need to be seen in their particular historical settings. Margaret Fitsimmons suggests that nature too cannot exist without social meaning.[42] Fitsimmons argues that "Nature as we know it was invented, in the differentiation of city and countryside ... in the abstraction of contemporary culture and consciousness from the necessary productive work of material life".[43] Haraway sees scientific debate as important as "a social process of producing stories, important stories that constitute public meanings". She says simply "science is our myth".[44] Science is still the most significant source of myths about nature.

Studies of the way in which scientific knowledge is socially constructed suggest that science does not provide society with the certainties it has come to assume. For example, Brian Wynne has explored the way science was invoked to provide assurances about public safety following the Chernobyl disaster.[45] There was widespread concern about lingering pollution by radioactive caesium-127 in the Lake District fells, and the associated contamination of lamb produced from the sheep that grazed there. This problem is a familiar one of environmental risk assessment. Conventional scientific approaches to risk involve making assumptions about context in order to come up with estimates of the nature and scale of the problem. Wynne showed that this approach was extremely misleading in the context of caesium in the Lake District, because (as is very often the case in real life) the scientists did not know enough. They made assumptions about soil conditions on the fells, and hence about the way the radioactive caesium-127 would behave, that proved inaccurate, and as a result their assessment of risk was flawed. It was announced that the problem of contamination was small and likely to be short-lived, but this, unhappily, proved incorrect.

Clearly, in this instance, the science of risk assessment generated the "wrong" answer. It did so because the scientists concerned lacked critical knowledge, but more seriously they did not realise how significant their ignorance was. Wynne argues that the real problem with the risk-assessment process was the way science handles the uncertainty that is embedded in scientific ignorance. He argues that indeterminacy always underlies scientific "knowledge", even when that knowledge is based on incredibly thorough work. We deal with that uncertainty by hiding behind a comfortable vision of science as a source of clear "answers", and by physically and politically allowing scientists (the proverbial "men in white coats") to close up into a private research community. Within that community, scientists decide how to conceive of problems and what to measure to explore them.

Scientific ideas are not free-floating, but are a social construction. Scientific judgements ultimately depend on "human judgement of what variables are and are not important".[46] Scientists talk among themselves, in a complex technical language, and what they think is expressed and constrained within a circuit of social commitments and conventions. Both scientists themselves and the wider community provide arenas where ideas about science are formed, debated and re-organised. Here is our system for providing Donna Haraway's "stories" about nature: myths to live by (or, in the case of the persistence of Chernobyl fallout in our meat supply, to worry about). In these arenas, scientific ideas about ecosystems, or "biodiversity", are tightly interwoven with broader ideas about natural beauty, naturalness or the desirability (and desirable limits) of ecological change. Ideas about conservation are formed and refined in response to the volatile combination of these diverse elements.

With our slight and transient knowledge of what is actually "out there" among species, populations, ecosystems and landscapes we create stories or myths which we then empower to affect the way we think about nature. Our stories about nature are conditioned both by shifting concepts of ecology, and the social context within which scientific ideas are produced. They can, of course, be shocked by new observations. That is why we are so upset to discover that, for example, chimpanzees hunt and eat monkeys, or that dolphins in the Moray Firth have been mugging harbour porpoises.[47] New stories rise to replace the old.

It might seem that the idea that nature is socially defined removes all foundation from conservation. As Donald Worster says:

> if nature is nothing but a bewildering panorama of changes, many of them induced by human beings going back to ancient hunters setting fire to the bush, and if our attitudes toward nature are themselves demonstrably in a state of constant flux, so that yesterday we hated wolves and today we love them, then what should conservation mean?[48]

This is an important question. Clearly the changes in the ways ecologists understand the dynamics of change, and in our understanding of the social context of scientific understanding, must have significant implications for conservation? Do they undercut the institutions that have been built up with such effort and determination over the last half century? Do the ideas that have guided conservationists for so long have to be abandoned? Or is there a way forwards that can use these ideas to provide a new dynamic for conservation action?

I argued in Chapter Five that conservation is not about "preserving the past" in any simple sense, or protecting pieces of countryside in a particular state. Conservation is about handling change, and about the transition from past to future. Here I have suggested that our understanding of nature, too, is "made", by science and by society. That creative process is of central importance to conservation. Conservation is about nature, but it is also inextricably about culture. Conservation is not about trying to stop the "human impact on nature", but about negotiating that impact. The implications of this for conservation are taken up in the next chapter, starting with a discussion of the importance to conservation of the cultural values of nature.

CHAPTER SEVEN

Nature and the Wild

Wildness is drained away through "wise management"
Neil Evernden[1]

The end of nature?

Conservation in the UK has grown up without a coherent philosophy, a cultural and scientific rag-bag of passion, insight and good intentions. Thinking about conservation has also, as we have seen, developed with a set of practical concerns (rare species, characteristic habitats, beautiful landscapes) and a set of recognised and institutionalised activities (particularly the complex pattern of British protected areas). However, underneath this established pattern, conservation floats on a maelstrom of diverse ideas. Science provides a handy recipe book, but it cannot tell us what to make in nature. Furthermore, its ideas about how the ingredients of ecosystems fit together have changed, which is rather unnerving. So how do we find ideas on which to base conservation?

Writing in 1969 about "the theory of conservation", Norman Moore suggested that conservation ultimately rested on one of two value judgements: "Either we conserve wildlife because we believe it exists in its own right, and has intrinsic value, or we do so because we believe wildlife is valuable to Man who is himself valuable — or we can conserve it for both reasons".[2] Conservationists in the UK have drawn on both moral and aesthetic arguments for conservation. It has been a particular task for British conservationists to emphasise "the integrity of social and natural values in a market economy".[3] In the government document, Biodiversity: the UK action plan, the point is made very simply: "we believe that a culture which encourages respect for wildlife and landscapes is preferable to one that does not". The conservation of species and habitats, as much as the conservation of landscapes, depends on the fact that "they are beautiful or because they otherwise enrich our lives".[4] Nature is seen to be important for its aesthetic value, its value for recreation, its value for science and education. It is also commonly held that nature has an important psychological contribution to human life, particularly for urbanised humanity.[5] These are essentially *cultural* values of nature.

Edward O. Wilson has suggested that we are hard-wired by the process of evolution to need other species. He has coined the word "biophilia" for this idea of a genetically based affinity with nature,[6] defining it as "the innate tendency to focus on life, and life-like processes". In his book *The Biophilia Hypothesis*, his co-editor Stephen Kellert argues that biophilia "proclaims a human dependence on nature that extends far beyond the simple issue of material and physical sustenance to encompass as well the human craving for aesthetic, intellectual, cognitive and even spiritual meaning and satisfaction".[7]

The idea of biophilia is far from being fully explored, and the intellectual challenge in making tight theoretical sense of the broad notion is great. As Wilson himself points out, "the manifold ways in which human beings are tied to the remainder of life are very poorly understood, crying for new scientific inquiry and a boldness of aesthetic interpretation".[8] Nonetheless, the message is clear, and it is a familiar one to conservationists; humans need other species. At the end of *The Biophilia Hypothesis*, Stephen Kellert writes of his "skepticism regarding the human capacity to thrive in a biologically depauperate world that has countenanced and abetted in the massive destruction of life".[9]

The cultural dimension of conservation may be obvious in the case of landscape, but it is also central to the debate about biodiversity. When the government comes to say why the UK's biodiversity is "special and significant" in Biodiversity: the UK action plan, it points to the way in which human-imposed and evolutionary change have interacted since the end of the last glaciation to produce distinctive assemblages of plants and animals, and the way these have been shaped by traditional countryside management practices. The key point is what we see of ourselves in nature — the fact that the countryside "tells a story of our changing relationships with other species, if we take the trouble to find and interpret the clues".[10] Richard Mabey made the same point in his classic book *The Common Ground*. He writes "the intricate fabric of our landscape is the result of a weaving together of human and natural life that spans five millenia".[11] His book opens with a long quotation from John Clare, and ends with the unforgettable reminder of the annual rhythms in nature in the return of swifts to British summer skies. It is an eloquent statement of the cultural importance of nature.

We create nature, both in a direct ecological sense, and in a wider cultural sense. Species and ecosystems have a cultural importance in the UK because they record our own human past. Nature has value because of the history of interaction with us, and our forebears. Lars-Erik Liljelund writes: "Our emotional ties to an area of nature, a particular sort of natural environment or even a single species fulfil far greater needs than the purely material, and deserve our respect and must be taken seriously." The purpose of conservation is therefore to "hand on to the next generation an environment that is no less rich than the one we ourselves inherited".[12]

We attach ideas to nature, and we weave stories around them that have human significance. We are a sentient, articulate, *archiving* species. We make meanings of the fabric of the Earth and its living organisms for ourselves. Culture has power, in this sense, over nature. And culture puts nature in boxes, "the glue cementing past, present and future humans together in a community of alienation from the rest of the world from which they arise, in which they participate with other entities, and to which they organically return through death".[13]

The conservation of biodiversity, just like conservation of landscape, is important because of the cultural value of nature. Habitats and species, like landscapes, acquire cultural value like any other historical object through human use, and human association. Yet at the same time the value of nature relies on the fact that it is *not* human, that it is "natural". Is the value of nature not destroyed by the extent of human involvement in its creation, and the weight of cultural associations we attach to it? In his book, *Green Political Theory*, Robert Goodin seeks to develop a "green" theory of value. He argues that there is indeed particular value in naturally occurring processes that do not involve human agents. People value these natural processes (and the products of those processes, co-evolved species and ecosystems) because they provide a larger context that sits outside their own lives. The involvement of human hands in these processes does diminish their value.[14] But as we have seen, the influence of human hands has been virtually ubiquitous in the UK.[15] Furthermore, we quite clearly value very highly ecosystems where human hands have been particularly influential, for example in the landscapes of National Parks. How can nature be valued because it is "natural" and outside the sphere of human action, when much of it is quite obviously within that sphere?

Nature writers in North America generally leap off at this point to talk about "wilderness". This has enormous cultural resonance, and is the source

101

of much confusion, as well as being enshrined in the USA's 1964 Wilderness Act.[16] In Bill McKibben's passionate book, *The End of Nature*, he wrote "we have killed off nature — that world entirely independent of us which was here before we arrived and which encircled and supported our human society".[17] Of course, as he puts it, "there's still something out there". We have not ended rain, or clouds. McKibben explains "when I say nature I mean a certain set of human ideas about the world and our place in it". The change has come about because of human changes in the global atmosphere, and although it is too soon to predict future climates, "the *meaning* of the wind, the sun, the rain — of nature — has already changed". "A child born now", he says, "will never know a natural summer, a natural autumn, winter or spring". We may ignore the implications of this change for a while, but in the end "our mistaken sense of nature as eternal and separate will be washed away and we will see all too clearly what we have done".[18]

What have we done? I suspect that McKibben suffers from the selective blindness of many North Americans of European extraction, and sees the only human impact as that of industrial society and economy within the last century or so. He feels that the extent of human influence on global biogeophysical processes is so profound that "The walk along Mill Creek, or any stream, or up any hill, or through any woods, is changed for ever, changed as profoundly as it was when it shifted from pristine and un-tracked wilderness to mapped and deeded and cultivated land".[19] The pre-Columbian presence, with its culture and cosmology, its fire and its hunting, is forgotten. These people do not count as damagers of naturalness, for they are deemed to be "natural" themselves.[20]

This romantic conceit is more or less impossible in Britain, where settlement happened millenia ago. We do not have a view of a "wild" nature suddenly transformed, but a view of nature manipulated, cultured, and steered over many centuries. For us there has been a recent decline (in diversity, in the extent of semi-natural habitat, in landscape beauty), but it is decline from an equilibrium where people had an important (and largely positive) role. Bill McKibben laments that "we have made every spot on earth man-made and artificial", with the result that even though "wildness, and the idea of wildness, has outlasted the exploration of the entire globe", it is gone. In the UK, nature, in that sense, has been gone a long time.[21]

Chapter Five argued that the countryside is nature known, and human-made, a "nature" made by culture. Chapter Six added the argument that the "nature" of ecosystems and species is equally a cultural creation, a human concept and a human artefact. And yet none of these are only human-made, in the sense that a motorway, or a photograph, is human-made. Does the fact that human hands have been so influential in directing the form of nature in the UK mean that there is no difference in the value of a piece of chalk downland and a new motorway? There is, of course, a difference, and it is a highly significant one for conservation. As Robert Goodin points out in *Green Political Theory*, it lies in the degree of their naturalness.[22] Downland is more natural than a motorway, and as a result its natural value is greater. Chalk grasslands, or hedgerows, are not the pure work of non-human processes, but neither are they created independently of those forces. Such fragments of nature may have acquired cultural values (in the history of a parish, for example), but they also have value for their naturalness, derived from the ecological processes that were guided by their human managers. Their natural values and their cultural values combine in their creation, and their importance for conservation stems from this partnership. Human hands have touched them, but done so *"lightly* or if you prefer, *lovingly"*.[23] Conservation action must be built upon an appreciation of the balance between these two dimensions of nature's values, those that derive from its separateness from human action, and those that derive from the history of active human association with it. Conservation has to involve making choices about change, and the challenge is to make those choices in ways that are, in Donald Worster's words, "consistent with our best ethical reasoning, consistent with our inescapable dependency on other forms of life".[24]

Nature and the wild

In making these choices about change, conservationists must, somehow, avoid the illusion that nature can be contained completely by human plans. Conservation is more than merely a branch of resource management. There must be space within conservation for an acceptance of the wildness of nature. We classify and analyse nature with our science, we construct and disassemble ecosystems with technology in planned and unplanned ways, and increasingly we make and remould even species themselves through biotechnology. We treat nature as something that can be bought and sold, and yet there is something within it that is not contained by this treatment. There is an "otherness" of nature that breaks out of those bounds. It is this otherness, this innate capacity to be an active agent, that conservation must meet and address.

Nature on one level is constrained by human action, and lives in the spaces created by human economy, society and culture, but on another level its very naturalness consists in its capacity to survive and act *outside* human control. Carolyn Merchant writes: "the nature that science is supposedly representing is not a stable backdrop to human production, but is unstable and continually changing, not just as a transformed human landscape, but in actively resisting and accommodating to human interventions". "Nature" is socially constructed, but there is also something beyond that construction. In Merchant's words, nonhuman nature is also "active, alive, and above all real".[25] Nature acts around and outside human actions, and in this lies its vital wildness.

Science is built on a philosophical platform that makes nature separate from human society, in the words of Margaret Fitsimmons, something "external and primordial".[26] The Enlightenment placed nature in opposition to a series of other categories: nature versus society, culture and nurture. Nature was the "non-human", the "other".[27] And yet there is a continuity with this "other" that is a repeated theme of writing that tries to explore human interactions with other species. The philosopher Erazim Kohák writes:

> I think only a person wholly blinded and deafened, rendered insensitive by the glare and the blare of his own devices, could write off that primordial awareness of the human's integral place in the cosmos as mere poetic imagination or as "merely subjective".[28]

Our place in that world suggests a fellowship with other species that transcends the nature/culture boundary, the 'us and it' of human and non-human. Kohák remarks how curious it is "that the notion of a fundamental discontinuity between humans and their natural world should come to appear evident". However, it has, and this idea of separation between human and natural has dominated Western thought and underpinned and justified the ruthless exploitation of nature. It is argued that different views of nature dominate non-modern worldviews, for example those of aboriginal North Americans.[29]

Conventional thinking separates and distances us from nature. Neil Evernden points out that "through our conceptual domestication of nature, we extinguish wild otherness, even in the imagination".[30] And yet that "otherness" is right there, as close and as individual as another human person, and we are connected to it: "left beyond, in nature, are all our fellow beings with whom we have shared our evolutionary existence".[31] Nature is something that can be experienced, very directly, and this experience is the spark from which wider ethical concerns about nature can grow — it is a vital root of conservation. Neil Evernden says, we can "actually encounter the other beings *as* other, as living subjects of significance", although to do so "requires some loosening of the conceptual bindings of nature so that subjectivity can flow back in, like water to a scorched garden".[32]

Many nature writers, from Richard Jefferies to Annie Dillard, have argued as much. In *The Tree*, John Fowles criticises the way we so easily turn nature into a "thing": a species, a landscape, something we can use. In the process we lose "its presentness, its seeming transience, its creative ferment and hidden potential." He says, "as long as nature is seen as something outside ourselves, frontiered and foreign, *separate*, it is lost both to us and in us".[33] Ian McHarg, inspiration for the pragmatic professionalism of Landscape Architecture, was clear about the place of the power of nature in his own work. He said that *Design with Nature* was:

a personal testament to the power and importance of sun, moon, and stars, the changing seasons, seedtime and harvest, clouds, rain and rivers, the oceans and the forests. They are with us now, co-tenants of the phenomenal universe, participating in that timeless yearning that is evolution, vivid expression of time past, essential partners in survival and with us now involved in the creation of the future.[34]

We are part of nature, and yet we need the "otherness" of nature. It is always there, enduring our attempts to direct it by science and technology and to tame it with our cultural constructions. Evernden speaks of "the impact of the realisation that there is an other, something in experience which cannot be contained in the self and is, therefore, uncanny — and *wild*". People need that sense of the wild, and conservation needs that contact between individual people and other species and landscapes. It needs the energy that flames out from the recognition of nature. As Neil Evernden says, "to encounter the wild other, to greet another, 'I am', is to accept the other's existence in one's life world". That is the beginning of conservation. This is also the basis of the notion of the intrinsic rights of nature, and is fundamental to the thinking of deep ecology, for example in the works of people such as Arne Naess and George Sessions.[35] The currency of such ideas among conservationists should perhaps not be surprising.

This "other" nature is beyond our control. Its "otherness" has the capacity to shock us. Sometimes it does so pleasurably as when we see buddleia seedlings with roots sunk into rail line ballast, or ferns clutching damp brickwork on car-park walls. We welcome the power of the patterns and rhythms of nature that brings migrating birds half way across the Earth to appear in battered bushes in busy urban parks, or dump in spectacular falls on remote islands. Nature can be so astonishingly unexpected — as I learned one morning years ago on Fair Isle, when I went out to find the place alive with wrynecks, with not a decent tree for hundreds of miles. We welcome too the capacity of nature's "otherness" to strike root in our consciousness, seeded by important and memorable but often *little* things.[36]

At other times the "other" in nature shocks and alarms us. Richard Nelson points out that we may be "elevated by the beauty of nature, cling to it, crave to protect it, but we cleave to the coldness of stone, the storm that carries us away without knowing, the waters that kill without reason".[37] Even in the UK, nature can act far beyond our capacity to predict or control, as when the "Great Storm" ripped out half the woods of southern England, or the "hundred-year" floods that make and remake river channels and roar across the croplands and urban development on floodplains. Conservation must hold on to this sense of the power of nature active and effective, and not (or not completely) under human control.

Using nature

Nature *is* of enormous value, because of its role as a cultural archive, a record of human endeavour and husbandry, and because nature has a wild non-human otherness that stands apart from human values. I want to go on to talk about how we can work to build these two dimensions into the work of conservation in the UK. However, first I must take time to consider a third, and much more prosaic, way of viewing nature. For we also value nature because it is useful. To hark back to the story with which I opened this book, whether we like to eat Norfolk mussels (or to sell them), or we value the coastal protection afforded by the salt marshes where they live, nature does have a measurable economic value.

Conservation is increasingly being justified on utilitarian grounds. *Biodiversity: the UK action plan*, for example, justifies the inevitable costs of conservation chiefly by arguing that wild species are economically useful.[38] Wild species can be used as a commodity (mussels, for example), for developing new crops (e.g. disease- or frost-resistant plants) or as feedstocks for industrial products (for example the eternal grail of cures for cancer). They can also be used non-consumptively, for example in supporting tourism or through "natural functions" such as flood control by river wetlands.

In *The Diversity of Life*, Edward O. Wilson has a chapter on "Unmined Riches", in which he sets out the conservationists' utilitarian stall impeccably. Here are the wild plant sources of successful pharmaceutical treatments, such as the rosy periwinkle of Madagascar (source of drugs to treat human cancer), or the Pacific yew (source of taxol, also used against human cancer), and the potential new food crops. Wilson urgently points out that the race is on to develop new ways "to draw income from the wildlands without killing them, and so give the invisible hand of free-market economics a green thumb".[39] Wilson's passion about the human-induced extinction spasm that is marking the end of the second millennium, the breaking of "the crucible of evolution", is matched tightly to this pragmatic argument for conservation of the economic usefulness of nature.

Utilitarian justifications for conservation have a logic neatly crafted for the boardroom and the Reagan/Thatcher generation. However, at first sight they appear somewhat strained in the context of the UK. With the exception of sea and game fishing and, locally, game shooting, no harvesting of wild species is economically important.[40] Nature's economical usefulness in the UK is rather different, and it derives from the application of environmental economics.

In the wake of the work by David Pearce and his colleagues in *Blueprint for a Green Economy*,[41] economic calculations have begun to be widely extended to nature in the UK, particularly in the context of debates about sustainability. The distinction between natural and human-made capital, and the idea of defining sustainability in terms of maintaining constant capital stocks over

106

time, have gained a great deal of currency.[42] There has been particular interest in the concept of "critical natural capital", referring to that part of natural capital that cannot be replaced if lost (or at least, not within feasible time-frames), and cannot therefore be substituted with human capital or compensated for by positive projects elsewhere. English Nature, for example, has defined "ancient woodland", as critical natural capital because it represents native biodiversity which cannot readily be replaced. Other habitats which could in theory be recreated are denoted "constant natural assets". English Nature's aim is to protect critical natural capital (by opposing damaging development and land uses), while trying to maintain stocks of natural features to ensure an increasing level of "net natural assets".[43]

The adoption of the terminology and thinking of environmental economics represents the first steps towards a systematic attempt to provide a consistent and quantifiable basis for defining conservation value. Although the English Nature proposals are rather vague as to detail (it is not clear, for example, whether the SSSI system would be critical natural capital or part of "constant natural assets"), the approach is steadily gaining ground in British conservation, among local authorities as well as the national agencies. Hampshire County Council, for example, are arguing in their Strategic Plan that all identified "County Wildlife Sites" should be regarded as critical natural capital. Such an approach, in theory, would deflect development pressures away from such sites, although this would not necessarily result in their protection, but would rather push the argument about their designation upstream to the stage of plan preparation and approval.[44]

Some conservationists have been attracted by the potential of economic methods to place monetary values on wildlife, nature reserves and other areas of natural habitat and landscape. The idea of this is that if the economic value of nature can be determined in this way, the costs and benefits of different land use options can be calculated and efficient and "rational" planning can take place. Approaches include the measurement of direct and indirect impacts of conservation on local economies, for example through tourism and employment.[45] Other methods are to measure the travel costs of visitors to sites (either directly or perhaps measuring the value of the time taken to travel), or using a method called "contingent valuation" to find out how much people would be prepared to pay for conservation. A study of the Mar Lodge estate in the Cairngorms used contingent valuation to estimate its value to the people of Scotland. The preservation of the wildlife, landscape and public access on the estate was estimated to be worth £109m, and preservation without access £61m. In this case the valuation approach (intended only to produce order-of-magnitude figures) supported the view that conservation of Mar Lodge was very important to the people of Scotland.[46]

There may be practical gains for conservation in the attempt to put a monetary value on wildlife or landscapes. It is certainly entertaining academically, but it does bring very real dangers. Some of these are pragmatic. As Simon Bilsborough comments, "the real worry is that such valuation exercises, typically producing low values for wildlife, will be used to promote inappropriate development on SSSIs and other sites under the guise of sustainable development".[47] As Kate Holland and Alan Rawles argue, "if it can be shown that *even on economic grounds* the case for conservation makes sense, all to the good". But it may well not always be so. Economic analysis might argue against the conservation of nature, and if it does, it is no good the conservationist-turned-economist suddenly asking for the rules to be changed back so that the game can be replayed on stronger ground.[48]

Other problems with an economic approach to conservation are more fundamental. Attempts to place a monetary value on nature confuses the values people have as consumers with those they hold as citizens. Neo-classical economic theory assumes that all preferences line up on a single scale, but this is not so. We may choose one thing as consumer (for example the chance to drive on new motorways), while as citizens we might prefer the woods and fields that would have to be destroyed to build them.

As the American philosopher Bryan Norton points out, to use economic arguments is to admit that species have value as commodities, and once it is accepted that this is an adequate measure of worth, other arguments about non-economic values of nature tend to be lost.[49] This is perhaps the fundamental problem with using environmental economics to justify conservation, "bringing together nature and the market".[50] Many conservationists would probably share Ian McHarg's scorn of a worldview built on economics. He wrote in *Design With Nature*, "We have but one explicit model of the world and that is built upon economics ... Money is its measure, convenience is its cohort, the short term is its span, and the devil may take the hindermost is the morality".[51]

The debate between the reductionism of environmental economics and broader ideas about the intrinsic values of nature is a kind of late-twentieth-century British re-enactment of the struggle within American conservation in the first decades of the century.[52] Opposing the pragmatic "resource management" approach of Gifford Pinchot's conservation was the preservationist passion of John Muir. Both the utilitarian arguments of the forester and public servant Pinchot and the moral arguments of Muir have left their legacy within the conservation movement. Sometimes they have seemed reconciled. In particular, Aldo Leopold managed to deal with the contradictions between his training as a scientific technical "manager" of nature and his instincts to respect and love it.[53] His ideas changed over time, but he was also very flexible. Like other successful pragmatic environmentalists (Rachel Carson for example), Leopold emphasised different values in different situations. In political and policy arenas, he emphasised human-oriented arguments, and, Bryan Norton argues, did so "without apparent remorse and with great effect on events".[54] Bryan Norton suggests that the diversity of values inherent in environmentalism is a strength and not a weakness. Both human-centred and intrinsic values in nature should lead us "to do all we can to save species and representative ecosystems".[55] Quite different ideas about nature, biocentric and utilitarian, can and do lead to quite similar aims in conservation.

Derek Ratcliffe, too, sees the need for these arguments to be in balance. He draws a distinction between the strictly utilitarian concern to maintain the natural capital (and the flows of benefits from them) for consumption by people, and the broader utilitarian view, which embraces human aesthetic and spiritual purpose.[56] Conservationists have to continue to press their case with governments and vested interests (on a global scale as much as nationally), and to appeal to the wider audience of ordinary people. The best way to do both is by stressing self-interest, the first of his approaches. But this alone is not enough. In the long run, permanent support for conservation will depend on the success of an appeal "to a deeper feeling for nature as something valued for its intrinsic interest and inspirational significance". People need to be persuaded to "respect nature for its own sake".[57]

Community with nature

Whether we choose to take Bryan Norton's pragmatic line or not, and whatever importance we give to justifications for conservation on the grounds of its measurable economic value, there is no doubt about the importance of the cultural connection between people and nature to the future of conservation. The existence of this connection, this fellow-feeling, explains much of the power of the conservation movement. The maintenance of that connection must be the first pragmatic task of conservation action, and arguably it may also prove the most valuable. Here we come to the start of the circle that is conservation. We need to work to regain our links with nature — with other species, and with natural processes. We do not, most of us, plough land or cut trees any more. As we discussed in Chapters Four and Five, most of us live urban lives, distanced from the "nature" with which formal conservation is concerned.

In towns and cities, and increasingly in rural areas, people live in a way that is divorced from natural rhythms of seasons or ecology, and from any direct economic link to land or water resources. Houses are warm in winter, food comes from supermarkets and not from our own labour, and lives are dictated by access to technology and not by the natural environment. Except for occasional droughts, blizzards or floods, and London's traditional "leaves on the line", most people's lives are run quite independently of nature. Urban parks are still largely manicured, and landscape architects offer a grim and standardised diet of *Berberis* and a few other hackneyed perennials in their plantings. Corporate nature is chosen for its ease of maintenance and its hostility to errant pedestrians.

Television and video games provide new myths about nature, and they are very different from the old, divorced from the past and from direct experience. Sonic the Hedgehog is probably now more widely recognised among children than Mrs Tiggywinkle, although neither perhaps have much to do with the real denizen of woods and gardens. Both have been relentlessly merchandised. If the futurologists are right, we will be offered, and will hungrily consume, more and more technologies of alternative reality. Cultural commentators suggest that we are living already in a postmodern world, where all is signs and shifting meanings — a world of virtual reality, composed of images and simulacra flashing across flickering screens.

People do not see, understand or relate to nature as they did. We relate to it at a distance, in bursts, or by remote control, in cyberspace, creating and consuming images of nature and countryside. Large numbers of people have little interest even in this abstracted, safe and digital facsimile of nature. When people do experience nature, it is most often in their armchair, through television. Real wildlife, and real countryside, may not measure up. A couple of years ago the BBC ran live television coverage of badgers inside their sett. It was amazing television, the baby badgers cute and the context dramatic and compelling. But you do not see badgers like that in the wild. Badger-watching in my experience is often a matter of a few grunts and a flash of fur in the dark, not intimate insider views of family life, and yet that fleeting encounter amidst the midges is real, and experienced directly, not vicariously by a camera crew and a TV presenter. For all their virtuosity and educative potential, nature programmes on television offer a view of nature that is all too often unreplicable in everyday life. Even as we watch in close-up, we are distanced from nature. That distance matters a great deal, because it is contact with nature that creates our awareness of its value. It is from this contact, with other species and particular places, that we construct our vision of the countryside.

Conservation must make its primary task the building of direct links between people and nature. This task is well advanced in National Parks, nature reserves, and other places where investments have been made in "countryside interpretation", but it can begin anywhere. In many ways the greatest need is among those who cannot, or do not, visit the countryside. Conservation is nowhere perhaps more important than it is in school playgrounds, gardens and parks, the "small worlds" of children.[58] The opportunities are legion, from school nature reserves to city greenspace created on derelict land, and in the potential for re-imagining the "grass-with-trees" of city parks.

Tree-planting, be it in a National Forest or an inner city, is particularly important. Trees have a particular resonance in British popular consciousness, perhaps due to their size, longevity or long history of usefulness. Tree-planting makes a contact between people and the wild, between human communities and nature. When we wish to commemorate a momentous event or person, we plant a tree. The archives of local newspapers are full of photographs of the great and the good, posed with bent back over a shining spadeful of soil, topping out the mulch on a freshly-planted sapling. As David Nicholson-Lord comments, tree-planting can be "an act of lifelong significance to a child".[59]

We need to re-establish contact with nature, and rekindle the sense of its otherness, the wonder and the surprise of it. We must not, therefore, let our conservation become too technocratic, too slickly predictable, too much of a routine. Nature does have the capacity to surprise us, and we need to work to create conditions where people — particularly young people — can engage with it. We cannot expect to be able to predict exactly how this will happen, but it is quite likely to challenge our conventional ways of thinking. It may well not come from any of our careful plans about biodiversity, about ecological regeneration, about landscape ecology. The engagement of people and nature will be both vital and dynamic, and may quite well be stimulated by throwing rocks in the sea, or planting a conker, or watching a grey squirrel in a "trees-and-grass" urban open space. We have to build conservation in such a way that it can provide these contacts, and can meet these kinds of simple but fundamental human needs. Conservation must demonstrate the links from these direct values of nature to the other more remote or more specialised attributes of nature that our conservation has long been designed to provide.

For most people, the place of this contact with nature is likely to be predominantly urban. Despite the cultural resonance of the countryside, particularly to the English upper-middle class (discussed in Chapter Five), the countryside is certainly not something with universal appeal in the UK. It is a foreign country to a great many people, whether the growing urban underclass, ethnic minorities, or just "Essex woman" (or man) who expects simply to see nature unreel past the windscreen. I have written in this book chiefly of nature outside the built-up environment, for that is where natural ecosystems and landscapes are at their richest. But nature is also there in cities, as vital and sometimes even more powerfully than outside. When I was a child, my bus to school went past the Thames in London, and I remember still my awareness of the rising and falling tide, the vast expanse of sludge, boulders and jetsam at low tide, and the heaving power of the river at full flood, and the eagerness with which I scanned the assembled gulls and ducks for the glimpse of something unusual.

Much of our conservation is built on images of the city's capacity to destroy. In *Design with Nature*, Ian McHarg wrote of his shock at the expansion of Glasgow following the Second World War. He wrote emotively of "the smear of Glasgow" that had moved out over woods he had known as a child: there were "no more fox and badger, squirrel and stoat, weasel and hedgehog but now only cat and dog, rats and mice, lice and fleas"; even the physical process of the landscape had gone, "the burn is buried and water now is the gutter trickle and spit". McHarg knew as well as anyone how much people needed the homes created in the expanded city, but he was also in no doubt about the importance of nature as part of urban life. As he wrote, "we need nature as much in the city as in the countryside".[60]

This was also the vision of Nan Fairbrother in *New Lives, New Landscapes*. People need a living space with space for living nature. Such ideas began to be implemented on the ground in the 1970s in some of the New Towns, and in other developments such as the William Curtis Memorial Park in London.[61] Urban conservation became a powerful force in the UK in the 1980s, with the establishment of the London Wildlife Trust and the many Urban Wildlife groups, and the establishment of the Fairbrother Group in 1985 to draw together their interests. In *The Greening of the Cities*, David Nicholson-Lord traces the roots and the dimensions of the achievements of the urban conservation movement, from nineteenth-century urban parks to twentieth-century city farms, school playgrounds and derelict-land restoration projects. Urban conservation has often been innovative in its approach. One example of this is Groundwork. This began in 1981 as "Operation Groundwork", funded by the Countryside Commission on the urban fringe of St Helens and Knowsley on Merseyside. The aim was to develop programmes that linked environmental, social and economic regeneration, working in partnerships with the community and with business. The approach was expanded in 1982 to five other areas of the northwest, and by 1995 there were 40 Groundwork Trusts around England and Wales.[62]

Urban conservation is about nature too, but it is in many ways quite different to its country cousin. There is no space for pastoral imagery here; it is tough, pragmatic and human-focused. David Nicholson-Lord celebrates the possibility of transcending our desire to escape the city, suggesting instead the notion that we might "bring wilderness back into our homes and our minds and our settlements, and thus make it more than wilderness".[63]

People in cities, and those outside whose lives are distanced from it, can find and engage with nature, and can make what we now perhaps lack: "hands-on visceral contact with other forms of life".[64] And they can do so in surprising ways. One way is through art. Earth art, eco-art, community art, drama, poetry or sculpture — all are playing a role in opening up people's awareness of nature, and their channels of communication with each other about the relations between people and nature. For example, the Kirklees Waymarker Project in West Yorkshire has involved placing a series of waymarks on a 72-mile network of paths. In each case, an artist was briefed to create something with the community that took "its inspiration from the character and spirit of the locality, and its form from direct relationship with

112

the landscape". Schoolchildren and site visitors were drawn into the creation of the works, sometimes conceptually, sometimes physically, and from this engagement with the art it is argued that engagement with place and with the environment has developed.[65]

There are many such examples of art-in-nature and art-in-community. Martin Spray, introducing a collection of accounts of such art, suggests that "the intention of much environment-orientated (and other) art appears to be to provoke the 'Child Within' until his grown-up guardian has to give in".[66] The "child within" may see with a steady eye things (not least about nature) that are too easily hidden. The opening-up of hidden dimensions of nature is the theme of the arts and environment group "Platform", set up in the 1980s, which has worked to awaken awareness of local communities to the rivers that run in tunnels below the streets of South London. In November 1983 they unveiled a micro-hydro turbine (something more usual in Himalayan rivers than South London) at the mouth of the River Wandle, where it pours out of its pipe and into the Thames. The electricity generated will eventually light the hall in the local primary school. A bell has been hung (from the Whitechapel Bell Foundry) that rings with the tides. Here is nature brought home to urban communities, a deliberate link back to the free-running river and the mills that it powered, before the city swallowed it.[67]

Conservation has to take seriously the challenge of doing something about the increasing distance between people and nature, and particularly the irrelevance of nature within urbanised lives and urban spaces. We have to rebuild contact with nature, and re-establish a place for nature in popular culture. We can do it gradually, by accretion and by attraction. It is no good arguing that the flea-ridden wild hedgehog in the garden is better than its virtual-reality cousin in the megadrive, but we *can* argue that it is different, and important: alive, and quite other from ourselves.

Conservation has changed a great deal in the half century since the basic structure was laid down at the end of the Second World War, but we have changed more. If we do not tackle the issue of our cultural distance from nature, no amount of tinkering with protected area systems will be of much use. There are two sides to this. To be narrowly pragmatic, conservation will succeed only if there is a real cultural concern for nature. To be a little more fundamental, if the cultural values of nature become reduced to an abstraction, locked in a video disk, we will have lost something of enormous human significance. The task for conservation is therefore to foster and build up this community of experience, the daily recognition of the existence and the otherness of nature: its actions, its values, and its rights.

I believe that the depth and vigour of people's contact with and understanding of nature is fundamental to conservation, and that the maintenance of cultural connections between people and other creatures and landscapes is a task on which conservation should invest far more effort than it has done in the past. This perhaps seems rather an esoteric suggestion, but I believe it to be vital. However, it can only be part of an agenda for the future of nature. There must also be a place for more pragmatic concerns, not least of which is the protection of particular pieces of nature in particular places. Here too, however, there are new ideas that can revitalise our thinking. These are the subject of the next chapter.

CHAPTER EIGHT

The Conservation Landscape

*The goal of land use planning should be to create means by which local communities can
creatively express their particular natures. Local values can be protected, however, only as part
of a larger context, a vast continent-wide mosaic composed of complex, overlapping
management cells and their environing systems*
Bryan Norton[1]

Reconnecting the landscape

Conservation in the UK has been characterised by the distinction between
protected and unprotected places — between land designated because it is
thought to be particularly valuable, and that left to drift on the stormy seas of
economic change, to endure or thrive as it may. Some protected areas are
strictly protected and managed for conservation (National Nature Reserves for
example). Others have much less protection, for example Sites of Special
Scientific Interest (SSSIs) or Heritage Coasts, that are little more than
spatially bound indicative strategies for planning, and a focus for recreational
management. Some protected areas are designated under international treaties
(World Heritage Sites or Biosphere Reserves, for example), others under EU
legislation (SACs and SPAs, for example; see Chapter Three), others

nationally or regionally.[2] However, the division between all of these and undesignated land has been fundamental to policy-making, and much of our thinking about conservation in the UK. In this we are not unusual, for the establishment of protected areas has been the common strategy for conservation worldwide, since the first American National Parks established in the late nineteenth century. The World Conservation Union now recognises over 9800 protected areas worldwide.[3]

Whatever their limitations, there is no doubt that protected areas will remain at the heart of conservation action in the UK. This is not only because we have invested far too much effort in entrenching the idea of protected areas into legislation, into the bureaucratic structure of government, and into the minds of landowners and naturalists to be able to abandon it, but also because it is difficult to see how else to deal with the accumulated biological and cultural values of the pieces of nature that have endured over generations in our changing land. The advantages of an approach involving protected areas are numerous. Protected area designation recognises that some places are more important than others for conservation (whether that judgement is made in terms of biodiversity, landscape or heritage), and they allow resources to be prioritised. Protected areas are an established concept, powerful in political debate and appealing to the general public.

However, protected areas also have disadvantages.[4] A conservation strategy based on protected areas can make a holistic approach to conservation more difficult, encouraging the view that conservation is a sector or a land use. Their existence can also imply that the needs of conservation have been met, making it harder to achieve integrated policies that cut across economic sectors and make a difference to national policies. Protected areas tend to be treated as separate entities from surrounding land, soaking up available conservation resources. Protected area boundaries are often arbitrary lines on maps, created by accidents of land tenure and the financial circumstances of conservation organisations, irrelevant to natural processes and environmental problems (pollution, for example). Furthermore, once a protected area is established, government agencies and the general public "begin to think that they have a free license to do whatever they want outside of its boundaries", which makes semi-natural habitat even more isolated and fragmented.[5]

Protected areas are a necessary part of a future conservation strategy but they are not sufficient. An editorial in the journal *Conservation Biology* in 1992 called for conservation biologists to expand beyond their own "reserve mentality". The reasoning was partly pragmatic, reflecting a view that protected areas of all kinds are likely to become harder to acquire, but it was also argued that many species do not need special protected areas, but "can coexist with reasonable amounts of intelligently managed commodity production and recreation".[6] In their book *Conservation for the Twenty-First*

116

Century, David Western and his collaborators suggest that one of the ways to make protected areas more effective is to integrate conservation into wider land use.[7] In this chapter, I want to look at this possibility, the idea of moving conservation out beyond the boundaries of protected areas, and of starting to conceive of conservation of the whole landscape.

The importance of extending conservation in this way has been recognised in the UK since the 1970s. There has been increasing concern for the management of land outside protected areas, in what is usually referred to as the "wider countryside". The Countryside Commission was established in 1968 with a concern for the whole countryside instead of just National Parks and Areas of Outstanding Natural Beauty, and the Nature Conservancy began to emphasise the importance of the way land outside the SSSI system was managed at around the same time. The immediate concern was the recognition that the protected area system was not, on its own, sufficient to achieve the survival of the species within it. In *Nature Conservation and Agriculture* (published in 1973), the NCC pointed out that NNRs and Local Nature Reserves covered only some 0.8 per cent of Great Britain, and that many plants and animals in nature reserves needed to be supported by populations outside protected areas to remain viable.[8]

In this report, the Nature Conservancy outlined an approach to habitat conservation that had the establishment and management of NNRs and SSSIs (through partnership with owners) at its centre, but also included much more widespread collaboration with other land users in the wider countryside so that "as much nature conservation is achieved on the better habitats on unscheduled land as is compatible with their primary uses". Derek Ratcliffe emphasised that SSSIs were not sufficient to achieve the objectives of nature conservation, and that there was also "a need to conserve the much greater part of the national capital of wildlife and habitat which lies outside this relatively small sample".[9] The NCC, the Countryside Commissions, and their successor agencies, have developed their concern for the wider countryside through the 1980s and 1990s, as have other organisations, notably the Farming and Wildlife Advisory Groups (FWAGs).[10]

The industrialisation of agriculture (discussed in Chapter Four) has everywhere tended to produce landscapes that are limited in their diversity. In parts of the country where agricultural intensification has wrought extensive changes, such as the prairies of East Anglia, the vast bulk of land is of limited diversity and conservation interest because of the clearance of hedges and trees, "improvement" of grassland and wetland, constant cultivation and application of pesticides of various kinds. Within this landscape, habitats are fragmented and protected areas of all kinds are isolated. However, even here, fragments of semi-natural habitat and landscape features do remain, and provide some kind of link between protected areas. The best surviving fragments are often places left out of the planning of high-tech farmers and

117

incoming urban migrants, existing on the margins of their properties. Such places include grasslands in churchyards and on road verges, and hedgerows, copses and small patches of unimproved land on farms. The network of habitat is skeletal in such areas, but in other parts of the UK where economic restructuring has proceeded less far (for example in Wales or Northern Ireland), the matrix of habitats in the "wider countryside" is far richer, and designated sites are less isolated.[11]

The density and ecology of this mosaic of landscape features is of great significance to the effectiveness of the protected areas that exist within the landscape, but perhaps more importantly it determines what wildlife the landscape as a whole can sustain, and it is also critical to the visual appearance of the landscape. Established protected areas are important, but conservation must move vigorously to address the management of the wider mosaic of habitats and landscapes within the countryside. The traditional concern for individual protected areas must be transformed to a concern for whole landscapes. We need, in the words of Roger DiSilvestro, to begin "formulating a remedy to fragmentation".[12]

The ecology of landscapes

Protected areas, like other bounded ecosystems or fragments of habitat, do not exist in a vacuum. Their ecology is not only influenced by processes going on within them, but by larger-scale processes outside. The field of landscape ecology offers a simple framework for understanding the idea that different physical elements within the landscape are connected.[13] This connection may relate to physical processes (for example, water flow in a river basin), or to physical juxtaposition and the capacity of organisms to hop from one piece of habitat to the next. Landscape ecologists argue that it is useful to analyse the physical structure of landscape, and that this provides a sound basis for understanding ecological processes and ecological change. They point to ideas such as MacArthur and Wilson's theory of island biogeography as evidence of the way in which this approach can be developed. That work, of course, long preceded formal statements about "landscape ecology".[14]

Landscape ecology provides a neat framework for understanding why we need to see protected areas in relation to their surroundings, and to one another. MacArthur and Wilson showed that the number of breeding species on islands tends to stabilise at a level determined by rates of immigration and extinction, and that these are controlled by isolation and island size. Large islands close to a continental source tend to have more species than small isolated islands. Subsequently, conservation biologists took up this idea and extended it. First the theory was applied to terrestrial habitats (e.g. mountains and isolated montane floras), then to isolated habitat fragments and to strategic questions about the selection of nature reserves. It was argued that reserves should be as large as possible, and if small they should be close together and connected by corridors of similar habitat.

There is now a large literature on island biogeography theory, and its application to conservation. There has been much discussion about what the theory can say about the size and spacing of reserves, and particularly the question of whether a single large reserve is better or worse than several small ones, and also discussion about the theory itself.[15] The implications for conservation of genetic change in small isolated populations are also recognised.[16] In the UK context, debate about reserve size is somewhat academic, since reserve purchase tends to be driven by threat of destruction and availability of funds, and areas of semi-natural habitat tend to be isolated already.[17] However, there is general agreement that isolation and the size of habitat fragments are important influences on the probability of extinction, and need to be taken seriously in conservation planning.

The Institute of Terrestrial Ecology has carried out studies over a number of years on songbird populations in 164 woods in West Cambridgeshire and surrounding counties. These woods are isolated from each other, and range greatly in size. They include ancient woodlands like Monk's Wood NNR, and newer plantings. The study shows that the number of breeding species depended most on woodland area, and increased rapidly up to 2 ha. The rate at which species became extinct and were re-established in individual woods was also greatest in small woods. Small woods seem therefore to have both fewer breeding species, and bird populations that fluctuate more from year to year. However, patterns vary of course between bird species. The numbers of pairs of some species (e.g. wrens) rise linearly with woodland area, while those of others with more specialised habitat requirements (e.g. marsh or long-tailed tits) do not. Different species also vary in their ability to cross open fields to re-colonise isolated woods. This work suggests that where new woods are planted, their value for conservation of birds will be greatest if they are as large as possible (at least 2 ha), and planted in groups to benefit species that are willing to cross between them.[18]

Nature reserves and other habitat fragments are not true islands, but lie in a matrix of other land. It is now recognised that the characteristics of that land have great significance for the patch it surrounds. The ITE woodland study found, for example, that the number of bird species in a wood was related to the length of hedgerow within 0.5 km of the wood. The success with which protected areas maintain populations of the species they contain may depend as much on surrounding land use as on management within the protected area itself.

Studies of the habitat requirements of individual species suggest that it may be possible to define the kind of mix of habitat types and land uses that are necessary to allow them to survive. This has been done for some species, such as the badger and the lapwing, through an analysis of present distributions. The detailed attributes of this "conservation landscape" are of great importance if the role of protected areas within the wider landscape is to be understood. The requirements of some species may perhaps be met only through specially managed protected areas. Some may survive quite well if forms of land use are adjusted to provide the landscape they require, while yet others may need a combination of both protected areas and appropriately managed surrounding land to survive.[19]

There is also growing interest in the structural elements of landscapes and in the idea of connectivity, or the extent to which landscape elements are linked to each other. Habitat "corridors" (defined by Richard Hobbs as linear features distinct from surrounding vegetation that connect at least two patches that were connected in historical time[20]) have received particular attention. Highly connected landscapes may provide a buffer against fragmentation and extinction by allowing populations to interact and re-colonise following local extinction. Corridors such as hedges and patches of scrub between woodlands may provide "stepping stones" for mobile species such as birds, and the "nodes" where landscape elements meet may be of particular importance.[21]

We should probably not get carried away by the messages of landscape ecology for conservation planning. We still know too little about what comprises a barrier to movement for different species (even of well-studied groups like birds), and there is much to learn about the interactions between "corridors" such as hedgerows and adjacent or even more distant fields or other landscape elements. The notion that habitat corridors are effective elements in conservation planning is widely accepted, but in fact the evidence that organisms do actually move along them to recolonise isolated patches is still rather limited. More research is needed lest a lot of effort is put into the establishment and management of corridors to little good effect. Richard Hobbs suggests (based on his work in Australia) that at least we need to think carefully about corridor design in the context of specific target species. The "retro-fitting" of corridors in an already fragmented landscape (as in lowland areas of the UK) is likely to be costly, but the retention of existing linkages in the landscape is sensible, if only for their value as further elements of semi-natural habitat within the wider landscape mosaic.[22]

Small isolated fragments of semi-natural habitat within protected areas are clearly insufficient on their own to achieve the conservation of biodiversity. Conservation energy must also be directed at the wider landscape. It must engage with both the problems of the general management of land (e.g. questions of surface and groundwater quality, the impact of chemical sprays and other forms of biocidal pollution) and with the biodiversity and beauty of the whole landscape, not just the protected areas that sit like lone jewels within it. The existence within this landscape of other areas of habitat (small wetlands, streams and ponds, field headlands, hedges or woods) will, if the science of landscape ecology is right, increase the conservation value of protected areas nearby, as well as providing valuable habitat and landscape features in their own right.

Gaps and maps

In order to tackle the fragmentation of habitat and the degradation of landscape, we need to look beyond the boundaries of protected areas at the land around them. We also need to start to think in terms of functionally linked *systems* of protected areas. Again, this requires a landscape-scale perspective. The conventional approach to selecting SSSIs and NNRs emphasises their place in a representative series of habitat types. This is rather like stamp collecting. The selection of "last best example fragments" has an important place in conservation, but it is not enough.[23] I do not think it is what Aldo Leopold had in mind when he said that "the first rule of intelligent meddling is to keep all the pieces", because the important thing is not that we have "one of each" in our collection but that the collection has the capacity to endure and survive in a dynamic way. We need to consider the capacity of the protected area system to sustain and regenerate populations of wild species, and to do so without massive and continuous injections of money, time and technology. The system needs to *live*.

First, though, we need to find what DiSilvestro calls "holes in the protective net".[24] One approach that commands attention here is what is called in the USA "gap analysis", "a process of identifying unprotected species or wild communities by the indirect evidence of plant life". Gap analysis is based on the assumption that you can predict what species live in an area if you know what ecosystems are there. The method developed in the USA uses satellite-derived maps of vegetation and data on vertebrates and butterflies (the best-known taxonomic groups) to map ecosystems in a given region, and then to overlay this on a map of protected areas. In theory, this will identify under-represented ecosystems and habitats.

There are a number of problems with the "gap analysis" approach. One is that research shows that areas that are species-rich for some well-known taxonomic groups (birds or dragonflies for example) may not be species-rich for others. Studies of species distributions in the UK show that only 12 per cent of so-called "hotspots" (areas with high diversity) for birds and butterflies overlap.[25] Furthermore, while a vegetation-mapping approach has obvious potential for countries where existing knowledge of biodiversity is poor, and large areas of semi-natural habitat remain, it is perhaps less useful in the UK, where there is a mass of existing data on the distribution of many taxa, and species distributions are so extensively influenced by human action.

However, the amount of existing knowledge of natural history is such in the UK that it is actually relatively easy to predict what species will be present from a knowledge of habitat type, and the use of standardised survey techniques such as the National Vegetation Classification in conservation surveys is based on just this assumption. In Scotland, the rich archive of existing natural history knowledge is being used by Scottish National Heritage (SNH) in a project to identify biogeographic zones based on the distributions of six taxonomic groups (birds, diurnal insects, molluscs, flowering plants, mosses and liverworts). This kind of approach should allow both a scientifically sophisticated basis for SSSI selection (based for the first time on natural and not administrative boundaries), and some kind of "gap analysis".[26]

English Nature have moved rather faster in a similar direction to SNH. They have defined and published a map of "Natural Areas", to "provide a framework for securing public support and greatly improve our ability to deliver effective action with our partners for conservation".[27] The aim of Natural Areas is to provide a framework for planning conservation that breaks away from the artificial constraints of administrative boundaries (counties and districts), which rarely follow divisions in land use, landform or ecology. Natural Areas are defined primarily in terms of geology, landforms, soils, and land use. In theory, each Natural Area will hold characteristic vegetation types and wildlife species, and support broadly similar land uses and settlement patterns. English Nature hopes also that they will "relate to a strong sense of place felt by people, particularly about the place where they live", although it is not clear how far this "sense of place" can be measured or taken into account.[28]

By May 1994, 92 terrestrial Natural Areas had been defined, plus 24 maritime Natural Areas. The latter represent a novel and important step forwards for UK conservation thinking. Coastal planning has for too long ignored natural processes of erosion and deposition (and through engineering tried to gainsay them). The coastal Natural Areas are based on the idea of a sedimentary cell, a unit of both sediment production (from eroding cliffs) and deposition (on spits and beaches). The terrestrial Natural Areas will also doubtless be useful, to provide a better alternative than county boundaries for selecting SSSIs, as the basis for defining corporate policies and delivering action, and a context within which to work with what English Nature likes to call its "partners" (landowners and tenants, local authorities, voluntary conservation organisations and local communities). English Nature will identify a "quality profile" for each Natural Area, set objectives and targets for the high-quality nature conservation resource (NNRs and SSSIs), and broader objectives for the wider countryside. The hope is that because Natural Areas will reflect the broad character of the land, they will encourage other interests to go along with the objectives of conservation plans and programmes.

These approaches have a lively parallel in the "Countryside Character" programme of the Countryside Commission, which involves the attempt to describe and delimit local landscapes within England, using a variety of criteria and professional landscape assessment.[29] A pilot "New Map of England" has been produced of the West Country, on a finer spatial scale than English Nature's Natural Areas. The Countryside Commission's mapping exercise took explicit account of survey information on what local people perceived about their own sense of natural area or landscape. The process produces a map of areas of landscape with "a cohesive, individual and identifiable character" and analytical descriptions of each landscape type and the key forces for change. Using these, the Countryside Commission will develop strategies for the conservation of the English landscape that (like English Nature) it hopes will command widespread support. The Landscape Character Programme will provide a common and analytically based framework for landscape conservation, reaching the length of England, for the first time, and will be used in all areas of the Commission's work.

In their different ways, each of these new initiatives provides the opportunity for innovative thinking about the relation of protected areas in the UK to one another, and to the wider landscape. The potential of this kind of approach has already been explored elsewhere in Europe, notably in the Nature Policy Plan of the Netherlands, and in the proposed European Ecological Network, EECONET.

The Dutch Nature Policy Plan was produced in 1990.[30] It is a strategic document that seeks to bring together all government policy for landscape and nature conservation. It reviews the problem of declining diversity of the natural environment, in terms of both species and the landscape. This is due to acidification, eutrophication, contamination, water-table decline, habitat fragmentation and neglect. The aim of government policy is "the sustainable conservation, rehabilitation and development of nature and landscape". The core of the strategy is a "national ecological network", which will include Core Areas, Nature Development Areas and Ecological Corridors. Core Areas will be those whose existing ecological value is of national or international significance. They will include forests, agricultural land, stream valleys, dunes, large lakes and marine offshore areas. "Nature Development Areas" will be those where there is a realistic chance of developing national or international ecological value, for example wet grassland, marshland and marshy woodland. They will be protected by existing measures, but major developments (roads or housing) will be excluded, and soil and water quality must be maintained. "Ecological Corridors" will be landscape structures that allow migration within and between Core Areas (e.g. between rivers and marshes). Their identification demands a high level of ecological knowledge, and is currently only possible for the badger, red deer, otter and game fish. Buffer zones will be established, for example to protect water quality or to prevent desiccation, or to provide protection against air pollution. The National Ecological Network will be achieved through geographically and thematically defined projects, and measures will range from the systematic application of existing legislation (the Nature Conservation Act) to substantial land acquisition and integrated and innovative application of other measures such as the EC Hill-farming Directive.[31]

The EECONET initiative bears much of the stamp of the Dutch Nature Policy Plan. The idea was discussed in a report by the Institute for European Environmental Policy (IEEP) in 1991.[32] This argued that nature conservation policy in Europe should move from species to habitats, from sites to ecosystems, and from national to international measures. Many species already depend on habitats in many different countries in passing across Europe on migration, and the reality of climatic change demands that conservation provides the space, not only for this existing migration to continue, but also for natural adaptation to climatic change to take place. This demands international action to define a network of sites, and that these sites are connected ecologically. An international ecological network is therefore proposed to include areas of core habitat, buffer zones to protect them and ecological corridors that allow movement between these core areas. The IEEP report points out that "the development of a coherent European ecological network can only be achieved if the framework for nature conservation is determined by the ecological structure of Europe rather than its political geography".

The notion of a network of protected areas, and of the importance of their connectedness, seems now to be widely accepted internationally within Europe. The conference on "Conserving Europe's Natural Heritage: Towards a European Ecological Network", held at Maastricht in the Netherlands in November 1993, called for a European Biological and Landscape Diversity Strategy and a European Ecological Network. The European Community environmental database, CORINE, and extensive national data holdings on species and ecosystems, allow some kind of biogeographical zonation (what one Dutch team call the "ecological main structure" of Europe).[33] The World Conservation Union's Action Plan for Protected Areas in Europe, *Parks for Life*, endorsed the EECONET Declaration, and its proposal to develop and implement a European Biological and Landscape Diversity Strategy and to use EECONET as a conceptual framework to help organisations set pan-European priorities.[34]

Obviously, the lack of detailed knowledge of either species biology or local circumstances is going to make the definition of core and buffer zones and corridors slow and complex. Nonetheless, the principle that protected areas must be conceived of and planned to be part of a functioning network is one that deserves extensive support and imaginative implementation in the UK. Furthermore, it is clear that the network of sites within the UK must not be conceived of in narrowly parochial terms, but must reach out beyond the individual countries of the UK, to the European and even to the global scale. The future capacity of natural ecosystems to persist in the UK will depend on the success with which our protected areas can knit together with others into a functioning whole.

Creative conservation

If there is one word that sums up the new thinking we need to bring to the task of tackling the fragmentation of nature in the UK, it is creativity. We need to be creative in our approach to protected areas, and we also need to be imaginative. The relentless tide of habitat and biodiversity loss, and the homogenisation of landscapes, can be tackled. The task has two dimensions. We have great experience with the first, the battle to stop damaging change and further fragmentation, both on a site-by-site basis and through tackling their causes. We have as yet less experience with the second, the challenge of re-integrating fragmented landscapes through creative conservation: the retention and rehabilitation of existing habitat remnants and the revegetation of key landscape elements.[35]

The last decade has seen increasing interest in the creation of habitats from scratch, outside as well as inside protected areas. One of the first attempts to create whole habitats was the work of the Ecological Parks Trust in the late 1970s. The William Curtiss Memorial Park, on an empty building site next to Tower Bridge, contained tiny areas of chalk grassland and other habitats, all being established on substrates literally trucked in for the purpose. That site is buried under concrete now, but it showed what could be done, and in an unpromising place. Present understanding of habitat creation owes a great deal to experience with the replanting of degraded industrial land (particularly spoil heaps with toxic residues), and to wildlife gardening. There is also a lot of experience with particular habitat restoration challenges such as the attempt to reinstate heathland vegetation over buried pipelines, courtesy of the oil and gas extraction in Dorset.

There is now a broad portfolio of techniques for habitat creation, re-creation or restoration.[36] The terms used in work of this kind tend to be rather confused, partly because of the philosophical debate about naturalness and the possibility of restoring it.[37] There is a continuum of techniques. At one end lies habitat creation, putting in place totally new assemblages of species and ecosystems, either on the basis of what what is already there, or starting from scratch. Chris Baines distinguishes between "ecological habitat creation" (which aims to replicate real habitats, and demands great care), and "political habitat creation", which is concerned with simpler habitats with immediate popular appeal. This demands equal skill, and perhaps a little more verve and imagination, but less concern to imitate existing habitats.[38] In the former

125

category would lie newly planted broadleaved woodlands, or newly dug wetlands. In the latter would come attempts to restore robust vegetation cover to heavily used urban spaces or polluted land.

Habitat re-creation or restoration involves attempting to put back what is believed to have been in a place before, perhaps vegetation that has been present within living memory. This might involve the re-establishment of heathland vegetation or grassland on land cleared for arable cultivation within the present century, or the re-establishment of hedgerows or wetlands. A third technique is habitat re-habilitation, which involves taking action to enhance the status of existing habitats by undoing degradation and damage. This might include removing invasive or planted species, changing nutrient or water levels in soils, or dealing with transboundary pollution. Such work is familiar to conservationists as part of protected area management, but is somewhat more novel as a strategy within the wider countryside.

These techniques have become very fashionable. Conservationists see them as a way of fighting back against the inexorable loss of semi-natural habitat in the countryside, and there is no doubt of their importance in future conservation strategies. Developers (be they mining corporations, supermarket chains, or the Department of Transport) are also attracted to them. They see the possibility of providing a new habitat to replace something inconveniently in the way of their plans, and thus get the conservation lobby off their backs. The techniques also fit the rhetoric of "sustainable" or "green" development, suggesting a mechanism by which development can go ahead and any damage to species and habitats (and hence landscape) can be compensated for by creative conservation. Many conservationists fear that developers will argue that natural habitats (SSSIs, for example, or ancient woodlands) can be re-created relatively simply. If it is easy to replace threatened habitat, then surely this gives a green light to any developer able to hire a plausible ecologist with an optimistic plan and a tool-kit of simple habitat-recreation skills. As one observer put it, we might in this way allow "the destruction of irreplaceable parts of our heritage in exchange for bare ground scattered with a wild-flower mix, or for a planting scheme of oak and hazel saplings".[39]

The recent rush of enthusiasm for seeking planning gain from developers, and for environmental compensation more generally, has certainly stimulated interest in habitat creation. However, there is a great deal of loose talk about what can be done. For example, while it is quite possible to establish a grass sward containing wild flowers, this does not make the result an adequate replacement for a piece of established chalk grassland, in either a biological or a cultural sense. There is more to chalk grassland than flowers. The full complement of insects would be rather harder to establish, and strip lynchets effectively impossible. By the same token, it is possible to plant a woodland with a mix of trees matching that of local ancient woodlands, but the resulting wood would, in the short term at least, hold only the most superficial aspects of the conservation values of the sites it attempts to mimic. One particularly controversial approach is habitat translocation, the idea of moving whole habitats to new sites. One example of this is the attempt to establish a 6 ha woodland using trees and ground flora transported from Darenth Wood SSSI in Kent, an ancient woodland about to be destroyed by a cement quarry. Similar approaches have been tried in many places with pieces of species-rich grassland. Such dramatic "rescues" may have some success, but will remain controversial.[40]

Despite the very real pitfalls, there are enormous benefits to be had in both attempts to replicate existing semi-natural habitats, and in the creation of new habitats that are beautiful, or that contain elements of semi-natural ecosystems, or that are simply more diverse than the communities they replace. The potential of a creative approach to conservation was demonstrated half a century ago by the work done at Minsmere in Suffolk by the RSPB. The reserve includes reclaimed fields that were re-flooded to prevent enemy landings during the Second World War. Control of water levels and salinity, and the excavation of the lagoon of the Scrape have created a wetland bird reserve of unprecedented importance, its value designed, created and sustained by human action. The creation of new habitat offers a significant means of putting natural elements back into the landscape, filling in gaps between existing protected sites, and creating diversity, interest and beauty.

Habitat creation and enhancement has become an increasingly important element in conservation thinking in the UK. In 1984 the NCC's *Nature Conservation in Great Britain* gave the idea of the "enhancement of the resource of nature" their cautious approval. In the 1980s the Environmentally Sensitive Area (ESA) programme gave a sudden boost to both the idea and the practice of habitat creation, with restoration options on both chalk grassland and heathland, for example in the South Downs and the Breckland ESAs. There are also extensive restoration options under the Countryside Stewardship Scheme (although uptake on all of these has been very small).

There are technical problems, of course. In the case of attempts to establish or re-establish both heathland and grassland on arable land, there is a particular problem of excessive soil fertility. Abandonment of land leads to a coarse weedy flora. The excess fertility has to be stripped out by planting and harvesting a series of nutrient-demanding crops (barley, for example), without fertilisation. After a few years of this, the land can then be re-seeded with a mix of wild plants.[41] However, even when this creative process is undertaken with great care, there can be problems. There is increasing concern about the presence of non-local and even non-native plant seeds in commercial "wild flower" seed mixes.[42] Such mixes tend to come as a standard package, and there is concern that local ecological distinctiveness may be broken down, established patterns of plant distribution confused, and genetic variation eroded and homogenised.

These are, perhaps, rather arcane risks when set against the remorseless erosion of semi-natural habitats across the country, but they merit attention. The problem can beset even serious and professional habitat restoration projects. One example is the work of the Magog Trust, which was established in 1989 to purchase 66 ha of arable land on the southern edge of Cambridge, on what are known locally as the Gog Magog Hills. The Trust has attempted to re-establish chalk grassland on the site, sowing part with a mix of 5 grasses and 12 flowering plants, and part with a standard mix of 5 grasses. The resulting grassland contains a number of odd species. Some might be part of a buried seed-bank at the site (for example cornfield knotgrass or fool's parsley). Others have almost certainly come in with the seed mix, such as the cornflower (whose colour suggests a horticultural origin), the corn marigold and the fodder burnet. John Akroyd, writing in *Nature in Cambridgeshire*, suggests that "if the current use of wildflower seed continues without any control or even question, it is bound to have a detrimental effect on the flora".[43]

The solution, of course, is to demand that habitat recreation schemes use only local seed and plant sources. A brisk industry is now developing to supply "native" genetic stock for tree-planting programmes. Ironically, perhaps, the chief problem is the volume of material needed. The collection of seed from local protected habitats can create environmental impacts. To draw another example from close to home, the Wildlife Trust for Bedfordshire recently purchased 79 ha of land on the chalk of the Chilterns. Part of this is chalk grassland, lying within Deacon Hill SSSI, but there is 40 ha of arable land. Here the Trust is trying to re-establish chalk grassland. It originally planned to do this using seed from the SSSI collected by vacuum, but English Nature vetoed this on the grounds that the vacuum collection would damage grassland insects. Instead, the "new" chalk grassland will have to be colonised naturally by plants from the adjacent SSSI. On this site, at least, habitat restoration is going to be a long, slow process.

Despite the technical problems and pitfalls, habitat creation and recreation has a vital role to play in beginning to turn back the long history of habitat fragmentation in the countryside, and also to enhance the value of existing protected areas. At Minsmere in Suffolk, for example, the RSPB is continuing to develop creative conservation, with an ambitious plan to dig out parts of the reedbed that are becoming too dry to create new lagoons, while at the same time allowing new reedbeds to develop on the Scrape nearby. The two habitats will then be managed together on a 15–20 year rotation to optimise the mix of habitats for breeding birds. The RSPB is also attempting a major heathland restoration project on 160 ha of arable land nearby, purchased in 1989.[44] There is no doubt that habitat creation and re-creation is here to stay.

Reintroducing nature

The logical partner of the idea of creating whole habitats is to target resources on particular animals and plants, and work to bring them back to old haunts. This can be done in two ways. The first is uncontroversial, and that is by creating the right ecological conditions for them, and waiting. The second is more radical, and involves deliberate reintroductions. The encouragement of recolonisation by species whose range is restricted is simply an extension of conventional conservation management; rather in the way that reserve managers provide nestboxes for pied flycatchers in Welsh oak woodlands. This approach is widely adopted. It lies at the core of the attempt by the Wildlife Trust's "Otters and Rivers Project" to expand the range of the otter in England and Wales. The hope is that improvements in water quality and provision of places for otters to feed and breed in riparian wetland habitats will encourage them to consoliate and extend their range.[45]

Such species-targeted habitat enhancement is now well-established, for example in the work of the Game Conservancy to promote the idea of leaving unsprayed headlands on field margins to increase insect populations that can provide food for the now uncommon grey partridge. New ideas of habitat enhancement have also entered commercial forestry, for example in the restructuring of forests to create a mosaic of small stands of timber, and different planting and management of ride edges, stream sides and wetlands.[46] The Forest Authority gave a Woodland Management Merit Award to the Ffrwdgrech Estate, near Brecon in Powys, in 1993, for the extent to which it had achieved a natural forest structure of varying age and size classes. It was also (no small matter) highly profitable.

Enthusiasm for creative conservation aimed at specific species is growing. A prime example is English Nature's innovative "Species Recovery Programme". Its aim is to reverse the decline of populations of plants and animals under threat of extinction. In 1995 there were projects aimed at 29 different species. They included a number of spectacular species, such as the lady's slipper orchid, the bittern and the large blue butterfly, as well as others that are perhaps more obscure, such as the spangled water beetle (known only from one site in Hampshire) or the strapwort (with one site in Devon). The list also includes three very well-known and popular species, which occur in a number of locations: the red squirrel, the dormouse and the natterjack toad. It is perhaps surprising to find such widespread species included within the programme, but it can be argued that work with species like these, whose habitat requirements are well-known, is "cost-effective", and that work with them will yield some return fairly rapidly, and thus makes good business sense. Furthermore, conservation programmes need public support, and this is helped if the species chosen have appeal. Between the familiar cuddly mammals and the bizarre wartbiter cricket (known only from three sites in southern England) the Species Recovery Programme is perfectly designed to capture the attention of the media, and to impress and amuse both public and politicians. "Species recovery" fits perfectly the soundbite culture of British public life.

However, this kind of conservation is expensive. English Nature's Species Recovery Programme absorbs about 3.5 per cent of English Nature's Grant-in-Aid, a total of no less than £1.4 million, a figure that bears comparison with the £6.6 million spent on 150 different National Nature Reserves, covering a total of 59,000 ha. Of course, action to save one species may well help others, for example if it leads to better management of woodland or heathland habitats. Nonetheless, however attractive the good news of "species recovery", its high cost means that this approach needs to be handled very carefully. It must not be allowed to suck up resources and energy that are more effectively used elsewhere.

Once established, species can move rapidly to colonise suitable habitat. This is well demonstrated by the expansion of the range of the osprey in Scotland since it first re-established itself in Speyside in 1954. In the 1994 season, 95 pairs bred, producing 146 young.[47] There is even speculation that the osprey might breed once again in England. There is more to recovery than habitat, of course. With birds of prey, deliberate persecution is still a major cause of mortality, as is theft by egg collectors. Such pressures can themselves be a reason for believing that the natural recovery of a population should be given a helping hand. They have been the main reason for the re-introduction of the red kite in England and Scotland, well outside its normal breeding range in Wales. It is as if the pressure of illegal killing has prevented the spatial expansion of the Welsh population. Once lifted over the ring of persecution, the bird seems to thrive. In 1994, there were 107 pairs in Wales, and they reared 98 young; in England 20 pairs raised 37 young and in Scotland eight pairs raised 13 young. The red kite seems well on the road to recovering its former territory: certainly, I have seen it recently where I did not expect to.[48]

The classic case of an attempted reintroduction in the UK in recent decades has been the white-tailed sea eagle. This went extinct through persecution in the nineteenth century (shooting, trapping, egg-collecting and poisoning), and although the habitat of the West Highlands remained broadly favourable, there seemed little prospect of natural recolonisation from the only stable European population, in northern Norway. The sea eagle met the guidelines for re-introductions laid down in 1979 by the UK Committee for International Nature Conservation, and a serious attempt at reintroduction was begun in the 1970s on the island NNR of Rhum. Between 1975 and 1985, a total of 85 sea eagle chicks were imported from Norway, and 82 survived to be released on Rhum. Only eight have been reported dead (two by poisoning), and it is estimated that up to 80 per cent survived their critical first year flying free. The first successful breeding took place in 1985, and by 1987

17 clutches had been found. Ten pairs of sea eagles held territory in 1994, and four pairs succeeded in raising five young. The sea eagle is apparently starting on the road back to permanent re-establishment.[49]

Butterflies have been particularly attractive candidates for release since the nineteenth century, with attempts to release new (and often quite unsuitable) species, to translocate species that have gone locally extinct, or to reintroduce species that have disappeared altogether from the UK. A study for the World Wide Fund for Nature reviewed 323 introductions, involving 43 butterfly species in 47 counties (mostly in Southeast England).[50] This is probably just the tip of the iceberg, for a great many introductions have gone unrecorded. The most commonly released species is the marsh fritillary, with 54 attempts, from which several populations still survive. Many introductions have failed, for example repeated attempts to re-establish the swallowtail at Wicken Fen between 1955 and 1965, and in 1975.[51] Intensive research is obviously the key to success in such introductions. The successful release of the large blue at secret sites in southwest England in the 1980s followed detailed studies of life cycle and habitat requirements of the caterpillars' ant hosts. Such re-introductions are exciting, but of course the cost can be considerable.

There have been many other attempted reintroductions to the UK, and many attempts to introduce totally new species. Most have been somewhat clandestine (the most controversial being the large cats, released exotic pets, that people believe roam the countryside), and most have failed. The experience with exotic species released to become serious pests (coypu, mink and giant hogweed spring to mind) is a reminder of the dangers of casual releases. Some introductions have been long naturalised and accepted (like the pheasant or the red-legged partridge), or have at least some supporters (like the grey squirrel or the rabbit). Others, like the rhododendron or the Himalayan balsam, have fans among the general public but are usually reviled by conservationists.[52]

Putting the pieces together

The need to counteract the fragmentation and the loss of diversity of the rural landscape is obvious. Ecologically, it is possible to talk of the need for new habitat networks to link conservation sites, for habitat creation, and for creative approaches to landscape and biodiversity. But how are these things to be brought into being? Crudely, who will do the work of re-creating nature, and who will meet the cost? Until relatively recently there was no easy answer to this question, but there are now mechanisms in place that offer some kind of start in the vast job of re-integrating nature. They have been created as a direct result of the crisis of agricultural over-production in Europe discussed in Chapter Four, and from the response of the Ministry of Agriculture, Fisheries and Food (MAFF) since the mid-1980s to arguments from conservationists, supported to some extent by free-marketeers, about the need to reform the Common Agricultural Policy's system of agricultural support, and to reduce its damaging effects on the countryside.

The future for farming in Europe is one of contraction. Studies of agriculture across Europe suggest that the squeeze on agriculture will continue, both because of international price competition and increasing yields on the largest farms on the best land. One Dutch study assessed four future scenarios for rural areas in Europe, making different assumptions about the extent of free trade, regional development, and environmental protection. All of them suggested that the future would see increasing land surpluses and further job losses in agriculture. In the UK it has been calculated that at present levels of intensity of production, very large areas of land could be removed from agricultural production without a disastrous effect on self-sufficiency in food production — perhaps as much as 2.5 or 3 million ha.[53] There is, across the EC, a surplus of production, and (unless agriculture "extensifies", or reverses the trend towards more intensive production) a surplus of land. There is also a very large budget for agricultural support. It is this which provides a possible engine for the reconstruction of the countryside.

The first schemes to use agricultural money on any scale to support conservation on farmland were the Environmentally Sensitive Areas (ESAs), established in the mid-1980s, and followed by a whole range of other measures. The forerunner of the ESAs was the Broads Grazing Marsh Conservation Scheme. This was launched in 1985 by the Countryside Commission on an experimental basis for three years, with joint funding from MAFF. It involved flat-rate payments, and proved popular with farmers (90 per cent of eligible farmers taking it up). With MAFF support, an EC regulation allowing member states to aid farming in "environmentally sensitive areas" was passed later in 1985, with a further regulation allowing Community money to be used for such support in 1987. MAFF moved swiftly to establish ESAs under the Agriculture Act 1985.[54]

The NCC and Countryside Commission responded with some enthusiasm to the idea of ESAs, and produced a list of 150 candidate ESAs. This was subsequently shortened to 14, and 6 were announced in England and Wales in August 1986. The scheme was extended in 1987, and by 1988 there were 11 in England, 2 in Wales and 8 in Scotland.[55] All these schemes were renewed in 1992 and 1993, and 6 new ESAs announced in 1994. ESAs now cover substantial areas of both lowland and upland throughout the UK, from the Suffolk River Valleys to the Antrim Coast, the Shetland Islands to Ynys Môn. Their remit has progressively widened to embrace historical features and access.

ESAs were established in areas whose environmental quality was threatened by agriculture, but whose character could be maintained if appropriate farming practices were adopted. Flat-rate payments were offered to farmers who agreed to adhere to simple and environmentally appropriate management regimes. Conservation groups have by and large welcomed ESAs, as have farmers able to enter the scheme voluntarily and thereby do something to combat falling agricultural returns. The scale and speed of the ESA programme is remarkable. The ability of the programme to continue to attract farmers will depend on the responsiveness of the price signals in relation to the wider agricultural economy. The economic costs of the programme will also depend on patterns of production and trade.[56]

There has perhaps not been very close review of the effectiveness of the programme in conservation terms. It is not clear how far those farmers entering an ESA agreement are simply those whose management already meets the prescriptive guidelines (and hence where the money may bring no new benefits for conservation), nor has enough scientific work yet been done to demonstrate whether the rather crude management criteria set for each ESA are actually delivering the conservation benefits intended. Small variations in the timing and intensity of grazing can have significant impacts on plant species, and landscape can be changed within ESAs in many important ways that are quite unaffected by the ESA agreement. It is therefore not clear how effective ESA payments are for conservation. It is unlikely that conservationists would have welcomed ESAs so openly had the money been available to them to spend in other ways.

Two other initiatives deserve particular attention for their potential in habitat management and creation. The first is another idea of the Countryside Commission's, Countryside Stewardship. This is run in association with English Nature, English Heritage and the Ministry of Agriculture. It tackles the criticism of ESAs that farmers might be getting money without doing any more than they were already. Countryside Stewardship is a programme offering landholders the chance to enter voluntary agreements by which they receive flat-rate payments for changes in land management that will promote conservation. These might sustain the beauty and diversity of the landscape, improve and extend wildlife habitats, conserve archaeological sites and historic features, improve opportunities for enjoying the countryside, restore neglected land or landscape features or create new wildlife habitats and landscapes. Agreements can apply to a range of English landscapes, including chalk and limestone grassland, lowland heaths, waterside land, the coast, uplands, historic landscapes and traditional orchards. Stewardship agreements can also be made in designated Community Forests, to restore hedgerows and in pasturelands of Hereford and Worcester and the Culm Measures of Devon and Cornwall.[57]

Payments under the Countryside Stewardship Scheme are at set flat rates, but they are discretionary, which means that the Commission does not have to give them unless the management proposed is positive, and (for example) combines a number of improvements for conservation and recreation on land that is already of conservation value or adjoins such land. Thus, for example, a payment of over £200 per hectare per year can be paid for the management of historic water-meadows. This is only applicable to sites with controlled irrigation (i.e. not grazing marshes), and the owner would have to prepare a ten-year management plan giving full historical details, specify what restoration work is required on sluices etc., specify the proposed grazing management and proposed provisions for public access.

Several of the Countryside Stewardship provisions allow for the re-creation of habitats. In the case of heathland, land adjacent to existing heath can be entered assuming its soil is suitable, and appropriate management (cutting and grazing) is carried out. A supplementary payment can be made for more intensive management, including measures to reduce soil fertility and control invasive species. There are similar provisions for the re-creation of grassland on cultivated land, either by natural regeneration or sowing of grass-seed mixes. There is money also for hedge-planting, and for the creation of grass margins in fields that link fields managed under another part of the scheme, alongside restored hedges, or to provide wildlife corridors or to buffer streams or other habitats from agricultural activities. These measures provide a financial base for a wide range of creative conservation proposals.

Countryside Stewardship was launched in June 1991. By 1994 almost 4000 contracts had been signed, covering 800 km^2 (plus 920 miles of hedgerow). It is too early to assess its success in conservation terms, but clearly expenditure is being much more closely targeted than in the ESA scheme. In June 1994, the Secretary of State for the Environment announced that when the Countryside Stewardship Scheme had ended its pilot phase in 1996, it would be handed over to the Ministry of Agriculture. This indicates success of a sort, and presumably (as with the ESAs), MAFF will now take on and expand the initiative.

Countryside Stewardship has one fault, however, and that is that money is once again being devoted only to small parts of the rural landscape. This problem is avoided by another innovative scheme, developed by the Countryside Council for Wales, *Tir Cymen*.[58] This experimental scheme is operating in three trial districts (Meirionydd, Dinefwr and Swansea). It is a voluntary scheme that offers farmers annual payments for following positive management guidelines, and standard payments towards capital works. However, unlike ESAs and Countryside Stewardship, the whole farm must be entered into the scheme. This avoids the flaw in both the other schemes (and in set-aside) that farmers are free to intensify production on parts of their holding not covered by the agreement. The farmer must observe a code of good practice for the whole farm, must keep rights of way free and avoid water pollution. In addition, they must follow set, positive management guidelines for all moorland and heathland, all broadleaved woodland, all unimproved coastal land and grassland (but not grass leys or reseeded pasture), and selected boundary features (walls, hedges, banks etc.). The farmer can also opt to enter land as arable field margins for wildlife, wild grazing for geese or swans or new permissive access paths. Support is available for capital expenditure on such things as boundaries, paths, trees, scrub or bracken control, the removal of eyesores and the installation of nestboxes.

It remains to be seen whether *Tir Cymen* will be judged a success, whether it might be extended across Wales, or even into the rest of the UK. Certainly it represents an important attempt to devise a specific programme extending conservation across the whole landscape. Increasingly, non-governmental organisations are pursuing the same broad objective, seeking constructive ways to move the agricultural industry away from intensification, and the rural landscape in directions more favourable to wildlife and landscape beauty. In 1991, for example, both Friends of the Earth and the RSPB published papers on the future of agriculture, whose names speak for themselves: *Off the Treadmill* and *A Future for Environmentally Sensitive Farming.*[59]

In 1992 the range of environmental schemes aimed at farmers was expanded considerably under an agri-environment package agreed at the same time as the EC's Common Agricultural Policy was reformed, through what is referred to as the MacSharry Proposals. This reform began to reduce support prices to levels closer to world market prices, particularly in cereals. Farmers were compensated for the reduced price support with area- and headage-based payments. A compulsory set-aside programme (15 per cent of arable acreage) was also established as a condition for eligibility for the new arable payments.[60]

National governments were left some freedom as to how to implement the agri-environment package. In the UK, seven new measures intended to promote environmentally friendly agriculture were announced in 1993. These included the designation of six new Environmentally Sensitive Areas (extending the total area of ESAs to over a million ha, 10 per cent of agricultural land) and measures to improve public access to ESAs and set-aside land, a Moorland Scheme to reward farmers outside ESAs for reducing stocking levels, a long-term set-aside scheme that would create and improve wildlife habitats, a scheme to encourage farmers to convert to organic production (without pesticides or inorganic fertilisers) and the creation of 30 Nitrate Sensitive Areas where farmers would be compensated for changing land management to reduce nitrate inputs to water tables.[61]

The new measures have not been received with particular rapture by conservationists.[62] These schemes do involve considerable sums of money being invested in agriculture in ways that begin to halt and even reverse the damage of intensification, and clearly a number of these proposals go some way to meet conservation objectives for rebuilding the countryside. However, conservation organisations still argue that the reforms of the Common

Agricultural Policy have not gone far enough, that many of them are not good value for money, and that the various schemes need to be far more closely targeted on conservation objectives, so that it is clear what they are trying to achieve, and whether they are doing it.[63]

The present measures for the reconstruction of the countryside are starting to put pieces of the puzzle back together, but they are only piecemeal. Efforts are targeted at particular landscape features — at farm woodlands under the Woodland Grant Scheme, and hedgerows under the Hedgerow Incentive Scheme, and the various habitats addressed by Countryside Stewardship. Hopes of larger-scale reconstruction of the countryside as a result of land surplus to needs for agriculture being set aside (taken out of crop and livestock production) as a "conservation reserve" have been disappointed.[64]

Set-aside has happened, but not in a very helpful way. A voluntary scheme has operated since 1988, and the compulsory scheme since 1992. However, under these schemes the set-aside land rotates round the farm, which means that the only areas of new habitat created are ephemeral, and a common effect is to make farmers increase the intensity of production on the remaining land (thus negating the programme's main purpose of production-limitation). Furthermore, in 1993 MAFF watered down the management requirements on set-aside land. It now seems clear that this set-aside land is of limited conservation benefit, and the programme an expensive way of achieving very little. The provisions for long-term set-aside under the Habitat Improvement Scheme announced in 1992 offer more scope. This is non-rotational, and is leading to the planting of willow and poplar plantations, and to natural regeneration in fields that favours some birds and small mammals.[65] It still falls short, however, of the possibility of larger-scale and longer-term reversion of land from agriculture. Much of the work of combating the fragmentation of nature remains to be done.

136

CHAPTER NINE

Nature, Landscapes, Lives

When you find a people who believe that man and nature are indivisible, that survival and health are contingent upon an understanding of nature and her processes, these societies will be very different from ours, as will their towns, cities and landscapes
Ian McHarg[1]

People and protected areas

The physical isolation of protected areas and the fragmentation of nature in the countryside have been discussed in Chapter Eight, as have some of the ways in which that fragmentation can be tackled. However, protected areas are very often not only isolated physically, they are also isolated institutionally, cut off from local people and local economic interests. If conservation is to be successful, we need to re-integrate conservation into the local economy. Just as we need to reach out beyond the confines of protected areas into the whole landscape, we need to build links between protected areas and the needs and economic lives of the communities around them.

The need to make close and effective links between protected areas and local people has become the dominant theme of international thinking on conservation in the last decade. It was the central theme of the Fourth World Parks Congress in Caracas in 1992, and is a fundamental element in the World Conservation Union's action plan for protected areas in Europe, *Parks for Life*. The new approach "puts protected areas at the centre of strategies for

137

sustainable development, concentrates on the linkages between protected areas and the areas around, and focuses on the economic benefits that such areas can bring".[2] The Fourth World Parks Congress identified seven purposes for protected areas, and in addition to the traditional concern to safeguard areas of outstanding natural wealth, natural beauty or cultural significance, and to maintain biodiversity, these included the need to provide homes for human communities with traditional cultures and knowledge of nature, and to provide economic benefits to local and national economies, and models of sustainable development that can be applied elsewhere. *Parks for Life* calls for all European governments to revise their approach to protected areas to incorporate this new thinking.

The need to build conservation onto the need and interests of local people has been stimulated by a range of studies from around the world.[3] Indeed, in many parts of the Third World, it is not now considered an option to try to achieve conservation without involving local people. In Africa it is widely argued that "conservation will either contribute to solving the problems of the rural poor who live day to day with wild animals, or those animals will disappear".[4] Most strategies to build harmonious relations between protected areas and surrounding people are based on one or more of three basic ideas. The first is the notion of separating a core area where human use is prohibited from outside areas, where human use is unregulated, by creating an intermediate or buffer zone. This approach is particularly associated with Biosphere Reserves, introduced under the UNESCO Man and the Biosphere Programme. This is often closely linked to the second idea of trying to derive financial flows from wildlife within the protected area to compensate or reward those living near the reserve. This might involve either non-consumptive use, usually through wildlife tourism, or consumptive use through commercial hunting, either by foreign sport hunters on safari, or meat for domestic sale. The third idea is to do away with the notion of exclusion altogether and explore the potential of local people *as* conservationists.

Buffer zones are usually seen as a way of protecting a reserve by ensuring appropriate management of surrounding land. Within them "appropriate" development activities can be begun, often labelled "integrated conservation and development" projects or "conservation-with-development" projects. Such activities might be used to deflect the economic interests of people living close to a protected area from economic opportunities within it that are now illegal (e.g. hunting), or a means of compensating people forced to leave the reserve and locate outside. Experience with the first generation of such projects is somewhat disappointing. Buzzwords like "participation" or "bottom-up" planning do not guarantee success, and while concepts such as "the local community" and "traditional resource use" trip easily off the tongue, they are more elusive in practice. Integrated conservation and development projects can be expensive, and cannot be hurried.[5]

In the UK, the message about local communities and conservation has been accepted, but more easily by some conservationists than others. Traditionally, the "great divide" between landscape and nature conservation also separated attitudes to people. In landscape conservation there has been little difficulty in implementing the ideas current in the 1940s about the dependence of natural beauty on appropriate human management. The role of protected areas in sustaining the local economy has long been a vital feature of conservation in National Parks as well as Areas of Outstanding Beauty, Heritage Coasts and other designated areas. The importance of local interests in decision-making in National Parks is achieved by elected members on National Park Planning Committees and Boards.[6]

Wildlife conservationists, on the other hand, have more often found themselves opposing economic development in and around protected areas. The Nature Conservancy Council frequently found itself being portrayed as the enemy of local people and economic activity. Whether making by-laws to restrict bait-digging on Lindisfarne, proposing a Marine Nature Reserve on Loch Sween, opposing peat mining for whisky distilling on Islay, or opposing afforestation in the "Flow Country" of Caithness, the NCC found itself at loggerheads with local opinion and local interests through the 1980s. The restrictions inherent in the list of "potentially damaging operations" for SSSIs also made them unpopular with landowners in a way that could easily be construed as opposing legitimate economic activity. Clumsy footwork by the NCC, and orchestrated opposition, produced a great deal of bad press about the adverse impacts of conservation on local people.

Of course, the picture has changed considerably. The NCC's successor agencies are much more sophisticated in their public relations, and have put a great deal of effort into wooing landowners and setting up more efficient and transparent procedures for dealing with their "customers" and "partners". In Wales, for example, the Countryside Council took the simple and yet enormously symbolic step of adopting a bilingual policy, and took the risk of locating their headquarters in the Welsh-speaking heartland of Bangor rather than the high road to England in Cardiff.[7] There is also a self-conscious attempt to offer a synthetic and people-oriented view of the unified task of landscape and wildlife conservation. CCW picturesquely describes its goal, for example, as "a beautiful land washed by clean seas and streams, under a clear sky; supporting its full diversity of life, including our own, each species in its proper abundance, for the enjoyment of everybody and the contented work of its rural and sea faring people". Beyond the hype, and the fashionable rhetoric of "the customer", all sectors of conservation in the UK are taking the needs of local people increasingly seriously.[8]

Conservation and the community

In a number of European countries, links between protected areas and local people are particularly strong, and are fundamental to the whole approach to conservation. A prime example of this is the French *Parcs Naturels Régionaux*. These represent an approach to conservation very different from the eight French National Parks (which are centred on wilderness zones in the mountains), or the 80 or so small and strictly protected Réserves Naturèlles.[9] The Parcs Régionaux were conceived in the 1960s chiefly as a means of tackling regional decline, and were intended to respond to local and not central government initiatives.[10] Parcs Régionaux have multiple functions: the protection of heritage, social and economic development, welcoming, educating and informing the public and carrying out research. They are created by the Conseil Régionale; the proposal is set out and agreed by all local authorities (regions, departments and communes), and the different partners draw up a contract, the charter, which binds its signatories for ten years. The charter delimits the park and provides a ten-year development plan. The park is then approved by the Minister of the Environment (advised by a standing commission), and confirmed by decree. The Parc Régional's life can be extended at the request of the Region, and the partners, and status could be withdrawn by the Minister if it fails to fulfil its objectives.

There were 27 Parcs Régionaux in France in 1994. They include areas of intensively managed land such as the Pas de Calais or the Montagne de Reims, areas of wetland such as the Brenne, the Brière, the Marais Poitevin or the Camargue and areas of hills or mountains such as Livradois-Forez, the Volcans d'Auvergne or the massif of the Vercors. They have to be areas that have a clear and strong local identity, that are seen to possess distinctive and rich natural and cultural values, and distinctive heritage and landscape. It is hoped that as a result they will have an integrity that can be recognised both by visitors and by local people.

The Parcs Régionaux are essentially put forward by local people, or at least local authorities. They are managed by a body comprising all the local authorities concerned (the Conseils Régionaux, the communes and the Conseils Généraux), with a team of 15–30 permanent staff. Finance comes from the region (35 per cent), the departments (28 per cent), the communes (20 per cent), the Ministry of the Environment (12 per cent) and other ministries (5 per cent). In 1992, the Parcs Régionaux had a total budget of 217 million francs.

The areas designated as Parcs Régionaux have fragile landscapes, under pressure from either economic depression and emigration, or from excessive tourist numbers. Park managers can develop projects to protect natural features and landscapes, to develop local cultural heritage, to promote economic activity (for example tourism that respects the environment) and to develop facilities and sources of information for visitors. The approach is to promote conservation through appropriate development. The parks are therefore as likely to be promoting local cheese as local wildlife, and will probably be trying to explore the links between the two (via, for example, traditional systems of agriculture and indigenous knowledge). In Normandie-Maine, for example, local cider and perry production was promoted, meeting socio-economic and cultural objectives (maintaining a traditional farm sector, and local appreciation of history), promoting tourism (for example through a "route de poiré"), and maintaining the landscape and wildlife value of old orchards.[11]

In the Parcs Régionaux, nature and landscape therefore exist in a kind of seamless continuum, traditions, economic life, landscape and wildlife, all, in theory, advancing hand in hand. Conservation in the Parcs Régionaux means a legal commitment voluntarily entered into by all parties, and moreover one that provides a tight and integrated link between people, landscape and nature.

Another outstanding example of the integration of protected areas and local people comes from Italy, and the Abruzzo National Park. This was created in 1923, and covers 440 km^2, with a further 600 km^2 buffer zone. It lies in the Apennines, and contains four peaks over 2000m in height. It is remarkable in particular because it contains populations of between 70 and 100 brown bear and 40–50 wolves as well as chamois and many other species. It is visited by about 2 million people a year, has 5 villages within its boundaries and 13 more nearby. The key to the success of Abruzzo lies in the establishment of a strict zonation system combined with the demonstration of real economic benefits of the park for local communities. It is estimated that some 210 billion lira is generated in the local economy because of tourism, plus 100 billion lira of direct government expenditure.[12]

In many ways, Abruzzo was pioneering sustainable development before the World Conservation Strategy was written. In the 1960s it was under severe pressure, but a new initiative to steer tourist pressure away from high-impact activities (such as ski resorts) began to show local communities that, in the words of Franco Tassi, "defending better conservation and use of the park would mean larger and surer incomes and lead to a better future for the park as well".[13] Economic decline in the Apennines and inspired leadership has kept the park and its remarkable landscapes and wildlife intact. Indeed, in 1989, the village of Rochetta and three neighbours voted to be included in the park, extending its area by ten per cent.[14]

The interests of conservation and those of local people can be combined, if planning is innovative enough and the legislative framework is flexible. It was certainly the perception of those planning for National Parks in the UK in the 1930s and 1940s that conservation and development need not lie in any simple opposition. Indeed, they saw a creative tension between the need for preservation (stopping urban sprawl or the "despoliation" of the countryside, for example) and the realisation of the importance of rural economy and society. As explained in Chapter Two, the central concern of National Parks was always, first and foremost, for outstanding natural beauty, or as the 1945 Ramsay Committee elegantly put it "the austere grandeur of mountain and moor, the varied beauty of glen, woodland and running water". But John Dower recognised in 1945 that conservation might also have broader purposes. British National Parks, he wrote, would be different from those in the USA or elsewhere because they were both human-made and lived-in. In the National Parks, he thought established farming use should be effectively maintained.[15] Dower did not see a fundamental threat from agriculture to the natural beauty or the wildlife of the countryside. The real threats were seen to be excessive numbers of visitors and large-scale development, such as forestry, military training or mineral extraction. The Hobhouse Committee in 1947 believed that farming and essential rural industries should be allowed to "flourish, unhampered by unnecessary controls or restrictions" in National Parks, while appropriate facilities for visitors should be developed.[16]

Thinking about National Parks in Scotland was from the first sensitive to the desirability of economic development. The 1945 Ramsay Committee saw afforestation as quite compatible with the use of an area as a National Park. They did not contemplate any general restriction on agriculture, and envisaged promotion of fish farming and rural industry. Furthermore it attempted to calculate the economic value of tourism in the proposed Scottish parks. It suggested that an enlightened National Park administration should aim "to preserve the continuity of rural life".[17] The 1947 Ramsay report took a similar view, proposing development plans for each National Park to show areas to be devoted to each major land use, wildlife, agriculture, forestry or hydro-electric development.[18]

Despite the scope and attractiveness of this vision (as we saw in Chapter Two), opponents of National Parks have prevented their creation in Scotland to this day. However, the English and Welsh National Parks have been held up internationally as a prime example of the ways in which cultural landscapes can be sustained and conserved. Within the National Parks and AONBs established over the last 45 years, an admirable balance has been struck between a concern for the economic wellbeing of rural communities, the desirability of preservation and the needs of the urban visitor.

One of the main ways in which local economies can benefit from conservation is through tourism. As the Abruzzo example shows, not all tourist development is compatible with conservation, but there is increasing awareness of and interest in the notion of "sustainable tourism". The approach of the National Parks in England and Wales again provides an example of this kind of approach in practice. One example would be the Peak District Integrated Rural Development Project. This seven-year research project worked in two villages and two valleys within the Peak District National Park between 1981 and 1988 to devise an approach to development that integrated social, economic and environmental interests. The project developed three "principles": *individuality* (looking at rural areas individually, as a source of economic strength, social identity and environmental character); *involvement* (getting local communities to conceive and plan their own future); and *interdependence* (looking at rural areas as a whole rather than in isolation). The project set up a scheme of grants and £185,000 was spent on 105 projects (worth, with other funds, £0.5m), creating 60 new full-time jobs and helping 43 community schemes.[19] This is an example that could be applied more broadly.[20]

For wildlife conservationists in the UK, public access has very often been an anathema. Great energy was (and is) devoted to dealing with the ecological impacts of visitors' feet on nature reserves, and of course the whole SSSI system is essentially private, sites being notified on private land with no presumptions about access, and the schedules of sites essentially unavailable to the general public. However, all the government conservation agencies have made significant strides towards a more open policy, and now have a similar range of concerns for access to reserves and the wider countryside. English Nature devoted an issue of its magazine to showing "how English Nature is encouraging people to visit nature reserves", and the National Audit Office review reported that they were attempting "to progress from their predecessor's low key approach to the public and have recognised that National Nature Reserves may provide opportunities for increasing public understanding and enjoyment of nature".[21] There is also, as we saw in Chapter Seven, increasing awareness of the links between economies and conservation, and as I shall explore below, growing concern to link conservation to the welfare of local communities.

Conservation and the coast

There is considerable potential in the involvement of local people in making decisions about protected areas in the UK. One of the best examples of this approach in action comes, perhaps rather surprisingly, from the least developed dimension of conservation in the UK, the marine environment. I have argued above (in Chapter Three) that existing measures for marine conservation are inadequate. As English Nature notes rather ominously, "statutory mechanisms such as Marine Nature Reserves or Special Areas for Conservation may take many years to achieve the protection of subtidal areas because of the lengthy consultation procedures".[22]

The Worldwide Fund for Nature argues that the problems are so serious as to need new legislation.[23] Their proposed Marine Protected Areas Bill is built

143

on an integrated approach to conservation that embraces not only the needs of marine wildlife, but also the conservation and sustainable use of marine economic resources (fish stocks) and wider cultural purposes (for example education and enjoyment). The core of the proposal is for a Marine Protected Areas Authority to propose and manage Marine Protected Areas (MPAs), and to make by-laws to regulate their use. These MPAs could extend from one metre above the highest astronomical tide down to the seaward limits of United Kingdom controlled waters, and the proposed Authority would have powers to deal with all the threats to marine ecosystems that disable present conservation initiatives: fishing, navigation (e.g. of oil tankers around Skomer or the Shetlands), use of leisure craft, diving, and pollution. These are radical proposals, and have implications not only for existing *de facto* right-holders on the seas such as fishermen and divers, but also for international maritime law.

Meanwhile, progress is being made in marine conservation not through the awkward existing statutory designation of Marine Nature Reserve (MNR), but through much more participatory approaches. Notable among these is the work at Strangford Lough in County Down, Northern Ireland. Strangford Lough is a remarkable place, a huge inlet of the sea, some 150 square kilometres in extent, of which half is inter-tidal. Its northern edge lies just 6 km from the outskirts of Belfast, and about 600,000 people live within an hour's drive. The Lough is 30 km long, and up to 8 km wide, but is connected to the sea by an 8 km long channel, Strangford Narrows. The Lough is shallow, mostly less than 10 metres, and there is a fantastic range of habitats on the seabed and the shore, from rock and areas of high exposure (the tide runs at up to 4 metres per second in the Narrows) to areas of fine sediments and sandy beaches. The marine and intertidal plant and animal communities are rich, there are important populations of migratory birds (sometimes including 60–75 per cent of the world's population of light-bellied Brent geese in winter) and breeding common seals. People, of course, use the Lough extensively, trawling for queen scallops and prawns, potting for lobsters and crabs, growing oysters and Manila clams, harvesting seaweed for food and as fertiliser and all kinds of waterborne and coastal recreation, from jet skiing through scuba diving to bathing. The Lough is also intensively used for research and teaching, and is also a dump for sewage and other wastes.[24]

Strangford Lough has all the complexity and the conservation importance of the rest of the UK coast within its bounds. In 1988 the Department of the Environment for Northern Ireland declared its shores as an Area of Special Scientific Interest (ASSI). This awoke concern among local communities that traditional uses of the Lough might be prevented, a concern only balanced by that of conservationists that changing use (especially agricultural pollution, trawling for shellfish and fish farming) was causing irreparable damage. In 1992 a Strangford Lough Management Committee was established to bring together all stakeholders. By 1994, this had defined principles for use in a management plan (covering, for example, development, fisheries, aquaculture, recreation and agriculture). It was actively seeking to find a practical strategy for combining development and conservation, its policy on fishing for example supporting a "locally based long term sustainable, commercial fishery". Through words like these, and through the work of local committees of active parties, marine conservation can be pushed forwards. The model is applicable much more widely in conservation across the UK. Success depends on the ability of such groups to forge new partnerships, and make people take uncomfortable decisions. It also depends, perhaps more than these things, on their ability to make government listen and act, rather than hiding behind bland words.[25]

There are similar innovatory approaches to marine and coastal conservation elsewhere in the UK. English Nature, for example produced a *Strategy for the Sustainable Use of England's Estuaries* in 1993, as part of its *Campaign for a Living Coast*. This suggested the development of "fully integrated estuary management plans", and the establishment of "estuary management groups" to guide and implement them. Scottish Natural Heritage has launched the "Focus on Firths" initiative, building on an idea that the Scottish Wildlife Trust initiated in the Moray Firth. It will seek to set up a local forum for each Firth, starting with the Moray, the Solway and the Firth of Forth. The idea is that a "round table" approach will allow a consensus to emerge between statutory bodies, local communities and businesses, to "identify and agree the aims and goals for management of the area, identify and seek to resolve conflicts, and formulate policies and options for integrated and balanced management". Each forum will review the environment and environmental problems of its Firth, develop a management strategy, and draw up an Action Plan.[26]

There are obvious limits to the "round table" approach, for it can so easily produce nothing but talk. Nonetheless, the renewed interest of the statutory bodies in marine conservation, and the creation of local environmental groups focused on marine areas (such as the Welsh group Cyfeillion Bae Ceredigion, the Friends of Cardigan Bay), suggests some potential. Other initiatives are also stressing the need for a co-operative approach. Marine Consultation Areas have been identified in Scotland and, in 1992, applied also to England and Wales. English Nature has identified 13 candidate MCAs around the English coast, from the Farne Islands via the Wash and the Solent to Morecambe Bay. There is also interest in England in the idea of "Voluntary Marine Nature Reserves".[27]

Lives and landscapes

The protected areas planned in the 1940s and developed in the years that followed were the the finest landscapes and the most outstanding areas of natural habitat remaining. There was no conception that they might become isolated from the rest of the countryside, either ecologically or in terms of their isolation from the logic of the economic activities around them. However, this is precisely what happened, as we saw in Chapters Three and Four. Agriculture industrialised, and brought standardisation and homogeneity in the countryside. Conservation fought to remove small pieces of particular diversity and importance from the controlling logic of production, and locked them instead into a regulated environment of conservation management.

Whether on the coast or inland, there is no doubt that the future of conservation in the UK will be through *integration* and not isolation. Conservation and the economic and social wellbeing of rural people cannot be tackled effectively in isolation from one another. The restructuring of the agricultural industry, described in Chapter Four, means that they are increasingly and very intimately interdependent. In many areas of Europe, particularly those with smaller farms, maintenance of conservation interest is going to demand continued agricultural activity, and there is likely to be increasing common ground between conservation and agriculture.[28] This is particularly so in areas with smaller and more marginal farms such as Northern Ireland, Wales, Scotland and the North and West of England.

This does not necessarily mean that all small farmers work in ways that promote conservation. Research has shown the dangers in making casual assumptions about the uniformity of interests, motivation and resources of small farmers.[29] However, it does mean that if conservationists want to influence the management of land beyond protected sites they are going to have to engage directly with the managers of that land. In doing so, they are going to have to concentrate on the conservation resource, and the economic and other needs of the farmer. Julian Clark and David Baldock argue that we need to find ways of delivering more integrated farming and conservation policies that are "flexible enough to take account of regional differences".[30] By building the partnership between conservation and the local economy, and by being explicit about conservation targets, real gains are possible.

The best example of this approach is probably the collaboration between the RSPB and the Scottish Crofters Union to propose a new approach to crofting, designed to enhance both the economic and cultural life of crofters, and the conservation of the enormous diversity and richness of the wildlife and scenery of their land.[31] The two organisations might be unexpected bedfellows, given the poor press of conservation in parts of the Highlands, but they present a thoughtful and unified case with great clarity and force. The interest of the RSPB stems from the fact that the crofting counties of north and northwest Scotland, the Hebrides, Orkney and Shetland, hold a remarkable number of rare breeding birds. Most poignant, perhaps, is the corncrake, whose range has progressively shrunk through the present century, forced out by agricultural change. In 1938 it occurred from Cornwall to

Shetland. Now it is extinct in all but the crofting counties, with a population of less than 500 pairs in Great Britain. The survival of the corncrake depends on the mosaic of hay meadows, iris beds and reeds that characterises the Hebridean croft, and its future is therefore inextricably bound up with the economic future of crofting. The argument is true for more than corncrakes. As *Crofting and the Environment* puts it:

> traditional management techniques, practised over very many crofting genera-
> tions, have ... preserved the flower-rich machairs of the Hebrides. Indeed
> management of this type is essential to maintain this internationally unique
> resource — abandonment or intensification would quickly result in the loss of
> this environmental interest.[32]

Crofters have gained little from the bonanza of agricultural production subsidies over the past forty years. Social and economic conditions are poor in the crofting townships, and investment is badly needed. Yet the conventional production-based agricultural support policies are not effective in meeting the needs of small multi-occupation crofting households, and the low-intensity agriculture that sustains the remaining corncrakes. Where grants are taken up they lead to the intensification of production, fertilisation and re-seeding of hay meadows and more mechanisation, and they place crofters on the same treadmill of production as lowland farmers, and expose them to the same pressures of debt and agricultural recession.

Crofting and the Environment outlines an economically sustainable future for crofting, and it is one with profound conservation benefits. The vision for crofting in the year 2010 is to have more crofts occupied, more young people in crofting and more local employment. In agriculture the vision involves fewer sheep, more cattle and more forestry. Behind this vision is the principle that crofters should be remunerated for the public goods they supply, and chief among these are the wildlife and scenery of the worked environment.

To achieve this goal, what is needed is a new system of economic support for crofting. This should achieve three things. First, it should increase the overall level of public support for crofting (and ensure that crofting areas get a good share of European CAP money). Second, these payments should be based on the principle of cross-compliance, such that support payments are tied explicitly to the provision of environmental benefits (management that helps corncrakes, for example). Third, there is a need to simplify drastically the bewildering range of support schemes that exist at present, and put them under a single co-ordinating agency. Other specific measures include the extension of the present ESAs, a premium payment for late-cut hay or silage, and the proposal that townships which make conservation plans should become eligible for extra grants, for example for the establishment of woodland.

In a sense, the details of these and other proposals do not matter. The important thing is that they argue for a new and positive approach to crofting that tries to maximise both local economic and social benefits and conservation gains, in a coherent and integrated way. Crofting support and crofting administration need reform to meet both people's needs and conservation goals. The potential for innovative collaborative solutions to old problems is there for the taking. There is the opportunity to integrate the conservation of nature and landscape, and social development: the chance to link nature, landscape and lives.

Planning whole landscapes

If conservation and local economies are to be integrated, we will need to plan the countryside in new ways. Protected areas overlap on the ground and in their aims. Different agencies toss protected area boundaries down on the map, and many end up on top of each other. The result is a confused policy environment for conservation action. It is not surprising, therefore, to find suggestions for the integration of different protective designations. These include the idea of a single Heritage Area, that would encompass places of particular wildlife, landscape, archaeological, historical and recreational or educational value. This could be managed by a new (and presumably very powerful) Ministry, and would sweep away all previous designations into a single simple system.[33]

A similar, and perhaps more realistic, idea is Tim O'Riordan's notion of three broad "veils" of new classifications, laid down across the existing maelstrom of countryside designations. He proposed this in 1983, as part of the UK's response to the World Conservation Strategy, *Earth's Survival: a Conservation and Development Programme for the UK*. O'Riordan suggested that the landscape should be classified into three categories, Heritage Sites, Conservation Zones and Agricultural and Forestry Landscapes. Heritage Sites would be areas with "special and irreplaceable nature conservation qualities (of wild or semi-natural vegetation), and/or significant natural beauty", and would enjoy "the strongest possible safeguards against undesirable alteration". They should include SSSIs, parts of National Parks and equivalent areas and Heritage Coasts and some AONBs, and might cover 10 per cent of the land surface. There should be a new package of grants and financial compensation to maintain existing incomes from the land, and suitable tax arrangements. The proposed Conservation Zones would cover a larger area (20 per cent of the land surface) and might enclose or link Heritage Areas. Similar financial and tax arrangements would be put in place, to achieve similar conservation objectives, but with a greater emphasis on environmentally benign land use (e.g. traditional farming) and the maintenance of the local economy. Within Agricultural and Forestry Landscapes, these economic activities would predominate, but O'Riordan argued that there was a need for "conservation ethos and practice" in these areas also if the aims of the World Conservation Strategy were to be realised.[34]

These suggestions were not formally taken up, but as we have seen in Chapter Eight, agricultural and conservation policy have begun to fit this pattern as agricultural grants have swung away from support for activities that damage wildlife and landscape (e.g. hedgerow removal) towards support for the creation of landscape features (e.g. hedgerow planting and farm woodlands) and environmentally benign agricultural management.[35] O'Riordan himself now believes that we are close to being able to manage landscapes as a totality. The Ministry of Agriculture has taken over the ESA programme, and will shortly also take the innovative Countryside Stewardship Programme from the Countryside Commission. While the Countryside Commission and English Nature remain separate in England, the integrated organisations for wildlife and landscape conservation in Scotland, Wales and Northern Ireland offer some promise of integrated policies. There are new approaches to planning, for example by the National Rivers Authority, which has adopted the model of the Catchment Management Plan. Perhaps also geographical information systems will allow co-ordination of resource management and cultural and economic requirements in an effective planning of whole landscapes.[36]

Landscape ecology, as discussed in Chapter Eight, offers a number of insights into ways in which landscapes might be planned as a whole.[37] A landscape-ecology approach to planning might work with two overall aims, the first to seek to maintain ecological processes in the landscape, and second to promote a socio-economically viable landscape.[38] From these a series of specific aims might be developed that would seek to safeguard and enhance existing regional and local landscapes, and ensure that their key features are regenerated; to upgrade over-simplified and damaged landscapes and increase their diversity; to create and maintain a framework of rural habitats which form coherent, regionally distinctive and ecologically connected structures, and to design individual landscape units to maximise amenity and ecological benefits.

The potential for integrated planning at a landscape scale may now exist, but the supposed British genius for improvisation will be much needed if integration is to be achieved in the face of entrenched and much less co-ordinated ways of working. So far, the apparent convergence in what different government agencies and ministries are trying to do in the countryside owes more to institutional competition to control the vast amount of money that is poured out by the CAP than to any real integration of policy.

At present the physical and economic isolation of conservation areas is mirrored in the institutional isolation of conservation. The work of conservation organisations, planning authorities and the government departments supporting rural industries (agriculture, forestry) are separate, and links to those ministries responsible for transport, defence or mineral extraction are more remote still. There is a need to integrate policies across government, so that conservation is not simply a sectional interest fighting others, but a coherent part of wider government strategy.

Each sector of the rural economy can be transformed and made more socially productive, and at the same time produce a landscape far more diverse and rich for conservation. Changes in sectors such as forestry are well understood, and clear and persuasive cases have been made for both an extension of the area of forested land and radical changes in the way forestry is planned and carried out. In the early 1990s, RSPB, Wildlife Link and Scottish Wildlife and Countryside Link published papers outlining future forestry strategies for the UK.[39] Both suggested better land-use planning, and particularly more careful avoidance of land better unforested, more planting (particularly of hardwoods) in the lowlands on arable land, and the adaptation of plantation design and management to take account of the interests of recreation and conservation. The keynote of this thinking is sustainability, the argument that an environmentally based forestry policy can be at the same time ecologically sustainable, economically viable and politically acceptable.

However, it is not only rural economies that need to be refashioned to build more space for nature. Conservation measures can begin to build a new rural landscape, but the integration of nature, landscape and economy needs to stretch further than the farm and the village, back down the tentacles of economy and society that bind urban and rural, town and country, together.

Chapter Four described the way in which the rural economy and conservation are locked into the same global processes of economic and cultural change that have transformed the urban and industrial economy of Britain. Close links bind urban consumers to rural change and specific pressures on the countryside. We drive new cars on new roads (even if we do so to "get away from it all" on a nature reserve), we visit out-of-town supermarkets (even if it is to buy "green" products). Chapter Five discussed the links between concern for the countryside and mainstream environmentalism and environmental protest. Problems of conservation cannot be separated from the wider debates about economy and society. The conservation of nature cannot be achieved unless we confront the uncomfortable truths, and start to do at a national scale what we can conceive of doing around protected areas or on lonely farms: integrating nature and economy.

150

Much can be done for nature within the conventional world of wildlife and landscape conservation, and familiar debates about the countryside. These things are important, and I have focused on them in this book. However, in the final analysis, they are not enough. You can have conservation without sustainability up to a point, but only if you can develop tunnel vision, and accept conservation as a technical activity producing limited editions of nature to human design. This book has argued that it is both possible and desirable to embed that technical competence within a deeper cultural and economic context, where nature is able to maintain its own place and pattern around human lives, and where people can engage with it as part of their normal lived experience. That places conservation firmly in the context of debates about sustainability and the "green economy".[40]

The concept of sustainable development was drawn into the international arena to keep the peace between industrialised countries and the Third World in the run-up to the Stockholm Conference in 1972, and developed by the international organisations IUCN, UNEP and WWF in the *World Conservation Strategy* (WCS) in 1980.[41] Thinking about sustainability was developed through the report of the World Commission on Environment and Development, *Our Common Future* (in 1987) and the follow-up to the WCS, *Caring for the Earth* in 1991, before its appearance in *Agenda 21* at the Rio Conference in 1992.[42]

The World Conservation Strategy called for action on three fronts. The first of these was the maintenance of "essential ecological processes", and the ecosystems ("life-support systems") on which they depend. The second was the preservation of genetic diversity, both as an "insurance" (for example against crop diseases), and an investment for the future (e.g. crop breeding). The third objective was "the sustainable development of species and ecosystems". The maintenance of ecological processes demands the rational planning and allocation of land uses. The conservation of genetic diversity demands site-based protection of ecosystems and the timely creation of banks of genetic material.

The elements of the sustainable development ideas in *Our Common Future* extended the ideas in the WCS to combine environmental and development concerns (e.g. poverty and basic needs and the need for continued economic growth to achieve environment–development objectives). *Caring for the Earth* picked up themes from both the preceding documents, but added a critical ethical strand to the sustainability debate. It set out nine "principles to guide the way towards sustainable societies". Its central argument was much the same as that of its predecessors, although more carefully and fully expressed:

> we need development that is both people-centred, concentrating on improving the human condition, and conservation-based, maintaining the variety and productivity of nature. We have to stop talking about conservation and

151

development as if they were in opposition, and recognise that they are essential parts of one indispensable process.[43]

The documents produced at the United Nations Conference on Environment and Development at Rio de Janeiro, the *Rio Declaration* and the much larger *Agenda 21* develop existing thinking about sustainable development. So too does the EC's Fifth Environmental Action Plan, also adopted in 1992, *Towards Sustainability*. This focused on five key economic sectors: agriculture, transport, energy, industry and tourism, although it also emphasised cross-sectoral policy change. In theory all EC policy-making will have an environmental dimension, with particular emphasis on re-use and recycling, secure waste disposal and efficient energy use. The Action Plan should therefore not only embrace both conservation and agricultural policy, but link these coherently through to transportation, industry and social change.[44]

In the UK, attention has been focused on the government's response to the Rio process, four volumes published early in 1994: *Sustainable Development: the UK strategy, Biodiversity: the UK action plan, Climate Change: the UK programme* and *Sustainable Forestry: the UK programme*. In his introduction to the *Sustainable Development* volume, the Secretary of State for the Environment wrote that the UK was "determined to make sustainable development the touchstone of its policies". Some measure of that commitment is the fact that, whereas the 1989 White Paper *This Common Inheritance* was a solo effort by the Department of the Environment (and its ideas were as a result hugely constrained by Whitehall's capacity for evasion), the 1994 volumes were signed by every major minister in government.

The vision of sustainable development to which the British government signed up is cornucopian, that the fruits of economic power and an industrialised way of life can be achieved without environmental cost. The Secretary of State called for policies such that "our economy can grow in a way that does not cheat our children", attempting to float a thoroughly conventional economic strategy on the high tide of popular aspirations about sustainability. This minimalist "business-as-usual" view of sustainability is being challenged in various ways by more radical perspectives. A number of conservation NGOs have proposed much more demanding and hard-hitting agendas for change, for example the Council for the Protection of Rural England's *Sense and Sustainability*, and the Worldwide Fund for Nature's *Changing Direction*.[45] Fundamental questions will have to be addressed. These include the long-term sustainability of economic growth and the equity of present patterns of production and consumption, both between poor and rich today, nationally and globally, and between generations.

There is also increasing interest in sustainability by local authorities (for example in the development of "Local Agenda 21" as a response to the Rio Conference at the local level), and a determination to involve local communities in the debate.[46] Once that happens, grassroots concerns, such as asthma and air quality or nitrates in drinking water, run rapidly up the agenda and start to highlight fundamental flaws in the organisation of economy and society.

Scottish Natural Heritage, alone of the government conservation agencies, is charged with promoting sustainability. The Natural Heritage (Scotland) Act 1991 charges it to "have regard to the desirability of securing that everything done, whether by SNH or any other person, in relation to the natural heritage of Scotland is undertaken in a manner which is sustainable".[47] SNH has developed a set of five guidelines for sustainability. These state that non-renewable resources should be used widely and sparingly, and at a rate that does not restrict the options for future generations; that renewable resources should be used within their capacity for regeneration; that the quality of the natural heritage as a whole should be maintained and improved; that action should be based on the precautionary principle; and that the costs and benefits (both material and non-material) should be distributed equitably. SNH has also co-sponsored a study of Etterick and Lauderdale District in Borders Region to see how these principles work out in practice.[48]

The other conservation agencies have also produced papers on sustainability, and are starting to build their work around the key words and concepts.[49] The agendas of conservation and sustainability are becoming increasingly closely entwined. David Western and colleagues, writing in *Conservation for the Twenty-First Century*, argue,

> the extinction crisis has reached the point where it is no longer possible for thoughtful people to consider the situation manageable by professional wildlife managers and park professionals alone. In order to conserve significant diversity in the earth's biological resources beyond the year 2100, action is needed by society as a whole.[50]

That action must extend well beyond a technocratic concern for conservation science and countryside planning. Bolder initiatives to tie improved landscape and habitat conservation into rural economics are needed, but they must be matched with similar initiatives to link nature into the urban industrial economy, and to the lives of ordinary people.

Bioregionalism and conservation

I argued in Chapter Seven that the awakening of human awareness of nature was the fundamental task of conservation. Integration of conservation into national and local economic life, and to the needs and aspirations of local communities, must embrace this cultural awareness of nature. From this awareness must come a determination to act with respect and consideration, fellow-feeling, not just with other individual creatures but with the wider environment. It is this that can provide the energy to drive both specific changes in land management for conservation and the deeper changes demanded by the challenge of sustainability. Conservation's link to economy and society must begin with the individual, and an individual response. Ian McHarg reminds us "the ecological view requires that we look upon the world, listen and learn".[51] Chris Bonington recognises this in rock-climbing, saying that:

> the ethic of accepting the natural line of the rock, of the climber becoming attuned to and merging with the environment rather than imposing his or her will on it by hammering in bolts, is one that is essential not only for the narrow field of climbing, but in our whole approach to the natural world.[52]

In one of the essays published after his death as *A Sand County Almanac*, Aldo Leopold outlined the notion of a "land ethic", which still resonates within the conservation movement. He suggested an extension of the boundaries of community to the land, including soil, water, plants and animals. A land ethic would make humans members and citizens of the land-community, not its conquerors.[53] Wendell Berry, American farmer, poet and polemical visionary for the environment, captures this same sense when he proposes the idea of "kindly use" of land. He says conservation that involves "understanding, imagining and living-out the possibility of 'kindly' use' " can reconcile both the contradictions within itself, and the lunacies of industrial agriculture. Kindly use demands intimacy with the land: "kindly use depends on intimate knowledge, the most sensitive responsiveness and responsibility".[54]

Intimacy with nature is a challenge for conservation, but also offers new horizons. Neil Evernden writes: "It is an amazing prospect, to dwell in a world in which each element is potentially meaningful, and which must be read like a book, not dismantled like a machine".[55] Writing about hunting-fishing-gathering communities in North America, Richard Nelson argues that "a deep, pervasive, ubiquitous, all-embracing affinity with life" lies at their core. He suggests that conservation practices of the Koyukon Indians (such as voluntary constraints on hunting) are based:

> partly on knowledge of ecological dynamics, partly on moral principles and spiritual beliefs. They emerge from a worldview that strongly opposes unrestrained exploitation of an environment that is not only finite and changeable but also aware. 'The country knows,' an elder told me. 'If you do wrong things to it, the whole country knows. It feels what's happening to it. I guess everything is connected together somehow, under the ground.'[56]

Knowing nature in its turn demands a particular commitment to *place*. North American nature writing is particularly strong in its evocation of place and wild nature, perhaps because of freedom from the bucolic and pastoral elements of so much British nature writing. One of the most remarkable examples of this is Annie Dillard's evocation of the very ordinary landscapes of the eastern USA in *Pilgrim at Tinker Creek*. All the wildness of nature is there, within a small and remarkably domesticated compass. She writes "The creeks — Tinker's and Carvin's — are an active mystery, fresh every minute".[57]

Place is an important theme of the mostly North American movement of Bioregionalism. This was popularised in the mid-1970s by Raymond Dasmann and Peter Berg of the Planet Drum Foundation, and more recently by Kirkpatrick Sale in his book *Dwellers in the Land*. A movement has developed in the USA through meetings such as the Ozark Area Community Congress and the North American Bioregional Congress.[58] Bioregionalists hold that society should be organised according to "bioregions", natural features of the Earth (life forms, species and topography), and they urge "living in place", by which is meant living according to what occurs naturally, rather than through dependence on industrialised production systems. Learning to "live-in-place" demands a process of "reinhabitation":

> becoming native to a place through becoming aware of the particular ecological relationships that operate within and around it. It means understanding activities and evolving social behaviour that will enrich the life of that place, restore its life-supporting systems, and establish an ecologically and socially sustainable pattern of existence within it.[59]

Gary Snyder speaks of the need to:

> learn our natural system, learn our region, to such a degree that we can be sensitive across the centuries and the boundaries of cultures. We should know what the life-cycle of salmon is, or what grows well here, but also become sensitive to what songs you might sing if you thought like a salmon. That's the learning that brings the place visibly into culture.[60]

This is perhaps all rather fanciful. Bioregionalism is much criticised, particularly where its politics begin to veer towards "ecofascism". It is also criticised because of the practical problems of looking for "natural" boundaries for bioregions, particularly in densely settled and long-inhabited land where human boundaries have practical, cultural and even ecological significance. Bioregionalism is easier to conceive in a world of cabins in the woods than it is in the inner city, or in the intensively farmed commuterlands of southern England.

However, there is a core in bioregionalism that is important to thinking about conservation in the UK. People do recognise place, and the challenge of "living in place" is of considerable relevance to us. Donald Alexander, for example, assesses the potential of the bioregional approach in southwest Ontario in Canada, and argues that urban catchments might provide a realistic context within which to develop a bioregional consciousness. The metabolism of the city drives change in the surrounding countryside, and as he points out, "any movement for bioregional sanity has to come to grips with the reality of urban areas".[61] The same approach could work in the UK.

An emphasis on place is central to conservation. I described in Chapter Four how processes of globalisation and associated cultural change have undone our sense of place, bringing about "a new dynamics of re-localisation".[62] The Lancaster Leisure Landscapes study team argues that not only are specific places seen to be threatened by industrialised methods and globalisation, but those processes threaten the sense of place itself.[63] A bioregional conservation must therefore foster a sense of place, of localness. The National Trust has certainly taken this perspective on board, titling the consultation paper arising from the Countryside Policy Review, Linking People and Place.[64] Interestingly, the Leisure Landscapes team suggests that conservation initiatives are attractive to people precisely because they do stress locality, and thereby seem to challenge "the massive processes of physical and economic change and commodification in Britain in the 1980s and early 1990s".

One British response to the erosion of "sense of place" is the idea of "local distinctiveness", provided by the work of the organisation Common Ground.[65] This was founded in 1983 to promote "the importance of our common cultural heritage — common plants and animals, familiar and local places, local distinctiveness and our links with the past", and also "to explore emotional value of these things", by building practical and philosophical links between conservation and the arts.[66] Common Ground's work, promoting the idea of parish maps, organising "Apple Day", campaigning to spread awareness of the importance of old orchards and traditional fruit varieties, or promoting "tree dressing", has certainly caught both newspaper headlines and people's imaginations. Local authorities have latched onto such thinking as a way of promoting identity and conserving "heritage", for example in the provision of grants to re-establish the Worcestershire Black Pear.

Another conservation initiative that attempts to stimulate local initiative and values (albeit from the top down) is Rural Action. This is run by a partnership of governmental and non-governmental organisations (including, interestingly, the Rural Development Commission). It was launched in 4 counties in 1992, and operated in 40 by 1995. It supports community environmental projects, which might be put forward by any group (from youth clubs to the Women's Institute, amenity societies to schools). It organises a free visit from one of some 800 organisations that form a "Rural Action network", and it offers project grants. Since its launch, some 1250 projects have been supported, ranging from local recycling schemes to support for studies or public displays to provide a catalyst for community action for environmental improvement.[67]

156

The County Naturalists Trust movement, which mostly sprang into life in the 1950s and 1960s, is another example of conservation action drawing on such a sense of locality. Concern about declining species and habitats was expressed through the establishment of Naturalists' Trusts in county after county (Chapter Two). Through the 1980s the Wildlife Trusts worked hard to try to build on this base in the "local community". Interestingly, while their influence grew, particularly with local government, their membership and income growth was relatively modest compared to other more centrally organised groups, modelled more closely on business corporations, and using state-of-the-art commercial skills to acquire members and promote their aims.[68] Must conservation abandon its own injunction to "think global, act local" by copying globalised business to organise globally and just *look* local? There are choices ahead if conservation is itself to "live in place".

CHAPTER TEN

Releasing the Wild

Wildness is not "ours" — indeed it is the one thing that can never be ours. It is self-willed,
independent, and indifferent to our dictates and judgements
Neil Evernden[1]

Wilderness and wildness

I have tried to argue the case in the last two chapters that we need to think
more creatively about conservation. We need to understand and work to
sustain the linkages between species and ecosystems that comprise
biodiversity, and underpin the natural beauty of the countryside, and we
need to use techniques of habitat creation and reconstruction innovatively and
on a large scale. In the past fifty years, conservation in the UK has been
restricted in its imagination. All the enormous energy sunk into conservation
efforts has been focused on a small conceptual and spatial canvas, addressing
in particular the many complex problems of protected areas. We need to begin
to envisage conservation anew, working at the scale of the landscape. We
should capture some of the spirit of the Wildlands Project in the USA, a
proposal for creative conservation on a continental scale. This argues, in
unashamedly emotional terms, that we need to "heal" the land, to "allow the
recovery of whole ecosystems and landscapes".[2]

I have spoken in Chapter Eight of the potential for work of this kind. On a small scale, existing measures such as Countryside Stewardship or *Tir Cymen* (or even set-aside if it was managed differently) allow some measure of habitat reconstruction. We can also begin to create specific habitats, on nature reserves or degraded land, or in cities. There is no reason not to see these ideas grow in boldness and extent. Existing measures are already being put together at the scale of the landscape, for example in the Countryside Commission's National Forest. This will not recreate the forest where an apocryphal squirrel could run from Severn to Wash without touching the ground, but there are going to be a great many trees. In theory there will be about 30 million of them, planted on private land (by private landowners) across 500 square kilometres of the English Midlands. The result will be a patchwork, still a fragmented landscape, but with every piece of the mosaic that is improved, the space for nature is increased. It is still early days, but this idea shows boldness and imagination.[3] Other initiatives offer a similar promise. In the fenland of East Anglia, for example, a project to re-create fenland habitats, Wet Fens for the Future, is being developed collaboratively by local authorities and governmental and non-governmental bodies.[4] Conservation needs more such imaginative thinking.

We might also be more bold in restoring extinct species, re-introducing some of the larger animals that have gone extinct, but have inhabited Britain since the end of the last glacial. There were serious proposals to reintroduce the beaver to the UK in the late 1970s. It has been done successfully, and without undue ill effect, in other European countries, for example in the Rhone Valley in France. Beavers are hardly coypu, or mink. If they could be driven to extinction by medieval technology they are hardly like to pose an unassailable threat in the twenty-first century.

But why stop at beaver? Why not reintroduce wild boar, or wolves, lynx or bear, and their prey species?[5] There is experience of large carnivore reintroductions elsewhere in Europe. There have been a number of attempts to reintroduce the lynx to the Alps, of which three (two in Switzerland) have been successful, and there is a strong movement for its introduction to the Apennines, in the Abruzzo National Park, which of course sustains populations of both wolves and bears despite a high intensity of human use.[6] There is a programme to re-establish the wolf in Yellowstone National Park in the USA, with an extensive compensation system for farmers whose livestock are killed. But wolves awaken strong emotions, both in the USA and in Europe, not least for their bad press in fairy tales. Perhaps there is room for wolves in the UK, perhaps not. Certainly, there are other species that are less controversial, and as Tim Nevard says, we are very parochial in our thinking. We need a little boldness in our attempt to rebuild the economy of nature.

I have argued in Chapter Nine that we also need to rebuild a place for people in the conservation landscape. On one hand, economic opportunities for rural communities can be built into plans for creative conservation; on the other it is vital to link conservation to wider issues of economic and social life. We need to begin to build new landscapes — human landscapes, rich and diverse, inhabited and yet wild. If we can work with nature over larger areas, at the scale of the whole landscape, we have the chance to regenerate not only "wild" nature itself, but also communities and economies. Two organisations demonstrate something of what might be done, and the scale of the changes needed if we are to tackle the impoverishment of nature.

Both are concerned with the regeneration of forests in Scotland. "Reforesting Scotland" was established in 1991 to promote awareness of the problem of deforestation in Scotland, to put this in context (for example drawing parallels with rainforest loss), and to promote ecological restoration, sustainable forestry, integrated land use and rural development. They write:

> we have lost beauty and wildness along with an understanding of the true nature of the landscape and the biological potential of our country.... Loss of the climax vegetation and soil degradation together with extractive land uses and the intensification and loss of control of land and its ownership have reduced options and opportunities for many rural communities. Now is the time to reverse that trend.[7]

Reforesting Scotland co-ordinated the Scottish Forestry Charter in 1992, which proposed a major reforestation programme, the formulation of land use and rural development plans, and land reform. They also ran an innovative Study Tour of Western Norway as a way to "think constructively about the future for Scotland's rural areas". The patterns of land-use in Norway, including an extensive and diverse forest, reflected optimum use of biological potential, "in stark contrast to much of Scotland which, with a few exceptions, is a deforested landscape and a land in a state of active degradation".[8]

"Trees for Life" is the Findhorn Foundation's tree programme, and has a specific focus on the regeneration of the Caledonian Pine Forest. The long-term vision is the ecological regeneration of a substantial area in the Highlands. Trees for Life have begun on a small scale, with a deer exclosure in Glen Affric, and are working with the Forestry Commission to plant seedlings raised from local cones. This work parallels that of Scottish Natural Heritage and the RSPB, the latter of which now owns the vast Abernethy Forest in Speyside, and are pushing for measures to expand pine forests in the Beauly Catchment, Strathspey and Deeside.[9] Alan Watson comments: "what is needed now is a quantum leap in scale, to begin the process of ecological restoration over a larger area in the Highlands in a co-ordinated fashion to rescue and regenerate this vital part of Scotland's natural heritage".[10]

These initiatives are not alone. In Snowdonia the idea has been floated of Coed Eryri, Forest of Snowdon. This is a vision of forest regeneration, of alder, ash, oak and rowan in place of Sitka spruce and lodgepole pine and bare hills. But it is also more, a vision of revitalised communities and a new relationship with nature.[11] In Scotland the Green Party produced its *Rural Manifesto for the Highlands* in 1989, where the idea of a restored Great Wood of Caledon was situated firmly within a social and economic vision of community control and land reform. A new forest economy could create prosperity and beauty, "transforming a distantly governed and grant-manipulated society into an economically viable, self-determined and just one".[12] The challenge for conservation is to conceive of the restoration of whole ecosystems and the empowerment of communities together — a conservation that embraces not just the challenges of ecology and landscape, but with them engages also those of political economy.

But where, in this new conservation landscape, is there a place for wildness? We have growing skills to create and restore habitat, and to predict how biodiversity and landscape will evolve under changing incentives and innovations. But these skills are those of the biological and landscape engineer. You could say that this approach to conservation is gardening on a vast scale. It offers the chance for us to craft a new landscape to meet the newly recognised needs of biodiversity, and to create and restore desired features of past landscapes. The importance of this as a theme in conservation is very great, as I have argued in Chapters Five and Six. But gardens, and pastoral landscapes, are by definition places that exclude the wild — indeed that are defined in opposition to it. And yet, as I have suggested in Chapter Seven, wildness is a vital element of both the appeal and the importance of conservation.

Some people have argued that the way to find a place for the wild is to re-create wilderness, by which I mean the abandonment of presently managed land to processes of ecological change on a very large scale. Allowing this to happen on a small scale — in field corners, or nature reserves — is not very controversial, but doing it over large tracts of country certainly is. The idea of *creating* wilderness is, as Norman Henderson comments, almost universally rejected as a policy option.[13] It is seemingly an anathema to many conservationists to consider letting nature go, allowing arable land to revert to scrub and woodland, allowing grazed hills to reforest, although the idea has its persistent advocates.[14] There is also a very real (and proper) sensitivity to the whole idea in the UK, particularly in Scotland, where the appearance of wilderness was achieved by the clearances, and in many cases the forced eviction of communities who would probably now be called "indigenous peoples". The word wilderness unlocks both fierce philosophical debates (see, for example, Chapter Seven), and strong emotions. It is anyway something of a red herring, for as Neil Evernden comments, "at root it is wildness that is at issue, not wilderness".[15] It is the wild for which we need to find room.

Caution about the abandonment of land is partly about the loss of control. Much of our conservation is based very precisely on the idea of control: on the application of science to predict change and technology to steer it. Ecologists have in the past blithely borrowed concepts and words from economics and from engineering to describe nature. From economics have come words and ideas such as "producers", "consumers" and "efficiency", and using them ecologists have interpreted ecological change as working like a modern industrial consumer society. From engineering, ecologists have taken concepts of thermodynamics, equilibrium and control. Nature has been seen as a homeostatic system, maintained by processes of internal feedback, and susceptible to external control.

As I have argued in Chapter Six, in building their ideas on ecology, conservationists have absorbed these kinds of ideas uncritically. They have left conservation with a strong legacy of an instrumentalist view of nature. However, these ideas are being challenged by the ideas of non-equilibrial ecology. Now when ecologists look at nature they see "instability, disorder, a shifting world of upheaval and change that has no direction to it".[16] Many ecologists do not now see nature as a "balanced economy" or a homeostatic system, but nature as system remains a central motif in ecology, and the conservation of nature widely seen to be the science of controlling that system. But what if nature is more ragged than that, more complex and multi-functional, more chaotic? As Johan van Zoest comments: "If nature were a system, man could regard himself as an engineer or doctor. If nature is a game, man should take the position of a player in the game, whose only advantage is that he can think a few steps ahead".[17]

Letting nature run

We will not find the wildness of nature through the planning and creation of habitats and landscapes. These things are valuable, indeed vital to the future, but they are not enough. For the wildness of nature we must have regard to natural *processes* and not simply the static notion of natural *places*.[18] We need, if you like, not only to re-create nature in specific forms and places but also to conserve the capacity of nature to re-create itself. One of the problems with ideas about habitat creation and even species reintroductions is that they are often inherently *static*. It is accepted that such environments need managing, or re-creating, but the assumption is that we can set up a new ecosystem like some great clock, and that when we let it go it will run, except for regular oiling and winding. However, as we saw in Chapter Six, nature is not really like that. It has its own dynamics, and functions outside and independently of our interventions.

The audacious vision of the American "Wildlands Project" is built on the principle that native species should be allowed "to flourish within the ebb and flow of ecological processes, rather than within the constraints of what industrial civilisation is content to leave alone".[19] Its approach is familiar, seeking to develop large protected areas surrounded by buffer zones and linked by corridors. What is new is the scope and scale of its vision. Their aim is to "allow for change". They want to enable ecological and evolutionary processes to continue, and this means making enough space for nature to allow ecological disturbance regimes (fire, or pest outbreaks) to happen, to provide room for ecological responses to climatic change, and to sustain trans-continental migration (both annual migrations, and also long-term fluctuations of range).

New ideas of "non-equilibrium" ecology question intensive conservation management that seeks to control "natural" processes. Thus standard approaches to sand-dune management are based on the control of ecological change and dune stabilisation. This kind of intensive management is ineffective since it also leads to loss of early successional stages in dune ecosystems. Johan van Zoest urges the "management of processes rather than patterns" in sand dunes.[20] He advocates the relaxation of control over the processes active in dunes, a process he calls "gambling with nature". His metaphor of nature as a game, rather than a controllable system, suggests that the best management strategy is not to try and control populations and communities, but to play the game, albeit with a deep (and scientific) understanding of both the ecological rules of play and the role of chance processes.

One of the most important sources of disturbance in ecosystems is the working of physical processes in the landscape, particularly processes of erosion and deposition.[21] The conservation of geomorphological features has always been part of the work of the Nature Conservancy and its successor bodies. In some cases these features are static (indeed, many important sites are relics of former climatic regimes, for example the last glacial period). Other geomorphological features, however, are highly dynamic. Sand dunes are a prime example of this, and as Alfred Steers and Arthur Tansley fully recognised when they wrote about the conservation of Scolt Head or Blakeney Point in the 1940s, you cannot "preserve" such features from natural processes of erosion and deposition. Their very existence depends on such natural change, and disturbance must be seen as part of the "nature" with which conservation is concerned.[22] What you can do, of course, is to protect them, both from direct exploitation (for example quarrying of sand or shingle), and from indirect human-induced change (for example offshore dredging, or starvation of sediment by inappropriate coastal defence works). Conservation then becomes the task of protecting processes of natural change from incompatible changes in economy and technology.[23]

Both the abundance and distribution of organisms and the appearance of the landscape can also be controlled by natural physical processes. This is obviously true of coastal environments (sand dunes, shingle beaches or salt marshes for example), but it is also true elsewhere, from mountain-tops affected by freeze-thaw processes to lowland woodlands affected by storms that cause trees to fall. The link between process and ecology is particularly clear in the case of rivers, where characteristic species and communities are maintained within different parts of the channel and the floodplain by processes of erosion and deposition, and by patterns of over-bank flooding and groundwater recharge. If those processes are changed, ecological changes are likely to follow.

Public authorities with responsibilities for whole river catchments were established under the Land Drainage Act 1930, but in the ensuing sixty years their efforts have been almost exclusively aimed at "hard engineering" solutions to the problems of flooding: changing the course, cross-section and regime of rivers, with concrete banks and flood channels, culverts and various forms of river control. The impact on riparian and aquatic ecosystems, wildlife and landscape has been vast, and negative. This, allied with the problem of pollution, has meant that UK rivers have become steadily less natural and less diverse. There has been a growing awareness of the need for new approaches to river engineering that benefit wildlife, and yet fulfil flood control and other needs. Considerable expertise has been developed, codified for example in *The Rivers and Wildlife Handbook*.[24]

Many conventional engineering "solutions" prove ineffective, On the River Dee, for example, river-bank collapse has been expensively tackled by building toe-armour, rock groynes and using geotextiles. In some stretches this has actually made the problem worse, because they impede drainage from floodplain sediments, and encourage banks to fail. Stretches of rivers lined with willows tend to be stable.[25] The notion of getting engineering effects "for free" is of course very attractive — allowing natural features and processes to do the job of flood storage or bank anchoring, instead of using heavy-duty engineering.

An important step forwards in the conservation of environments linked to rivers is the idea of river restoration, for example in the work of the independent group called the "River Restoration Project".[26] This work involves nothing less than the attempt to re-establish the natural processes and behaviour of rivers. Different meanings can be attached to "restoration", as with habitat re-creation (see Chapter Eight). The River Restoration Project defines "restoration" to mean a complete structural and functional return to the natural "pre-disturbance" state. A lesser target would be "rehabilitation", a partial return to the same pre-disturbance state. Both these are rather sophisticated forms of "habitat enhancement", by which is meant any structural or functional improvement.[27]

The river restoration approach involves the redesign and reconstruction of the physical form of a river such that natural processes of erosion and deposition can begin themselves to recreate aquatic and riparian habitats, and

165

the wildlife and landscape that goes with them. The approach has been extensively used in Germany and Denmark. There is no uniform methodology, because techniques have to be closely adapted to local circumstance. In agricultural areas, streams have often suffered from straightening, loss of riffles and pools, loss of floodplains and riparian wetlands, and loss of riparian and aquatic vegetation. Typical restoration work might include: the establishment of buffer strips along the stream (to cope with agricultural run-off) and measures to establish appropriate vegetation upon them (planting or natural succession with control of grazing); reduction of bank slopes, re-configuration of the channel to make it meander (once it does, it will tend to hold this form, and the variety of bank and channel features it brings); the establishment of riffles and pools (e.g. by putting gravel or stones into the river bed). Other techniques may include widening or deepening of the river channel.[28]

In the UK, most experience to date relates to the natural recovery of stretches of river that have been heavily engineered in the past, although experience of deliberate intervention to promote recovery is growing. One study lists 60 stretches of river where natural channel recovery is taking place, in some of which engineers are helping it along.[29] The River Cherwell in Oxfordshire, for example, was widened in 1967, but has been steadily silting up on the inside of bends ever since. On the River Lyde in Hampshire, a similar process was helped by narrowing the over-widened channel from 9m to 5–6m, leaving a wider channel at a higher level to pass flood flows. Artificially straightened rivers also tend to "recover" naturally. They are unstable, and bends and meanders tend to re-establish themselves. This process too can be helped, for example by installing rocks or some other material as flow-deflectors to create sinuous flow patterns and re-establish natural sequences of riffles and pools. In each case, re-adjustment of channel form can allow re-establishment of in-stream and riparian physical processes, and this can create suitable ecological conditions for plant and animal communities to come back.

The River Restoration Project argues that there is considerable potential for much more extensive restoration of British rivers, and it has funding for work on the River Cole near Swindon and the River Skerne near Darlington, in partnership with the National Rivers Authority. River restoration work needs to extend beyond a "hands-off" approach to the natural recovery of form and process of channels to embrace active restoration of both channels and floodplain habitats (fens, meadows, pools or forests), and the connections between the two. There is a particular need for the restoration of natural hydrological regimes.

River restoration represents more than a novel and cost-effective approach to river management, and more too than a neat way to increase biodiversity and improve landscapes. It is also indicative of a new philosophy of environmental management; one that is more technically informed, and more perceptive, than the one it succeeds, to be sure, but also one which places the human manager in the frame with the natural process. It is, ultimately, the beginnings of an approach to an environmental management partnership with nature. Environmental management does not have to mean total control of nature. No longer is technology expected to provide the weapons of subjugation of natural processes. Instead of trying to subjugate nature, the new philosophy of "soft" engineering attempts to define ways to live round nature, using its own biogeophysical feedback systems.

There are other initiatives that share this new approach to nature. One example is the idea of moving from a policy of trying to prevent the erosion of soft coasts through expensive (and often futile) engineering structures towards a more adaptive policy of "managed retreat".[30] The maintenance of sea-walls is vastly expensive, and will get both more expensive and technically more difficult if sea-levels rise as anticipated. Where it is not feasible to go on protecting low-lying farmland (and under conditions of agricultural surplus) the sea wall might be set back to allow salt-marsh vegetation to re-establish itself on formerly reclaimed land and provide a natural defence against the sea. This would have the conservation benefit of replacing salt marshes lost to sea-level rise. Already there are experiments in Essex, where a sea wall has been breached deliberately to study whether salt-marsh will regenerate in this way.

English Nature and the Countryside Council for Wales are developing an approach to coastal conservation and management based on the idea of sedimentary cells, stretches of coast within which changes do not affect adjacent cells. Their idea is to prepare Coastal Zone Management Plans that take account of the impact of "hard engineering" coastal defences on adjacent areas. Protecting eroding cliffs, for example, may simply starve nearby depositional coasts (shingle spits or beaches for example) of sediment, and make coastal defence in these locations prohibitively expensive. This approach matches that of local authorities in England and Wales, which have formed local groups to promote integrated coastal management.[31] A strategic approach is required that takes account of the natural processes of erosion and deposition, and the way these vary over time (seasonally and between years), both to make sea defence affordable and also to maintain the diversity of coastal habitats and landscapes. On the North Norfolk coast, for example, the RSPB reserve at Titchwell contains a mix of freshwater, saline and brackish habitats on farmland abandoned following a breach of the sea wall in 1953. Breaches of sea-walls are a real problem of this coast (the shingle ridge at Cley was breached in 1978 and 1993, for example), and research suggests that there is considerable potential for cost-effective creative conservation at a number of points along the coast.[32]

Another ingenious idea is the use of "biomanipulation" in freshwater aquatic management. Such techniques have been used in some of the Norfolk Broads to restore clear water conditions. The Broads have long suffered from excessive levels of phosphates in the water due to pollution from sewage and agricultural activity. This has resulted in poor water quality, loss of characteristic species and algal blooms, and serious impacts on both the wildlife conservation status and recreational value of the Broads. Measures were taken to reduce pollution at source, but too much phosphate was already locked into the system (particularly in the sediments) to allow the water bodies to recover. The first attempts at tackling the problem directly involved the isolation of selected broads from river water (and further pollution) and the removal of sediments excessively rich in phosphate by pumping. This brought only modest improvement, and algal blooms persisted. Biomanipulation was then attempted, to reduce predation of the zooplankton that themselves fed on algae. Fish that consumed zooplankton (particularly roach fingerlings) were removed from the isolated broads, increasing zooplankton numbers and reducing phytoplankton. Clear water returned.[33] Clearly restoration is possible in these degraded ecosystems, given sufficiently detailed ecological knowledge, detailed work and careful monitoring.

Methods such as soft engineering and biomanipulation, and the new approaches to planning coastal management and river restoration all involve a specific concern for natural physical and biological processes. It is this which is particularly important for conservation. It can bring us three things. First, it suggests how to build an effective approach to conservation for the whole landscape. We currently organise conservation within administrative boundaries — counties, regions and countries — and not natural ones. Conservation must become much more responsive to natural boundaries in its planning, both in the voluntary and the statutory sector. The various "mapping" projects discussed in Chapter Eight (the Countryside Commission's "Countryside Character" project, Scottish Natural Heritage's "Biogeographic Zones" and English Nature's "Natural Areas") go some way towards achieving this, but they are static rather than dynamic.

We need to build conservation much more closely around the spatial frameworks of natural process within the landscape, and make our "natural unit" thinking embrace the *dynamics* of nature as well as its static biogeography. English Nature's organisation of its coastal conservation work in terms of sedimentary cells is one such approach. Another is the use of the river basin in conservation planning, for example in the catchment-based approaches of the National Rivers Authority and some Wildlife Trusts. Such approaches could be adopted much more widely. I wonder, for example, what would happen if the Wildlife Trusts built all their planning on river catchments rather than the artificial (and fluctuating) boundaries of counties. Such an approach might be rather awkward in marketing terms, but as I have argued in Chapter Nine (reflecting thinking about bioregionalism) that it might awaken much wider awareness of nature among ordinary people. My point here is that such an awareness of the natural dynamics of nature might both generate exciting new thinking about conservation, and more effective action.

The second thing that these new approaches do is to provide further evidence that conservation must move outside the straitjacket of protected areas. Despite the degradation of rivers in the UK, it has not proved easy to fit the remaining stretches of relatively undeveloped rivers into the mould of our protected area system. Of the 6628 river systems in Scotland, only 16 have been notified as SSSIs because of their riverine interest specifically.[34] The situation is slowly being improved, and the statutory conservation agencies are starting to focus attention on river SSSIs, but to date rivers have been badly served by our conservation system. So too have other environments (like the coast) whose characteristics are created by dynamic natural processes. We cannot conserve such places without conserving the large-scale physical and biological systems that influence them. We certainly cannot do it cheaply (any more than we can cheaply maintain eroding sea walls), and in many instances we will not be able to do it at all. If nothing else, the vast scale of the ocean–atmosphere system that we have influenced through CO_2 emissions reminds us that we have to build conservation on a firm understanding of natural processes at the largest of scales.

The third thing that these new approaches can teach us is the need to work with nature in an interactive way, and not to stand outside it like some remote technocratic ecological engineer. We might understand enough about the way natural systems function to make a good job of undoing the constraints our industrialism have placed upon it (in the case of rivers for example we apparently do know enough to replace concrete banks with gravel and vegetation), but we still do not know very much. It would be the utmost arrogance to think that we could replace natural processes. The critical point about river and stream rehabilitation is that it works with and not against natural stream processes: "artificial shaping may start the rehabilitation process, but it can never be a substitute".[35]

The same approach must permeate the whole field of habitat creation and re-creation. What is being created is not a series of finished products, like stamps in an album, but a series of places where nature and natural processes can work. If you like, what this kind of "conservation" is doing is facilitating nature, and not making it — being creative on behalf of nature, not trying to build nature in particular pre-planned forms as if we were budding engineers with a spanner and a kit of parts. The capacity of rivers, for example, to make and maintain their own channels, and their own ecosystems, is a vital feature of their naturalness. This, as much as the fact that they may or may not contain rare species or characteristic habitats, or fit classic images of landscape beauty, is something that conservation needs to take very seriously indeed. Whether we want to paddle, or photograph dragonflies or catch pike (or simply to hear water chuckle as it moves: a rare pleasure in my part of the world), we need clean and free-running rivers. To do this, and to apply the approach more widely, we need a new and more dynamic approach to the conservation of nature.

We must allow nature space to be itself, to function, to build and tear down. This is necessary for straightforward technical reasons, because otherwise our clever conservation plans may be thwarted, but it is also necessary because this is where the wildness of nature finds its place in our conservation. Nature *acts* outside our plans. We must be prepared to allow nature to act. Our conservation must recognise that it does so, and not seek to corral it within the bounds of either our predictive conservation science, or within the frameworks of our bureaucratic or business-management models.

Conservation in the UK has long sought to maintain diverse fragments of past patterns of organisms and associations of organisms and landscapes. We try to stop the clock of ecological change, to freeze patterns of ecological and landscape evolution. But even as we do so, nature is *re*created (both ecologically and culturally) around us. Nature takes new forms, new patterns, as "naturally" as it assumed the patterns that we wanted to conserve. These too have value, and as we interact with them that value will be overlain and enhanced by cultural links and associations. Conservation must include an element of partnership with nature as well as attempts to define, control, manipulate and reproduce it. Our conservation must make space for nature's otherness alongside all the activities aimed at reaching human goals set in terms of habitat loss, biodiversity or landscape beauty.

Future conservation: some principles

I have tried to argue in this book that we need a new approach to conservation. For years now, debates about conservation, both within and outside the conservation movement, have been specific, detailed and intense. The fury of those debates has forced us too deep in our bunkers to be able to see the horizon clearly. The conservation movement is literally entrenched in its thinking, and we need to sit up, stop the fireworks, and think again about the things that make conservation important, and what this "nature" is that we fight so hard to sustain.

So, what principles for conservation action can be drawn from the kaleidoscope of words and ideas about conservation discussed in this book? I think that four key aims can be identified. The first is that we need *to maintain*

170

the diversity of landscapes and ecosystems. Existing protected areas will be vital to achieving this, and the shortcomings of the protected area system will need to be tackled. It is probably too complicated, with too many overlapping designations, and certainly the measures actually to protect protected areas from destruction are inadequate in a number of ways. There are also important habitats and landscapes left inadequately protected, notably in marine environments. The problems facing the protected area system need to be addressed effectively and quickly, particularly if the EC Habitats Directive is to have its intended effect. Management of protected areas also needs to be improved, as do the provisions for linking protected areas with local communities and economies.

However, the approach of designating protected areas cannot stand alone. We need to build on existing protected areas to create a much more extensive and effective programme of conservation. This must embrace the needs of nature outside special places, and start to create and restore habitats and landscapes across the whole countryside, and bring appropriate management regimes into play. We can only maintain the diversity of landscapes and ecosystems by being creative, imaginative and opportunistic. We must use the oddball bundle of measures available to support habitat creation and restoration, while arguing for more sweeping and coherent measures. We must create a landscape within which both the particular features of protected areas and more general aspects of habitats and landscapes are sustained. We must disdain no opportunity to enhance the diversity and beauty of the countryside, while planning for and dreaming about larger and more integrated opportunities to create landscapes that are at the same time inhabited, natural and wild.

The second principle is that we should *build room for nature into economic life.* Human influence on other species is now so pervasive that only those aspects of nature that can endure the assaults of our changing economy will endure. We must not allow our concern for nature to be confined to protected areas, nor believe that the expansion of those protected areas over more and more land (the "spreading green slime" of conservation designations bemoaned by local councillors in Orkney in the 1980s) is the same as admitting nature to the *entire* landscape. Nature is everywhere, and nature conservation is therefore something that must be pursued everywhere and must be built into the weave of human life. You can only go so far in imagining the future of conservation without coming up against the constraint of current patterns of production and consumption. If we are to be serious about conservation, we will have to widen our debate to consider changes in the way economy and society are organised. The shape of future nature will be determined by the choices we make about living standards, economic growth and economic organisation. The wildlife and landscapes that my children will be able to enjoy as adults will be limited to those for which we are willing to find space.

The need to be creative in our approach to conservation must therefore extend to these links between nature and economy. We should plan to ensure that new economic activities create new landscapes and habitats of value, in both special places and ordinary ones. This will demand work locally, with rural communities and in cities and suburbs, to build sustainable local economies, but it will also demand work nationally and internationally (most obviously within Europe) to create larger-scale economies where there is space for nature. Our economy will generate new ecological patterns, new landscapes, and we must work to direct the forces of change in ways that sustain both nature and ourselves.

The third principle is an extension of the second, that we should *build connections between people and nature*. Conservation must be woven into everyday life. It is people that create the cultural values of nature, and it is through this contact that we come to understand other species and ecosystems, and the place of people in the landscape. Particular features in the countryside (Ancient Woodlands, chalk grasslands, Lakeland Fells or machair) might now be valued as national treasures, but they were created by ordinary economic activities. Those activities have changed, yet we believe the things themselves have a value that arises from both their diversity and from what they tell us about our past. By conserving them as objects, and locking that conservation into rhetoric about national heritage, biodiversity or natural beauty, we distance ourselves from them. We need to re-establish the links between people and nature.

As I have argued in Chapters Three and Seven, the relations between people and the countryside in the UK have changed beyond all recognition, even in the half century since our conservation institutions were founded at the end of the Second World War. Britain is urbanised culturally as never before, and people have become increasingly distanced from nature. It is a vital task for conservation to bring nature back to people. This needs to be done physically through initiatives to put plants and animals back into urban environments and by making buildings and townscapes that place people in contact with natural processes and forms, and also by finding ways for people to make contact with living creatures and diverse landscapes. There is a saying in the field of Third World development, that if you give someone a fish they have food for a day, if you teach them to fish they have food for life. Too often, nature is offered to people as fish — a product, an experience. We need to find ways to teach people to fish for themselves in the natural world.

What we see and experience of nature will affect what we feel about it, and the way in which we engage with it. Unless people feel the value of nature, it will be treated as a mere commodity, to be bought and sold, built and done away with as profit dictates. If we only notice nature when it is packaged and dramatised in full colour on the TV, or when we spray something on it because it is spoiling our perfect vegetables, we will cease to see conservation

172

as any more than one among a range of commodities that can be purchased by the wealthy to enhance their leisure time.

One problem of our past attempts to set aside protected areas is that it has created a specialised "conservation landscape". This has been planned, tended and paid for in almost complete isolation from the remaining "working landscape" of production. We seem to have accepted uncritically the notion that nature is no longer (as it was in the past) something whose patterns in particular places were created locally by the daily work of ordinary people. It is refashioned in response to wide-ranging social and economic changes, and in response to the plans of increasingly large and remote organisations. Conservation organisations have changed and restructured to acquire influence in this new global corporate world, which obviously opens up exciting possibilities. Yet there are also risks, even if these efforts are successful. Nature could so easily be reduced to something consumed in special places, with protected areas a rather specialised version of the "Astroturf landscape" of the golf-course, where nature is controlled and made to yield predictable products; somewhere to use binoculars and wear waxed cotton, and leave the golf clubs and loud trousers in the car.

The final principle that I would suggest is therefore that we need to *allow nature to function, and create conditions for it to do so.* As well as being far more inventive in looking for ways to build diverse and valuable landscapes and ecosystems, and looking for ways to integrate conservation with both economic and cultural life, we have to learn to allow natural systems to function *as* natural systems. This is, in a sense, the closing of the circle of my argument. It is in the capacity of nature to function outside human planning that its vital wildness is found. It is this wildness which provides the dynamic of the connection between people and nature, that drives concern for conservation, and which provides the political impetus to place nature high on the agenda of public policy. The natural functioning of nature is also, as I have argued in this chapter, increasingly obviously an essential element in conservation planning.

These four principles are very simple. They represent developments of past practice, and are already visible in some conservation action. Nonetheless, the challenge of putting them into practice is considerable. We have to look beyond protected areas to bring conservation into the whole landscape, which will demand new skills, new ideas, new "partners", to use the current jargon. We have to link conservation to economic life, taking seriously the challenge that this will offer to consumerist lifestyles. We have to confirm and establish cultural links between people and nature, which means taking people seriously in the places where they live and work and go to school, and enabling them to engage with "nature" even in its most restricted and plainest forms, particularly in cities. We also have to take seriously the importance of the wildness and "otherness" of nature, which will demand on the one hand being courageous in embracing new scientific ideas, and on the other being willing to explore the cultural dimensions of nature. Finally, we have to work to create places whose natural value will be clear both to ourselves and to future generations, and where there are opportunities for nature to create its own futures.

A place for the wild

Cambridge used to lie on the edge of an enormous wetland, that stretched as far as the Wash. No more, of course. The fens had a lively economy, based on fish and gathered products, salt, grazing and arable farming. In the seventeenth century it was drained by enterprising capitalists, "adventurers". Two enormous artificial channels were built across it, from Earith to Denver, the Old Bedford River and the Hundred Foot Drain, by the Dutch engineer Vermuyden under the patronage of the Duke of Bedford. Between these two channels lie the Ouse Washes, an area of seasonally-flooded land that acts as a vast flood-storage reservoir to protect surrounding land from winter inundation. That land is drained, and highly productive, but sinks further every year as pumps suck it dry, peat soils oxidise and the silts blow away.

Very few fragments of wet fen survive, and these that do are all owned by conservation bodies and are declared National Nature Reserves.[36] Wicken, Woodwalton and Holme Fens have all been reserves since the early part of the century, slowly drying out and losing open fen habitats to woodland. Holme Fen NNR is now a mature woodland of silver birch, but was once part of Whittlesey Mere, one of the last pieces of the East Anglian Fens to be drained. In recent years, enormous management effort has been put into stopping vegetation succession. The boundary ditches of Wicken and Woodwalton Fens reserves have been waterproofed with clay or butyl rubber so that they can be used to store floodwater pumped off surrounding farmland, thus keeping the fen wet and the farmland dry. At Wicken a lake has been dug in Adventurers Fen, which was reclaimed for arable in the Second World War, in the hope that natural fenland succession can begin again, and the Nature Conservancy Council has done the same at Woodwalton and Holme Fens. The new collaborative project, Wet Fens for the Future, is proposing to promote similar activities on a larger scale.[37]

The established fenland nature reserves reflect the history of conservation in microcosm. They are the last fragments of a formerly much more extensive ecosystem. Economic changes that seemed at the time (except to the local fensmen) perfectly normal and appropriate destroyed the vast ecosystem of which they were once part, and very late in the day their value was recognised by early conservationists. They were acquired for conservation, "saved" from destruction, but of course deteriorated rapidly because of both transboundary

174

influences (the drainage around them) and because of natural succession. Costly cycles of management have been prescribed to hold back succession, and major programmes instituted to keep them wet, and as new problems have emerged (for example nutrient enrichment from agricultural runoff), they have been identified, and addressed. Their isolation and limited size have been tackled through imaginative habitat creation schemes. The attractiveness to people of the nature they contain has been recognised (at least at Wicken) by encouraging access, and by building a long boardwalk suitable for visitors of all abilities.

Fragments of nature like Wicken Fen, precious and isolated, tightly and imaginatively managed and much visited, represent one part of the conservation of nature. It is the longest established, and the most familiar. Outside these reserves lies the rest of the fens. Here the old wetland plants and animals are mostly long gone, and with them the landscape of water, scrub and woodland. Nonetheless, what is left is remarkable in its own right, a wonderfully stark landscape of straight lines and vast skies. At its heart lie the Washes. They are wholly human-made, and moreover created by the Duke of Bedford's engineers to serve his hunger for profit by better drainage of the wild wetland that preceded them.

However, the Washes are no blot on the conservation landscape, for they provide an astonishing resource for conservation. In summer the land is grazed, and ruff and black-tailed godwit breed; in winter they flood from bank to bank, and thousands of wildfowl flight in from the Arctic. The by-product of the adventurers' arrogant engineers is the creation of a new wetland landscape on a large scale. It does not in any sense replace what was lost by their draining, but it is a very real resource for conservation in the modern landscape.

Land in the Washes is mostly divided into small parcels. Many have been bought by the Wildlife Trust, the RSPB and the Wildfowl and Wetlands Trust, who all have extensive reserves. On winter weekends I often go with my children to the Wildfowl Trust visitor centre at Welney, on the eastern side of the washes. Here there is a vast hide overlooking the floods. Right in front of it the Trust has dug a huge shallow lagoon, where large numbers of waterfowl congregate. This is an artificial habitat par excellence: a wetland within a wetland, both human-made. What makes it more bizarre is that part of the hide has a glass front, so that members of the Trust can sit in comfort to watch the birds as they fly in to feed on old potatoes and split grain, and (even worse) the lake is floodlit on winter evenings. The Trust advertises the chance to see swans by floodlight, and people come in from all over England to see them.

It may be bizarre, but it is magnificent. On a cold afternoon last November there were six hundred whooper swans, 400 Bewick swans, a thousand wigeon and countless other ducks on the flooded washes. What is more, they can be seen, and identified and pointed at and enjoyed. It is an amazing place to take children: an opportunity to explain something of the magic of other species, and the wild symmetry of their migration. The artificiality of the lake, the hide and the floodlights intersect incongruously but with remarkable effectiveness with the natural rhythms of migration, and the needs of the birds for a place to feed and roost.

The Washes of the Ouse and the Nene offer a new opportunity for nature, a station on the vast international flyways that stretch from the Arctic to the Cape of Good Hope. The swans that come in winter fly north to the tundra to breed in the brief Arctic summer, while the swallow that nests in the hides in summer is gone before they arrive, south over Europe and the Mediterranean to the African savanna. Each time I visit the Washes, I am amazed at the scale of the movements that these birds make, and the chance that brings them within the range of my home. I am struck too by the extent of the Washes themselves, a vast feature slashed across the landscape of East Anglia. Each time the swans return, it is a reminder that it is possible to turn even forces of destruction to benefit. We can rebuild a landscape where nature can flourish, we can create a world of diversity and beauty, a land wild yet peopled. We have remarkable resources and opportunities. All we need is the imagination, and the determination, to make a place for the wild.

Postscript

Progress in conservation?

Since *Future Nature* was published in 1995, debate about the future of the countryside and of conservation in the UK has continued to be both live-ly and imaginative. The broader context for these debates has also changed, both in ways that could be foreseen (for example, the decline of public subsidy for agriculture, and climate change), and in ways that could not (for example, the succession of crises to hit the agricultural industry). A new complexion of economic forces is driving change in the country-side, and new ideas in conservation are broadening the role conservation is being asked to play in negotiating the transition from past to future.[1]

There have been several changes in the government's management of conservation in the UK. The English countryside conservation agency (the Countryside Commission) was merged with the Rural Development Commission to form the Countryside Agency.[2] This was then placed, with the English wildlife conservation agency (English Nature), under the new Department of Food, the Environment and Rural Affairs (DEFRA).[3] The national conservation bodies Scottish Natural Heritage (SNH), the Countryside Council for Wales (CCW) and English Nature survived the ten-year anniversary of their creation unchanged, at least in structure.[4] Devolution, in the creation of the Scottish Parliament and the Welsh Assembly Government, has had a significant impact on conservation across the UK. In Wales and Scotland, conservation agencies have grown much closer to politicians. The economic and employment agenda has become much more important, and there is greater recognition of the cul-tural dimensions of rural landscape and conservation. Non-governmental organisations (NGOs) have major offices in Cardiff and Edinburgh to engage with the new political leaders. Distinctive national styles and strategies in conservation are starting to emerge.

Nationally, the condition of conservation sites has continued to deteriorate, despite the armoury of designations available and the care being focused on the collection of data — indeed, arguably, some of the recorded damage has come to light as a result of more careful monitoring rather than being due to new or more destructive land management. Nonetheless, the conservation estate has certainly not prospered since 1995. In England in 2001–2002, for example, only 57 per cent of the 4102 Sites of Special Scientific Interest (SSSIs) were in good condition, and over 18 per cent were declining in quality.[5] Several had been partly destroyed. The depressing story of habitat loss presented in the first edition of *Future Nature*, only too familiar to conservationists, is still current. There are also worries that momentum has been lost in declaring National Nature Reserves (NNRs), or in declaring reserves that are not already being managed by organisations such as the National Trust or Wildlife Trusts. Norman Moore argues that expenditure on NNR acquisition and management during the 1990s was only half that in the 1970s, and points out that state ownership of reserves emphasises not only the importance of the sites themselves but also the importance of conservation in the life of the nation.[6]

The marine environment has continued to be missed by conservation policy. Peter Marren points out that conservation interest tended to stop at the high water mark until about 1987, when the Nature Conservancy Council (NCC) began to survey shallow marine habitats. The resulting Marine Nature Conservation Review has been used to identify candidate Special Areas for Conservation (SACs) under the European Union (EU) Habitats and Species Directive, and the science effort has spawned an array of Habitat and Species Action Plans. Little progress was made with Marine Nature Reserves (MNRs): Lundy was declared in 1986, Skomer in 1990 and Strangford Lough in 1995. Plans to designate Loch Sween in Argyll were abandoned in the face of entrenched opposition from fish catchers and farmers.[7] Meanwhile, the evidence of environmental degradation in the seas around the British isles is legion: over-fishing and the collapse of finfish populations; pollution from farmed salmon; shellfish poisoning due to algal blooms; the death of dolphins and porpoises in fishing nets; repeated oil pollution incidents; and the release of radio-nuclides in the Irish Sea. The Wildlife Trusts run an energetic Marine Campaign, pushing the government for an integrated marine policy that is ecosystem based.[8] Although there is more awareness of the importance of the UK's marine ecosystems than there was 20 years ago, and plenty of people out diving to look at them, there is little effective progress to date on their conservation.

A number of terrestrial species have experienced a significant downturn in fortune; inevitably, most publicly debated is the case of birds.[9] The decline in numbers of common species, such as the house sparrow and song thrush, as well as farmland species, such as the skylark, linnet and corn bunting, has caught public attention. In 1999, the government published a White Paper *A Better Quality of Life* that included among its 15 "headline" indicators an index of the populations of 100 breeding bird species. Woodland species have declined by 22 per cent on average since the mid-1970s, and farmland birds by a grim 46 per cent. The jury is still out on the causes of these declines, with widespread popular suspicion of slug killer and garden pesticides, and the depredations of sparrowhawks and magpies (the new bugbears of suburban bird-lovers). There is debate about the future significance for biodiversity of genetically-modified crops. Broadly, however, the story is clear: the enmity of intensive agriculture for birds and their biodiverse prey is obvious; the broader demands of human society on other species and their habitats remain insatiable. In birds, UK conservation has acquired a highly public barometer of at least one dimension of human demands on nature.

It is not, of course, all bad news. Choughs bred in Cornwall for the first time for 50 years in 2002, and ospreys bred in the Lake District. Welsh red kites have at last begun to expand their range during the previous 20 years.[10] Many of the various efforts at "species recovery" have also borne some fruit, despite the scepticism of some observers (including me). The 1994 government report *Biodiversity: the UK Action Plan*, which grew out of the Rio Conference, committed government to produce costed action plans for key habitats and species (unfelicitously known, to the acronym-lovers of inner conservation circles, as Habitat Action Plans — HAPs — and Species Action Plans — SAPs). These have been produced, through the work of numerous governmental and non-governmental partners, such as Plantlife, whose Back from the Brink programme was launched as early as 1991. There is also a good coverage of "Local Biodiversity Action Plans" (LBAPs in the trade). Information on species distributions is now becoming available on the web.[11] Views of the usefulness of this whole enterprise vary quite widely.[12]

Without doubt, the Biodiversity Action Plan (BAP) process has helped to draw different organisations together, and has encouraged a focus on the needs of critically endangered species.[13] By 2000, 436 species action plans had been prepared, although, by 2001, not a single target had been reached.[14] The ecological requirements of species such as black grouse or stone curlew, the red squirrel or sand lizard, Deptford pink or narrow-leaved helleborine are now much better known. Managers of protected habitats can, in theory, at least feed this new science into their plans or use this new knowledge to drive land acquisition or restoration programmes (as, for example, in the case of the bittern). The BAP methodology has also, arguably, been good for conservation's public image — a clever move to re-invent what might have seemed an old-fashioned concern for obscure species in the language of business planning and enterprise: conservation as understood at business school. Certainly, biodiversity action planning was used effectively by conservation to bid for money in the new enterprise culture of government of the 1990s. Perhaps this alone is sufficient justification: that it provided a new and urgently needed "big idea" in difficult times.

At the same time, it can be argued that BAPs have soaked up a great deal of energy and money, and produced a blizzard of paper, while confusing and distracting the conservation community. Peter Marren comments that "the exponential growth of Species Action Plans has produced a mass of detail, but lacks any real ethical and philosophical foundations, and ignores common sense".[15] He suggests that the BAP has become a monster, sucking in resources to employ "an army of head-scratching indoor technicians": maybe the real success of the BAP is as a job creation scheme. James Robertson complains:

> *What amazes me is that conservationists think that all you need is yet more regulation, dictat and bureaucracy. Want to save the marsh fritillary? Write an action plan, then write an implementation plan, then write a policy in a Local Plan. Yet, no one wants to help solve the real problems of how to graze an overgrown "rough" divided between three owners in a corner of Anglesey.*[16]

Arguably, it is still the multiple decisions of landowners (whether conservation organisations or not) that really determine whether wildlife can survive or even prosper. BAPs are necessarily abstracted from this world of practical decision-making.

There is one sense, though, in which the most exciting shifts in conservation relate precisely to this, to the rising number of people showing an interest in nature. Membership of conservation organisations has continued to rise in the face of sluggish or declining growth in more overtly campaigning environmental organisations. Thus, the Wildlife Trusts had a combined membership of 225,000 in 1995, which rose to 343,000 in 2000 and 413,434 in 2002. The Wildlife and Wetlands Trust membership rose above 100,000, and the Woodland Trust above 115,000 in 2002. The Royal Society for the Protection of Birds (RSPB) has more than one million members, the National Trust more than three million.[17] Furthermore, although many people are armchair naturalists, the rise of "citizen's science" has persuaded many people, particularly children, to look directly at nature as they count, measure and watch it. The RSPB's Big Garden Birdwatch, which has run for 25 years, had 262,000 participants in 2002, and the 2002 Homes for Birds survey with BBC Radio 4 evoked 10,000 responses, over half on the internet.[18]

Wild Scotland?

Scotland has seen a number of distinct changes, most notably the creation of the first National Parks. The National Parks Scotland Act 2000 allowed their establishment, a mere 55 years after they were first proposed, by the Ramsay Committee.[19] Scotland was left out of the post-war provisions for National Parks, and when the intention to declare the first, Loch Lomond and the Trossachs National Park, was announced in 1997, it sparked renewed debate about the form such designations should take.[20] Arguably, having managed so long without National Parks, Scotland had developed alternative (and possibly more democratic) ways to balance demands on critical mountain areas. The Loch Lomond and the Trossachs National Park was finally opened in July 2002, covering 1800 square kilometres. It was soon followed by a second. The Scottish Parliament passed the designation order for the Cairngorms National Park in 12 December 2002, with a view to establishment by March 2003 and operation by September. The long-standing arguments about the Cairngorm Plateau, and particularly the level of tourist and ski development that is appropriate at altitude, made debate about this park sharp and lively. The long-opposed funicular railway on Cairngorm was opened in December 2001. The exclusion of the Drumochter Hills and part of central Deeside (in fact, all of the land in Perth and Kinross) from the park ensure continued controversy.[21]

The Scottish hills provide a complex battleground of conflicting ideologies. Mountaineers see them as wilderness; landowners are interested in deer stalking and estate revenues; local communities emphasise the need for employment; and conservationists wish to maximise the biodiversity of their ecosystems. The challenge of representing all of these interests within a coherent policy is considerable. The debate over the whole idea of "wilderness" in the Scottish context (where memories of the Highland Clearances are sharp) is challenging for conservation and is potentially highly divisive.[22] The continuing dominance of the large estates, and the existence of absentee landlords, adds a further dimension.[23] The debate over the number of red deer in Scotland, and the need to cull them to reduce overgrazing, demonstrates something of the complexity of the land and conservation issue in the Highlands.[24]

The obverse of the desire of conservationists to reduce deer is their enthusiasm for re-planting "native" woodland, particularly with local Scots pine. Considerable progress has been made by organisations such as Trees for Life, the John Muir Trust, the National Trust for Scotland,

181

Scottish Natural Heritage and the Forest Enterprise.[25] The enthusiasm with this reforestation of Scotland, about which I wrote in the first edition of *Future Nature*, is now becoming matched by concern at what James Fenton describes as "the single-minded obsession with trees that is stalking the country".[26] The proposal by Scottish Natural Heritage to cull deer on the island of Rum to allow for the re-establishment of forest on its many bogs is just one example of battle lines being drawn, with debate about both palaeo-environmental evidence, scientific interest and the future of local communities.[27]

Farming nature

Agriculture has been hit by a succession of crises since the mid-1990s. The first was the outbreak of bovine spongiform encephalopathy (BSE), discovered in December 1986. BSE is a chronic disorder of the nervous system in cattle and has been associated with a similar transmissible disease in humans, Creutzfeld-Jacob Disease (CJD).[28] The outbreak is now understood to be the result of feeding animal offal containing nerve and brain tissue to cattle, a practice that was itself the fruit of economic restructuring in the livestock meat commodity chain. It was associated with the near collapse of consumer confidence in the UK and restrictions in export markets.[29] Just under 1000 cases of BSE were confirmed in the UK in 2002, and 11 deaths from new-variant CJD.[30]

The outbreak of foot and mouth disease in the UK in 2001 was both more public and more immediately catastrophic.[31] The ultimate source of the disease is still unknown, but its origin in a pig unit in North-East England is established. From here it spread rapidly, reflecting the scale and speed of livestock movements prior to slaughter (a marketing pattern that appears to have caught the Ministry of Agriculture and its vets completely by surprise). The virus spread through wind-borne contagion to sheep on a neighbouring holding, and then through the movement of diseased animals (both pigs to holdings in Essex and Kent and sheep), people and vehicles, widely throughout England, Wales and the southern counties of Scotland. Over four million animals were culled, with up to half a million a week at the peak, with slaughter and disposal undertaken by the army. The media offered gruelling pictures of distraught farm families and vast pyres of slaughtered animals, and were quick to level accusations of ignorance, injustice, corruption and bad faith on all parties, particularly on the government.[32]

The smallholder livestock sector was devastated, and so, too, was the rural tourist economy. The damage, in this case, was done by the bizarre closure of the countryside to visitors. The impacts were devastating and unsettling to established ideas about the countryside. I drove across Dartmoor at mid-morning just after Easter 2001, the road eerily deserted, police tape across any parking spot, and the residual smell of burning on the air. This landscape was more than an agricultural factory floor, temporarily emptied of visitors: the wheels had come off the rural economy, and suddenly the complexity of the linkages between people and landscape was revealed. I suggested in 1995 that there was a chance for our imaginations and our policy to "link nature, landscape and lives" (see Chapter 9). The opportunity and the need for such a holistic vision was reinforced by the foot and mouth epidemic. The integration of social development, and the conservation of nature and landscape, of agriculture and recreation, of town and country, was not just a cosy vision, but a vital and urgent need

As John Bowers pointed out, with his customary acerbity, the foot and mouth outbreak proved what conservationists had long known, that the rural economy was not dependent on agriculture. He argued that "taking land out of farming will not devastate rural England, nor undermine the base of tourism — it might even enhance it. It will, of course, change the landscape and the ecology".[33] The crisis opened disturbing vistas for conservationists, which challenged the holistic thinking that had developed about the integration of biodiversity, society, economy and landscape. Should conservationists fight to maintain farming in marginal areas of the UK, or accept structural change and seek to create a new conservation landscape? How should we balance the economic interests of small hill farmers, and the landscape, historical and ecological values of the land that they have created over time, against the possibilities of large-scale restoration of wildlife habitats, such as upland scrub and woodland — free at last from the damaging effects of overgrazing from subsidised sheep flocks?[34] Should conservationists lament the loss of traditional sheep flocks in the Forest of Dean or the Cumbrian fells, or welcome the new ecological possibilities and new landscapes, and think creatively about the opportunities for new policy frameworks for agriculture, conservation and rural economies?[35] Could conservationists deliver on their claim of being the friends of the small family farmer?

The animal health crises were not the only threats to established policy for British agriculture. The quiet introduction of genetically-modified (GM) crop trials, and the British public's resulting fear of "Frankenstein foods", became important issues in the decline in confidence in the UK agriculture industry during the late 1990s. This crisis led for the first time to mass consumption of organic food, one of the few profitable sectors of the agricultural economy. Much of that food had to be sourced abroad, and its consumption was easily condemned as an elitist fad, since price premiums placed it beyond the reach of poorer households. Opposition to GM farm trials, and fear of cross-pollination of nearby (particularly organic) crops, grew. Debate was focused by the trial (and acquittal) in 2000 of Greenpeace activists for harvesting GM crops on a Norfolk farm. Attitudes on both sides of the debate have hardened, with trials continuing and research seeking to differentiate "biodiversity impacts" (for example, on farmland birds) from wider environmental concerns.[36]

Behind all these crises lay the prospect of profound changes in the Common Agricultural Policy (CAP). By the late 1990s, substantial reform was taken for granted, although its shape remained unclear and the subject of extensive analysis and advocacy.[37] The European Commission (EC) published proposals for reform, in 1997, implementing them as Agenda 2000 in March 1999. They went some way to devolving powers to national governments in order to decide how to direct area payments — for example, to favour cross-compliance and positive environmental outcomes.[38] This created opportunities for conservationists wishing to promote policy that favoured conservation and rural livelihoods against traditional production goals in the UK, although it left all of the detail open.

The most positive feature of Agenda 2000 was the Rural Development Regulation, which integrated rural development and agri-environment issues. It allowed national governments to move to a system of support for rural areas based on social, environmental and economic objectives, rather than simply production, and recognised the social and environmental importance of agriculture. The English response in 2000 suggested that the Ministry of Agriculture, Fisheries and Food (MAFF) recognised the potential of integrated rural development to support farmers and rural communities, and to protect and enhance landscape, and was responding positively to this challenge both in its approach and the level of funding proposed. The devil, as ever, lay in the detail.[39]

The context for the reform of the CAP is not only the way in which it dominates spending by the EU and drains national exchequers, but the impact of global moves towards free trade. The impact of the World Trade Organisation (WTO) is being felt keenly by European governments. It is not easy to predict how farmers will respond to agricultural liberalisation — and, therefore, its impacts on the countryside — but they are likely to be locally specific and economically significant.[40] The expansion of the European Community eastwards, as agreed at the Copenhagen Summit in December 2002, offers further challenges. The nature of reform of the CAP remains a central issue to conservation in the UK in 2003, and there are no easy solutions to the complex issue that it raises.

In the wake of the foot and mouth crisis, the UK government finally broke up the post-war monolith of MAFF, creating the Department of Food, the Environment and Rural Affairs (DEFRA) in 2001. In theory, this was supposed to allow better integration of policy for the agricultural industry, rural areas, food quality and environment. Commentators were sceptical as to whether DEFRA's new package would do anything to change the old culture within.[41] DEFRA also established a Policy Commission on the Future of Farming and Food under Sir Donald Curry. This reported, in January 2002, to cautious enthusiasm from farmers and conservationists. It set out clear ideas of the potential for CAP reform, and recommended an extension of environmental schemes and continued support for organic farming. However, there was frustration that its analysis and recommendations were not more radical.[42] It recommended shifting 10 per cent of agricultural subsidies into environmental schemes, still less than the 20 per cent under current EU rules that could be spent on rural development, organic farming and other environmental schemes. Arguably, it also did little to address the issues of trade and the power of supermarkets.

However, the paperwork has been reasonably encouraging, from a conservation perspective at least. The England Rural Development Programme (2000–2006), for example, aims to extend the area covered by agri-environment schemes (Countryside Stewardship Scheme, Organic Farming Scheme, Woodland Grant Scheme and Farm Woodland Premium Scheme); it continues the Environmentally Sensitive Areas Scheme and provides a new Hill Farm Allowance Scheme. These are all proven measures for providing outcomes that maintain or enhance the countryside, at considerable cost to the taxpayer. Countryside Stewardship, for example, covers a range of landscape and habitat types, including arable land (measures such as field boundaries and headlands), old meadows, limestone and chalk grasslands, old orchards, waterside land and coastal areas.[43] In Wales, the whole-farm Tir Gofal Scheme launched by the Countryside Council for Wales in March 1999, building on the pilot Tir Cymen agri-environment scheme, offered payments on 66,000 ha in its first year. A budget of UK£16.4 million was approved by the Welsh Assembly for 2003–2004. Both private landowners and large conservation organisations have become adept at harnessing agri-environment payments to conservation objectives, often by acquiring farms and pushing the boundaries of their management to favour wildlife over production. At Abbots Hall Farm in Essex, for example, over UK£0.4 million over ten years under Countryside Stewardship and ESA schemes have allowed re-creation of 80 ha of salt marsh under "managed retreat" of old sea walls.[44]

Key challenges for conservation, however, remain. Firstly, these initiatives are delivered piecemeal to separate farm businesses, or even to small parts of farms; there is a need to link them at the landscape scale.[45] Secondly, as pointed out in the first edition of *Future Nature* (see Chapter 9), there is a need to find a way to relate these broad schemes to the smaller site scale of individual SSSIs in order to prevent their isolation in a blanket of mediocrity. Here, on the ground, it has proved harder to break the mould. An anonymous critic, the "Thinking Worm", despairs of making effective use of the multitude of disparate schemes to deliver conservation on the ground. Mountainous bureaucracy dogs every step (astonishingly, the DEFRA Countryside Stewardship brochure, in full colour, runs to 62 pages, plus four attached annexes).[46] The Thinking Worm suggests that any "agri-environment scheme that is prescribed in Whitehall (let alone Brussels), rather than prioritised locally and on its own local merits, will fail to deliver an environmentally improved landscape".[47] Christopher Lowell responds by pointing to DEFRA's staff, suggesting that "if there is to be a new, positive sensitivity to the agri-environment, it is the people giving the advice who must change, or be changed".[48]

Claiming the countryside

Government rural policy has certainly developed under Labour since 1997. The Countryside and Rights of Way Act (CROW Act) 2000 brought to a slightly anticlimactic end many decades of pressure for reform of the Wildlife and Countryside Act 1981. It finally took steps to close loopholes in protection for SSSIs, an issue that Friends of the Earth, in particular, had been campaigning for since the passage of the 1981 Act and its various amendments.[49]

The CROW Act also incorporated provisions for public access to open land in England and Wales. This had been unfinished business since the mass trespasses of the 1930s, and a measure deeply resented by landowners and long dreamed of by ramblers.[50] Part I of the act allowed access for walkers over open, uncultivated land. However, this must first be designated "access land" (common land, mountain and moorland over 600 m, heathland or downland) by the Countryside Agency and the Countryside Council for Wales and a process of public consultation. This process will take considerable time.

With unfortunate timing (just before the foot and mouth outbreak), the Labour government also published a new English rural White Paper in November 2000, "Our Countryside: The future — a fair deal for rural England".[51] This ranged widely, from discussions about the need for rural services and transport, and affordable rural homes, through agriculture and market towns, to conservation and ecological restoration. On conservation, the paper was open-minded and creative. It outlined targets to reverse the decline in farmland birds by 2020 and bring 95 per cent of nationally-important wildlife sites into favourable condition by 2010, as well as new planning guidelines for wildlife sites, conservation and biodiversity. It proposed a new biodiversity strategy for England to carry forwards species and habitat action plans, a new hill farm allowance scheme and a review of policy on "alien" and invasive species. There was the obligatory engagement with issues of local decision-making, and a commitment to "thinking rural". Rural society, economy, politics and nature were all present in an ordered and businesslike whole. Was this a recipe for joined-up government, for policy that seamlessly linked town and country, nature and industrial agriculture? Was the Labour government credible in its appeal to the old rural Tory heartland?

Not if headlines and popular politics are to be believed. The plight of rural Britain has become a major political issue. The root cause of this has been the relentless squeeze on farm incomes, particularly among small hill farmers hardest hit by foot and mouth, and arguably least well represented by the National Farmers' Union. By the end of 2002, the *average* farm income in the UK was being quoted in the press as UK£5000 per year, and much less for small hill farms. The strong, global over-production of temperate foods and the contracting CAP were creating a severe agricultural recession and, in places, real hardship. Despite public subsidy of the order of UK£3 billion per year, farming was in crisis.[52]

The immediate anger of farmers' groups to the looming agricultural crisis was allied with wider concerns about the decline of rural services (threatened closure of rural post offices, loss of rural bus services and rising rural house prices) and, above all, with the perceived urban challenge to rural ways of life. The rise and growing prominence of urban–rural migration and the growth in green field housing led to a "circling of the wagons" around what was truly "rural" and against the influx of "townies".[53] These issues predated the change of government in 1997; but the election of a Labour government more distanced politically from old Conservative rural heartlands and committed to legislation about hunting with hounds focused political energy. Brilliantly harnessing these disparate sources of concern, the Countryside Alliance has orchestrated a coherent anti-government political phenomenon, bringing together a coalition of interests based on loose notions of the rural.[54]

The roots of the Countryside Alliance lie in the Countryside Movement, established in November 1995 to "put the country's side", with former MP Sir David Steel as its figurehead. This grew from a desire of some reformers within the British Field Sports Society (BFSS) to broaden their appeal and supporter base. The Countryside Movement folded in 1996 due to lack of funds, and its successor, the Countryside Alliance, was formed at a BFSS board meeting in March 1997. The prospect of legislation about fox-hunting stimulated it to organise the Countryside Rally, in July 1997, and the Countryside March, in 1998. The prominent role of farmers in the highly effective public protests about high fuel prices in September 2001 gave some inkling of the political space for public protest against the government. The Countryside Alliance's political alchemy was to link support for the freedom to hunt with opposition to "urban" influence (even among middle class rural in-migrants) and to protest at the economic plight and loss of cultural traditions of the countryside. It is claimed that the Liberty and Livelihoods March in London, in September 2002, was attended by over 400,000 people. It brought issues of rural economy, society and environment to the political centre stage.

Producing solutions for the countryside

Arguments about the need to deliver integrated change in livelihoods and landscapes, which gained widespread acceptance during the 1990s and were reflected in the first edition of *Future Nature*, are still valid. The scope of the challenge in the countryside is clear. Following the 2002 London march, my local newspaper quoted the local MEP as saying "we want less bureaucracy and fewer imports of food from the Third World. The whole structure of rural affairs should be looked at, such as policing and schools in rural communities."[55] Leaving aside the parochialism of such views in the light of the developing world's rural poor, and the depth of venom for Labour and the animal welfare lobby of the pro-hunting movement, the Countryside Alliance has identified a complex and urgent set of issues. The problems are diverse, and solutions will clearly have to be holistic.

New thinking has edged into government policy. Thus, in addition to its various agri-environment schemes, the England Rural Development Programme (2000–2006) also launched four new schemes — for rural enterprise, processing and marketing, the energy crops and vocational training. The Rural Enterprise Scheme offers grants to promote "sustainable, diversified, enterprising rural economies and communities".[56] The Processing and Marketing Grants Scheme offers one third of the cost of projects to help farmers and others to process their produce at source. The Energy Crops Scheme seeks to encourage the planting of biomass fuels (including coppice woodland), while the Vocational Training Scheme offers up to 75 per cent of the cost of training in business, marketing, information technology or environmental land management.

Numerous projects and initiatives are attempting to demonstrate the economic feasibility and environmental merits of small rural enterprises and products. From farms, these include obvious things such as food and drink, with niche markets for cider, cheese and many other products. Farmers' markets have proved a success in many areas as both consumers and farmers seek an alternative to the oligopoly of the large supermarket chains. Despite the scepticism of the Food Standards Agency, organic farming continues to grow in popularity. The benefits of organic production for wildlife has been established by the British Trust for Ornithology and others, and the sector is expanding.[57] Organic vegetable "basket" schemes are linking producer and consumer in new economic networks.

Wood and woodland products can also provide opportunities for employment and small-scale manufacturing with clear environmental benefits.[58] Such "micro-enterprises" are also attractive to cash-strapped conservation organisations, for example Wildlife Trusts, whose large woodland holdings can start to yield some kind of economic return. They can also be socially inclusive — for example, the National Trust's welcome of Travellers on the Stackpole Estate in Pembrokeshire.[59] Such innovations in thought and action may seem a wonderful idea, but they can also be quite divisive. Even a superficial reading of the Countryside Alliance and the interests it represents makes clear that novel and challenging ideas may not instantly play well among rural communities. The Stackpole experience bears this out.

One example of support for these new enterprises is the Countryside Agency's Eat the View initiative. This arose as a response to a challenge by the Prime Minister in March 2000 to assist consumers to understand the connections between the food they buy and the countryside they value, and to work with others to develop projects in order to achieve this aim and improve the market for regional produce.[60] It aims to increase public understanding of where food and other countryside products come from, facilitate marketing and increase demand for products that will allow land managers to diversify and adopt more sustainable management practices. One element in this initiative is local distinctiveness, a theme of innovative rural thinking for some years — for example, in the work of Common Ground (and even English Nature's Natural Areas and the Countryside Agency's Countryside Character Initiative).[61]

In February 2001, the government published a Planning Policy Guidance note on *The Countryside — Environmental Quality and Economic and Social Development*.[62] This set out how the government's objectives for rural areas (as expressed in the 2001 rural White Paper) should be reflected in land use planning in England and Wales. The development of specific policies was left up to local authorities, through their development plans in the light of local circumstances, and to government departments and statutory agencies. The centrepiece of this guidance was the idea of sustainable development, demanding a balance between the need for change in rural areas while maintaining and enhancing environmental quality (for both visitors and local people). Recognition is given to the links between wealth creation and environmental quality in the countryside. New development should "respect, and where possible enhance, the environment in its location, scale and design".

There are more radical vision of land and livelihoods, notably the The Land is Ours (TLIO) campaign, which addresses public access to land, the resources of the land and decision-making about their use.[63] TLIO's campaigning style is very direct. In May 1996, activists occupied 5 ha of derelict land on the banks of the Thames in Wandsworth, highlighting the misuse of urban land, lack of affordable housing and the deterioration of the urban environment. In July 1999, activists claimed the site of a former hospital in Norwich as common land, marking the 450th anniversary of Kett's rebellion against the enclosures. In April 1999, 300 activists marched to St George's Hill, Weybridge, Surrey, to erect a memorial stone to the Diggers, 350 years after the initial occupation of this site.

TLIO emphasises three issues: firstly, land for homes (space for low-cost and self-designed housing in cities; places for Travellers and low-impact settlers in the countryside); secondly, land for life (the protection and reclamation of common space; reform of planning and public enquiries; mandatory land registration; community ground rents and a right to roam); thirdly, land for livelihoods (farming without catastrophe; subsidies and planning for small-scale, high-employment, low-consumption land uses). A sub-group ("Chapter 7") focuses explicitly on sustainability and planning, lobbying for firmer guidance on what makes developments sustainable; on policies to promote low-impact developments, self-built homes and workplaces; and on alternatives to car-based urban development. They are interested in safeguarding urban land for sustainable low-profit use (for example, affordable housing, workshop space and yards, markets, independent shops, public transport facilities, allotments, community projects and gardens). They want the public's right to appeal against major development proposals strengthened, and major agricultural activities brought within the planning system.[64]

New ways of living and working in the countryside may require shifts in land ownership. This is already a widespread opinion in rural Scotland. The community buy-outs of crofting land in Scotland, notably the island of Eigg and in Assynt in Wester Ross, open up interesting and challenging new possibilities.[65] Community ownership and initiative provides no guarantee of economic efficiency or enhanced conservation status; but it has repeatedly emerged as critical to effective and sustainable solutions.

Countryside with chips

Integration may be the universal watchword among those declaring new agendas for conservation and the countryside, but there are challenges to the whole concept of "rural" areas. My journey to work involves a half-hour bicycle ride, sandwiched between an endless stream of commuters' cars and bleak East Anglian fields. This provides a strange and varied commentary on nature and society, on sustainability and consumption. There is wildlife to be seen — a muntjack deer on a road verge late on a February night, apparently watching the traffic, and again six months later in the same place, dead; lapwings most winters (although only ever in one corner of the same field); arctic thrushes milling around the uncut hawthorn hedges like teenagers restlessly window-shopping on a Saturday afternoon. Alongside these, the unending river of cars streaming to work, and then home, is a reminder of the way in which urban and rural are stitched together into a fabric of society that makes the achievement of sustainability an almost unimaginable utopia.

Cambridge, of course, is booming. In villages and on the city's edge, development intensifies, the pawl of urbanisation clicking inexorably home. Villages are increasingly becoming commuter settlements, both for local high-tech companies and for London. Everywhere, farms are being redeveloped as offices for new-economy enterprises, their yards filled with new cars, their buildings full of computers and bright lights. Rural roads sport the cool graphics of the new enterprise economy, and provide a dense warren of rat-runs for commuters on the run to work, schools, supermarkets or home. The car and the internet are the logistic muscular system that powers new rural–urban lifestyles. The micro-chip is the seed of a new rural ecology, and the harvest is cars, houses, tarmac and consumption.

The neatness of the Countryside Agency's injunction to "eat the view" highlights something important about the relations between town and country in the UK. While farmers like to portray themselves as the victims of "a vendetta by heartless urban dwellers who do not understand rural life", the old familiar distinctions between "town" and "country" do make decreasing sense.[66] Commuting, second homes, weekend breaks and urban niche markets are stitching town and country together (even in remote regions of the country) by means of information technology, speeding delivery trucks and the all-pervasive private car. "Urban" and "rural" are cultural categories, not economic ones. Any contemplation of the future of conservation in Britain must surely seek to re-think them.

For conservationists, the traditional distinction between town and country constrains innovation and imagination. Chris Rose has even suggested that it may be time to campaign against "rural England". Writing in the Independent, he says: "80 per cent of England is farmland and most of that is green — but effectively as dead as concrete."[67] Rose objected to the government's mixture of policies, its attempt to micro-manage change in the countryside, its "incrementalist regime of minor tweaking". He rejected rural policy as "old-fashioned, backward looking and mock traditional". Big problems call for brave solutions, "a vision and architecture as big as the founding principles of town and country planning itself". Above all, he argued that the very distinction drawn between "urban" and "rural" inhibited policy development.

We certainly need new and innovative ways in which to understand and build links between urban and rural. Chris Rose is right that they are far less separate than we have tended to think, and the Rural and Urban White Papers produced in 2000 and 2001 accord very different status to nature conservation.[68] Yet, urban conservation has been one of the success stories of the last 30 years, and urban sites (especially derelict land) can attract diverse and attractive wildlife communities — they, in their turn, can appeal to urban people.

Green spaces (and green "brown spaces") in urban areas are central to any agenda of opening conservation to a wider community — for example, among ethnic minorities and young people. Arguably, the bird table is the single most important invention in the history of Western conservation, and the RSPB's membership demonstrates the capacity of urban and suburban birds to awake in people a sense of the value of nature. Initiatives in inner city areas to make garden plots available, or to meet the environmental needs of disadvantaged people, are vital in re-connecting people to the environment.[69]

Certainly, if one could measure it, the contribution of nature to national quality of life is primarily expressed in urban areas. In the language of environmental economists, nature provides a wide range of services, mostly consumed by people who live in urban areas. This understanding became part of thinking about the British countryside during the later 1990s through the idea of "environmental capital". This has been developed as Quality of Life Capital, a joint initiative of the Countryside Agency, English Nature, English Heritage and the Environment Agency.[70] The aim of the approach is to provide a way of delivering sustainable development by identifying the ways in which particular areas (or particular landscape features) contribute to human well-being. One such contribution might be in the form of economic benefits, but the idea of Quality of Life Capital is wider. The aim of the approach is to provide a systematic and transparent framework, suitable at all scales of decision-making, which can integrate environmental, social and economic issues. The approach emphasises the possibility of improving quality of life rather than simply accepting the status quo, and it tries to value the commonplace as well as the unusual and rare. It also seeks to be transparent and open to the concerns of local people (rather than being a tool for remote "expert" planners). Quality of Life Capital is designed to be integrated with other tools and processes, such as Environmental Impact Assessment, Sustainability Appraisal, and Community Planning.

Urban and rural areas are complementary dimensions of one problem — of sustainability. Chris Rose urges the importance of the much-hated suburb. What is wrong with suburbs? Sneered at by politicians, the media, professional conservationists and Countryside Alliance supporters alike, Chris Rose suggests that they are, in fact, the cutting edge of the problem of unsustainability. Far from seeking to maintain the separation of country and town, we should combine the two. We should create "ecological settlements", where problems of wildlife, housing, energy, transport and community are solved together. The Poundbury settlement, an urban extension to Dorchester, offers one much discussed example of a sustainable settlement because of its association with the Prince of Wales. However, there are many others: communal (such as the South Devon Co-Housing Group); developed by Housing Associations (for example, the Beddington Zero Energy Development in Sutton); and many individual projects.[71]

This all suggests that we should be wary about the compartmentalising of "rural" areas and, indeed, of "conservation". They cannot easily or reliably be separated, either conceptually or practically. We need to move away from piecemeal policies to think holistically about "ecologically-intelligent development" for both rural and urban areas. We need to imagine new forms of community and new ways of living with the land. Low-impact development needs to move from the lunatic fringe into the mainstream of architecture and planning.[72] We need to understand the challenge of sustainability to planning, seeing the links between proposals for new roads or super quarries in the Western Isles.[73] As the Royal Commission on Environmental Pollution noted in its report on environmental planning in March 2002, town and country are interdependent, and integrated spatial planning should embrace both within one frame.[74]

Conservation as restoration

If one change stands out from the 1990s, it was the gradual dawning of the thought that conservation strategies could move beyond the traditional idea of protecting habitat towards thinking about its restoration. The ideas and methods of "restoration ecology" grew among scientists and conservation practitioners on both sides of the Atlantic. The restoration of ecosystems in many ways provided a new metaphor for conservation, and certainly a new challenge for conservation for the new millennium.[75] In the UK, the 2001 Rural White Paper announced that the Biodiversity Strategy for England would set targets for the re-creation and enhancement of threatened habitats and species habitats.[76]

Habitat creation and restoration have begun to be a normal part of the portfolio of British conservation planners, reversing the twentieth century's unrelieved experience of habitat loss. In the Cambridgeshire Fens, for

example, there are several projects that seek to establish new large wetlands around existing isolated reserves. Cambridgeshire lies in what
Adrian Colston refers to as England's "black hole", a county where barely any semi-natural habitat survives, and there are, as a consequence, few
areas worth designating as conservation sites. The only solution in such a
biodiversity desert is, arguably, to start again through habitat creation.[77]
And where better than adjacent to one of the remaining fragments of habitat, where a larger area of wetland might help prevent the extinctions that
biogeographic theory suggests are inevitable in the small and isolated
nature reserve of the late twentieth century? Populations of wildlife
species are small, and are vulnerable both to random events and to gradual environmental changes that even obsessively energetic management
regimes cannot wholly prevent (particularly falls in water tables). At
Wicken, for example, many species have disappeared over the last 200
years, the most famous of which is probably the swallowtail butterfly, but
also birds such as the Montagu's harrier and marsh warbler, and plants
such as the lesser bladderwort, fen orchid and marsh helleborine.[78] The
large copper butterfly has also gone from Wicken and from Woodwalton
Fen, where protracted efforts at re-introduction over many decades have
failed.

The idea of large-scale wetland creation in the fens grew from the
Cambridgeshire County Council's 1988 Rural Strategy. A wide range of
partners then developed the Wet Fens for the Future Project, eventually
launched in 1996.[79] Two large wetland restoration projects are now being
developed. Between Huntingdon and Peterborough, the Great Fen Project
aims to restore 3000 ha of habitat to re-connect Woodwalton Fen and
Holme Fen National Nature Reserves. The project is a partnership
between Huntingdonshire District Council, English Nature, the
Environment Agency and the Wildlife Trust for Cambridgeshire, and it
aims to combine nature conservation with tourism and other economic
activities, and to store winter water for the protection of the Middle Level
System and the homes, farms and businesses that depend upon it. In 2000,
the Wildlife Trust secured UK£20,000 from the World Wide Fund for
Nature-UK (WWF-UK), and in September 2001 English Nature secured
UK£1 million for the project and commenced experimental scrub removal
at Woodwalton Fen.[80]

Wicken Fen is also starting to grow. Having laboured for almost a century to optimise habitat management at Wicken, during the late 1990s the
National Trust changed tack and launched a major long-term land acquisition programme. There was some precedent for this, undoing the effects
of agricultural reclamation. Adventurer's Fen, adjacent to Wicken Fen,
immortalised by Eric Ennion, was drained and reclaimed for agriculture
during the Second World War in response to the national drive to increase

food production.[81] During the 1950s, it was acquired by the National Trust, its fields were allowed to become waterlogged, and a lagoon was excavated. The National Trust's current initiative is, however, much bolder, both in extent and conception.

The National Trust proposes to acquire up to 3700 ha of farmland to the south of Wicken Fen, including most of the catchment supplying water to the present reserve. The area is a patchwork of over 100 farms, and the vision is that as the high costs of land drainage (as soils shrink, and sea levels rise) and decline in the agricultural sector in the UK bite, farmers may be willing to sell. The plan was to acquire land slowly (over the next century); but uptake has been astonishingly fast, and land acquisition has already begun.[82] The National Trust purchased Guinea Hall Farm, (47 ha of land east of the existing reserve) in October 2000 and Burwell Fen Farm (168 ha) in October 2001.

The restoration of wetland in farmed fenland could potentially bring other benefits. Amidst Cambridgeshire's intensive agricultural landscapes, Wicken Fen offers a strong sense of wildness in its fen, woodland and open water. At the same time, it provides a reminder of the historical depth of human management of the fen in the history of peat and sedge cutting (recorded from the fifteenth century), and in the restored eighteenth-century fenman's cottage, the working wind pump (originally used for draining peat trenches) and the old brick pits and kilns.[83] The new wetland will lie just north-east of the city of Cambridge, the fastest growing hub of the UK's fastest growing region.[84] If it were possible to create direct access (for example, for bicycles) to Wicken from Cambridge, a major recreation area could be added to the pressurised Cambridge Green Belt.[85] The extended reserve could also provide jobs for the depressed rural fens, both directly and through multiplier effects from demand from visitors for accommodation and food.

Restoration and creativity

But what should a 'restored' fen be like in the twenty-first century? The restoration of species-rich, low-productivity fen from species-poor but highly productive arable land is technically highly problematic. Hydrology, nutrient status and vegetation are closely linked. Key challenges are the removal of nutrients from soils, the re-wetting of the peat and the issue of habitat fragmentation and the dispersal (or re-introduction) of species lost during agricultural intensification.[86] In practice, the restoration of Wicken will have to be pragmatic and driven by the needs and opportunities of each patch of land, many of which may initially be isolated from others. Patches of land obtained at an early stage may only later be connected

together. The result is likely to be a mosaic of habitat patches with disturbance regimes that allow the formation of different habitat elements, from
open water to wet woodland. Such a landscape might not look much like
the sanctuary for late nineteenth-century *Lepidoptera* that Rothschild
might have imagined when he started donating bits of the fen to the
National Trust.

Nonetheless, the new wetland should provide a place for all, or most
of, the elements of the fauna and flora of recent centuries. And if it does
not, does it matter? This should not be an attempt to create a particular
set of habitats. The new wetland will be, indeed, that, new: a created space
where human managers and other species interact under quite novel
ground rules. What is being restored is a terrain for future decisions and
engagements. Here, conservation involves choosing to set the terms of
that engagement at a particular level — one much more favourable to
nature than the current alternative, where nature is confined to cracks
within an agricultural factory floor, squeezed by expanding towns.

In many ways, the whole idea of the "restoration" of nature is problematic.[87] In places such as the UK, where the human impact is so extensive, the idea that society might choose to undo particular human impacts
is appealing. Perhaps the role of conservation is to wind back the tape of
damaging interventions and "restore" nature to its former glory. But
nature is not a fixed and static thing. Nature, left alone, flourishes, and can
and does restore itself.[88] The complexion of plants and animals in a particular place changes independently of human action. Nature forms and
re-forms in response to human action in ways that are novel and stretch
beyond the scope of particular human impacts themselves. The human-
made is, in a curious but profound sense, also natural.

Where human impacts are very great — for example, a felled woodland or a polluted stream — it may be possible to speak about the "pre-
disturbance state" of an ecosystem, and (if the research has been done) it
may be possible to identify what that state might have looked like. But the
huge time depth of the human signature in British landscapes makes for
particular problems. Is it possible to speak of a time before human disturbance? Yes, in theory, if one went back to the pre-Neolithic period; but we
will never know much detail about the exact patterns of ecosystems, climate and human impacts in such remote times.[89] The target states of
restored ecosystems are, by any standards of judgement, social.

The British experience with river restoration is interesting here.
Throughout the twentieth century, river management in the UK has been
typified by heavy-handed engineering approaches aimed at flood control.
These ideas began to shift during the 1980s, and more environmentally-
enlightened approaches to rivers began to be established.[90] Jeremy
Purseglove's *Taming the Flood* helped to change both public and profes-

sional ideas, and the idea of river restoration emerged.[91] The River Restoration Project developed prominent projects on the River Cole near Swindon and Skerne near Darlington.[92]

In the case of rivers, river and floodplain habitats can be created either in-situ (in what one might unkindly call gardening), or by the restoration of natural processes of erosion and deposition that will, in their turn, create the conditions for habitat development.[93] In the latter case, the outcome of a project is harder to predict. Inevitably, most river restoration projects in the UK have taken place on a small scale on relative slow-flowing and docile rivers, where created or re-created physical features tend to stay where they are put. Restoration targets are the result of careful discussion with local stakeholders. On the River Cole, old maps were used to re-establish the former course of the river. However, the landowner (the National Trust) needed to conserve a historic water mill; so although channel dimensions were reinstated, water flow within the channel was controlled by a sluice gate. Inundation of the floodplain was prevented, and a low ground-water level was maintained. The River Restoration Project's Skerne site was close to a large housing area, and was designed after close consultation with local people to include a hard stream-side path.

Restored nature, therefore, inevitably bears the imprint of human design. For this reason, some conservationists regard restoration as a Trojan horse. There are certainly risks in the growing ease with which planners, developers and ecologists assume that ecosystems can be assembled, partly dis-assembled and reconstructed to suit human ideas of what is natural. Such a managerial approach has disturbingly strong parallels to the confident re-shaping of nature to fit human ends that was a feature of industrial engagements with nature throughout the nineteenth and twentieth centuries.[94] Is restoration the final logical element in ecological managerialism, an attempt to specify exactly what form "natural" nature should take?[95] A belief that restoration is possible can, itself, potentially legitimise environmental destruction.[96] Moreover, creative restoration to mitigate habitat loss demands the sacrifice of undamaged habitats of a different kind.[97] A good example of this is the creation of a wetland nature reserve on the Gwent Levels in Wales as some kind of mitigation for the loss of inter-tidal mudflats in Cardiff Bay, flooded by the Cardiff barrage.[98] The Gwent Levels had their own landscape and ecological values which could themselves have been the subject of sympathetic restoration, rather than being the target of wetland creation to compensate for losses elsewhere.[99] There is a sense in which it is bizarre to see management interventions as a way of restoring nature to a more "natural state". As John Cairns sharply observes, "If management is the disease, how can it be the cure?"[100]

197

However, there is no doubt that both the scale and the competence of ecological restoration is expanding rapidly. Restoration techniques are attractive to many different interests, to determined developers looking for an argument in favour of their proposals, to beleaguered planners trying to balance environmental impacts and economic gains, and to conservation planners trying to undo centuries of unsustainable human demands on nature. Ecological restoration is here to stay — it has its own journals and its own (albeit still largely American) learned society; its annual conference came to the UK in 2001.[101]

However, the real implications of restoration for conservation are more profound than this role as a new "technique" for conservation implies. Arguably, restoration represents a new way of understanding relations between society and nature. John Cairns asks: "Are restoration ecologists merely running a series of environmental 'body-shops' that repair damaged ecosystems without appreciable effects on either rates of ecological destruction or human society's set of guiding beliefs?"[102] The answer has to be no: restoration is both less and more than good landscaping of society's numerous demands on nature.

It is less, because it is never possible to undo human impacts. It may be possible to create an illusion of naturalness by clever landscape design and management, or to distract even expert observers by creating something exciting or new. However, the authenticity of "restored" ecosystems remains highly questionable.[103] As was argued in Chapter 6, ecosystems — certainly, all ecosystems in the UK — are, in Arthur Tansley's terms, "anthropogenic", human-influenced hybrids of human and non-human agency.[104] Restoration allows the terms of engagement of conservation and industrial society to be re-set, in particular places, but it cannot "undo" human action, simply compound it.

But this is also why restoration can also be more than simply a new and clever technique for environmental mitigation. It is precisely because human action cannot un-hybridise transformed nature that it is so exciting. The things that conservationists value in non-human nature in the UK are mostly very direct products of human action. The idea of "protecting nature" provides a limited metaphor to guide conservation in the future precisely because it limits the terms of engagement between human and non-human. Conventional conservation allows only reservation (to keep the forces of destruction at bay) and, in the British case, careful (scientific) intervention management, where this can be proved to enhance diversity. This essentially confines conservation debate to a tiny proportion of the landscape, that alphabet soup (NNRs, SSSIs, SPAs and SACs and the rest) that have been described elsewhere in this book.

We have allowed conservation to be a land use in the UK. From the 1980s onwards, it tentatively crept outside nature reserves onto private land, clutching management agreements and a fistful of euros paid for by agricultural surpluses. In the process, the wider terms of engagement between society and nature were left to find their natural course, resulting in the drab urban sprawl and ecologically-impoverished countryside with which we are only too familiar. It is this engagement that the idea of restoration can re-vivify. Restoration can provide a metaphor to guide human engagements with nature, a statement of intent about the terms of the future relationship, a glimpse of how things might be.

Restoration makes us look backwards to the way things were, drawing on the stories science tells us, but also on the many other myths that pattern our thinking about ourselves and our past. Does not the name of the National Forest deliberately seek to establish a cultural identity by awakening ideas of an imagined past, more confidently retrospective Robin Hood than wishfully modernist Millennium Dome?[105] Does not the excitement of the London Wetlands Centre in a great curve of the Thames, on the site of the old Barn Elms Reservoir in south-west London, in part reflect a sense of London as a city built around the river, of the floodplain that underpins the teeming financial powerhouse of the global financial system?[106] Is not the bizarre sight of Landlife's fields of wild flowers around Liverpool housing estates a deliberate reminder of the impoverishment of our urbanised lives and silent countryside, and a statement about the possibility of something better?[107]

Introducing the wild

The growing enthusiasm for creation and restoration of nature has given new life to a long-running debate about introductions and "alien" species. The attempt to extirpate the ruddy duck (ironically, accidentally introduced by one of the greatest conservationists of the twentieth century, Peter Scott) is a good example of the complexities of introductions, however benignly intentioned. The ruddy duck is popular in the UK, but a menace to biodiversity in countries such as Spain because it is spreading and hybridising with the white-headed duck. Welcome the alien, or protect the native: the choice is interesting.[108]

The conventional approach within conservation emphasises the risks of introducing species into the UK, classically pointing to rhododendron, mink and grey squirrel as examples of the risks, and species such as Himalayan balsam, the Australian swamp stonecrop or the zander as examples of the challenge.[109] A number of commentators continue to urge caution. They fear that introduced species will run amok, out-competing indigenous species, as the Australian swamp stonecrop does in waterways, or predating them, as the humble hedgehog has in the Outer Hebrides.

They also fear the dilution of indigenous gene pools with new DNA that has not evolved to deal with local conditions, most obviously perhaps in the spread of "wild meadow" plant mixes, often from continental European seed sources.

The language of this debate is interesting — the very phrase "alien species" resonates strongly and adversely with many people. It has disturbing parallels with political attitudes to immigration and seems defensive, exclusive, even racist. Are we, as a recent Plantlife publication put it, "At War with Aliens" in conservation as in politics?[110] It is a disturbing thought, and suggests that there is as much culture as ecology in such thinking, with possibly not very comfortable overtones. There is a long history of new species becoming established members in the fauna and flora of the UK. We have a wonderfully mongrel biota, with many species culturally accepted through long association. While everyone might hate muntjac deer, species such as the brown hare are among the most charismatic in the public eye.

Richard Mabey's *Flora Britannica* demonstrates how rapidly new plants become accepted, and the *New Atlas of the British and Irish Flora* carefully describes and maps newer, as well as older, non-human citizens.[111] It distinguishes between "archaeophytes" (introduced before 1500) and "neophytes" (introduced after 1500), and it maps the distribution of alien and native stock separately for almost all species. Its editors note that no other wildlife atlas (especially the recent bird or butterfly atlases) has managed to distinguish between natural and human-supported distributions. They also point out that there is no register of plant and animal introductions, not even those done under the supposedly scientific Biodiversity Action Plan (BAP) process.[112]

If we accept that restoration targets are social, what is wrong with thinking boldly about re-introductions? As Adrian Colston likes to point out, why not graze the enlarged Wicken Fen wetland with something like its Pleistocene ungulate fauna?[113] There is increasing interest in such introductions. Beavers are grazing a fenced paddock in a nature reserve in Kent, and plans by Scottish Natural Heritage and the Forest Enterprise to re-introduce them in Argyll are well advanced. Wild boar have managed to re-introduce themselves in southern England, although opinions are sorely divided as to the appropriateness of their action. They are widely regarded as a menace to public safety, although they have their admirers. Lynx and large black cats also appear to be at large in the British countryside, again to some public alarm. Nonetheless, the idea of re-introducing wolves to the Scottish Highlands (where, hopefully, their appetite for deer will exceed that for sheep) is being discussed.[114]

Of course, there is another side to this debate. Nature has a way of puncturing the plans of those who claim to know nature's business. Nigel

Ajax-Lewis points out the irony of the introduction of Swedish and Spanish red kites to England and Scotland, just as the Welsh population was starting to expand: one result is that we will never now see Welsh birds above the Chiltern beechwoods. Peter Marren is equally amused at the self-motivated return of choughs to Cornwall, forestalling the razzmatazz of a proposed release of captive birds, or the osprey's sly nesting in the Lake District ignoring the huge, sponsored and very public efforts to establish it at Rutland Water.[115] More seriously, the current enthusiasm for introductions represents a take-over of the "apartness" of nature. Marren fears for the "pseudo-wild Britain" that is being created, suggesting that introductions (even those sanctioned by the unimpeachable industrial standard of the Biodiversity Action Plan) are eroding any meaningful concept of naturalness.

These are important issues. How much effort should we put into policing the purity of our biodiversity? How important is it to use only local seed sources in new planting projects? How much energy should we expend in removing species that people like and that are good at colonising the nutrient-rich, mobile and isolated habitats we have created around ourselves, particularly in semi-urbanised settings? Arguably, we need to think hard about the conditions for learning to accept new species.[116] And if those species are not entirely docile, so be it. For myself, I feel rather sympathetic to those advocating a re-wilding of Britain, accepting what Peter Taylor calls "a frisson of risk", and the odd boar or lynx in the woods.[117] I am quite certain that conservation needs the challenge of considering the possibilities.

Conservation and climate change

One reason why conservationists may need to think more creatively in the twenty-first century is the challenge of climate change. The idea that human activities influence climate has been increasingly widely accepted since 1995. The Intergovernmental Panel on Climate Change (IPCC) is no longer routinely portrayed as some wild environmentalist organisation — rather, as the world's best shot at wise judgement of the human signature on the atmosphere, on warming and on the consequences of action and inaction.[118] Even the USA, apparently terminally in thrall to its oil industry, has finally accepted that society is contributing to global warming, and before the Johannesburg Summit in September 2002 (the World Summit on Sustainable Development), Canada broke ranks among the global refusniks and agreed to accept the Kyoto Protocol.[119]

Conservation planning clearly has to work from the premise of climate change, probably unprecedentedly rapid and certainly complex in its effects.[120] Mean annual temperature in Europe has risen by 0.8° Celsius (C) during the twentieth century. The 1990s were the warmest decade on record in the UK: the mean temperature for the period from January to March was 5.6°C during the 1990s, compared to 4.2°C in the 1960s; October 2001 was the warmest October on record, with the average temperature for the month 3°C higher than usual.[121] Climate is likely to change in spatially complex ways. Models suggest that in the next 50 years the length of the growing season in Europe will increase by up to three months in central Europe, and fall by up to three months in southern Europe.[122]

Climate change affects the timing of recurrent biological events, such as budding, flowering and bird migration, through the biological and physical factors that influence them. Changes in the timing of these events will vary for individual species, and may affect the success of reproduction and change the balance of competition between species, particularly local and exotic species. Such phenological changes in response to climate change could have serious consequences for wild species (for example, because it influences the length of the growing season), as well as for agriculture, forestry and gardens (for instance, because of frost damage and the severity of crop disease and pest attack). There could be impacts on water and nutrient budgets and the biological sequestration of carbon.

For many naturalists and gardeners in the UK, the evidence of climate change is before their eyes. The UK Phenology Network records that trees are coming into leaf sooner, and some typical spring flowers are increasingly being seen coming into bloom in November and December. Butterflies are appearing earlier, and chiffchaff and blackcap are increasingly over-wintering in the UK.[123] Historical data on phenology exist from the records of individual naturalists and from the national network established by the Royal Meteorological Society in 1875, which ran until 1948. The work was revived by Tim Sparks of the Natural Environment Research Council (NERC) Centre for Ecology and Hydrology in 1998, and expanded in 2000 with the Woodland Trust. Over 18,500 people across the UK are now registered with the UK Phenology Network.[124]

Observed and predicted climate change must be central to thinking about future conservation strategies.[125] Some effects are potentially positive — for example, the expansion northward of some temperature-limited species such as butterflies. Modelling studies, however, suggest that impacts are likely to be highly complex.[126] Arctic–alpine and montane plant communities are likely to be most acutely threatened by future climate change.[127] Models show them losing most ground, followed by pine woodland and beech woodland in the south. Some species will be little affected, because they are already widely distributed, or their northern range margins do not change (for instance, cross-leaved heath, cleavers, great crested newt and yew). Other species, particularly those limited by altitude or latitude, were predicted to expand — for example, great burnet, sea purslane and large skipper. A third category of species that is likely to lose ground comprises those species currently of wet or moist habitats in southern England because of predicted Summer droughts (for example, tall cotton grass and marsh valerian).

Climate change will have significant impacts on coastal habitats regarding sea level rise and increased storminess.[128] Low coasts (especially salt marshes) risk inundation, and soft cliffs, shingle beaches and sand dunes face enhanced rates of erosion. The impacts of such changes on property and agriculture, as well as on nature conservation and landscape, are obvious; but the proper conservation response is less easily decided. National planning guidelines now recognise the need to live with coastal erosion and deposition rather than blindly trying to stop it. The National Trust has accepted the possibility of losses of land and features, and is embracing managed retreat (or just accepting coastal erosion) at a range of properties, notably at Porlock in Somerset.

Climate change has also been implicated in public discussions of urban flooding. The serious floods of 2001 and 2002 brought river flood-plains to policy attention across the UK. Too many cities, and too much recent urban development, have been allowed on floodplains: they would be more valuable in a more natural state as free flood-balancing reservoirs.[129] Planners are having to rediscover the concept of catchment-scale planning, a trend likely to be enhanced considerably when the EU Water Framework Directive comes into force. It is not just planners who have to learn to think about non-living nature. The concept of catchment management has hardly registered in a conservation world obsessed with site safeguard and designation. Few wetland SSSIs or reserves have boundaries determined by the hydrological unit. Conservation needs to rediscover the physical environment.[130] Sea levels will rise and river-flooding patterns will change, and conservation has to think through how to respond.

It is hard to second-guess climate change. It is a problem that does not fit comfortably into reductionist thinking about the security of threatened species and habitats. It does, however, reward imaginative lateral thinking. One clear response is the awareness of the importance of giving nature room for manoeuvre. A conservation landscape comprising small, isolated, specialised blocks of habitats is unlikely to be very useful in a twenty-first century where unknown patterns of climate change unroll complex patterns of ecological change. Species can move, but they need somewhere to move to. Animals and plants need corridors to leapfrog across inhospitable terrain; but, above all, nature needs *space*. There is, for this reason, increasing recognition that one element of future conservation strategies must be large areas.[131] This is not a new concept — in many ways, the idea reflects that of the Conservation Areas proposed by the Huxley Committee in 1947.[132] It is part of the logic of large-scale restoration in the Cambridgeshire Fens, or in Scotland, discussed elsewhere in this book

There are those for whom conservation can only mean the established methods of protecting nature in the formulations and habitats that have been co-created with human action over many centuries: the "classic preservation with management" model. There are others who are excited by letting go, floating with future possibilities. One dimension of this is a concern with natural processes. As I say in *Future Nature*, "we need...not only to recreate nature in specific forms and places, but also to conserve the capacity of nature to recreate itself".[133] Peter Marren argues that much of the apparent confidence of plans such as the BAP stems not from closeness to nature, but from distancing ourselves from it. In their "pretended omniscience", we are starting to usurp the natural world.[134]

Conservation needs to make space for nature to be itself. Nature has agency — it does things. Some we like (sunsets, birdsong, bluebell woods); others we tend to feel threatened by (for example, floods, gales and retreating coastal cliffs). However, it is nature's capacity to make and re-make itself that is both the source of its diversity and resilience and, in many cases, the source of our wonder at it. My guess is that people engage with nature much more readily when it does things, and much less when conservationists package it. As Kay Milton observes, "nature doesn't just do things, it does things to us".[135] We may not entirely like the ways in which people react; but at least it reflects a direct engagement with nature and a recognition that nature matters. And if conservationists have a different view, at least it opens up the debate. With our technology, and even in our conservation management, we have taken over nature's freedom to be itself. We need to give it back.

Living in place

Near to where I live in Cambridgeshire, a large new settlement has been built in a greenfield site to meet the relentless demand for new houses. To serve it, a new dual carriageway road has been built, cutting through a narrow band of woodland beside the old Bedford Road. This, presumably, had no designated "importance" for wildlife; but it was one of those blessed places where, in May, you could see bluebells from the public road — that uniquely British ecological delight, a sea of ethereal blue, repeating the open Spring sky above in the dark base of the wood.[136] I cannot drive past it now without reflecting bitterly on the tight links between our lifestyles

and our impacts on nature. Tarmac replaces woodland; cars replace bluebells. It is not an exchange about which to feel comfortable, especially
from behind the wheel of a car.

The root of the unsustainability of the modern globalised world is consumption — the excessive demand for material objects way above and
beyond those necessary for survival, beyond even what global and local
ecosystems can provide space for and can break down. Consumption and
waste are the twin poles of modern society, the rock and the hard place. In
East Anglia, we are running out of holes in which to put rubbish. Waste
management is a major industry, and landfill an increasingly visible influence on landscape — a running reminder of the way our power to consume outstrips our ability to deal with its consequences. The landfill tax is
a new source of finance for conservation projects; landfill mountains are a
new feature of the lowland English horizon.[137]

Jay McDaniel offers a rather neat description of what he calls "the religion of consumerism". He says:

> *Its god is economic growth for its own sake; its priests are the
> public policy-makers who provide access to growth; its evangel-
> ists are the advertisers who display the products of growth and
> try to convince us that we cannot be happy without them; and
> its church is the shopping mall.*[138]

Ironically, of course, we have increasingly allowed nature to become something that people consume. Standard conservation practice suggests that
nature can be found in particular places (reserves), and in those places we
devise a nature experience to make sure that those visiting are satisfied.
We educate, inform and amuse; but we also charge and, increasingly,
develop merchandise to enhance the nature consumption experience. The
most popular nature reserves have to compete with shopping for the public gaze and to pay for themselves, and they do it by offering a rich consumer experience. Some of the most creative developments in conservation involve new economic activities that build directly on nature (for
example, whale-watching enterprises).[139] However, it is worth pausing to
reflect that while Lakeside Thurrock or Bluewater have a lot of shop and
a little green space, and the RSPB reserve at Minsmere has a tiny shop and
a lot of space, it is disturbing that the difference between them is, in some
respects, so narrow.

Ruby, the girl who came to save and educate Ada Monroe in Charles
Frazier's novel *Cold Mountain* had a strong sense of the needlessness of
many manufactured things, and of travel, allied to a powerful sense of
place:

There was not one thing in a place like France or New York or Charleston that Ruby wanted. And little she even needed that she couldn't make or grow or find on Cold Mountain. She held a deep distrust of travel, whether to Europe or anywhere else. Her view was that a world properly put together would yield inhabitants so suited to their lives in their assigned place that they would have neither need nor wish to travel. No stagecoach or railway or steamship would be required; all such vehicles would sit idle. Folks would, out of utter contentment, choose to stay home, since the failure to do so was so patently the root of many ills, current and historic. In such a stable world as she envisioned, some might live many happy years hearing the bay of a distant neighbour's dog and yet never venture out far enough from their own fields to see whether the yap was from hound or setter, plain or pied.[140]

I can readily identify with the bioregional sentiments being expressed here. There is much for UK conservation to learn from Ruby's worldview for its conduct in the twenty-first century.

Ian Christie calls for "a politics of reverence" for the Earth.[141] He suggests that we should promote learning based on the idea of revelation, "grounded in experience, learning that can influence personal values and heighten empathy". He believes that we should seek to link different people, create programmes of experiential learning, create participatory initiatives and take decision-makers away from their normal environments. The vital element here is how people engage with nature — indeed, whether they do so at all.

Nature has become remote from the lived experience of the vast majority of people in the UK. Ecosystems are most commonly the subject of aesthetic reflection, remote from physical involvement, particularly through the medium of television. There are arguments to be made both for and against such "virtual nature". Without it, most people would be oblivious of nature and uncaring, and the best can be both disturbing and potentially empowering.[142]

The way in which children engage with nature is particularly important. British children are better at recognising imaginary Pokémon characters than wildlife. They leave primary school able to name 80 per cent of Pokémon characters, but only 50 per cent of common wildlife types.[143] Children, like adults, only recognise what they have encountered. Rivers, for example, are outside the experience of many London children and mean little to them. However, when children get the chance to visit rivers, for play or study, they come alive, and with them come ideas about what they should be like (clean and fun to play in, for example).[144] Martin

206

Mulligan emphasises the importance of childhood in human relationships with the more-than-human world:

> *If you ask adults when and how they lost their childhood propensity to be enchanted by the non-human, they struggle for an answer; yet each of us, in our personal journeys, probably mirrors the evolution of Western culture in its journey from a reliance on intuitive knowledge to the dominance of the rational.*[145]

Kay Milton shows that childhood experiences of nature are important to today's conservationists.[146]

There are clear issues here for those responsible for formal education, where there are fears that biological fieldwork may be a dying practice in schools, driven out by the demands of the curriculum and by fears of safety and litigation.[147] There is a real challenge for those in conservation education, in families or in communities to get their enthusiasms across and to make connections with nature that work for children and adults.[148]

Sense of nature is necessarily tied closely to sense of place. John Cameron asks whether it is possible "to engender love of place as a means of achieving conservation objectives"?[149] If so, he suggests that it could be a profound counter-balance to more conventional conservation metaphors about fear of loss and the consequences of unsustainable acts, sermons about improved behaviour, or visions of ecological utopia. He asks: "What if educators and conservationists did see it as their mandate to foster deeper place attachment among students and the general public?" Experience teaching a course in "sense of place" at the University of Western Sydney suggests that it is possible to instil a sense of place in people, at least in some people. What Cameron's work seeks to promote is "an inclusive sense of place, in which experiencing a deeper relationship with one place opens one up to a deeper affiliation with all places" — a growing awareness of multiple stories of place. He urges a "place-responsive culture". Surveys of nature by local people contribute directly to their sense of belonging to place, and to their concern for the way in which it is managed.[150] As Kay Milton points out, "knowledge generates emotion"; knowledge of nature is a source of love of nature.[151]

Re-imagining our place in nature

In early April this year, I was awoken morning after morning by the sound of a cuckoo calling. While not a natural early riser, I reflected that to hear this organic alarm clock was a remarkable privilege. I was brought up in south-west London, and while there were chaffinches and sometimes tawny owls to be heard in the road, there was never a whisper of a cuckoo. Like buzzards on the wing, the cuckoo was for me a bird that others knew, an inhabitant of countryside beyond the urban fringe, to be listened for on holidays and excursions. Despite its pride of place in the national consciousness, a marker of the arrival of Spring and grist for the old-fashioned newspaper letter writer, I never heard a cuckoo regularly until we moved to our present house five years ago.[152]

The thing that makes hearing the cuckoo so important is that it goes and comes back. It is a Summer visitor, its Winter spent far away to the south. Like the swifts over the house and the fieldfares that infest the hawthorn hedges along my route to work, the cuckoo's arrival betokens for me not Spring and the endless round of the seasons, but the capacity of life to endure what humans throw at it. Somehow, these migrants have returned again, back from distant Summer or Winter homes, across landscapes re-fashioned by human action, cities, factories, farmed fields, through skies criss-crossed by air corridors and in places thick with pollution. We are well past the days when radar operators on the English coast mistook flocks of birds for enemy aircraft formations, and we have those rather dismal maps of "ringing recoveries" to show us how far and wide migration systems stretch.[153] But we do not know exactly how they do it: how they infiltrate our built environments; how they profit by our accidental munificence in providing habitat to rest and feed; how they endure the bleak and inert landscapes that we sometimes create.

But they do. Year on year they return, turning up (and waking us up) as they go about their daily lives. The cost in evolutionary terms is huge. I remember years ago a bizarre week on Fair Isle in late September. In addition to a remarkable fall of wrynecks, a great grey shrike, a lanceolated warbler and a hapless White's thrush all turned up on this lonely rocky island.[154] What were they doing there, terminally off course, and disorientated? What was their fate once they had served scientific enterprise by being ringed, and satisfied the fascinated gaze of a handful of birdwatchers? They flew off and died, of course, probably dropping into the hard green sea.

Whatever we feel about it, migration is a percentage game. There is nothing personal about the arrival of cuckoos or fieldfares in their familiar places: there are new faces every year. Nature blows a great deal of flesh and blood on a vast experiment every time these long-distance migration systems click into action in the turning year. What is personal is our reaction to them, the things they tell us about ourselves, our own thinking or imagining, the world we have re-fashioned.

To me, what the arrival of these migrants betokens is simply this: Nature is still there; it is still possible for individual animals to navigate the human-dominated globe and find a space. Humans may annex 40 per cent of the products of the biosphere, and have transformed almost the whole face of the Earth. Nature is officially dead.[155] And, yet, the cuckoo comes to wake us from sleep, the fieldfares to stride the Winter fields, and the swifts to scream in the dusk of a Summer night. The planetary interconnections are still in place; the Arctic, Mediterranean and the Sahel are still all spun together by the weird lacework of evolution.

Moreover, their departure and return marks our own place in nature. It is a reassurance that our rationalising genius is not yet perfected. Our industrialisation of production and consumption, our eagerness to span the Earth in search of novelty and profit, our desire to suck in the services and products we desire from ecosystems and people across the Earth — all these things are yet encompassed by nature. The claims we make on the biosphere are not yet so great that we leave no "waste" for nature's share.

It seems to me that the critical question for conservation is not really about biodiversity, but about us. It is nature's capacity to be itself that matters, and conservation is about setting the terms of the engagement between people and nature. Migration matters because it demonstrates that nature still exists in place — its place, my place. We choose to be where we are; or, at least, we can choose to some extent to behave the way we do in the place where we find ourselves. There is no right way to do conservation. There are only choices. Conservation is possible when we become aware of those choices. Ultimately, I see conservation as the outworking of those choices in our own lives, and in the social and economic systems of which we are part.

Notes and References

Introduction to the Revised Edition

1   The classic works on the draining of the fens are by the geographer Clifford Darby. H.C. Darby (1940) *The Medieval Fenland*, Cambridge University Press, Cambridge; H.C. Darby (1956) *The Draining of the Fens*, Cambridge University Press, Cambridge; H.C. Darby (1983) *The Changing Fenland*, Cambridge University Press, Cambridge.

2   See, for example, E. Duffey (1970) "The management of Woodwalton Fen: a multidisciplinary approach" in E. Duffey and A.S. Watt (eds) *The Scientific Management of Animal and Plant Communities for Conservation*, Blackwell, Oxford (pp.581–597). Contemporary wetland management methods are reviewed by W.J. Sutherland and D.A. Hill (1995) in *Managing Habitats for Conservation*, Cambridge University Press, Cambridge.

3   In 1899 the National Trust was itself less than four years' old; see J. Sheail (1976) *Nature in Trust: the history of nature conservation in Britain*, Blackie, Glasgow; and D.J. Bullock and H.J. Harvey (1995) (eds) *The National Trust and Nature Conservation: 100 years on*, The Linnean Society, London. The most complete historical account of Wicken Fen is by L. Cameron (2001) entitled *Anthropogenic Natures: Wicken Fen and histories of disturbance 1923–43*, Ph.D. thesis, University of Cambridge, Cambridge; but see also L. Cameron (1999) "Histories of disturbance", *Radical History Review* 74: 4–24, and L.F. Friday (ed.) *Wicken Fen: the making of a wetland nature reserve*, Harley Books, Colchester. Wicken Fen has its own website at www.wicken.org.uk/.

4   J.M. Lock, L.F. Friday and T.J. Bennett (1997) "The management of the Fen", pp.213–254 in L.F. Friday (ed.) *Wicken Fen: the making of a wetland nature reserve*, Harley Books, Colchester.

5   L.F. Friday and B.H. Harley (2000) *Checklist of the Flora and Fauna of Wicken Fen*, Harley Books, Colchester.

6   However, the National Trust's thinking about Wicken has been transformed; see the Postscript to this book, and Adrian Colston "Beyond preservation: the challenge of ecological restoration", pp.247–267 in W.M. Adams and M. Mulligan (2003) *Decolonizing Nature: strategies for conservation in a post-colonial era*, Earthscan, London.

7   E.R. Lankester (1914) "Nature reserves", *Nature* 93(2315): 33–35 (p.34)

8   See also J. Sheail (1998) *Nature Conservation in Britain: the formative years*, The Stationery Office, London, and P. Marren (2002) *Nature Conservation: a review of the conservation of wildlife in Britain, 1950–2001*, HarperCollins, London (New Naturalist Series 91).

9   The development of the protected area system in the UK is described in Chapter 2.

10   W.M. Adams (1996) "Creative conservation, landscapes and loss", *Landscape Research* 21(3): 265–276.

11   Most notably M. Shoard's (1980) *The Theft of the Countryside*, Temple Smith, London; but see also P. Lowe, G. Cox, M. MacEwen, T. O'Riordan and M. Winter (1986) *Countryside Conflicts: the politics of farming, forestry and food*, Gower, Aldershot; and W.M. Adams (1986) *Nature's Place: conservation sites and countryside change*, George Allen and Unwin, Hemel Hempstead.

12   These are described in Chapter 8.

13   S. Festing (1996) "The third battle of Newbury-war in the trees", *Ecos: A Review of Conservation* 17(2): 41–48

14   See Chapter 3; see also, for example, P. Evans (1996) "Biodiversity: nature for nerds?", *Ecos, A Review of Conservation* 17(2): 7–12.

15   See Chapter 9.

16   See, for example, A. Parfitt (1995) "Letter from a LA21 activist", *Ecos: A Review of Conservation* 16(3/4): 48–51, and A. Keller (1996) "Sustainability in the Scottish Borders", *Ecos: A Review of Conservation* 17(3/4): 30–41.

17   The 1995 Act is reviewed by T. Burton (1995) "The Environment Act 1995: blessing or bane", *Ecos: A Review of Conservation* 16(3/4): 3–6, and the White Paper by C. Potter (1995) "Tomorrow's countryside?" *Ecos: A Review of Conservation* 16(3/4): 7–9.

18   M. Spray (1995) "Other ways of telling", *Ecos: A Review of Conservation* 16(1): 1; see also other articles in this issue.

19   BANC was established in 1979. See www.banc.org.uk.

20   I am grateful to John Cameron, Laura Cameron, Adrian Colston, Katherine Hearn, Rob Jarman, Martin Mulligan, Rick Minter, David Russell and Steve Trudgill for conversations and ideas while I have been thinking about this revised edition, and to Franc Hughes, Rob Jarman, Rick Minter, Adrian Phillips and David Russell for their careful reading of the new material. Sins of omission and commission are mine alone.

21   K. Milton (2002) *Loving Nature: towards an ecology of emotion*, Routledge, London. Kay Milton was on the advisory committee for the BANC 'Future Nature' project.

22   Not least in conservation; see Susan Pipes (1996) "Environmental information on the internet", *Ecos: A Review of Conservation* 17(2): 63–6.

23   They are discussed in Chapter 4, although many trends have accelerated since 1995, and many new innovations have contributed to the nature and pace of change.

24   N.W. Moore (2002) *Oaks, Dragonflies and People: creating a small nature reserve and relating its story to wider conservation issues*, Harley Books, Colchester (p.105).

25   W.M. Adams (2001) "Joined-up conservation", *Ecos: A Review of Conservation* 22(1): 22–27.
26   I am grateful for this phrase of David Abram's from M. Mulligan (2003) "Feet to the ground in storied landscapes: disrupting the colonial legacy with a poetic politics", pp.268–289 in W.M. Adams and M. Mulligan (eds) *Decolonising Nature: strategies for conservation in a post-colonial era*, Earthscan, London.
27   D.W. Orr (2002) "Four challenges of sustainability", *Conservation Biology* 16: 1457–1460.

Chapter One   Finding Nature

1   Thomas Sharp (1940) *Town Planning*, Penguin Books, Harmondsworth, (p. 28).
2   Countryside Commission (1993) *Heritage Coasts in England and Wales*, Countryside Commission and Countryside Council for Wales, Cheltenham (CCP 252). The development of the seaside resort is described by John Urry (1990) *The Tourist Gaze: leisure and travel in contemporary societies*, Sage, London.
3   SSSIs are notified in England under the Wildlife and Countryside Act.
4   Until 1994 the Norfolk Wildlife Trust was the Norfolk Naturalists Trust. English Nature was created in 1991 when the Nature Conservancy Council was split up, and is responsible for biological and geological conservation in England. UNESCO is the United Nations Educational, Scientific and Cultural Organisation. Ramsar sites are designated under the Ramsar Convention on "Wetlands of International Importance especially as Wildfowl Habitat", signed in 1973. The full title of the EC Birds Directive is the European Communities Council Directive of April 1979 on the Conservation of Wild Birds. The Habitats Directive is discussed in Chapter Three.

Chapter Two   Constructing Conservation

1   John Dower (1945) *National Parks in England and Wales*, Cmd. 6628, HMSO, London, para 97.
2   The most thorough account of the history of conservation in the UK is by John Sheail (1976) *Nature in Trust: the history of nature conservation in Britain*, Blackie, Glasgow. More generalised accounts of the twentieth-century history of conservation are given by David Evans (1992) *A History of Nature Conservation in Great Britain* (Routledge, London), and W.M. Adams (1986) *Nature's Place: conservation sites and countryside change* (Allen and Unwin, Hemel Hempstead).
3   J. Sheail and W.M. Adams (1980) *Worthy of Preservation: a gazetteer of sites of high biological or geological value, identified since 1912*, Discussion Papers in Conservation No. 28, Ecology and Conservation Unit, University College London.
4   By the Royal Society for the Protection of Birds in 1942, the British Ecological Society in 1943 and the Nature Reserves Investigations Committee in 1945.

5   This committee was chaired by Julian Huxley, and its report published in 1947 (*Conservation of Nature in England and Wales*, Cmd. 7122, HMSO, London). See John Sheail (1976) *Nature in Trust: the history of nature conservation in Britain*, Blackie, Glasgow; and J. Sheail (1995) "War and the development of nature conservation in Britain", *Journal of Environmental Management* 44: 267–283. The proposed reserves are listed by Sheail and Adams in *Worthy of Preservation: a gazetteer of sites of high biological or geological value, identified since 1912*, Discussion Papers in Conservation No. 28, Ecology and Conservation Unit, University College London.

6   J.A. Steers (1926) "Scolt Head", *Transactions of the Norfolk and Norwich Naturalists' Society* 12(1): 84–86. An appreciation of Steers's work is given by David Stoddart (1987) *Alfred Steers, 1899–1987: a personal and departmental memoir*, Department of Geography, University of Cambridge.

7   J.A. Steers (1944) "Coastal preservation and planning", *Geographical Journal* 104: 7–18 (quote p. 16). The Ministry of Town and Country Planning was established in 1943.

8   J.A. Steers (1946) "Coastal preservation and planning", *Geographical Journal* 107: 57–60.

9   Max Nicholson (1970) *The Environmental Revolution: a guide to the new masters of the world*, Hodder and Stoughton, London, p. 180 (Penguin edition 1972).

10 The development of planning is described by J. Barry Cullingworth and Vincent Nadin (1994) *Town and Country Planning in Britain: eleventh edition* (Routledge, London); see also G.E. Cherry (1982) *The Evolution of the Planning Acts* (Longman, London), and the series of articles in *The Planner* Volume 60 No. 5 (pp. 675–702).

11 The response of planners and conservationists to urban sprawl is discussed in depth in John Sheail (1981) *Rural Conservation in Inter-war Britain*, Oxford University Press, Oxford.

12 John Sheail (1981) *Rural Conservation in Inter-war Britain*, Oxford University Press, Oxford.

13 The first National Park was Yellowstone in the USA, created in 1872. Accounts of the origins of US National Parks are given by R. Nash (1983) *Wilderness and the American Mind*, (Yale University Press, New Haven) and R.L. DiSilvestro (1993) *Reclaiming the Last Wild Places: a new agenda for biodiversity*, Wiley, New York. National Parks in the British Empire are described in Fitter, R.S.R. (1978) *The Penitent Butchers*, Collins, London.

14 Both still exist. The Commons Preservation Society is now the Open Spaces Society. The origins of the National Trust are described by Jennifer Jenkins and Patrick James (1994) *From Acorn to Oak Tree: the growth of the National Trust 1895 1994*, Macmillan, London.

15 See Tom Stephenson (1989) *Forbidden Land: the struggle for access to mountain and moorland*, Manchester University Press, Manchester.

16 John Sheail (1976) *Nature in Trust: the history of nature conservation in Britain*, Blackie, Glasgow.

17 Argyllshire in 1936, Forest of Dean in 1939. A third park, Gwydir in Snowdonia, followed in 1940. It is interesting that Lord Bledisloe, Parliamentary Under-Secretary to the Minister of Agriculture and a landowner in the Forest of Dean was

so enthused by his experience of National Parks on a visit to the USA and Canada in 1925 that he proposed a National Park in the Forest of Dean in a letter to the Prime Minister in 1928 (John Sheail (1981) *Rural Conservation in Inter-war Britain*, Oxford University Press, Oxford, p. 115).

18 See John Sheail (1976) *Nature in Trust: the history of conservation in Britain*, Blackie, Edinburgh; John Sheail (1981) *Rural Conservation in Inter-war Britain*, Oxford University Press, Oxford, and J. Sheail (1995) "War and the development of nature conservation in Britain", *Journal of Environmental Management* 44: 267–283.

19 Lord Justice Scott (1942) Committee on Land Utilisation in Rural Areas, Cmd. 6378 (HMSO, London).

20 John Sheail (1976) *Nature in Trust: the history of conservation in Britain*, Blackie, Edinburgh, p 105.

21 John Dower (1945) *National Parks in England and Wales*, Cmd 6628, HMSO, London. Dower's work is assessed by J. Sheail (1995) "John Dower, national parks and town and country planning in Britain", *Planning Perspectives* 10: 1–16.

22 Sir J. Douglas Ramsay (1945) *National Parks: a Scottish Survey; Report by the Scottish National Parks Survey Committee*, Cmd. 6631, HMSO, London. Ramsay also chaired a second committee that reported in 1947, *National Parks and the Conservation of Nature in Scotland: report by the Scottish National Parks Committee and the Scottish Wild Life Conservation Committee*, Cmd. 7235, HMSO, London.

23 John Dower (1945) *National Parks in England and Wales*, Cmd. 6628, HMSO London (quote from para. 13, emphasis in original).

24 The proposed Scottish parks were Loch Lomond and the Trossachs; Glen Affric, Glen Cannich and Strath Farrer; Ben Nevis, Glen Coe and Black Moor; Cairngorm; Loch Torridon, Loch Maree and Little Loch Broom. The "reserves" were Knoydart and Ben Lawers.

25 J. Sheail (1993) "The management of wildlife and amenity — a UK post-war perspective", *Contemporary Record* 7: 44–65.

26 Sir Arthur Hobhouse (1947) *National Parks Committee*, Cmd. 7121, HMSO, London; The Scottish Committee was appointed in 1946, chaired again by Sir J. Douglas Ramsay (Sir J. Douglas Ramsay (1947) *National Parks and the Conservation of Nature in Scotland: report by the Scottish National Parks Committee and the Scottish Wild Life Conservation Committee*, Cmd. 7235, HMSO, London).

27 Paradoxically, perhaps, this apparent weakness eventually became a strength in the changed climate of the 1980s; see Adrian Phillips (1994) paper to the Conference at the University of Cardiff, 9 November 1994 on *The Merits of Merger*, unpublished ms.

28 J. Sheail (1995) "War and the development of nature conservation in Britain", *Journal of Environmental Management* 44: 267–283.

29 A.G. Tansley (1945) *Our Heritage of Wild Nature: a plea for organized nature conservation*, Cambridge University Press, Cambridge (p. 41).

30 Julian Huxley (1947) *Conservation of Nature in England and Wales*, Cmd. 7122, HMSO, London; James Ritchie (1949) *Nature Reserves in Scotland: final report*, Cmd. 7814 (HMSO, London).

31 Julian Huxley (1947) *Conservation of Nature in England and Wales*, Cmd. 7122,

HMSO, London, (para 192). The role of science in conservation is discussed further in Chapter Six.

32 See David Evans (1992) A History of Nature Conservation in Britain, Routledge, London; D. Poore and J. Poore (1992) Protected Landscapes in the UK, Countryside Commission, Cheltenham (CCP 362).

33 Ann MacEwen and Malcolm MacEwen (1982) National Parks: conservation or cosmetics? Allen and Unwin, Hemel Hempsead, (p. 24); the relevant part of the Act is Section 11.

34 For details on the background to and debate of this Bill, see W.M. Adams (1986) Nature's Place: conservation sites and countryside change, Allen and Unwin, Hemel Hempstead.

35 Adrian Phillips (1993) "The Countryside Commission and the Thatcher years", in A. Gilg (ed.) Progress in Rural Policy and Planning, Belhaven, London.

36 The Broads is not strictly a National Park, but functions under the Broads Authority as if it were one. It was confirmed in 1989.

37 See John Moir (1991) "National Parks north of the border", Planning Outlook 34: 61–7.

38 Under the Natural Heritage (Scotland) Act 1991.

39 Michael Scott (1992) "What future for the Cairngorms?", ECOS 13(2): 16–23.

40 IUCN (1994) Parks for Life: action plan for protected areas in Europe, IUCN, Gland, Switzerland.

41 Roland Smith (1994) "The call of nature tries a new voice", National Parks Today 38 (Autumn 1994), p. 8. It can be argued that AONBs offer many of the advantages of English and Welsh National Parks while avoiding some of their problems.

42 Under the Nature Conservation and Amenity Lands (Northern Ireland) Order 1985.

43 National Parks and Access to the Countryside Act 1949, para 23.

44 Sheail, J. (1975) Nature in Trust: the history of nature conservation in Great Britain, Blackie, Glasgow.

45 Nature Conservancy Council 16th Annual Report, 1 April 1989–31 March 1990, NCC, Peterborough.

46 John Sheail (1993) "The management of wildlife and amenity — a UK post-war perspective", Contemporary Record 7(1): 44–65. The contents of the "unpublished appendix" are listed by J. Sheail, and W.M. Adams (1980) Worthy of Preservation: a gazetteer of Sites of high biological or geological value, identified since 1912, Discussion Papers in Conservation No. 28, Ecology and Conservation Unit, University College London.

47 This work, and the opposition to it, is described by John Sheail in Pesticides and Nature Conservation: the British experience 1950–1975, (Clarendon Press, Oxford, 1985). A personal view of the work at Monk's Wood is given by Norman Moore (1988) in The Bird of Time: the science and politics of nature conservation, Cambridge University Press.

48 See J. Sheail (1993) "The management of wildlife and amenity — a UK post-war perspective", Contemporary Record 7: 44-65.

49 The life and battles of the Nature Conservancy are described by James Robertson in The Thin Green Line (unpublished ms).

50 Katrina Brown (1994) "Biodiversity", pp. 98-114 in D. Pearce (ed.) *Blueprint 3*, Earthscan, London.

51 See reports by Mike Harley in *Earth Science Conservation* No. 26 (September 1989), 28 (September 1990) and 29 (June 1991). See also NCC (1990) *Earth Science Conservation: a strategy*, NCC, Peterborough.

52 This proportion is similar to that in England, but much less than that in Wales (0.6 per cent) or Scotland (1.4 per cent) or Great Britain as a whole (K. Milton, 1990, *Our Countryside, Our Concern: the policy and practice of conservation in Northern Ireland*, Northern Ireland Environment Link, Belfast).

53 Palmer Newbould (1993) "Conservation", in R.H. Buchanan and B.M. Walker (eds) *Province, City and People: Belfast and its Region*, Greystone Books, Antrim, with the British Association for the Advancement of Science.

54 These are now being renotified Areas of Special Scientific Interest (ASSIs) under Article 24(1) of the Nature Conservation and Amenity lands (Northern Ireland) Order 1985; 20 ASSIs had been renotified by 1990 (K. Milton, 1990, *Our Countryside, Our Concern: the policy and practice of conservation in Northern Ireland*, Northern Ireland Environment Link, Belfast).

55 Prior to 1985, some 48 Areas of Scientific Interest (ASIs) had been declared.

56 The causes of the NCC's demise are complex, and controversial. See Peter Marren (1993) "The siege of the NCC: nature conservation in the eighties", pp. 283–300 in F.B. Goldsmith and A. Warren (eds) *Conservation in Progress*, Wiley; James Robertson's manuscript history of the Nature Conservancy, *The Thin Green Line*, provides both chapter and verse.

57 J. Sheail (1993) "The management of wildlife and amenity — a UK post-war perspective", *Contemporary Record* 7: 44–65.

58 The creation of new cultures for the new organisations (particularly in the case of English Nature) has proved interesting; see John Box (1994) "Changing the conservation culture", *ECOS* 15(2): 16–22 and the reply by B. Smith (1994) "Culture shock", *ECOS* 15 (3/4): 72.

59 The background to the merger is reviewed by Adrian Phillips in his address to a Conference at University of Cardiff 9 November 1994 on *The Merits of Merger*, unpublished ms. The phrase the "great divide" was coined by Ann MacEwen and Malcolm MacEwen (1982) *National Parks: conservation or cosmetics?* Allen and Unwin, Hemel Hempstead. The consultants also said that new agencies would need wholly new senior management teams, and it is rumoured that this punctured the enthusiasm of at least one of the agencies for the idea of merger.

60 The Secretary of State for Wales, John Redwood, cut the budget of the Countryside Council for Wales for 1995–6 by 16 per cent, and following a "Financial Management and Policy Review" planned to hive off their functions to local authorities. See Martin Spray (1994) "Welsh Agency cut back for carve up", *ECOS* 15 (3/4): 73–4.

61 E.M. Nicholson (1976) "The ecological breakthrough", *New Scientist* 72: 460–463.

62 John Sheail (1976) *Nature in Trust: the history of nature conservation in Britain*, Blackie, Glasgow.

63 Janet Dwyer (1991) *The County Wildlife Trusts: primary conservation CARTs*,

University of Cambridge Department of Land Economy Discussion Paper 30. The growth of the Wildlife Trusts is discussed by Philip Lowe and Jane Goyder in *Environmental Groups in Politics* (Allen and Unwin, Hemel Hempstead, 1981).

64 RSPB Annual Reports.

65 Peter Rawcliffe (1994) *Swimming with the Tide: the changing nature of national environmental pressure groups in the UK 1984–1994*, Unpublished Ph.D. Thesis, University of East Anglia; see also Peter Rawcliffe (1995) "Making inroads: transport policy and the British environmental movement", *Environment* 37(3): 6–20, 29–36. The membership data are from *Social Trends 24* (HMSO 1994), Section 9.2.

Chapter Three   Nature Lost

1 E. Ray Lankester (1914) "Nature reserves", *Nature* 93 (2315): 33–5 (p. 33).

2 Angela King and Czech Conroy (1980) *Paradise Lost? The destruction of Britain's wildlife habitats*, Friends of the Earth, London; Chris Rose and Charles Secret (1980) *Cash or Crisis: the imminent failure of the Wildlife and Countryside Act*, Friends of the Earth, London; Tony Juniper (1994) *Gaining Interest: the UK's wildlife wealth and the law*, Friends of the Earth, London; the RSNC appeal is described in *Natural World* 15 (Winter 1985); RSNC (1989) *Losing ground: habitat destruction in the UK*, RSNC, Nettleham; 1989; RSNC (1990) *Nature Conservation: the health of the UK*, RSNC, Lincoln; T.A. Rowell (1991) *SSSIs: a health check*, Wildlife Link, London.

3 Nature Conservancy Council (1984) *Nature Conservation in Great Britain*, NCC, Peterborough.

4 Catherine Caufield (1991) *Thorne Moors*, Sumach Press, St Albans (including a photographic essay by Fay Godwin).

5 This company is Fisons' successor in the horticultural peat business. The agreement was finalised in 1994, *English Nature* 15 (September 1994): 4–5. For background to the campaign, see Peter Rawcliffe (1994) *Swimming with the Tide: the changing nature of national environmental pressure groups in the UK 1984–1994*, Unpublished Ph.D. Thesis, University of East Anglia, Chapter Six.

6 George F.Peterken and Francine M.R. Hughes (1990) "The Changing Lowlands", pp. 48–76 in T.P. Bayliss-Smith and S.E. Owens (eds.) *Britain's Changing Environment from the Air*, Cambridge University Press, Cambridge.

7 Fuller, R.M. (1987) "The changing extent and conservation interest of lowland grasslands in England and Wales: a review of grassland surveys 1930-84", *Biological Conservation* 40: 281–300.

8 George F.Peterken and Francine M.R. Hughes (1990) "The Changing Lowlands", pp. 48–76 in T.P. Bayliss-Smith and S.E. Owens (eds) *Britain's Changing Environment from the Air*, Cambridge University Press, Cambridge.

9 John Sheail (1976) *Nature in Trust: the history of nature conservation in Britain*, Blackie, Glasgow.

10 *Biodiversity: the UK Action Plan*, Cm 2428, HMSO. The Biodiversity Convention definition comes from para 1.11.

11 Edward O. Wilson (1992) *The Diversity of Life*, Penguin Books, Harmondsworth

12 G. Wynne, M. Avery, L. Campbell, S. Gubbay, S. Hawkswell, T. Juniper, M. King, P. Newbury, J. Smart, C. Steel, T. Stones, A. Stubbs, J. Taylor, C. Tydeman, and R. Wynde (1995) *Biodiversity Challenge: an agenda for conservation in the UK*, Second Edition, published by Butterfly Conservation, Friends of the Earth, Plantlife, The Wildlife Trusts Partnership, the Royal Society for the Protection of Birds and the World Wide Fund for Nature, Sandy.

13 Katrina Brown (1994) "Biodiversity", pp. 98–114 in D. Pearce (ed.) *Blueprint 3*, Earthscan, London.

14 G. Wynne, M. Avery, L. Campbell, S. Gubbay, S. Hawkswell, T. Juniper, M. King, P. Newbury, J. Smart, C. Steel, T. Stones, A. Stubbs, J. Taylor, C. Tydeman, and R. Wynde (1995) *Biodiversity Challenge: an agenda for conservation in the UK*, Second Edition, published by Butterfly Conservation, Friends of the Earth, Plantlife, The Wildlife Trusts Partnership, the Royal Society for the Protection of Birds and the World Wide Fund for Nature, Sandy.

15 D.A. Ratcliffe (1984) "Post-medieval and recent changes in British vegetation: the culmination of human influence", *New Phytologist* 98: 73–100.

16 "Nationally rare" species are defined as occurring in 15 $10km^2$ grid squares or less, F.H. Perring and L. Farrell (1983) *British Red Data Book 1. Vascular Plants*, RSNC, Lincoln.

17 The balance between agriculture and conservation since World War Two is reviewed by J. Sheail (1995) "Nature protection, ecologists and the farming context: a U.K. historical perspective", *Journal of Rural Studies* 11: 79–88.

18 Lord Justice Scott (1942) Report of the Committee on Land Utilisation in Rural Areas, Cmd. 6378, HMSO, (paras 158, 160, 172). One member of the Committee, Professor S.R. Dennison, submitted a separate dissenting report.

19 Dower (1945) *National Parks in England and Wales*, (para 27).

20 Dower (1945) *National Parks in England and Wales*, (para 28).

21 For a good account of this process, see J.K. Bowers and P. Cheshire (1983) *Agriculture, the Countryside and Land Use*, Methuen, London. The industrialisation of agriculture is discussed further in Chapter Four.

22 N.W. Moore (1969) "Experience with pesticides and the theory of conservation", *Biological Conservation* 1: 201–207.

23 Richard Westmacott (1983) *Agricultural landscapes: a second look*, Countryside Commission, Cheltenham (CCP 168). See also A. Woods (1984) *Upland Landscape Change: a review of statistics*, Countryside Commission, Cheltenham (CCP 161) and Countryside Commission (1991) *Landscape Change in the National Parks* (CCP 359).

24 Marion Shoard (1980) *The Theft of the Countryside*, Temple Smith, London.

25 See Ann MacEwen and Malcolm MacEwen (1982) *National Parks: conservation or cosmetics?* Allen and Unwin, Hemel Hempstead; and W.M. Adams (1986) *Nature's Place: conservation sites and countryside change*, Allen and Unwin, Hemel Hempstead.

26 See David Goode (1981) "The threat to wildlife habitats", *New Scientist* 22 January 1981: 219–223, and Nature Conservancy Council (1984) *Nature Conservation in Great Britain*, NCC, Peterborough.

27 Norman W. Moore (1987) *The Bird of Time: the science and politics of nature conservation: a personal account*, Cambridge University Press, Cambridge; N.W. Moore (1962) "The heaths of Dorset and their conservation", *Journal of Ecology* 5: 369–371.

28 N.R. Webb (1980) "The Dorset heathlands: present status and conservation", *Bull. Ecol.* 11: 659–664.

29 Data on the extent of different woodland habitats are discussed in G.F. Peterken and H. Allison (1989) *Woods, Trees and hedges: a review of changes in the British Countryside*, Focus in Conservation No. 22, NCC, Peterborough. More recent studies of grassland include Fuller, R.M. (1987) "The changing extent and conservation interest of lowland grasslands in England and Wales : a review of grassland surveys 1930–84", *Biological Conservation* 40: 281–300; T.H. Blackstock, J.P. Stevens, E.A. Howe and D.P. Stevens (1995) "Changes in the extent and fragmentation of heathland and other semi-natural habitats between 1920–22 and 1987–88 in the Llyn Peninsula, Wales, UK", *Biological Conservation* 72: 33–44

30 G. Sinclair (1992) *The Lost Land: land use change in England 1945–1990*, Council for the Protection of Rural England, London.

31 C.J. Barr, R.G.H. Bunce, R.T. Clark, R.M. Fuller, M.T.Furse, M.K. Gillespie, G.B.Groom, C.J.Hallam, M.Hornung, D.C.Howard and M.J. Ness (1993) *Countryside Survey 1990: Main Report*, HMSO, London. The study excluded Northern Ireland. The sponsoring agencies were the Department of the Environment, the Nature Conservancy Council and the Natural Environment Research Council. See also R.M. Fuller, J. Sheail and C.J. Barr (1994) "The land of Britain, 1930-1990: a comparative study of field mapping and remote sensing techniques", *Geographical Journal* 160: 173–184; and articles in ECOS 15 (3/4), 1994.

32 Colin Barr, Chris Benefield, Bob Bunce, Heather Ridsdale and Margaret Whittaker (1986) *Landscape Changes in Britain*, ITE, Abbots Ripton.

33 Land cover is a term developed in remote sensing to describe what scanners and computers detect on the land surface. It is a convenient shorthand for land use and habitat type, although because of technical constraints the "land cover" data can differ significantly from either.

34 The phrase semi-natural vegetation was first coined by A.G. Tansley, and has long been current among British conservationists. It is used to mean vegetation that is influenced by human action and yet retains characteristics of vegetation communities that are presumed to have flourished prior to human management, and are conventionally referred to as "semi-natural". This useful, but somewhat problematic, phrase, and the idea of "naturalness" that lies behind it, are discussed in Chapter Five.

35 Fred Pearce (1995) "Sea life sickened by pollution", *New Scientist* 17 June 1995: 4; issues of marine pollution have recently been highlighted by the RSPB's "Marine Life Campaign".

36 Andrew Tickle (ed.) (1993) *The Acid Test for Plants: acid rain and British plants*, Plantlife, London.

37 Kate Bisset and Andrew Farmer (1993) *SSSIs in England at Risk from Acid Rain*, English Nature Science No. 15, Peterborough.

38   A. Tickle (1994) "Protected areas in Europe — the threat from acid rain", *ECOS* 15(1): 33–9.

39   D.A. Ratcliffe (1984) "Post-medieval and recent changes in British vegetation: the culmination of human influence", *New Phytologist* 98: 73–100.

40   See for example Chris Rose and Phil Hurst (1992) *Can Nature Survive Global Warming?*, WWF International, Gland; and Adam Markham, Nigel Dudley and Sue Stolton (1993) *Some Like It Hot: climate change, biodiversity and the survival of species*, WWF International, Gland, Switzerland; Countryside Commission (1995) *Climate Change, Air Pollution and the Countryside: summary of potential impacts*, Cheltenham (CCP458 FL).

41   Phil Gates (1994) "Climatic change: implications for conservation management", *ECOS* 15 (3/4): 29–34.

42   G.W. Elmes and A. Free (1994) *Climate Change and Rare Species in Britain*, ITE Research Publication No. 8, HMSO, London.

43   See, for example, Plantlife (1991) *Death Knell for Bluebells? Global warming and British plants*, (Plantlife, London); and Keith Clayton and Sue Austin (1993) *Climatic Change, Acidification and Ozone Changes: potential impacts on the English countryside*, unpublished ms.

44   NCC (1984) *Nature Conservation in Great Britain*, NCC, Peterborough, para 3.5.2.

45   The provisions of the 1981 Act are rather complex. There is a fairly full account in W.M. Adams, (1986) *Nature's Place: conservation sites and countryside change*, Allen and Unwin, Hemel Hempstead.

46   There were at that time 5,435 SSSIs in Great Britain, covering 1.71 m ha.

47   Ann MacEwen and Malcolm MacEwen (1983) "National Parks: a cosmetic conservation system?" in A. Warren and F.B. Goldsmith (eds) *Conservation in Perspective*, Wiley, Chichester.

48   These managment agreements include lump sum and annual payments for and leases for NNRs. Over 60 per cent of the total expenditure in 1989/90 was in England. The agreements cost on average £153 per ha in England compared to £49 in Scotland and £92 in Wales.

49   Tim Rice (1994) *Losing Interest: a survey of threats to Sites of Special Scientific Interest in England and Wales*, Friends of the Earth, London.

50   John Sheail (1976) *Nature in Trust: the history of nature conservation in Britain*, Blackie, Glasgow; P.M. Barton, and G.P. Buckley (1983) "The status and protection of notified sites of special scientific interest in South-East England", *Biological Conservation* 27: 213–242.

51   Terry A. Nowell (1991) *SSSIs: a health check*, Wildlife Link, London.

52   Robert Brown (1992) "Site protection in Northern Ireland; why is progress so slow?", *ECOS* 13(2): 30–35; see also Richard Nairn (1992) "Areas of Scientific Interest: time for a re-think?" *ECOS* 13(2): 36–40.

53   Environment Service (1993) *Target 2001: a programme for the survey, declaration and monitoring of Areas of Special Scientific Interest in Northern Ireland*, Environment Service, Belfast.

54   Damage and loss statistics for Scottish SSSIs between 1990 and 1994 were published by Scottish Natural Heritage in their 1993 Annual Report. The number of sites damaged is said to have fallen from 253 in 1990/1 to 161 in 1993/4.

Long-term damage occurred on over 30 sites each year. One SSSI was lost completely, in 1991.

55 The Joint Nature Conservation Committee's budget and staff are provided by the country agencies, the largest contribution coming from English Nature, whose headquarters are just down the street in Peterborough.

56 Sir W. Wilkinson (1992) "Site safeguard in Great Britain", unpublished ms, March 1992.

57 National Audit Office (1994) *Protecting and Managing Sites of Special Scientific Interest*, (Report by the Controller and Auditor General), HMSO, London (para 2.14).

58 Tony Juniper (1994) *Gaining Interest: the UK's wildlife wealth and the law*, Friends of the Earth, London.

59 By 1991, 29 Nature Conservation Orders had been made, there had been one prosecution for breaching NCO terms, and one compulsary purchase. T.A. Rowell (1991) *SSSIs: a health check*, Wildlife Link, London.

60 The list of sites was basically a continuously updated version of those listed in D.A. Ratcliffe (ed.) (1977) *A Nature Conservation Review*, Cambridge University Press, Cambridge (often referred to as "NCR Sites").

61 Ian Brotherton (1994) "SSSIs: betting on a busted flush?", ECOS 15(2): 33–7

62 Sir W. Wilkinson (1992) "Site safeguard in Great Britain", unpublished ms, March 1992 (p. 1).

63 NCC (1990) *16th Annual Report*, NCC, Peterborough.

64 The European Directive on the Conservation of Natural Habitats and of Wild Fauna and Flora (92/43/EC).

65 EC Directive on the Conservation of Wild Birds (79/409/EC)

66 Article 6 of The European Directive on the Conservation of Natural Habitats and of Wild Fauna and Flora (92/43/EC); see Hazel Phillips and Carol Hatton (1994) "Implementing the Habitats Directive in the UK", ECOS 15(1): 17–22, and Carol Hatton (1992) *The Habitats Directive: time for action*, World Wide Fund for Nature UK, Godalming.

67 RSPB (1992) *SSSIs in the 1990s: a check on the health of internationally important bird areas*, RSPB, Sandy, Beds. The two SPAs designated in Northern Ireland are Swan Island and Sheep Island.

68 Derek A. Ratcliffe (1994) *Conservation in Europe: will Britain make the grade? The status of nature resources in Britain and the implementation of the EC 'Habitats and Species' Directive*, Friends of the Earth, London. The 112 SACs considered were large enough to include 250 Nature Conservation Review sites.

69 James Fenton personal comment; RSPB (1995) *Possible Special Areas for Conservation (SACs) in the UK*, RSPB, Sandy.

70 Hazel Phillips and Carol Hatton (1994) "Implementing the Habitats Directive in the UK", ECOS 15(1): 17-22, (p. 21).

71 See Adam Cole-King (1993) Marine Conservation: a new policy area, *Marine Policy* 17(2): 171–185.

72 Susan Gubbay (1989) *Using Sites of Special Scientific Interest to Conserve Seashores for their Marine Biological Interest*, World Wide Fund for Nature, Godalming.

73 Philip Rothwell and Stuart Housden (1990) *Turning the Tide: a future for estuaries,*

RSPB, Sandy; *A Shore Future: RSPB vision for the coast* (not dated); see also R. Sidaway (1991) *A Review of Marina Developments in Southern England*, RSPB and WWF, Godalming.

74 The CFP is reviewed by Michael Holden (not dated) *The Future of the Common Fisheries Policy*, World Wide Fund for Nature, Godalming.

75 MNRs can be declared under Sections 36 and 37 of the Wildlife and Countryside Act 1981 and the Nature Conservation and Amenity Lands Order (Northern Ireland) 1985.

76 See, for example, Robert Brown (1992) "Site protection in Northern Ireland; why is progress so slow?", ECOS 13(2): 30–35.

77 Department of the Environment for Northern Ireland (1994) *Strangford Loch Proposed Marine Nature Reserve: guide to Designation*, DOE (NI), Belfast.

78 Edward O. Wilson (1992) *The Diversity of Life*, Penguin Books, Harmondsworth, p. 268.

79 *Ex situ* conservation is discussed in the context of other approaches by David Western, Mary C. Pearl, Stuart L. Pimm, Brian Walker, Ian Atkinson and David Woodruff (1989) "An agenda for conservation action", pp. 304–232 in D. Western and M. Pratt (eds) *Conservation for the Twenty-first Century*, Oxford University Press, London.

80 *Biodiversity: the UK action plan*, Cm 2428, HMSO, (p. 15).

81 *Biodiversity Challenge* was published by Butterfly Conservation, Friends of the Earth, Plantlife, Royal Society for Nature Conservation — the Wildlife Trusts Partnership, Royal Society for the Protection of Birds, World Wide Fund for Nature. A second edition was published in 1995: *Biodiversity Challenge: an agenda for conservation in the UK*, RSPB, Sandy.

82 Jeffrey A. McNeely, Kenton R. Miller, Walter V. Reid, Russell A. Mittermeier and Tony B. Werner (1990) "Strategies for conserving biodversity", *Environment* 32(3): 16–20, 36–40, (p. 20).

Chapter Four   Conservation and the Global Village

1 Nan Fairbrother (1970) *New Lives, New Landscapes*, The Architectural Press, London (Penguin Books 1972), p. 168.

2 These and subsequent energy figures come from *The Energy Report No. 1*, (1994) published by the Department of Trade and Industry (HMSO, London).

3 In the early 1990s there has been a sharply fought battle for market share in domestic energy supply between gas and electricity on the basis of their "cleanness". Interestingly, both industries have a long record of advertising their contributions to conservation, notwithstanding the impacts of their core business (as indeed does the oil industry). The nuclear industry has also sought to promote a "green" image through arguments based explicitly on the countryside.

4 These and subsequent data on consumer goods come from the *General Household Survey 1992*, Office of Population Census and Surveys (HMSO, London), table 2.34.

5 In 1993, 72 per cent of households owned video recorders; 33 per cent owned CD

players. The proportion of households with computers rose from 13 per cent in 1985 to 23 per cent in 1993. By 1970, almost three-quarters of British households had a refrigerator, nine out of ten had a washing machine and deep freeze, and half a tumble drier and a microwave oven.

6 *General Household Survey 1992*, Office of Population Census and Surveys (HMSO, London), tables 2.31–33.

7 These themes are explore in detail by Dick Hebdige (1988) in *Hiding the Light: on images and things*, (Routledge, London); and by Iain Chambers (1986) in *Popular Culture: the metropolitan experience*, (Routledge, London).

8 Data for 1992, *Social Trends 24*, (HMSO), p. 129.

9 It is not my point that everyone has these things, but that consumerism is so ubiquitous that these things have had profound effects on culture, regardless of individual capacity to obtain particular products.

10 Ignorance of the context of production is not new, but the scale of such ignorance and the significance of impacts are. See Ulrich Beck (1986) *Risk Society: towards a new modernity*, Sage Publications, London; (Published in English 1992).

11 David Harvey (1990) *The Condition of Postmodernity: an enquiry into the origins of cultural change*, Blackwell, Oxford.

12 Richard Peet (1987) "Industrial restructuring and the crisis of international capitalism", pp. 9–32 in R. Peet (ed) *International Capitalism and Industrial Restructuring: a critical analysis*, Allen and Unwin, London (p.19).

13 See Susan Strange's *Casino Capitalism* (Blackwell, Oxford, 1986); and David Harvey (1990) *The Condition of Postmodernity: an enquiry into the origins of cultural change*, Blackwell, Oxford. Time–space compression is discussed by Scott Lash and John Urry (1994) *Economies of Signs and Space*, Sage, London.

14 George Ritzer (1993) *The McDonaldization of Society: an investigation into the changing character of contemporary social life*, Pine Forge Press, Newbury Park, California.

15 Howard Newby (1993) "Social science and public policy", *RSA Journal LXLI* (5439): 365–372, p. 368; see also Scott Lash and John Urry (1994) *Economies of Signs and Space*, Sage, London.

16 Kevin Robins (1991) "Tradition and translation: national culture in its global context", pp. 21–44 in J. Corner and S. Harvey (eds) *Enterprise and Heritage: crosscurrents of national culture*, Routledge, London (p. 29).

17 See for example Dick Hebdige (1988) *Hiding in the Light*. The arguments for and against this notion are discussed by David Harvey (1990) *The Condition of Postmodernity* (Blackwell, Oxford). See also David Harvey (1993) "From space to place and back again: reflections on the condition of postmodernity", pp. 3–29 in J. Bird *et al.* (eds) *Mapping the Futures: local cultures, global changes*, (Routledge, London), and Scott Lash and John Urry (1994) *Economies of Signs and Space*, Sage, London.

18 Kevin Robins (1991) "Tradition and translation: national culture in its global context", pp. 21–44 in J. Corner and S. Harvey (eds) *Enterprise and Heritage: crosscurrents of national culture*, Routledge, London, (p. 25).

19 See, for example, Terry Marsden, Jonathan Murdoch, Philip Lowe, Richard Munton and Andrew Flynn (1993) *Constructing the Countryside*, UCL Press,

London. On industrial restructuring, see for example Ron L. Martin (1989) "The reorganisation of regional theory: alternative perspectives on the changing capitalist space economy", *Geoforum* 20: 187–201 and Meric S. Gertler (1988) "The limits of flexibility: comments on the post-Fordist visions of production and its geography", *Transactions of the Institute of British Geographers N.S.* 13: 419–32.

20 Nan Fairbrother (1970) *New Lives, New Landscapes*, The Architectural Press, London (Penguin Books 1972), p. 16.

21 These are discussed in depth by David Goodman and Michael Redclift (1991) in *Refashioning Nature: food, ecology and culture*, Routledge, London.

22 David Harvey (1990) *The Condition of Postmodernity: an enquiry into the origins of cultural change*, Blackwell, Oxford (p. 300).

23 Links between the farm business and landscape change are discussed in T.K. Marsden and R.J.C. Munton (1991) "The farmed landscape and the occupancy change process", *Environment and Planning A* 23: 663–676, and by Clive Potter (1986) "Processes of countryside change in lowland England", *Journal of Rural Studies* 2: 187–195.

24 There are good accounts of these processes in John Bowers and Paul Cheshire (1983) *Agriculture, the Countryside and land use: an economic critique*, Methuen, London, and Howard Newby (1980) *Green and Pleasant Land? Social change in rural England*, Penguin Books, Harmondsworth.

25 David Goodman and Michael Redclift (1991) *Refashioning Nature: food, ecology and culture*, Routledge, London, (p.92).

26 Graham Cox, Philip Lowe and Michael Winter (1986) "From state direction to self regulation: the historical development of corporatism in British agriculture", *Policy and Politics* 14: 475–490.

27 Terry Marsden, Jonathan Murdoch, Philip Lowe, Richard Munton and Andrew Flynn (1993) *Constructing the Countryside*, UCL Press, London.

28 Clive Potter, Paul Burnham, Angela Edwards, Ruth Gasson and Bryn Green (1991) *The Diversion of Land: conservation in a period of farming contraction*, Routledge, London (p. 8).

29 The implications of a "farm survival policy" for conservation are discussed by Clive Potter (1990) "Conservation under a farm survival policy" *Journal of Rural Studies* 6: 1–7; Set-aside is discussed in Clive Potter, Paul Burnham, Angela Edwards, Ruth Gasson and Bryn Green (1991) *The Diversion of Land: conservation in a period of farming contraction*, Routledge, London; see also RSPB (1991) *A Future for Environmentally Sensitive Farming* (RSPB, Sandy); and G.W. Furness, N.P. Russell and D.R. Colman (1990) *Developing Proposals for Cross Compliance: with particular application to the oilseeds sector* (RSPB, Sandy).

30 Hazel Phillips and Carol Hatton (1994) "Implementing the Habitats Directive in the UK", *ECOS* 15(1): 17–22. These countryside schemes are discussed further in Chapter Nine.

31 Department of Transport (1991) *Transport Statistics Report, National Travel Survey 1989/91*, HMSO, London.

32 Car ownership, and particularly multiple car ownership, is strongly concentrated in wealthier households. Data from *Myths and Facts: transport trends and transport policies*, Transport 2000, London (1984); and Department of Transport (1991)

Transport Statistics Report, National Travel Survey 1989/91, (Government Statistical Service, HMSO, London). See also Royal Commission on Environmental Pollution 18th Report (1994) *Transport and the Environment*, Cmd. 2674, HMSO, London.

33 Gordon Stokes, Phil Goodwin and Francesca Kenny (1992) *Trends in Transport and the Countryside: the Countryside Commission and transport policy in England*, Countryside Commission, Cheltenham (CCP 382).

34 L. Brook *et al.* (1992) *British Social Attitudes Cumulative Source Book* — the First Six Surveys, Gower, Bath, (Data reworked from S11, S30, and S31). The largest cause of change was seen to be the spread of built-up areas. Interestingly, 48 per cent of those interviewed thought new roads were a good thing, against 37 per cent who did not. The links between road building and environmentalism are discussed by Peter Rawcliffe (1995) "Making inroads: transport policy and the British environmental movement", *Environment* 37 (3): 6–20; 29–36.

35 Bob Tobin (1994) "Roads: cruel cuts for the countryside", *Natural World* 41, Autumn 1994, p. 15. The destruction of Twyford Down is discussed in Chapter Five.

36 In the mid-1980s, there were 1.2 cars per household in rural areas compared to 0.85 in London and rural people drove on average 321 miles per week.

37 Andrew Johnson (1994) "What's super about big quarries", *ECOS* 15 (3/4): 35–42.

38 See Terry Marsden, Jonathan Murdoch, Philip Lowe, Richard Munton and Andrew Flynn (1993) *Constructing the Countryside*, UCL Press, London.

39 Gordon Clark, J. Darrall, R. Grove-White, P. Macnaghten and J. Urry (1993) *Leisure Landscapes: leisure, culture and the English Countryside: challenges and conflicts*, Council for the Protection of Rural England, London (p. 34).

40 Thomas Sharp (1940) *Town Planning*, Penguin Books, Harmondsworth, (pp. 91–2.

41 Michael Dower (1965) *The Challenge of Leisure*, Civic Trust, London (p. 5).

42 J. Allan Patmore (1970) *Land and Leisure*, David and Charles, Newton Abbott (Pelican Books 1972).

43 Sponsors of the Day Visits Survey include the Countryside Commission, the Countryside Council for Wales, Scottish Natural Heritage, the Department of National Heritage, the Scottish and Welsh Tourist Boards, the Forestry Commission and British Waterways. Data are taken from the *Countryside Recreation Network News* 2(2): 7–12, February 1994. The 1993 survey excluded Northern Ireland.

44 An amendment to make the quiet enjoyment and understanding of the special qualities of the National Parks was inserted into the Environment Bill in the House of Lords in 1995, although subsequently removed in the Commons.

45 These issues are discussed in depth in Gordon Clark, J. Darrall, R. Grove-White, P. Macnaghten and J. Urry (1993) *Leisure Landscapes: leisure, culture and the English Countryside: challenges and conflicts*, Council for the Protection of Rural England, London. The quote is from p. 39.

46 Ken Worpole (1991) "The age of leisure", pp. 137–150 in J. Corner and S. Harvey (eds) *Enterprise and Heritage: crosscurrents of national culture*, Routledge, London (p. 147).

47 Howard Newby (1993) "Social science and public policy", RSA Journal LXLI (5439): 365–372, (p. 369).

48 John Corner and Sylvia Harvey (1991) "Mediating tradition and modernity: the heritage/enterprise couplet", pp. 45–75 in John Corner and Sylvia Harvey (eds) Enterprise and Heritage: crosscurrents of national culture, Routledge, London.

49 See G. Clark, J. Darrall, R. Grove-White, P. Macnaghten and J. Urry (1993) Leisure Landscapes: leisure, culture and the English Countryside: challenges and conflicts, Council for the Protection of Rural England, London. See also the National Trust's response to these issues in Linking People and Place: a consultation report (National Trust, 1995).

50 Philip Lowe, Judy Clark and Graham Cox (1993) "Reasonable creatures: rights and rationalities in valuing the countryside", Journal of Environmental Planning and Management 36: 101–115.

51 Alexander Wilson (1992) The Culture of Nature: North American landscape from Disney to Exxon Valdez, Blackwell, Oxford, (p. 43). Cultural dimensions of landscape in the USA and the UK are compared by Michael Bunce (1994) The Countryside Ideal: Anglo-American Images of Landscape, Routledge, London.

52 Shelagh J. Squire (1993) "Valuing countryside: reflections on Beatrix Potter tourism", Area 25(1): 5–10.

53 The implications of this courtship of the consumer are discussed by L.M. Benton (1995) "Selling the natural or selling out? Exploring environmental merchandising", Environmental Values 17(1): 3–22.

54 Max Nicholson (1987) The New Environmental Age, Cambridge University Press, Cambridge, p. 78.

55 The Society for the Protection of the Fauna of the Empire is still very active, as Fauna and Flora International, although it has changed a great deal. British colonial conservation is described briefly in my book Green Development: environment and sustainability in the Third World (Routledge 1990), and at greater length in John M. Mackenzie in The Empire of Nature: hunting, conservation and British imperialism, (1989, Manchester University Press, Manchester). See also Bernard and Michael Grzimek (1960) Serengeti Shall Not Die, Collins, London and G.A.W. Guggisburg (1966) S.O.S. Rhino, Andre Deutsch, London.

56 Robert Arvill (1967) Man and Environment: crisis and the strategy of choice, Penguin Books, Harmondsworth.

57 On the recent growth of environmentalism, see Peter Rawcliffe (1994) Swimming with the Tide: the changing nature of national environmental pressure groups in the UK 1984–1994, Unpublished ph.D. Thesis, University of East Anglia. See also Peter Rawcliffe (1995) "Making inroads: transport policy and the British environmental movement", Environment 37 (3): 6–20; 29–36.

58 Curiously, the environment remained a low political priority in polls, perhaps because the worldview of politicians is obsessively focused on conventional wealth-creation politics and the great game of Westminster, see Chris Rose (1993) "Beyond the struggle for proof: factors changing the environmental movement", Environmental Values 2: 285–298

59 The work referred to here is discussed in two chapters of the book Conservation in Progress, edited by F.B. Goldsmith and A. Warren (Wiley 1993), the first by

Carolyn Harrison ("Nature conservation, science, and popular values", pp. 35–49), and the second by Jacquelin Burgess ("Representing nature: conservation and the mass media", pp. 51–64). Other papers include C.M. Harrison and J. Burgess (1994) "Social constructions of nature: a case study of conflicts over the development of Rainham Marshes", *Transactions of the Institute of British Geographers* N.S. 19: 291–310; C.M. Harrison and J. Burgess (1992) "Rainham Marshes in the media", *ECOS* 13: 20–26 and Jacquelin Burgess, Carolyn Harrison and Paul Maiteny (1993) "Making sense of news about nature", pp. 115–134 in J. Burgess (ed.) *People, Economies and Nature Conservation*, University College London Ecology and Conservation Unit, Discussion Paper 60. The Rainham case and wider issues are discussed in detail by Burgess and Harrison in "The circulation of claims in the cultural politics of environmental change", in Anders Hansen (ed.) (1993) *The Mass Media and Environmental Issues*, Leicester University Press, London.

60 Stuart Hall (1991) "The local and the global: globalisation and ethnicity", in A. King (ed.) *Culture, Globalisation and the World System*, Macmillan, London.

Chapter Five   Culture and the Countryside

1 Alan Holland and Kate Rawles (1993) "Values in conservation", *ECOS: A Review of Conservation* 14(1): 14–19.

2 John Corner and Sylvia Harvey (1991) "Mediating tradition and modernity: the heritage/enterprise couplet", pp. 45–75 in John Corner and Sylvia Harvey (eds) *Enterprise and Heritage: crosscurrents of national culture*, Routledge, London, p. 53.

3 Thomas Sharp (1940) *Town Planning*, Penguin Books, Harmondsworth, (pp. 91–92).

4 John Urry (1990) *The Tourist Gaze: leisure and travel in contemporary societies*, Sage, London.

5 Raymond Williams (1993) *The Country and the City*, Hogarth Press, London (1st edition: Chatto and Windus, 1953); Michael Bunce (1994) *The Countryside Ideal: Anglo-American images of landscape*, Routledge, London; John Rennie Short (1991) *Imagined Country: society, culture and environment*, Routledge, London.

6 To NIMBYs ("Not in My Back Yard"), we might add NOTEs (the "Not Over There Eithers"); see Chris Blackhurst (1994) "NOTEs: the rural taste tyrants", *Observer* 21 August 1994 (p.3).

7 Nan Fairbrother (1970) *New Lives, New Landscapes*, The Architectural Press, London (Penguin Books 1972) (p. 106).

8 Nan Fairbrother (1970) *New Lives, New Landscapes*, The Architectural Press, London (Penguin Books 1972) (pp. 105, 106).

9 John Corner and Sylvia Harvey (1991) "Mediating tradition and modernity: the heritage/enterprise couplet", pp. 45–75 in John Corner and Sylvia Harvey (eds) *Enterprise and Heritage: crosscurrents of national culture*, Routledge, London, emphasis in original.

10 Stephen Daniels and Denis Cosgrove (1988) "Introduction: iconography and landscape", pp. 1–10 in Stephen Daniels and Denis Cosgrove (eds) *The*

Iconography of Landscape, Cambridge University Press, Cambridge (p. 1).

11 Kay Milton (1993) "Land or landscape — rural planning policy and the symbolic construction of the countryside", pp. 129–150 in M. Murray and J. Greer (eds) *Rural Development in Ireland*, Avebury, Aldershot, (p. 139).

12 Raymond Williams (1993) *The Country and the City*, Hogarth Press, London (1st edition: Chatto and Windus, 1953), (pp. 3 and 7–8).

13 Raymond Williams (1993) *The Country and the City*, Hogarth Press, London (1st edition: Chatto and Windus 1953) (p. 1).

14 Martin J. Weiner (1981) *English Culture and the Decline of the Industrial Spirit, 1850–1980*, Cambridge University Press, Cambridge.

15 On the lack of appeal of Western ideas about conservation in Africa see G.W. Burnett and Kamuyu wa Kang'ethe (1994) "Wilderness and the Bantu mind", *Environmental Ethics* 16(2): 145–160.

16 Quoted by Chris Smout (1991) *The Highlands and the Roots of Green Consciousness, 1750–1990*, Scottish Natural Heritage, (p.1).

17 Michael Bunce (1994) *The Countryside Ideal: Anglo-American images of landscape*, Routledge, London.

18 Phil Kinsman (1995) "Landscape, race and national identity: the photography of Ingrid Pollard" *Area* 27(4): 300–310.

19 David Matless (1990) "Definitions of England, 1928–89: preservation, modernism and the nature of the nation", *Built Environment* 16: 179–191.

20 Shelagh J. Squire (1993) "Valuing countryside: reflections on Beatrix Potter tourism", *Area* 25: 5–10.

21 W.G. Hoskins (1970) *The Making of the English Landscape*, Penguin Books, Harmondsworth (1st edition: Hodder and Stoughton, 1955), (pp. 298–299).

22 Vaughan Cornish (1932) *The Scenery of England: a study of harmonious grouping in town and country*, Council for the Preservation of Rural England, London, (p. 21). See also Michael Bunce (1994) *The Countryside Ideal: Anglo-American images of landscape*, Routledge, London; John Rennie Short (1991) *Imagined Country: society, culture and environment*, Routledge, London).

23 Martin J. Weiner (1981) *English Culture and the Decline of the Industrial Spirit, 1850–1980*, Cambridge University Press, Cambridge (p. 7).

24 Martin J. Weiner (1981) *English Culture and the Decline of the Industrial Spirit, 1850–1980*, Cambridge University Press, Cambridge, (pp. 49–50).

25 Portrayed, for example, in Kipling's poem *The Land*, in James Cochrane (ed., 1977) *Rudyard Kipling: selected verse*, Penguin Books, Harmondsworth.

26 J.A. Steers (1944) "Coastal preservation and planning", *Geographical Journal* 104: 7–18 (pp. 11 and 12).

27 Quoted in Edward Abelson (ed.) *A Mirror of England: an anthology of the writings of H.J. Massingham* (1888–1952), Green Books, Hartland. The quotes are from pp. 93–98. *Through the Wilderness* was published in 1935 by Cobden-Sanderson.

28 Here and subsequently, *sic*.

29 The development of Wordsworth's *Guide* and his other work is related to environmental thought by Jonathan Bate (1991) *Romantic Ecology: Wordsworth and the environmental tradition*, Routledge, London. The first edition under Wordsworth's name was in 1820, the most extensive in 1842.

229

30 Meredith Veldman (1993) *Fantasy, the Bomb and the Greening of Britain: Romantic protest, 1945–1980*, Cambridge University Press, Cambridge (pp. 113, 207).

31 See for example Dick Hebdige (1988) in *Hiding the Light: on images and things*, Routledge, London; and Iain Chambers (1986) *Popular Culture: the metropolitan experience*, Routledge, London, (p. 36).

32 Eric Hobsbawm (1994) *Age of Extremes: the short twentieth century 1914–1991*, Michael Joseph, London (Extract in the *Independent on Sunday*, 9 October 1994, pp. 4–10, quote p. 5).

33 Stephen Cotgrove and Andrew Duff (1980) "Environmentalism, middle-class radicalism and politics", *Sociological Review* 28(2): 333–351; see also S. Cotgrove (1982) *Catastrophe or Cornucopia: the environment, politics and the future*, Wiley, Chichester.

34 Raymond Williams (1993) *The Country and the City*, Hogarth Press, London (p. 9).

35 Samuel P. Hays (1997) *Beauty, Health and Permanence: environmental politics in the United States, 1955–1985*, Cambridge University Press, Cambridge (p. 36).

36 Peter Rawcliffe (1995) "Making inroads: transport policy and the British environmental movement", Environment 37(3): 16–20; 29–36. "Monkey-Wrenching" refers to physical attacks on property or machinery involved in the destruction of nature, and is taken from Edward Abbey's wonderful novel, *The Monkey Wrench Gang* (1975, J.B. Lippincott, New York).

37 Derek Langslow (1994), quoted in "Gardeners who walked on the wild side", *English Nature* No. 14: 10–11 (p. 11); see also Paul Evans (1995) "Wild at Heart", *Geographical* lxvii (5): 26–9.

38 Sir Magnus Magnusson (1994) *Scottish Natural Heritage, Annual Report 1992–3*, SNH, Edinburgh.

39 Alexander Wilson (1992) *The Culture of Nature: North American landscape from Disney to the Exxon Valdez*, Blackwell, London, pp.189–90 and 291.

40 Alan Holland and Kate Rawles (1993) "Values in conservation", *ECOS: A Review of Conservation* 14(1): 14–19.

Chapter Six   Making Nature

1   Svend Erik Larsen (1992) "Is nature really natural?", *Landscape Research* 17(3): 116–122 (p. 116).

2   Alexander Wilson (1992) *The Culture of Nature: North American Landscape from Disney to the Exxon Valdez*, Blackwell, London, pp.189–90, 291.

3   The classic work on this is by A.S. Watt and E.W. Jones (1948) "The Ecology of the Cairngorms: the environment and the altitudinal zonation of vegetation", *Journal of Ecology* 36: 283–304.

4   *Mountain Flowers* is by John Raven and Max Walters (Collins, 1956). An excellent and more recent (and equally evocative) book is Derek Ratcliffe's *Highland Flora* (Highlands and Islands Development Board, Edinburgh, 1977).

5   See for example N.G. Bayfield (1971) "Some effects of walking and skiing on vegetation at Cairngorm", pp. 469–485 in E. Duffey and A.S. Watt (eds) *The Scientific Management of Animal and Plant Communities for Conservation*, (Blackwell,

Oxford), and Adam Watson (1984) "Paths and people in the Cairngorms", *Scottish Geographical Magazine* 100: 151–160.

6   N.V. Pears (1967) "Present tree lines of the Cairngorm Mountains, Scotland", *Journal of Ecology* 55: 815–829.

7   Adam Watson (1983) "Eighteenth century deer numbers and pine regeneration near Braemar, Scotland", *Biological Conservation* 25: 289–306.

8   The conflict over deer, overgrazing and the contrasting ways in which nature and "the Highlands" are represented is discussed by Mark Togood (1995) "Representing ecology and the Highland tradition", *Area* 27: 102–109.

9   A.G. Tansley (1945) *Our Heritage of Wild Nature: a plea for organized nature conservation*, Cambridge University Press, Cambridge (p. 7–8).

10 A great deal of research on the ecology of the grasslands on Snowdonia was done under the aegis of the International Biological Programme, see D.F. Perkins (1978) "Snowdonia grassland: introduction, vegetation, climate", pp. 289-296 in O.W. Heal and D.F. Perkins (eds) *Production Ecology of British Moors and Montane Grasslands*, Springer Verlag, New York.

11 Arthur G. Tansley (1939) *The British Islands and their Vegetation*, Cambridge University Press, London; Arthur G. Tansley (1945) *Our Heritage of Wild Nature: a plea for organized nature conservation*, Cambridge University Press, Cambridge (p. 1).

12 Nature Conservancy Council (1989) *Guidelines for Selection of Biological SSSIs: rationale, operational approach and criteria; detailed guidelines for species groups*, Nature Conservancy Council, Peterborough (p. 10).

13 See, for example, Oliver Rackham's books: *Trees and Woodlands in the British Landscape* (Dent, London, 1976): and *The History of the Countryside* (Dent, London, 1986).

14 Oliver Rackham (1975) *Hayley Wood: its history and ecology*, Cambridge and Isle of Ely Naturalist's Trust, Cambridge. The category of "Ancient Woodland" is usually taken to include woods that have remained un-grubbed-up (even if clear-felled) since about AD 1600, effectively since the earliest map records. It is thought that many of them have been wooded since agricultural land was first cleared around them.

15 Interestingly, the Wildlife Trust of Bedfordshire and Cambridgeshire began commercial exploitation of coppice products again in the Winter of 1993/4.

16 George F. Peterken (1981) *Woodland Conservation and Management*, Chapman and Hall, London.

17 Robert P. McIntosh (1985) *The Background of Ecology: concept and theory*, Cambridge University Press, London (p. 77). F.E. Clements' work includes *Research Methods in Ecology* (University Publishing Company, Lincoln, 1905) and *Plant Succession: an analysis of the development of vegetation*, (Carnegie Institute, Washington D.C., Publication 290, 1916). Arthur G. Tansley's ideas are set out in "British ecology in the past quarter century: the plant community and the ecosystem", *Journal of Ecology* 27: 513–530.

18 Steward T.A. Pickett, V. Thomas Parker and Peggy L. Feidler (1992) "The new paradigm in ecology: implications for conservation biology above the species level", pp. 65-88 in P.L.Feidler and S.K. Jain (eds) *Conservation Biology: the theory*

and practice of nature conservation, preservation and management, Chapman and Hall, London.

19 There is a good summary of Britain's former vegetation in Peter Vincent (1990) *The Biogeography of the British Isles: an introduction*, Routledge, London. See also H.J.B. Birks (1986) "Late-Quaternary biotic changes in terrestrial and lacustrine environments, with particular reference to north-west Europe", pp. 3–65 in B.E. Berglund (ed.) *Handbook of Holocene Palaeoecology and Palaeohydrology*, Wiley, Chichester. .

20 Hazel Delcourt and Paul Delcourt (1991) *Quaternary Ecology: a palaeoecological perspective*, Chapman and Hall, London.

21 Peter D. Moore (1990) "Vegetation's place in history", *Nature* 347 (25 October 1990): 710. Similar dynamism probably characterises other geological periods, but our knowledge of them is much less detailed.

22 Donald Worster (1994) "Nature and the disorder of history", *Environmental History Review* 18(2): 1–16, (reprinted in Michale Soulé and Gary Lease (eds.) *Reinventing Nature: responses to postmodern deconstruction*, Island Press, Washington D.C.).

23 See S.T.A. Pickett and P.S. White (1985) *The Ecology of Natural Disturbance and Patch Dynamics*, Academic Press, New York; Steward T.A. Pickett, V. Thomas Parker and Peggy L. Feidler (1992) "The new paradigm in ecology: implications for conservation biology above the species level", pp. 65–88 in P.L.Feidler and S.K. Jain (eds) *Conservation Bioogy: the theory and practice of nature conservation, preservation and management*, Chapman and Hall, London (p. 70).

24 These ideas are discussed in H. Delcourt and P. Delcourt (1991) *Quaternary Ecology: a paleoecological perspective*, Chapman and Hall, London; and in Michael A. Huston (1994) *Biological Diversity: the coexistence of species on changing landcapes*, Cambridge University Press, Cambridge.

25 Robert M. May (1989) "Levels of organisation in ecology", pp. 339–363 in J.M. Cherrett (ed.) *Ecological Concepts: the contribution of ecology to an understanding of the natural world*, Blackwell, Oxford (for the British Ecological Society) (p. 339).

26 Johan Van Zoest (1992) "Gambling with nature? A new paradigm of nature and its consequences for nature management strategy", pp. 503–514 in R.W.G. Carter, T.G.F. Curtis and M.S. Sheehy-Skeffington (eds) *Coastal Dunes*, Balkema, Rotterdam, (p. 510).

27 The problem is parasites, and bad burning practices, although birds of prey still sometimes get the blame from keepers and myopic lairds; for the science see P. Hudson (1986) *Red Grouse: the biology and management of a wild gamebird*, Game Conservancy, Fordingbridge.

28 The British Ecological Society published a report on nature reserves in 1943. Tansley's fundamental book on British vegetation had been published as early as 1911 (A. G. Tansley (1911) *Types of British Vegetation*, Cambridge University Press, Cambridge). Tansley subsequently became the first Chairman of the Nature Conservancy. The work of Tansley and the British Ecological Society is described in J. Sheail, (1987) *Seventy-five Years in Ecology: the British Ecological Society*, Blackwell, Oxford.

29 E.M. Nicholson (1957) *Britain's Nature Reserves*, Country Life Limited, London (p. 20).

30 W.T. Williams (1958) "Conservation: is it important?", *Journal of the Institute of Biology* 5(4): 86–8.

31 E.M. Nicholson (1957) *Britain's Nature Reserves*, Country Life Limited, London, (pp. 26, 19).

32 Norman Henderson (1992) "Wilderness and the nature conservation ideal: Britain, Canada and the United States contrasted", *Ambio* 21(6): 394–399 (p. 397).

33 The Cow Green saga is described by R. Gregory (1975) "The Cow Green reservoir", pp. 14–201 in P.J. Smith (ed.) *The Politics of Physical Resources*, Penguin, Harmondsworth. A good introduction to research on the area is A.R. Clapham (ed.) *Upper Teesdale: the area and its natural history*, Collins, London. Earlier research includes C.D. Pigott (1956) "The vegetation of Upper Teesdale in the North Pennines", *Journal of Ecology* 44: 545–586, and H. Godwin and S.M. Walters (1967) "The scientific importance of Upper Teesdale", *Proceedings of the Botanical Society of the British Isles* 6: 348–351.

34 See Chapter Five.

35 S. Yearly (1993) "Standing in for nature: the practicalities of environmental organisations' use of science", pp. 59–72 in K. Milton (ed.) *Environmentalism: the view from anthropology*, Routledge, London.

36 Neil Evernden (1992) *The Social Creation of Nature*, Johns Hopkins University Press, Baltimore.

37 Quoted in J. Blunden and N. Curry (eds) (1985) *The Changing Countryside*, Croom Helm, London, (p. 117).

38 Julian Huxley (1947) *Conservation of Nature in England and Wales*, Cmd. 7122 (HMSO, London), (para 56).

39 Norman W. Moore (1987) *The Bird of Time: the science and politics of nature conservation*, Cambridge University Press, Cambridge (pp. 87–8).

40 A.G. Tansley (1945) *Our Heritage of Wild Nature: a plea for organized nature conservation*, Cambridge University Press, Cambridge (p. 6).

41 For example Donna J. Haraway (1991) *Simians, Cyborgs and Women: the reinvention of nature*, Free Association Books, London.

42 See for example Fitsimmons (1989) "The matter of nature", *Antipode* 21(2): 106–120; see also Neil Smith (1984) *Uneven Development*, Blackwell, Oxford; and Michael Redclift (1987) "The production of nature and the reproduction of the species", *Antipode* 19(2): 222–230.

43 Margaret Fitsimmons (1989) "The matter of nature", *Antipode* 21(2): 106–120 (pp. 106–8, emphasis in the original).

44 Donna J. Haraway (1991) *Simians, Cyborgs and Women: the reinvention of nature*, Free Association Books, London.

45 See Brian Wynne (1992) "Uncertainty and environmental learning: reconceiving science and policy in the preventative paradigm", *Global Environmental Change* June 1992: 111–127.

46 Robin Grove-White (1991) "The emerging shape of environmental conflict in the 1990s", *RSA Journal* 139 (5419) 437-447 (p. 442).

47 Neil Evernden (1992) *The Social Creation of Nature*, Johns Hopkins University Press, Baltimore, (p. 15). Film of chimpanzees hunting monkeys was incorporated

in David Attenborough's *Trials of Life* series on BBC. Dolphin violence was reported in *The Observer* on Sunday 4th December 1994 under the title "Dolphins born to a life of violence". Anna Bramwell has discussed the links between German fascism in the 1930s and ideas of nature in *Ecology in the Twentieth Century: a history* (1988, Yale University Press, New Haven).

48 Donald Worster (1994) "Nature and the disorder of history", *Environmental History Review* 18(2): 1–16 (p. 3).

Chapter Seven   Nature and the Wild

1 Neil Evernden (1992) *The Social Creation of Nature*, Johns Hopkins University Press, Baltimore (p. 122).

2 Norman Moore (1969) "Experience with pesticides and the theory of conservation", *Biological Conservation* 1: 201–207 (p. 203).

3 Philip Lowe, Judy Clark and Graham Cox (1993) "Reasonable creatures: rights and rationalities in valuing the countryside", *Journal of Environmental Planning and Management* 36: 101–115 (p. 103).

4 *Biodiversity: the UK action plan*, Cm 2428, HMSO, London (para 1.28).

5 See James Fenton (1984) "Even more about the purpose of nature conservation" *ECOS* 5(4): 39–41; and discussion in Kate Rawles and Alan Holland (1994) *The Ethics of Conservation*, unpublished ms.

6 Edward O. Wilson (1984) *Biophilia: the human bond with other species*, Harvard University Press, Cambridge, Mass (p. 1).

7 Stephen R. Kellert (1993) "Introduction", pp. 20–27 in Kellert and Wilson (eds) *The Biophilia Hypothesis*, Island Press, Washington D.C..

8 Edward O. Wilson (1992) "Biophilia and the conservation ethic", pp. 31–41 in Kellert and Wilson (eds) *The Biophilia Hypothesis*, Island Press, Washington D.C., (p. 40).

9 Stephen R. Kellert (1993) "Coda", pp. 455–6 in Kellert and Wilson (eds) *The Biophilia Hypothesis*, Island Press, Washington D.C..

10 *Biodiversity: the UK Action Plan*, Cm 2428, HMSO, London (paras 3.108 and 3.109).

11 Richard Mabey (1980) *The Common Ground: a place for nature in Britain's future*, Hutchinson, London, with the Nature Conservancy Council (p. 251).

12 Lars-Erik Liljelund (1991) "Conservationism's view of nature", pp. 9–20 in Lars J. Lundgren (ed.) *Views of Nature*, Swedish Environmental Protection Agency and the Swedish Council for Planning and Coordination of Research, Stockholm (p.14).

13 Patrick D. Murphy (1992) "Rethinking the relations of nature, culture, agency", *Environmental Values* 1: 311–320, (p. 312).

14 Robert E. Goodin (1992) *Green Political Theory*, Polity Press, Oxford.

15 And human hands have been far more influential elsewhere than many conservationists like to think, for example in the "wilderness" areas of North America, in Amazonia, or the savannas of Africa.

16 For a discussion of thinking about wilderness, see Roderick Nash (1983)

Wilderness and the American Mind, Yale University Press, New Haven, and Max Oeschlager (1991) *The Idea of Wilderness*, Yale University Press, New Haven.

17 Bill McKibben (1990) *The End of Nature*, Penguin Books, Harmondsworth, (p. 88).

18 Bill McKibben (1990) *The End of Nature*, Penguin Books, Harmondsworth, (pp. 7, 44, 55; emphasis in original).

19 Bill McKibben (1990) *The End of Nature*, Penguin Books, Harmondsworth (p. 84).

20 On the impact of pre-Columbian pre-industrial people, see Gary Paul Nabhan (1995) "Cultural parallax in viewing North American Habitats", pp. 87–101 in P.L. Feidler and S.K. Jain (eds) *Conservation Biology: the theory and practice of nature conservation, preservation and management*, Chapman and Hall, London (p. 70).

21 There is another way in which McKibben argues that "nature" has ended, in our increasing capacity to intervene directly in the genetic modification of organisms that was once the fruit of slow processes of evolution through genetic engineering. This is a more profound and unsettling argument, but is not pursued here.

22 Robert Goodin (1992) *Green Political Thought*, Polity Press, Oxford.

23 Robert Goodin (1992) *Green Political Thought*, Polity Press, Oxford (p. 53, emphasis in original).

24 Donald Worster (1994) "Nature and the disorder of history", *Environmental History Review* 18(2): 1–16 (p. 14).

25 Carolyn Merchant (1994) "William Cronon's Nature's Metropolis", *Antipode* 26(2): 135–140 (p. 139).

26 Margaret Fitsimmons (1989) "The matter of nature", *Antipode* 21(2): 106–120.

27 Both Raymond Williams and C.S. Lewis have written on the historical evolution of ideas of "nature", see C.S. Lewis (1967) *Studies in Words*, Cambridge University Press, Cambridge; R. Williams (1980) *Problems of Materialism and Culture*, Redwood Burn.

28 Erazim Kohák (1984) *The Embers and the Stars: a philosophical enquiry into the moral sense of nature*, University of Chicago Press, Chicago (pp 5, 6).

29 See, for example, Richard Nelson (1993) "Searching for the lost arrow: physical and spiritual ecology in the hunter's world", pp. 201–228 in Stephen R. Kellert and Edward O. Wilson (1993) *The Biophilia Hypothesis*, Island Press, Washington D.C. (p. 218).

30 Neil Evernden (1992) *The Social Creation of Nature*, Johns Hopkins University Press, Baltimore (p. 116).

31 Neil Evernden (1992) *The Social Creation of Nature*, Johns Hopkins University Press, Baltimore (p. 109). I am grateful to Kay Milton for her insights here.

32 Neil Evernden (1992) *The Social Creation of Nature*, Johns Hopkins University Press, Baltimore (p. 109).

33 John Fowles (1979) *The Tree*, The Sumach Press, St Albans, (pp. 53, 81, emphasis in original).

34 Ian McHarg (1969) *Design with Nature*, Natural History Press, Garden City, NY (p. 5).

35 On the intrinsic rights of nature see Holmes Rolston III (1988) *Environmental Ethics*, Temple, Philadelphia; for Deep Ecology see for example, Bill Devall and

George Sessions (1985) *Deep Ecology: living as if nature mattered*, Peregrine Smith, Salt Lake City; George Sessions (ed.) (1995) *Deep Ecology for the 21st Century*, Shambhala, Boston and London. See also James Fenton (1987) "The ecology of environmentalism: some ideas for discussion", ECOS 8(4): 28–33.

36 Martin Spray (1993) "Concerning little things", ECOS 14(1): 37–41.

37 Richard Nelson (1993) "Searching for the lost arrow: physical and spiritual ecology in the hunter's world", pp. 201–228 in Stephen R. Kellert and Edward O. Wilson (1993) *The Biophilia Hypothesis*, Island Press, Washington D.C. (p. 218).

38 *Biodiversity: the UK action plan*, Cm 2428, HMSO, London.

39 Edward O. Wilson (1992) *The Diversity of Life*, Penguin, Harmondsworth (first published Belknap Press, Harvard University Press, 1992) (p. 271).

40 The Biological Service proposed by the Huxley Committee in 1947 was to have advised upon and controlled the consumptive use of wild species (particularly game-birds, wildfowl and fish) for food or sport. The Nature Conservancy's studies of grouse stemmed from this vision.

41 David Pearce *et al.* (1988) *Blueprint for a Green Economy*, Earthscan, London.

42 Robert Constanza and Herman E. Daly (1991) "Natural capital and sustainable development" *Conservation Biology* 6: 37–46. This is the tip of a very large iceberg of literature. One way in is Edward B. Barbier, Joanne C. Burgess and Carl Folke (1994) *Paradise Lost? The ecological economics of biodiversity*, Earthscan, London; another is R. Constanza (ed.) *Ecological Economics: the science and management of sustainability*, (1991, Columbia University Press, New York).

43 English Nature Position Statement on Sustainable Development, November 1993.

44 Susan Owens (1993) "Planning and nature conservation — the role of sustainability", ECOS 14(3/4): 15–22.

45 A study of wildlife sites in three areas in Scotland, for example, suggested direct expenditures attributable to wildlife of between £0.67m (on 7 sites in Wester Ross) and £2.79m (on 12 sites in Perthshire). Wildlife on the reserves studied was estimated to account for between 2 per cent of tourist spending in Wester Ross and 11 per cent in Orkney; see J.R. Crabtree, P.K.M. Leat, J. Santarossa and K.J. Thomson (1994) "The economic impact of wildlife sites in Scotland", *Journal of Rural Studies* 10: 67–72.

46 Paul Cobbing and Bill Slee (1993) "A contingent valuation of the Mar Lodge estate, Cairngorm Mountains, Scotland", *Journal of Environmental Planning and Management* 36: 65–72.

47 Simon Bilsborough (1992) "The oven-ready golden eagle: arguments against valuation", ECOS 13(1): 46–50. See also the hilarious vision of the work of committees charged with wildlife valuation by James Fenton (1992) "Wildlife valuation", ECOS 13(4): 46–50.

48 Kate Rawles and Alan Holland, *The Ethics of Conservation*, unpublished ms, 21 March 1994 (p. 20, emphasis in original).

49 Bryan G. Norton (1989) "The cultural approach to conservation biology", pp. 241–246 in D. Western and M. Pearl (eds) *Conservation for the 21st Century*, Oxford University Press, London.

50 Philip Lowe, Judy Clark and Graham Cox (1993) "Reasonable creatures: rights and rationalities in valuing the countryside", *Journal of Environmental Planning and*

Management 36: 101–115 (p. 105).

51 Ian McHarg (1969) *Design with Nature*, Natural History Press, Garden City, NY.

52 Samuel P. Hays (1959) *Conservation and the Gospel of Efficiency: the progressive conservation movement 1890–1920*, Harvard University Press, Cambridge, Mass.

53 Bryan C. Norton (1991) *Toward Unity Among Environmentalists*, Oxford University Press, London.

54 Bryan C. Norton (1991) *Toward Unity Among Environmentalists*, Oxford University Press, London (pp. 82, 85).

55 Bryan C. Norton (1989) "The cultural approach to conservation biology", pp. 241–246 in D. Western and M. Pearl (eds) *Conservation for the 21st Century*, Oxford University Press, London (p. 243).

56 Derek Ratcliffe (1993) "A conservation rationale" *ECOS* 14(1): 10–15.

57 Derek Ratcliffe (1993) "A conservation rationale" *ECOS* 14(1): 10–15 (pp. 11, 14).

58 See David Nicholson-Lord (1987) *The Greening of the Cities*, Routledge and Kegan Paul, London.

59 David Nicholson-Lord (1987) *The Greening of the Cities*, Routledge and Kegan Paul, London (caption to a plate between pp. 56 and 57).

60 Ian McHarg (1969) *Design with Nature*, Natural History Press, Garden City, NY, (pp. 3–5)

61 Nan Fairbrother (1970) *New Lives, New Landscapes*, Architectural Press (Penguin 1972); the development of urban conservation is described by Lyndis Cole (1983) "Urban nature conservation", pp. 267–285 in F.B. Goldsmith and A. Warren (eds) *Conservation in Perspective* (Wiley, Chichester); and by Bob Smyth (1987) *City Wildspace*, (Hilary Shipman, London).

62 Peter Jones (1995) "Groundwork and the environmental management message", *Town and Country Planning* February 1995: 54–6.

63 David Nicholson-Lord (1987) *The Greening of the Cities*, Routledge and Kegan Paul (p. 230).

64 Gary Paul Nabhan and Sara St. Antoine (1993) "The loss of floral and faunal story: the extinction of experience", pp. 229–250 in Stephen R. Kellert and Edward O. Wilson (eds) *The Biophilia Hypothesis*, Island Press, Washington D.C..

65 Chris Cowen (1995) "Seeing the way", ECOS 16(1): 23–25.

66 Martin Spray (1995) "Other ways of telling", ECOS 16(1): 1–6. ECOS 16(1) is a special issue on *Art and the Environment*.

67 I am grateful to Ann Smith for information about Platform (who are based at 7 Horsleydown Lane, Bermondsey); see David Nicholson-Lord (1993) "Power from river to light school", *Independent* 10 November 1993, and Claire Dean (1993) "Power supply comes on stream", *Times Higher Education* 5 November 1993.

Chapter Eight   The Conservation Landscape

1 Bryan C. Norton (1991) *Toward Unity Among Environmentalists*, Oxford University Press, London (p. 183).

2 See Kevin Bishop, Adrian Phillips and Lynda Warren (1995) "Protected Areas in the U.K.: time for a new thinking" *Regional Studies* 29: 192–201; also Kevin

Bishop, Adrian Phillips and Lynda Warren (1995) "Protected for ever? factors shaping the future of protected area policy", *Land Use Policy* 12(4): 291–305.

3   Kevin Bishop, Adrian Phillips and Lynda Warren (1995) "Protected for ever? factors shaping the future of protected area policy", *Land Use Policy* 12(4): 291–305; see also Chapter Two.

4   These are discussed by Kevin Bishop, Adrian Phillips and Lynda Warren (1995) "Protected for ever? factors shaping the future of protected area policy", *Land Use Policy* 12(4): 291–305.

5   Peter F. Brussard, Dennis D. Murphy and Reed F. Noss (1992) "Strategy and tactics for conserving biological diversity in the United States", *Conservation Biology* 6: 157-159 (p. 158).

6   Peter F. Brussard, Dennis D. Murphy and Reed F. Noss (1992) "Strategy and tactics for conserving biological diversity in the United States", *Conservation Biology* 6: 157-159 (p. 158).

7   David Western, Mary C. Pearl, Stuart L. Pimm, Brian Walker, Ian Atkinson and David Woodruff (1989) "An agenda for conservation action", pp. 204–232 in D. Western and M. Pratt (eds) *Conservation for the Twenty-First Century*, Oxford University Press, Oxford (p. 313). They also suggest expanding the system to complete its coverage and improving management (looking at boundaries, law-enforcement, education and the balancing of conflicting aims).

8   Nature Conservancy Council (1975) *Nature Conservation and Agriculture*, NCC, London, UK (quotes from pp. 16 and 24).

9   D.A. Ratcliffe, (1977) *A Nature Conservation Review*, Cambridge University Press, Cambridge (p. 5).

10   Norman W. Moore (1987) *The Bird of Time*, Cambridge University Press, Cambridge; Graham Cox, Philip Lowe and Michael Winter (1990) *The Voluntary Principle in Conservation: the Farming and Wildlife Advisory Group*, Packard Publishing, Chichester.

11   W.M. Adams, N.A.D. Bourn and I.D. Hodge (1992) "Conservation in the wider countryside: SSSIs and wildlife habitat in eastern England, *Land Use Policy* 9: 235–248.

12   Roger L. DiSilvestro (1993) *Reclaiming the Last Wild Places: a new agenda for biodiversity*, Wiley, New York (p. 207).

13   See for example R.T.T. Forman and M. Godron (1986) *Landscape Ecology*, Wiley, Chichester.

14   Robert H. MacArthur and Edward O. Wilson (1967) *The Theory of Island Biogeography*, Princeton University Press, Princeton.

15   See, for example, J.M. Diamond (1975) "The island dilemma: lessons of modern biogeographic studies for the design of natural reserves", *Biological Conservation* 7: 129–145; D.S. Simberlof and L.G. Abele (1976) "Island biogeographic theory and conservation practice", *Science* 191: 285–286; C. Margules, A.J. Higgs and R.W. Rafe (1982) "Modern biogeographic theory: are there lessons for nature reserve design?" *Biological Conservation* 24: 115–128; T.M. Reed (1983) "The role of species–area relationships in reserve choice: a British example", *Biological Conservation* 25: 263–271; I.F. Spellerberg (1991) "Biological basis for conservation", pp. 293–322 in I.F. Spellerberg, F.B. Goldsmith and M.G. Morris (eds) *The*

Scientific Management of Temperate Communities for Conservation, Blackwell, Oxford.

16 C. Schonewald-Cox, S.M. Chambers, B. MacBryde and W.L. Thomas (1983) *Genetics and Conservation*, Benjamin Cummings, London, UK.

17 The same is in fact also true elsewhere: see Craig L. Shafer (1995) "Values and shortcomings of small reserves", *BioScience* 45(2): 80–88.

18 S. Hinsley, P. Bellamy and I. Newton (1991) "Habitat fragmentation, landscape ecology and birds", pp. 19–21 in *Report of the Institute of Terrestrial Ecology 1991–2*, ITE, Abbots Ripton.

19 The study of badgers is by P.Cresswell, S. Harris, R.G.H. Bunce, and D.J. Jeffries (1989) "The badger (*Meles meles*) in Britain: present status and future population changes", *Biological Journal of the Linnean Society* 38: 91–101; the study of lapwings is by H. Galbraith (1988) "Effects of agriculture on the breeding ecology of lapwings, *Vanellus vanellus*", *Journal of Applied Ecology* 25: 487–504.

20 Richard J. Hobbs (1992) "The role of corridors in conservation: solution or bandwaggon?", *Trends in Ecology and Evolution* 7(11): 389–392.

21 These ideas are reviewed by G.L.A. Fry (1991) "Conservation in agricultural ecosystems", pp. 415–443 in I.F. Spellerberg, F.B. Goldsmith and M.G. Morris (eds) *The Scientific Management of Temperate Communities for Conservation*, Blackwell, Oxford; Other studies include R.J. Hobbs (1990) "Nature conservation: the role of corridors", *Ambio* 19 (2): 94–5 and J. Baudry (1988) "Hedgerows and hedgerow networks as wildlife habitat in agricultural landscapes", pp. 111–124 in J.R. Park (ed.) *Environmental Management in Agriculture: European perspectives*, Belhaven Press, London; The importance of nodes for birds is discussed by P. C. Lack (1988) "Hedgerow intersections and breeding bird distribution in farmland", *Bird Study* 35: 133–136.

22 Richard J. Hobbs (1992) "The role of corridors in conservation: solution or bandwaggon?", *Trends in Ecology and Evolution* 7(11): 389–392.

23 Craig L. Shafer (1995) "Values and shortcomings of small reserves", *BioScience* 45(2): 80–88.

24 Roger L. DiSilvestro (1993) *Reclaiming the Last Wild Places: a new agenda for biodiversity*, Wiley, New York (p. 207).

25 J.R. Prendergast, R.M. Quinn, J.H. Lawton, B.C. Eversham and D.W. Gibbons (1993) "Rare species, the coincidence of diversity hotspots and conservation strategies", *Nature* 365 (23 September): 355–7. "Hotspots" were defined as the top 5 per cent of 10-km squares, ranked by number of species per square.

26 P.D. Carey, J.C.M. Dring, M.O. Hill, C.D. Preston and S.M. Wright (1994) *Biogeographical Zones in Scotland*, Scottish Natural Heritage Research Survey and Monitoring Report No. 26, Edinburgh; P.D. Carey, C.D. Preston, M.O. Hill, M.B. Usher, S.M. Wright (1995) "An environmentally-defined zonation of Scotland designed to reflect species distributions", *Journal of Ecology* 83: 833–846.

27 English Nature (1993) *Natural Areas: setting conservation objectives, a consultation paper*; and *Natural Areas: responses to English Nature's consultation document*, English Nature, Peterborough.

28 Keith Duff (1994) "Natural Areas: English Nature's new approach to conservation based on geology", *Earth Heritage: conserving our geology and landscapes* 1: 8–12 (p.

9).

29 Countryside Commission (1994) *The New Map of England: a celebration of the south western landscape*, CCP 444; and *The New Map of England: a directory of regional landscapes*, CCP 445, The Countryside Commssion, Cheltenham.

30 Ministry of Agriculture, Nature Management and Fisheries (1990) *Nature Policy Plan of the Netherlands*, The Hague.

31 Surprisingly, perhaps, it is envisaged that this might be applied to river forelands, grasslands on thick peat soils, hydrological buffer zones and areas with small fields on sandy soils.

32 Graham Bennett (ed.) *Towards a European Ecological Network*, Institute for Environmental Policy, Arnhem. EECONET is discussed by Kevin Bishop, Adrian Phillips and Lynda Warren (1995) "Protected areas in the U.K.: time for new thinking" *Regional Studies* 29: 192–207.

33 N.T. Bischoff and R.H.G. Jongman (1993) *Development of Rural Areas in Europe: the claim of nature*, Netherlands Scientific Council for Government Policy, The Hague.

34 IUCN Commission on National Parks and Protected Areas (1994) *Parks for Life: action for protected areas in Europe*, IUCN, Gland, Switzerland.

35 See R.J. Hobbs and D.A. Saunders (1991) "Re-integrating fragmented landscapes — a preliminary framework for the Western Australian Wheatbelt", *Journal of Environmental Management* 3: 161–167.

36 See G.P. Buckley (ed.) (1989) *Biological Habitat Reconstruction*, Belhaven, London; see also Robert A. Jarman (1995) "Habitat restoration — recanting the status quo", *ECOS* 16(2): 29–38, and other articles in the same issue. River restoration is discussed in Chapter Ten.

37 See for example Alistair Gunn (1991) "The restoration of species and natural environments", *Environmental Ethics* 13(4): 291–310, and Robert Elliot (1994) "Extinction, restoration and naturalness", *Environmental Ethics* 16(2): 135–144.

38 J.C. Baines (1989) "Choices in habitat creation", pp. 5–8 in G.P. Buckley (ed) (1989) *Biological Habitat Reconstruction*, Belhaven, London.

39 William Sutherland and Chris Gibson (1988) "Habitats to order", *New Scientist* 28 January 1988, p. 70.

40 See G.S. Down and A.J. Morton (1989) "A case study of whole woodland transplanting", pp. 251–257 in G.P. Buckley (ed.) (1989) *Biological Habitat Reconstruction*, Belhaven, London.

41 R.H. Marrs and M.W. Gough (1989) "Soil fertility — a potential problem for habitat restoraton", pp. 29–44 in G.P. Buckely (ed) (1989) *Biological Habitat Reconstruction*, Belhaven, London. For wildflower meadows, see for example, Alison Crofts (1994) *How to Create and Care for Wildflower Meadows*, The Wildlife Trusts, Lincoln.

42 John Akroyd (1994) *Seeds of Destruction: non-native wildflower seed and British floral biodiversity*, Plantlife, London; On "aliens", see also James Fenton (1993) "No more aliens", *Scots Magazine*, September 1993: 281–283.

43 John Akroyd (1992) "A remarkable alien flora on the Gog Magog Hills", *Nature in Cambridgeshire* 34: 35–42 (p. 41).

44 Geoff Welch (1994) "Digging and scraping", *Birds Magazine* 15(1): 17–20.

45 See for example Duncan Glen (1993) "The North Northumberland Otter Project: principle of habitat creation for otters", pp. 79–83 in I. Glimmerveen and A. Ritchie (eds) *What is the Value of River Woodland?* Institute of Chartered Foresters and the British Ecological Society, Edinburgh.

46 See, for example, M.A. Anderson (1989) "Opportunities for habitat enhancement in commercial forestry practice", pp. 129–146 in G.P. Buckley (ed.) *Biological Habitat Reconstruction*, Wiley, Chichester.

47 John Arlidge (1994) "Highland hawk set to swoop South", *Independent on Sunday*, 9 October 1994, p. 11.

48 Data from *Birds* 15(4), Winter 1994. My sighting was *en route* between Cambridge and Wallingford. The introduced kites mostly come from Scandinavian stock.

49 J.A. Love (1988) *The Reintroduction of the White-tailed Sea Eagle to Scotland 1975–1987*, NCC Research and Survey in Nature Conservation No. 12, Peterborough; J.A. Love (1983) *The Return of the Sea Eagle*, Cambridge University Press, Cambridge.

50 M.R. Oates and M.S. Warren (1990) *A Review of Butterfly Introductions in Britain and Ireland*, World Wide Fund for Nature.

51 Habitat management and better water-level control have now improved the availability of the larval food plant, the milk parsley; new attempts at re-establishment might fare better.

52 See: James Fenton (1993) "No more aliens", *Scots Magazine* September 1993: 281–283.

53 Clive Potter, Paul Burnham, Angela Edwards, Ruth Gasson and Bryn Green (1991) *The Diversion of Land: conservation in a period of farming contraction*, Routledge, London.

54 David Baldock, Graham Cox, Philip Lowe and Michael Winter (1990) "Environmentally Sensitive Areas: incrementalism or reform?" *Journal of Rural Studies* 6: 143–162.

55 Potter, C. (1988) "Environmentally Sensitive Areas in England and Wales: an experiment in countryside management", *Land Use Policy* 5: 301–313; D. Baldock, G. Cox, P. Lowe and M. Winter (1990) "Environmentally Sensitive Areas: incrementalism or reform?" *Journal of Rural Studies* 6: 143–162.

56 The ESA programme is reviewed at length in Martin Whitby (ed.) (1994) *Incentives for Countryside Management: the case of ESAs*, CAB International, Wallingford.

57 Countryside Commission (1994) *Countryside Stewardship: handbook and application form*, CCP 453, Countryside Commission, Cheltenham.

58 *Tir Cymen: a farmland stewardship scheme* (1992), Countryside Council for Wales, Bangor.

59 Friends of the Earth (1991) *Off The Treadmill: a way forwards for farmers and the countryside*, FoE, London; RSPB (1991) *A Future for Environmentally Sensitive Farming*, RSPB, Sandy.

60 CEC (1991) *The Development and Future of the Common Agricultural Policy* — proposals of the Commission of European Communities, COM (91) 238, CEC, Brussels.

61 Caroline Saunders (1994) *Agricultural Policy: an update*, University of Newcastle

upon Tyne, Department of Agricultural Economics and Food Marketing, Working Paper 6.

62 Paul Wynne (1992) "The missed opportunities for CAP reform", *ECOS* 13(3): 20–24; Paul Wynne (1994) "Agri-environment schemes: recent events and forthcoming attractions", *ECOS* 15(3/4): 48–52.

63 See for example Vicki Swales (1994) "Incentives for countryside management", *ECOS* 15(3/4): 52–57.

64 See Clive Potter, Paul Burnham, Angela Edwards, Ruth Gasson and Bryn Green (1991) *The Diversion of Land: conservation in a period of farming contraction*, Routledge, London.

65 Amelia Craighill and Emily Goldsmith (1994) "A future for set-aside?", *ECOS* 15(3/4): 58–62.

Chapter Nine Nature, Landscapes, Lives

1 Ian McHarg (1969) *Design with Nature*, Natural History Press, Garden City, NY (p. 33)

2 IUCN Commission on National Parks and Protected Areas (1994) *Parks for Life: Action for Protected Areas in Europe*, IUCN, Gland, Switzerland (p. 15).

3 See, for example, E. Kemf (ed.) (1993) *The Law of the Mother: protecting indigenous peoples in protected areas*, Sierra Club Books, San Francisco. The issue of people and parks is reviewed by M.Wells and K. Brandon (1992) *People and Parks: linking protected area management with local communities*, World Bank, Washington D.C..

4 J.S. Adams and T.O. McShane (1992) *The Myth of Wild Africa: conservation without illusion*, W.W. Norton and Company, New York (p. xix).

5 See for example M. Stocking and S. Perkin (1992) "Conservation-with-development: an application of the concept in the Usambara Mountains, Tanzania", *Transactions of the Institute of British Geographers N.S.* 17: 337–349.

6 The Edwards Committee's recommendation for independent boards did not challenge this, but rather sought to provide independent boards for each park, with their own budgets, free of the distractions of County Council business.

7 It was perhaps a mistake to be so far from the Welsh Office: on 2nd November 1994 the Secretary of State announced his intention to cut CCW down and devolve some its functions to local authorities (Parliamentary Question 2434/93/94).

8 See James Fenton (1989) "Democracy and habitat protection", *ECOS* 10(2): 9–11.

9 Fédération des Parcs Naturels de France (1994) *Centrale D'Argumentaires des Parcs Naturels Régionaux* (unpublished ms); David Baldock (1987) *The Organisation of Nature Conservation in Selected European Countries*, Institute for European Environmental Policy, London.

10 Contrasts with British National Parks are discussed by Janet Dwyer (1991) "Structural and evolutionary effects upon conservation policy performance: comparing a U.K. National and a French Regional Park", *Journal of Rural Studies* 7: 265–275. She compares the Brecon Beacons National Park with the Parc Régionale Normandie-Maine.

11 Janet Dwyer (1991) "Structural and evolutionary effects upon conservation policy performance: comparing a U.K. National and a French Regional Park", *Journal of Rural Studies* 7: 265–275.

12 Abruzzo National Park (1994) "Why the Park is Really Special", ms; Franco Tassi (1983) "Abruzzo's bears: reconciling the interests of wildlife and people in Abruzzo National Park, Italy", Proceedings of the Third World Congress on National Parks, Bali.

13 Franco Tassi (1983) "Abruzzo's bears: reconciling the interests of wildlife and people in Abruzzo National Park, Italy", Proceedings of the Third World Congress on National Parks, Bali.

14 Mary Ellen Chatwin and Lindsay Allen (1990) "Italy's Year of the Park", *WWF News* 68: 3; Grazia Francescato (1988) "Vivvere di Parco", *Airone* 92 (December 1988): 17–20; Grazia Francescato (1989) "Civatella fa scuola: il paese di Rocchetta ha scelto il parco", *Airone* 95 (March 1989): 14; (translated by the Parco Nationale d'Abruzzo).

15 John Dower (1945) *National Parks in England and Wales*, Cmd. 6628, HMSO London (para 4).

16 Sir Arthur Hobhouse (1947) *Report of the National Parks Committee (England and Wales)*, Cmd. 7121, HMSO, London (para 30).

17 Sir J. Douglas Ramsay (1945) *National Parks: a Scottish survey*, Cmd. 6631, HMSO, London.

18 Sir J. Douglas Ramsay (1947) *National Parks and the Conservation of Nature in Scotland*, Cmd. 7235, HMSO, London.

19 Ken Parker (1990) *Two Villages Two Valleys: The Peak District Integrated Rural Development Project 1981–88*, Peak District National Park, Bakewell.

20 See the Federation of Nature and National Parks of Europe (1992) *Loving Them to Death: the need for sustainable tourism in Europe's Nature and National Parks*, Report to European Commission by FNNPE Sustainable Tourism Working Group, Grafenau, Germany.

21 *English Nature* No. 15, September 1994; National Audit Office (1994) *Protecting and Managing Sites of Special Scientific Interest in England*, Report by the Comptroller and Auditor General, HMSO, London.

22 English Nature (1992) *The Seas of England: an agenda for action*; (1993) *Conserving England's Marine Heritage: a strategy*, English Nature, Peterborough.

23 Carol Hatton (1992) *The Habitats Directive: time for action*, World Wide Fund for Nature UK, Godalming, Appendix 1 (quote para 5.69).

24 Department of the Environment for Northern Ireland (1994) *Strangford Lough Proposed Marine Nature Reserve: guide to designation*, DOE (NI), Belfast.

25 Strangford Lough Management Committee, *First Report 1994*, Portaferry, Co. Down.

26 English Nature (1993) *Strategy for the Sustainable Use of England's Estuaries*, English Nature, Peterborough; Scottish Natural Heritage (1994) *Focus on Firths*, Edinburgh (pamphlet). See also K.A. Duncan, S. Kaznowska and D. d'A Laffoley (1992) (eds) *Marine Nature Conservation in Britain: challenge and prospects*, English Nature Science No. 5, Peterborough.

27 English Nature (1992) *The Seas of England: an agenda for action*; (1993) *Conserving England's Marine Heritage: a strategy*, English Nature, Peterborough.

28 Netherlands Scientific Council for Government Policy (1992) *Ground for Choices: four perspectives for the rural areas in the European Community*, The Hague.

29 See for example Clive Potter and Matt Lobley (1992) *Small Farming and the Environment*, RSPB, Sandy.

30 Julian Clark and David Baldock (1994) *Renewing the Farmed Landscape: a report to RSNC* — the Wildlife Trusts Partnership, Institute for Environmental Policy, London.

31 Tim Stowe and George Campbell (eds) (1992) *Crofting and the Environment: a new approach*, Scottish Crofters Union and the Royal Society for the Protection of Birds, Inverness. A similar line of thought is put forward for the whole of Scotland in RSPB (1993) *Agriculture in Scotland: farming for a living countryside*, RSPB, Sandy.

32 Tim Stowe and George Campbell (eds) (1992) *Crofting and the Environment: a new approach*, Scottish Crofters Union and the Royal Society for the Protection of Birds, Inverness.

33 S. Micklewright (ed.) (1988) *Sites for Science or Places for Heritage: problems with the SSSI designation and possible solutions*, University College London Discussion Paper in Conservation 47, London.

34 T. O'Riordan (1983) "Putting Trust in the Countryside" pp. 171–260 in *Earth's Survival: a conservation and development programme for the UK*, Kogan Page, London (pp. 242–3).

35 Bryn H. Green (1989) "Conservation in cultural landcapes", pp. 182-198 in D. Western and M. Pearl (eds) *Conservation for the 21st Century*, Oxford University Press, Oxford.

36 T. O'Riordan (1994) "Creating whole landscapes", *Countryside* No. 69 (September/October 1994) (p. 7).

37 See for example Paul Selman (1993) "Landscape ecology and countryside planning: vision, theory and practice", *Journal of Rural Studies*, 9:1–21; Anna M. Hersperger (1994) "Landscape ecology and its potential application to planning", *Journal of Planning Literature* 9: 14–29.

38 P.H. Selman and N.R. Doar (1991) "A landscape ecological approach to countryside planning", *Planning Outlook* 34: 83–8.

39 Roger M. Turner (1991) *Forests for the Future: integrating forestry and the environment, a discussion paper*, RSPB, Edinburgh; Simon Pryor (1992) *Future Forestry: a new direction for forest policy*, Wildlife Link, London.

40 See, for example, World Wide Fund for Nature (1994) *Changing Direction: towards a greener Britain*, WWF, Godalming; Michael Jacobs (1993) *Sense and Sustainability: land use planning and environmentally sustainable development*, Council for the Protection of Rural England, London.

41 International Union for the Conservation of Nature and Natural Resources, World Wildlife Fund (now Worldwide Fund for Nature) and the United Nations Environment Programme (established following the 1972 Stockholm Conference). Detailed accounts of this period are given in W.M. Adams (1990) *Green Development: environment and sustainability in the Third World* (Routledge, 1990) and J.S. McCormick, (1989) *Reclaiming Paradise: the global environmental movement*, Indiana University Press, Bloomington, Ind.

42 Brundtland, G. H. (1987) *Our Common Future*, Oxford University Press, Oxford, for the World Commission on Environment and Development); IUCN (1980) *The World Conservation Strategy*, International Union for Conservation of Nature and Natural Resources, United Nations Environment Programme, World Wildlife Fund, Geneva; IUCN (1991) *Caring for the Earth: a strategy for sustainable living*, IUCN, Gland; J. Holmberg, K. Thomson and L. Timberlake (1993) *Facing the Future: beyond the Earth Summit*, Earthscan/International Institute for Environment and Development, London.

43 IUCN (1991) *Caring for the Earth: a strategy for sustainable living*, IUCN, Gland (p. 8).

44 Janice Morphet (1995) "Towards a new environmental policy" *Town and Country Planning*, March 1995: 75–77.

45 Michael Jacobs (1993) *Sense and Sustainability: land use planning and environmentally sustainable development*, Council for the Protection of Rural England, London; World Wide Fund for Nature (1994) *Changing Direction: towards a greener Britain*, WWF, Godalming.

46 Local Government Management Board (1994) *Local Agenda 21, Principles and Process: a step by step guide*, Local Government Management Board, Luton.

47 Scottish Natural Heritage (1993) *Sustainable Development and the Natural Heritage: the SNH Approach*, Scottish Natural Heritage, Edinburgh. The Natural Heritage (Scotland) Act 1991 is the first mention of sustainability in British legislation.

48 Scottish Enterprise, Scottish Natural Heritage, Scottish Borders Enterprise, Borders Regional Council, Etterick and Lauderdale District Council and Rural Forum (1994) *An Area Sustainability Study of Etterick and Lauderdale*, Scottish Natural Heritage, Edinburgh.

49 English Nature produced a Position Statement in November 1993, the Countryside Commission in December 1993.

50 David Western, Mary C. Pearl, Stuart L. Pimm, Brian Walker, Ian Atkinson and David Woodruff (1989) "An agenda for conservation action", pp. 304–232 in D. Western and M. Pratt (eds) *Conservation for the Twenty-first Century*, Oxford University Press, Oxford (p. 317).

51 Ian McHarg (1969) *Design with Nature*, Natural History Press, Garden City, NY (p. 29).

52 Chris Bonington (1994) "To bolt or not to bolt", *The National Trust Magazine* 73 (Autumn 1994): 22–24 (p. 24).

53 Aldo Leopold (1949) *A Sand County Almanac and Sketches Here and There*, New York; "The land ethic" is reprinted in Paul Shepherd and Daniel McKinley (eds) (1969) *The Subversive Science: essays towards an ecology of man*, Houghton Miflin, Boston.

54 Wendell Berry (1977) *The Unsettling of America: culture and agriculture*, Sierra Club Books, San Francisco (pp. 30–1).

55 Neil Evernden (1992) *The Social Creation of Nature*, Johns Hopkins University Press, Baltimore (p. 43).

56 Richard Nelson (1993) "Searching for the lost arrow: physical and spiritual ecology in the hunter's world", pp. 201–228 in Stephen R. Kellert and Edward O. Wilson (1993) *The Biophilia Hypothesis*, Island Press, Washington D.C. (pp. 220, 224).

57 Annie Dillard (1976) *Pilgrim at Tinker Creek*, Picador, London (first published 1974) (p. 16).

58 Kirkpatrick Sale (1985) *Dwellers in the Land: the bioregional vision*, Sierra Club, San Francisco; see Donald Alexander 1990) "Bioregionalism: science or sensibility?", *Environmental Ethics* 12(2): 161–173.

59 Peter Berg and Raymond Dasmann (1978) "Reinhabiting California", in Peter Berg (ed.) *Reinhabiting a Separate Country: a bioregional anthology of northern California*, Planet Drum Foundation, San Francisco (quoted by Donald Alexander (1990) "Bioregionalism: science or sensibility?", *Environmental Ethics* 12(2): 161–173).

60 Gary Snyder (1990) "Regenerate culture!", pp. 12–19 in Judith Plant and Christopher Plant *Turtle Talk: voices for a sustainable future*, New Society Publishers, Philadelphia PA.

61 Donald Alexander (1990) "Bioregionalism: science or sensibility?" *Environmental Ethics* 12(2): 161–173.

62 Kevin Robins (1991). "Tradition and translation: national culture in its global context", pp. 21–44 in J. Corner and S. Harvey (eds) *Enterprise and Heritage: crosscurrents of national culture*, Routledge, London (p. 34).

63 Gordon Clark, J. Darrall, R. Grove-White, P. Macnaghten and J. Urry (1994) *Leisure Landscapes: leisure, culture and the English countryside: challenges and conflicts*, Council for the Protection of Rural England, London, (p. 39).

64 National Trust (1995) *Linking People and Place: a consultation paper*, National Trust, Cirencester.

65 Sue Clifford and Angela King (1993) *Local Distinctiveness: place, particularity and identity; essays for a conference*, Common Ground, London. Apple Day is 21st October.

66 Angela King and Sue Clifford (1985) *Holding Your Ground: an action guide to local conservation*, Maurice Temple Smith, London.

67 *Rural Action: the newsletter for Rural Action Networks*, No. 4 (April 1995).

68 In 1994 the Wildlife Trusts revised their national organisation and made major efforts to harmonise their names and logos. The Royal Society for Nature Conservation was re-styled "the Wildlife Trusts National Office". The work of the Wildlife Trusts (and other landholding conservation trusts) is described in Ian Hodge and Janet Dwyer (in press) *Conservation in Trust* (Wiley, Chichester).

Chapter Ten   Releasing the Wild

1 Neil Evernden (1992) *The Social Creation of Nature*, Johns Hopkins University Press, Baltimore (p. 120).

2 Dave Foreman, John Davis, David Johns, Reed Noss and Michael Soulé (1992) "The Wildlands Project: Mission Statement" *Wild Earth* special issue 1992: 3–4.

3 The National Forest is reviewed critically by Fred Pearce (1994) "Greening the heart of England", *New Scientist* 24 September 1994: 30–35.

4 Caroline Davies and Alison Kew (1995) "Wet Fens for the Future", *ECOS* 16(2): 38–41.

5   This is not a new suggestion; see for example T.D. Nevard and J.P. Penfold (1978) "Wildlife conservation in Britain: the unsatisfied demand", *Biological Conservation* 14: 25–44; D.W. Yalden (1986) "Opportunities for reintroducing British mammals", *Mammal Review* 16: 53–63; T. Nevard (1991) "Reintroducing large vertebrates — what benefits?", *ECOS* 12(3): 44–6; Laura Spinney (1995) "Return to the Wild", *New Scientist* 14 January 1995: 35–38. See also R. Dennis (1995) "Scotland's native forest — return of the wild", *ECOS* 16(2): 17–21.

6   Franco Tassi (1991) *Bentornate Lince: il retorno del lupo cerviero*, Centro Studi Ecologi Appeninci, Parco Nazionale D'Abruzzo (translated, F. Tassi, ms.).

7   *Reforesting Scotland*, unpublished brochure, Reforesting Scotland, Ullapool, Ross-Shire.

8   Reforesting Scotland (1993) *Norway and Scotland: a study in land use*, The Reforesting Scotland Norway Study Tour, May 1993, Reforesting Scotland, Ullapool, Ross-Shire.

9   RSPB (1993) *Time for Pine: a future for Caledonian Pinewoods*, RSPB, Sandy.

10 Alan Watson (1989) "Let the Caledonian Forest Flourish", *Resurgence* 133: 20–21.

11 P.J. Cedrown Taylor (1992) *Coed Eryri*, unpublished ms.

12 The Scottish Green Party (1989) *A Rural Manifesto for the Highlands: creating the Second Great Wood of Caledon*, Highland Green Party, Scourie, Inverness-shire.

13 Norman Henderson (1992) "Wilderness and the nature conservation ideal: Britain, Canada and the United States contrasted", *Ambio* 21(6): 394–399.

14 See, for example, Clive Potter, Paul Burnham, Angela Edwards, Ruth Gasson and Bryn Green (1991) *The Diversion of Land: conservation in a period of farming contraction*, Routledge, London; and Bryn Green (995) "Plenty and wilderness? Creating a new countryside", *ECOS* 16(2): 3–8, and other articles in this issue.

15 Neil Evernden (1992) *The Social Creation of Nature*, Johns Hopkins University Press, Baltimore (p.121).

16 This quote comes from an interview with David Cayley on the Canadian Broadcasting Corporation programme, *The Age of Ecology*, June 18th 1990. The wider issue of economics and ecology is discussed in Donald Worster (1977) *Nature's Economy: the roots of ecology*, Cambridge University Press, Cambridge.

17 Johan van Zoest (1992) "Gambling with nature? A new paradigm of nature and its consequences for nature management strategy", pp. 503–514 in R.W.G. Carter, T.G.F. Curtis and M.J. Sheehy-Skeffington (eds) *Coastal Dunes*, Balkema, Rotterdam (p. 511).

18 See S.T.A. Pickett, V.T. Parker and P.L. Feidler (1992) "The new paradigm in ecology: implications for conservation biology above the species level", pp. 65–88 in P.L. Feidler and S.K. Jain (eds) *Conservation Biology: the theory and practice of nature conservation, preservation and management*, Chapman and Hall, London.

19 Dave Foreman, John Davis, David Johns, Reed Noss and Michael Soulé (1992) "The Wildlands Project: Mission Statement" *Wild Earth* special issue 1992: 3–4.

20 Johan van Zoest (1992) "Gambling with nature? A new paradigm of nature and its consequences for nature management strategy", pp. 503–514 in R.W.G. Carter, T.G.F. Curtis and M.J. Sheehy-Skeffington (eds) *Coastal Dunes*, Balkema, Rotterdam.

21 Alan Werrity, John McManus, Vanessa Brazier and John Gordon (1994)

"Conserving our dynamic and static geomorphological heritage", *Earth Heritage* 1: 16–17.

22 S.T.A. Pickett, V.T. Parker and P.L. Feidler (1992) "The new paradigm in ecology: implications for conservation biology above the species level", pp. 65–88 in P.L. Feidler and S.K. Jain (eds) *Conservation Biology: the theory and practice of nature conservation, preservation and management*, Chapman and Hall, London.

23 Biological conservation is defined in this way by Donald Worster (1994) "Nature and the disorder of history", *Environmental History Review* 18(2): 1–16.

24 RSPB, NRA, RSNC (1993) *The New Rivers and Wildlife Handbook*, RSPB, Sandy.

25 Rod Jones and Stewart Campbell (1994) "The Dee meanders: a case of Dee-stabilisation", *Earth Heritage* 1:13–15.

26 A non-governmental organisation established in 1991 following a conference at the University of York on River Conservation and Management.

27 ECON (1993) *River Restoration Project Phase 1. feasibility study*, ECON, Norwich; Summary edited by Jeremy Biggs and Penny Williams, River Restoration Project, Huntingdon.

28 R.C. Petersen, L. B.-M. Petersen and J. Lacoursière (1992) "A building block model for stream restoration", pp. 293–309 in P.J. Boon, P. Calow and G.E. Petts (eds) *River Conservation and Management*,Wiley, Chichester.

29 A. Brookes (1989) "Recovery and restoration of some engineered British river channels", pp. 337–352 in P.J. Boon, P. Calow and G.E. Petts (eds) *River Conservation and Management*,Wiley, Chichester.

30 See for example K. Pye and P.W. French (1983) *Targets for Coastal Habitat Re-creation*, English Nature Science No. 13, Peterborough.

31 J.M. Hooke and M.J. Bray (1995) "Coastal groups, littoral cells, policies and plans in the U.K." *Area* 27(a): 358–368.

32 A.F. Brown, P.V. Rice, G.P. Radley, P.N. Leafe and P. Lambley (1994) "Towards a Strategy for the Conservation of Coastal Habitats in North Norfolk", *English Nature Research Report No. 74*, Peterborough; Noel Jones (1993) "Coastal cell studies: a basis for coastal zone management", *Earth Science Conservation* 32: 12–15.

33 Martin R. Perrow, (1992) "Biomanipulation in Broadland", pp. 335–337 in K.T. O'Grady, A.J.B. Butterworth, P.B. Spillet and J.C.J. Domaniewski, (1992) *Fisheries in the year 2000*, Proceedings of the 21st Anniversary Conference of the Institute of Fish Management, Aberdeen; Martin R. Perrow, Brian Moss and Julia Stansfield (1994) "Trophic interactions in a shallow lake following a reduction in nutrient loading: a long-term study, *Hydrobiologia* 275/276: 43–52.

34 A.E. Brown and D.L. Howell (1992) "Conservation of rivers in Scotland: legislative and organisational limitations", pp. 406–424 in P.J. Boon, P. Calow and G.E. Petts (eds) *River Conservation and Management*,Wiley, Chichester.

35 K. Kern (1992) "Rehabilitation of streams in South-West Germany", pp. 321–335 in P.J. Boon, P. Calow and G.E. Petts (eds) *River Conservation and Management*, Wiley, Chichester.

36 Wicken Fen is owned by the National Trust, Woodwalton Fen by the Royal Society for Nature Conservation, Holme Fen by English Nature.

37 Caroline Davies and Alison Kew (1995) 'Wet Fens for the Future' *ECOS* 16(2): 38–41.

Postscript

1   This phrase is from A. Holland and K. Rawles (1993) "Values in conserva-
    tion", *Ecos: A Review of Conservation* 14(1): 14–19. Hereafter, this journal
    (ISSN 0143-9073) is referred to simply as *Ecos*; see: www.banc.org.uk/
    ecosarta/artsindx.html.

2   The Countryside Agency website is www.countryside.gov.uk/index.htm.

3   The DEFRA website is www.defra.gov.uk.

4   The splitting up of the old Nature Conservancy Council is described in
    Chapter 2; but see also P. Marren (2002) *Nature Conservation: a review of
    the conservation of wildlife in Britain, 1950–2001*, HarperCollins, London
    (New Naturalist Series 91). The websites of the agencies are Countryside
    Council for Wales: www.ccw.gov.uk; English Nature: www.ccw.gov.uk;
    Scottish Natural Heritage: www.snh.org.uk; the Department of the
    Environment in Northern Ireland: www.doeni.gov.uk.

5   English Nature (2002) *Annual Report 2001–2002*, English Nature,
    Peterborough.

6   N.W. Moore (2002) *Oaks, Dragonflies and People: creating a small nature
    reserve and relating its story to wider conservation issues*, Harley Books,
    Colchester (p.89).

7   P. Marren (2001) *Nature Conservation: a review of the conservation of wildlife
    in Britain 1950–2001*, HarperCollins, London.

8   For the Wildlife Trusts Marine Campaign, the 2001 *Marine Update* report
    and the 2002 *Dying Seas Report*, see www.wildlifetrusts.org; see also the
    Marine Conservation Society: www.mcsuk.org.

9   Royal Society for the Protection of Birds, Joint Nature Conservation
    Committee, Wildlife and Wetlands Trust and British Trust for Ornithology
    (2001) *The State of the UK's Birds*, RSPB, Sandy, Bedfordshire.

10 Spanish and Swedish red kites were introduced in both England and
    Scotland from the 1980s with great success. They are now commonplace in
    the Chilterns and elsewhere. Nigel Ajax-Lewis urges caution in such intro-
    ductions, pointing out that this effort was both unnecessary and undesirable:
    N. Ajax-Lewis (2002) "Reintroductions: closing the stable door after the
    horse has bolted?", *Natur Cymru* 4: 4–7.

11 See the National Biodiversity Network Trust: www.nbn.org.uk.

12 See Geoffrey Wain's (2000) editorial in the special issue of *Ecos*, vol. 21, no.
    2, "Biodiversity Challenged", and articles in that issue, including R.
    Knightbridge (2000) "The UK BAP — five years on", *Ecos* 21(2): 2–8. See
    also the National Biodiversity Network Trust: www.nbn.org.uk.

13 J. Smart, R. Davis, J. Duckworth and M. Harper (2000) "Backlash against
    the BAP", *Ecos* 22(1): 8–12.

14 P. Marren (2001) *Nature Conservation: a review of the conservation of wildlife
    in Britain 1950–2001*, HarperCollins, London.

15 P. Marren (2000) "Did the bittern read the BAP?", *Ecos* 21(2): 43–46,
    quotes p.45.

16 J. Robertson (2000) "Killer subsidies: 'meditations on a future countryside'
    revisited", *Ecos* 23(3/4): 72–75, quote p.73.

17 *Independent*, 7 October 2002, p.6; for the National Trust, see www.national-trust.org.uk/main/nationaltrust.

18 M. Eaton, R. Gregory and A. Farrar (2002) "Bird conservation and citizen science: counting, caring and acting", *Ecos* 23(3/4): 5–13.

19 See Chapter 2; Sir J.D. Ramsey (1945) *National Parks: a Scottish Survey; a report by the Scottish National Parks Survey Committee*, HMSO London. The website of the Loch Lomond and the Trossachs National Park is www.lochlomond-trossachs.org.

20 C. Warren (1998) "National Parks for Scotland: the other side of the coin", *Ecos* 19(2): 62–70; see also C. Warren (2002) *Managing Scotland's Environment*, Edinburgh University Press, Edinburgh.

21 Details of the negotiations leading to the creation of the park and the views of Scottish Natural Heritage are available at www.snh.org.uk/strategy/nat-parks/sr-npc00b.htm. The history of development and opposition is well reviewed in P. Marren (2001) *Nature Conservation: a review of the conservation of wildlife in Britain 1950–2001*, HarperCollins, London.

22 See M. Toogood (2003) "Decolonizing Highland Conservation", pp.152–171 in W. Adams and M. Mulligan (2003) (eds) *Decolonizing Nature: strategies for conservation in a post-colonial era*, Earthscan, London.

23 See, for example, www.whoownsscotland.org.uk/latest_news.htm, and www.firstfoot.com/whowns/Who-Owns/who-ownsframemain.htm.

24 See the Deer Commission for Scotland: www.dcs.gov.uk.

25 See, for example, A. Watson Featherstone (1997) "The wild heart of the highlands", *Ecos* 18(2): 48–61.

26 J. Fenton (1999) "Scotland: reviving the wild", *Ecos* 20(2): 67–69.

27 See, for example, A. Samuel (2001) "Rum: nature and community in harmony?", *Ecos* 22(1): 36–45, and subsequent correspondence.

28 The Department of Food, the Environment and Rural Affairs BSE website is www.defra.gov.uk/news/issues/bse.asp. The full text of the government report on the BSE outbreak is at www.bse.org.uk.

29 In response to the spread of BSE, the feeding of ruminant protein to ruminants was banned in the UK in 1988. In response to the crisis, the controls were extended in 1996 to ban giving any mammalian meat and bonemeal to any farmed livestock. They were further extended in August 2001 to ban the feeding of any processed animal protein to any livestock intended for food production, in line with EU legislation. There are still allegations that meat intended for petfood is being fed to livestock (www.defra.gov.uk/news/latest/2003/petfood.htm).

30 The UK Department of Health records 115 "definite and probable" deaths from new-variant CJD since 1995–2002: www.fact.cc/BSE_Table.htm.

31 The Department of Food, the Environment and Rural Affairs report on the origins of the foot and mouth epidemic is available electronically on www.defra.gov.uk/news/2002/020620a.htm.

32 M. Pratt (2001) "The microbe and the media", *Ecos* 22(2): 2–6; M. van Eyk McCain (2001) "Smoke signals: getting the message from foot and mouth", *Ecos* 22(1): 79–83.

33   J. Bowers (2000) "Culling the livestock industry", Ecos 22(1):102–105 (p.105).

34   M. King (2001) "Any room for scrub?", Ecos 22(2) 21–24.

35   M. Spray (2000) "Living at the border", Ecos 22(1): 84–87; D. Harpley (2000) "A turning point in the fells", Ecos 22(1): 93–95.

36   See P. Chandler (2002) "Lies, damn lies and corporate spin: why don't we trust the biotechs?", Ecos 23(3/4): 65–71. The Greenpeace website is www.archive.greenpeace.org/~geneng. A government view is available at www.defra.gov.uk/news/issues/gmcrops.asp.

37   See C. Potter (1998) Against the Grain: 65-71agri-environment policy reform in the EU and US, CAB International, Wallingford, and C. Potter (2001) "Negotiating the transition: rural policy reform and the restructuring of agriculture", Ecos 22(2): 25–30.

38   M. Winter (1998) "CAP reform and the countryside", Ecos 19(2): 9.

39   A. Rutherford and K. Hart (2000) "The new rural development regulation: fresh hope for farming and England's countryside?", Ecos 21(1): 69–75.

40   See C. Potter (1998) "Agricultural liberalisation: opportunity or threat?", Ecos 19(2): 38–43, and C. Potter (2001) Against the Grain: agri-environment policy reform in the EU and US, CAB International, Wallingford.

41   See J. Robertson (2001) "Moving the deckchairs or changing course — will DEFRA make a difference?" Ecos 22(2): 7–14.

42   The report is at www.cabinet-office.gov.uk/farming. See J. Robertson (2002) "NFU fails to curry favour", Ecos 23(1): 43–45.

43   DEFRA (2003) The Countryside Stewardship Scheme and How To Apply, DEFRA, London. See www.defra.gov.uk/erdp/schemes/landbased/css/cssindex.htm.

44   DEFRA (2002) Agri-environment Schemes: Abbots Hall Farm, pamphlet, DEFRA, London.

45   T. O'Riordan, A. Lovett, P. Dolman, D. Cobb and G. Sünnenberg (2000) "Designing and implementing whole landscapes", Ecos 21(1): 57–68.

46   DEFRA (2003) The Countryside Stewardship Scheme and How To Apply, DEFRA, London.

47   The Thinking Worm (2002) "Meditations on a future countryside", Ecos 23(2): 52–60 (quote p.56).

48   C. Lowell (2002) "Don't prune the trees — replant the orchard", Ecos 23(3/4): 76–77.

49   See Chapter 3; see also M. Phillips and T. Juniper (2000) "What did you do in the campaign daddy? How the Countryside Act was Won", Ecos 21(3/4): 63–79. For the text of the Act see www.hmso.gov.uk/acts/acts2000/20000037.htm. For a review, see P. Marren (2001) Nature Conservation: a review of the conservation of wildlife in Britain 1950-2001, HarperCollins, London.

50   See, for example, the Ramblers' Association, www.ramblers.org.uk/index.html.

51   HMSO (2000) Our Countryside: the future – a fair deal for rural England, HMSO, London.

52   W. Hutton (2002) "Sorry, Phil Archer, but your time is up', *Observer*, 15 September, p.26. Figures for farm income are hard to assess; living costs and income from way-leaves and linked enterprises such as tourism have to be taken into account.

53   R. MacFarlane (1998) "One rally and a march, but whose countryside?", *Ecos* 19(1): 87–96.

54   The Countryside Alliance's website is www.countryside-alliance.org.

55   Robert Sturdy in the *Cambridge Evening News*, 23 September 2002, p.2.

56   Leaflet on the *England Rural Development Programme 2000–2006*, MAFF, 2002.

57   The Soil Association website is www.soilassociation.org.

58   See, for example, L. Nichol (2000) "Bodger and Badger: green livelihoods in the countryside", *Ecos* 21(1): 52–56; A. Nisbet (2000/2001) "Woods that work: job creation in wood product businesses", *Ecos* 21(3/4): 34–38; S. Blacker (2000/2001) "Silvanus and working woodlands: combining conservation with economic regeneration", *Ecos* 21(3/4): 39–43.

59   R. Ellis (2000) "Sustainable partnerships — a tale of benders, planners, alternative lifestyles and prejudice", *Ecos* 21(1): 49–51 (and volume 21(3/4): 44–46).

60   See www.eat-the-view.org.uk/, January 2003.

61   See Chapter 9. The Countryside Character Initiative is described at www.countryside.gov.uk/cci/default.htm.

62   *Planning Policy Guidance Note 7: The Countryside — Environmental Quality and Economic and Social Development*, 28 February 2001, updated 25 September 2001; see www.planning.odpm.gov.uk/ppg/ppg7.

63   See www2.phreak.co.uk/tlio.

64   For Chapter 7, see www2.phreak.co.uk/tlio/chapter7.

65   C. Dressler (2002) "Taking charge on Eigg — the benefits of community ownership", *Ecos* 23(1): 11–17, and I. MacPhail (2002) "Relating to land — the Assynt Crofters Trust", *Ecos* 23(1): 26–35.

66   Will Hutton (2002) "Sorry, Phil Archer, but your time is up", *Observer*, 15 September 2002, p.26.

67   C. Rose (2001) "The countryside is a myth", *Independent* 18 March; C. Rose (2000/2001) "Time to campaign against 'rural England'?", *Ecos* 21(3/4): 2–7.

68   P. Shirley (2001/2002) "Town and country: two nations separated by a common misconception" *Ecos* 22(3/4): 27–32. See HMSO (2000) *Our Towns and Cities: the Future. Delivering an urban renaissance*, The Stationery Office, London; and DETR (2001) *Our Countryside: the Future. A fair deal for rural England*, HMSO, London.

69   See, for example, K. Patterson (2001) "Experiencing deeply", *Ecos* 22(3/4):14–19, and K. Burningham and D. Thrush (2001) "Rainforests in perspective — exploring the environmental concerns of disadvantaged groups", *Ecos* 22(3/4): 20–26.

70   CAG Consultants and Land Use Consultants (1997) *What Matters and Why — Environmental capital: a new approach*, Countryside Commission Cheltenham. The Overview report on *Quality of Life Capital* and other reports can be downloaded from www.qualityoflifecapital.org.uk.

71 On Poundbury, see www.princes-foundation.org/foundation/projdir-uep-poundbury.html; on the South Devon Co-Housing Group, see www.lets-groworganic.co.uk/clearlight/co-housing.htm; for BedZED, see www.BedZed.org.uk; for one-house conversion experience, see www.campaignstrategy.org.

72 For example, R. Moyse (1999) "Low-impact development: a sustainable future for the countryside", *Ecos* 20(2): 59–64.

73 S. Owens and R. Cowell (2001) *Land and Limits: interpreting sustainability in the planning process*, Routledge, London. On the Harris super quarry, see A. McIntosh (2001) "Sabbath and the corporate mammon: concluding the Harris Superquarry debate", *Ecos* 22(1): 46–52, and K. Milton (2002) *Loving Nature: towards an ecology of emotion*, Routledge, London.

74 Royal Commission for Environmental Pollution (2002) *Environmental Planning*, HMSO, London (Cm 5459); available on the web at www.rcep.org.uk.

75 R.J. Hobbs and J.A. Harris (2001) "Restoration ecology: repairing the earth's ecosystems in the New Millennium", *Restoration Ecology* 9: 239–246. Reviews of restoration include A.J. Davy and M.R. Perrow (2002) *Handbook of Ecological Restoration*, Cambridge University Press, Cambridge.

76 Department of the Environment, Transport and the Regions (2001) *Our Countryside: the Future. A fair deal for rural England*, HMSO, London.

77 A. Colston (1997) "Conservation in a black hole", *Ecos* 18(1): 61–67.

78 A. Colston "Beyond preservation: the challenge of ecological restoration", pp.247–267 in W. Adams and M. Mulligan (eds) (2003) *Decolonizing Nature: strategies for conservation in a post-colonial era*, Earthscan, London.

79 C. Davies and A. Kew (1995) "Wet fens for the future", *Ecos* 16(2): 36–41; Wet Fens for the Future (1996) *Wet Fens for the Future — the value of wetlands for people and wildlife in the Fens*, RSPB, Sandy, Bedfordshire. This has been widely debated; see J. Aldred (1998) "Land use in the Fens: lessons from the Ely citizen's jury", *Ecos* 19 (2): 31–33.

80 See www.greatfen.org.uk/information.htm.

81 E.A.R. Ennion (1942) *Adventurer's Fen: the classic portrait of primitive fenland*, Methuen, London (reprinted Colt Books, Cambridge, 1996).

82 Ironically, the restoration of intensive farmland to good wildlife habitat in the UK is, in some instances, funding the intensification of agriculture (and the loss of wildlife habitat) in eastern Europe, where land is cheap and potential profitability large.

83 The history of the cottage is described at www.wicken.org.uk/fen.htm.

84 By the 1990s, Cambridge had become the centre of what analysts dubbed "Silicon Fen", a high-tech engine of economic activity and employment, as well as housing London commuters.

85 See www.sustainablecity.net/Resourceconservation/Wildlife/greenbelt.htm.

86 See T.P. Moorhouse (1999) "The restoration of fen habitats on former arable land: a literature review" at www.wicken.org.uk/newpage15.htm.

87 See W.M. Adams (2003) "When nature won't stay still: conservation, equilibrium and control", pp.22–246 in W. Adams and M. Mulligan (eds) *Decolonising Nature: strategies for conservation in a post-colonial era*,

Earthscan, London. See also A.D. Bradshaw (2002) "Introduction and philosophy" pp.3–9 in M.R. Perrow and A.J. Day (eds) *Handbook of Ecological Restoration*, Cambridge University Press, Cambridge.

88   See Christopher Craft's review of W.M. Throup (2002) (ed.) *Environmental Restoration: ethics, theory, and practice*, Humanity Books, Amherst, New York, in C. Craft (2002) *Conservation Biology* 16: 733–734.

89   See, for example, O. Sterba, J. Mekotova, M. Krskova, P. Samsonova and D. Harper (1997) "Floodplain forests and river restoration", *Global Ecology and Biogeography Letters* 6: 331–337.

90   RSPB (1994) *The New Rivers and Wildlife Handbook*, Royal Society for the Protection of Birds, Sandy, Bedfordshire, second edition.

91   J. Purseglove (1988) *Taming the Flood*, Oxford University Press, Oxford; see also A. Brookes (1996) "River restoration experience in northern Europe", pp.233–267 in A. Brookes and F.D. Shields Jr. (eds) *River Channel Restoration: guiding principles for sustainable projects*, J. Wiley and Sons, Chichester.

92   S. Eden, S.M. Tunstall, and S.M. Tapsell (2000) "Translating nature: river restoration as nature — culture", *Environment and Planning D: Society and Space* 18: 257–273; N. Holmes (1997) "River rehabilitation in the UK", *Ecos: A Review of Conservation* 18(2):33–40.

93   F.M.R. Hughes and S. Rood (2001) "Floodplains", pp.105–201 in A. Warren and J.R. French (eds) *Habitat Conservation: Managing the Physical Environment*, J. Wiley and Sons, Chichester.

94   W.M. Adams (2003) "Nature and the colonial mind", pp.16–50 in W. Adams and M. Mulligan (eds) *Decolonising Nature: strategies for conservation in a post-colonial era*, Earthscan. London.

95   These arguments are developed in W.M. Adams (2003) "When nature won't stay still: conservation, equilibrium and control", pp.220–246 in W.M. Adams and M. Mulligan (eds) *Decolonising Nature: strategies for conservation in a post-colonial era*, Earthscan, London.

96   See, for example, Richard Cowell (1997) "Stretching the limits: environmental compensation, habitat creation and sustainable development", *Transactions of the Institute of British Geographers* 22(3): 292–306.

97   J. Cairns Jr. (2002) "Rationale for restoration", pp.10–23 in M.R. Perrow and A.J. Day (eds) *Handbook of Ecological Restoration*, Cambridge University Press, Cambridge.

98   For those who like white elephant-watching, BBC Wales has installed a webcam on the National Assembly Building that shows the lake retained by the Cardiff Bay Barrage, 24 hours a day, at www.bbc.co.uk/wales/programmes/webcam.shtml. The barrage is described at www.data-wales.co.uk/baybarr.htm. The Gwent Levels Wetland Nature Reserve (439ha) is owned by the Countryside Council for Wales (CCW); see www.gwentbirds.org.uk/GLWR.htm.

99   The exchange was made the more odd because what was lost was feeding habitat for wintering waders, particularly a globally significant numbers of dunlin, while what was created was breeding habitat, particularly for ducks and one day, perhaps, bittern — interesting, but no substitute.

100   J. Cairns Jr. (2002) "Rationale for restoration", pp.10–23 in M.R. Perrow and A.J. Day (eds) *Handbook of Ecological Restoration*, Cambridge University Press, Cambridge (p.16).

101   The Society for Ecological Restoration was founded in 1988 (www.ser.org). *Ecological Restoration* was founded in 1981 and *Restoration Ecology* in 1993. It held its first meeting outside the USA in Liverpool in Autumn 2001.

102   J. Cairns Jr. (2002) "Rationale for restoration", pp.10–23 in M.R. Perrow and A.J. Day (eds) *Handbook of Ecological Restoration*, Cambridge University Press, Cambridge (p.16).

103   See, for example, R. Elliot (1997) *Faking Nature: the ethics of environmental restoration*, Routledge, London; and S. Eden, S.M. Tunstall and S.M. Tapsell (2000) "Translating nature: river restoration as nature—culture", *Environment and Planning D: Society and Space* 18: 257–273.

104   I have been much influenced by Bruno Latour's ideas about "hybrid objects", and am borrowing something of this idea at a simplistic level here because it seems to me to capture so well the dilemma of "nature" conservation in the UK. See B. Latour (1993) *We Have Never Been Modern*, Harvard University Press, Cambridge, Massachusetts.

105   See www.nationalforest.org.

106   See www.wwt.org.uk/visit/wetlandcentre.

107   See www.landlife.org.uk.

108   For the case for defence and prosecution, see T. Lawson (1996) "Brent Duck", *Ecos* 17(2): 27, and B. Hughes and G. Williams (1997) "What future for the white-headed duck?", *Ecos* 18(2): 15–26. See also K. Milton (2002) *Loving Nature: towards an ecology of emotion*, Routledge, London.

109   See, for example, A. Prowse (1997) "Himalayan balsam — problem or prejudice?", *Ecos* 18(2): 41–43; or P. Smith and J. Briggs (1999) "Zander — the hidden invader", *British Wildlife* 11(1): 2–8. The history of re-introductions is described by P. Marren (2001) *Nature Conservation: a review of the conservation of wildlife in Britain 1950–2001*, HarperCollins, London.

110   Plantlife (2000) *At War With Aliens*, Plantlife, London.

111   R. Mabey (1998) *Flora Britannica*, Chatto and Windus, London; C.D. Preston, D.A. Pearman and T.D. Dines (eds) (2002) *New Atlas of the British and Irish Flora*, Oxford University Press, Oxford.

112   D.A. Pearman, C.D. Preston and T.D. Dines (2002) "*New Atlas of the British and Irish Flora*", *British Wildlife* 14(1): 31–37.

113   Once cleared of scrub, 150 ha of the existing fen will be grazed by konig horses, perhaps similar to ancient tarpans; see www.wicken.org.uk/konig.htm.

114   These introductions and escapes are all discussed in *Ecos* 23(2), 2002. On beavers, see P. Taylor (pp.23–26); on lynx, see D. Bamping and M. Fraser (pp.9–13). On large cats, see P. Taylor in *Ecos* 23(2): 56–64. The re-introduction of wolves is discussed by R. Panaman in *Ecos* 23(2): 2–8 (and see www.wolftrust.org.uk).

115   N. Ajax-Lewis (2002) "Reintroductions: closing the stable door after the horse has bolted?", *Natur Cymru* 4: 4–7. P. Marren (2002) "Introductions: are we conserving species at the expense of nature?", *British Wildlife* 14(2): 77–82.

116 P. Green (2002) "Riparian alien plants: towards ecological acceptance?", *Ecos* 23(2): 34–42.

117 P. Taylor (2002) "Big Cats in Britain", *Ecos* 23(2): 56–64.

118 See www.ipcc.ch.

119 Canada ratified the Protocol in December 2002. The initiative was not entirely popular, notably in oil-rich Alberta; see www.planetark.org/dailynewsstory.cfm/newsid/17612/newsDate/5-Sep-2002/story.htm.

120 Climate change and impacts in Europe are reviewed by the EU Acacia Project; see M. Parry (2000) (ed.) *Assessment of Potential Effects and Adaptations for Climate Change in Europe*, Report of a Concerted Action of the Environment Programme of the Research Directorate-General of the Commission of the European Communities, University of East Anglia, Norwich.

121 Research on climate change in Europe is reviewed by the EU Acacia Project; see M. Parry (2000) (ed.) *Assessment of Potential Effects and Adaptations for Climate Change in Europe: Summary and Conclusions*, University of East Anglia, Norwich.

122 See www.dow.wau.nl/msa.

123 See, for example, J.F. Burton and T.H. Sparks (2002) "Flying earlier in the year: the phenological response of butterflies and moths to climate change", *British Wildlife* 13(5): 305–311.

124 See www.woodland-trust.org.uk/phenology/newsletter.htm. The initiative is linked to the European Phenology Network; see www.dow.wau.nl/msa.

125 See L. Hannah, G.F. Midgley and D. Millar (2002) "Climate change-integrated conservation strategies", *Global Ecology and Biogeography* 11: 485–495. For information on climate change research, see, for example, the work of the ESRC/NERC/EPSRC-funded Tyndall Centre at the University of East Anglia, www.tyndall.ac.uk.

126 P.M. Berry, T.P. Dawson, P.A. Harrison and R.G. Pearson (2002) "Modelling potential impacts of climate change on the bioclimatic envelope of species in Britain and Ireland", *Global Ecology and Biodiversity* 11: 453–462 (p.459).

127 J.E. Hossell, B. Briggs and I.R. Hepburn (2000) *Climate Change and Nature Conservation: a review of the impact of climate change on UK species and habitat conservation policy*, HMSO for Department for Environment, Transport and the Regions and the Ministry of Agriculture, Fisheries and Food, London.

128 See M. Lee (2001) "Coastal defence and the Habitats Directive: predictions of habitat change in England and Wales", *The Geographical Journal* 167: 39–56.

129 *Planning Policy Guidance Note 25: Development And Flood Risk*, 17 July 2001; see www.planning.odpm.gov.uk/ppg25/index.htm.

130 Not only water but air can be thought of in a catchment context: the impacts of upstream air pollution for conservation can be considerable (Rob Jarman, personal communication).

131 See, for example, J. Harvey (2001) "The role of large areas in nature conservation", *Ecos* 22(1): 13–18.

132 See W.M. Adams (1986) *Nature's Place: conservation sites and countryside change*, Allen and Unwin, London. Martin Holdgate drew my attention to this heritage in the context of climate change.

133 See Chapter 10, p.163.

134 See P. Marren (2002) "Introductions: are we conserving species at the expense of nature?", *British Wildlife* 14(2): 77–82.

135 K. Milton (2002) *Loving Nature: towards an ecology of emotion*, Routledge, London (quote p.51).

136 Cambourne was one of several new settlements proposed in Cambridgeshire during the 1980s, and the political momentum made the development of one, at least, inevitable. Cambourne was the only proposal that took conservation seriously. The Wildlife Trust (whose Conservation Committee I chaired) took the decision to work with the developers to protect and create habitat within the site.

137 W.M. Adams (1998) "Landforms, authenticity and conservation value", *Area* 30: 168–169. On the conservation implications of the income from the Landfill Tax, see T. Lawson (1997) "Lessons from the landfill tax", *Ecos* 18(3/4): 48–52.

138 J. McDaniel (2002) "Spirituality and sustainability", *Conservation Biology* 16: 1461–1464 (p.1462).

139 For whales, see www.physics.helsinki.fi/whale/europe/uk/uk.html.

140 C. Frazier (1997) *Cold Mountain*, Hodder and Stoughton, London (p.234).

141 Ian Christie (2002) "Sustainability and spiritual renewal: the challenge of creating a politics of reverence", *Conservation Biology*, 16:1466–1468.

142 And its photography is simply astonishing, as in the BBCs 1992/1993 series "Life of Mammals"; see D. Attenborough (2002) *The Life of Mammals*, BBC Books, London. On TV wildlife, see, for example, D. Ratcliffe (2000) "Image and reality: more reflections on TV natural history", *Ecos* 21(1): 80.

143 A. Balmford, L. Clegg, T. Coulson and J. Taylor (2002) "Why conservationists should heed Pokémon", *Science* 295: 2367.

144 S. Tapsell, S. Tunstall, M. House, J. Whomsley and P. Macnaghten (2001) "Growing up with rivers? Rivers in London children's worlds", *Transactions of the Institute of British Geographers NS* 33: 177–189.

145 M. Mulligan (2003) "Feet to the ground in storied landscapes: disrupting the poetic legacy with a poetic politics", pp.268–289 in W.M. Adams and M. Mulligan (eds) *Decolonising Nature: strategies for conservation in a post-colonial era*, Earthscan, London (quote p.285).

146 K. Milton (2002) *Loving Nature: towards an ecology of emotion*, Routledge, London.

147 S. Barker, D. Slingsby and S. Tilling (2002) *Teaching Biology in the Classroom: is it heading for extinction? A Report on Biology in the 14–19 Curriculum*, Field Studies Council and British Ecological Society, Shrewsbury.

148 For the conventional, try the RSPB's Wildlife Explorers and Phoenix (www.rspb.org.uk/youth/membership/); for the unconventional, try the Fairyland Trust (www.fairylandtrust.org).

149   J. Cameron (2003) "Responding to place in a post-colonial era", pp.172–196 in W.M. Adams and M. Mulligan (eds) *Decolonising Nature: strategies for conservation in a post-colonial era*, Earthscan, London (quotes pp.192, 193).

150   J. Gittins (2002) "Local Countryside Surveys — a route to learning caring and campaigning", *Ecos* 23(3/4): 19–24.

151   K. Milton (2002) *Loving Nature: towards an ecology of emotion*, Routledge, London (quote p.58).

152   And am lucky today, given the cuckoo's 33 per cent decline nationally between 1970 and 1999; see Royal Society for the Protection of Birds, Joint Nature Conservation Committee, Wildlife and Wetlands Trust and British Trust for Ornithology (2001) *The State of the UK's Birds*, RSPB, Sandy, Bedfordshire.

153   The classic source on this is C. Wernham, M. Toms, J. Marchant, J. Clark, G. Siriwardena and S. Baillie (BTO) (eds) (2002) *The Migration Atlas: Movements of the Birds of Britain and Ireland*, Poyser, London.

154   Referred to in Chapter 7.

155   The classic paper on human appropriation of terrestrial productivity is P.M. Vitousek, P.R. Ehrlich, A.H. Ehrlich and P.A. Matson (1986) "Human appropriation of the products of photosynthesis", *BioScience* 36: 368–373. Global impacts on biodiversity are analysed by B. Groombridge and M. Jenkins (2000) *Global Biodiversity: earth's living resources in the 21st Century*, World Conservation Press, Cambridge. Bill McKibben (1990) in *The End of Nature*, Penguin Books, Harmondsworth, argued that nature was dead.

Further Reading

Chapter One 　*Finding Nature*

Goldsmith, F.B. and Warren, A. (eds) (1993) *Conservation in Progress*, Wiley, Chichester.

Mabey, R. (1980) *The Common Ground: a place for nature in Britain's future*, Hutchinson, London, with the Nature Conservancy Council.

Moore, N. (1987) *The Bird of Time: the science and politics of nature conservation*, Cambridge University Press, Cambridge.

Tansley, A.G. (1945) *Our Heritage of Wild Nature*, Cambridge University Press, Cambridge.

Wilson, E.O. (1992) *The Diversity of Life*, Penguin Books, Harmondsworth (first published Belknap Press, Harvard University Press, 1992).

Chapter Two 　*Constructing Conservation*

Cullingworth, J.B. and Nadin, V. (1994) *Town and Country Planning in Britain: eleventh edition*, Routledge, London.

Evans, D. (1992) *A History of Nature Conservation in Great Britain*, Routledge, London.

MacEwen, A. and MacEwen, M. (1982) *National Parks: conservation or cosmetics?* Allen and Unwin, Hemel Hempstead.

Nicholson, M. (1970) *The Environmental Revolution: a guide to the new masters of the world*, Hodder and Stoughton, London.

Sheail, J. (1976) *Nature in Trust: the history of nature conservation in Britain*, Blackie, Glasgow.

Sheail, J. (1981) *Rural Conservation in Inter-war Britain*, Oxford University Press Oxford.

Chapter Three 　*Nature Lost*

Adams, W.M. (1986) *Nature's Place: conservation sites and countryside change*, Allen and Unwin, Hemel Hempstead.

Barr, C.J., Bunce, R.G.H., Clark, R.T., Fuller, R.M., Furst, M.T., Gillespie, M.K., Groom, G.B., Hallam, C.J., Hornung, M., Howard, D.C., and Ness, M.J. (1993) *Countryside Survey 1990: main report*, HMSO, London.

Bayliss-Smith, T.P. and Owens, S.E. (eds) (1990) *Britain's Changing Environment from the Air*, Cambridge University Press, Cambridge.

MacEwan, A. and MacEwen, M. (1982) *National Parks: conservation or cosmetics?* Allen and Unwin, Hemel Hempstead.

Shoard, M. (1980) *The Theft of the Countryside*, Temple Smith, London.

Wynne, G., Avery, M., Campbell, L., Gubbay, S., Hawkswell, S., Juniper, T., King, M., Newbury, P., Smart, J., Steel, C., Stones, A., Stubbs, T., Taylor, J., Tydeman, C. and Wynde, R. (1995) *Biodiversity Challenge: an agenda for conservation in the UK, Second Edition*, published by Butterfly Conservation, Friends of the Earth, Plantlife, The Wildlife Trusts Partnership, the Royal Society for the Protection of Birds and the World Wide Fund for Nature, Sandy.

Chapter Four   Conservation and the Global Village

Beck, U. (1986) *Risk Society: towards a new modernity*, Sage Publications, London.

Bowers, J. and Cheshire, P. (1983) *Agriculture, the countryside and land use: an economic critique*, Methuen, London.

Fairbrother, N. (1970) *New Lives, New Landscapes*, The Architectural Press, London (Penguin Books 1972).

Goodman, D. and Redclift, M. (1991) in *Refashioning Nature: food, ecology and culture*, Routledge, London.

Harvey, D. (1990) *The Condition of Postmodernity: an enquiry into the origins of cultural change*, Blackwell, Oxford.

Lash, S. and Urry, J. (1994) *Economies of Signs and Space*, Sage, London.

Marsden, T., Murdoch, J., Lowe, P., Munton, R. and Flynn, A. (1993) *Constructing the Countryside*, UCL Press, London.

Newby, H. (1980) *Green and Pleasant Land? social change in rural England*, Penguin Books, Harmondsworth.

Potter, C., Burnham, P., Edwards, A., Gasson, R. and Green, B. (1991) *The Diversion of Land: conservation in a period of farming constraction*, Routledge, London.

Wilson, A. (1992) *The Culture of Nature: North American landscape from Disney to Exxon Valdez*, Blackwell, Oxford.

Chapter Five   Culture and the Countryside

Bunce, M. (1994) *The Countryside Ideal: Anglo-American Images of Landscape*, Routledge, London.

Daniels, S. and Cosgrove, D. (eds) *The Iconography of Landscape*, Cambridge University Press, Cambridge.

Short, J.R. (1991) *Imagined Country: society, culture and environment*, Routledge, London.

Veldman, M. (1993) *Fantasy, the Bomb and the Greening of Britain: Romantic protest, 1945–1980*, Cambridge University Press, Cambridge.

Weiner, M.J. (1981) *English Culture and the Decline of the Industrial Spirit, 1850–1980*, Cambridge University Press, Cambridge.

Williams, R. (1993) *The Country and the City*, Hogarth Press, London (1st edition Chatto and Windus, 1953).

Chapter Six   Making Nature

Delcourt, H. and Delcourt, P. (1991) *Quaternary Ecology: a palaeoecological perspective*, Chapman and Hall, London.

Evernden, N. (1992) *The Social Creation of Nature*, Johns Hopkins University Press, Baltimore.

Haraway, D.J. (1991) *Simians, Cyborgs and Women: the reinvention of nature*, Free Association Books, London.

Huston, M.A. (1994) *Biological Diversity: the coexistence of species on changing landscapes*, Cambridge University Press, Cambridge.

McIntosh, R.P. (1985) *The Background of Ecology: concept and theory*, Cambridge University Press, London.

Peterken, G.F. (1981) *Woodland Conservation and Management*, Chapman and Hall, London.

Pickett, S.T.A. and White, P.S. (1985) *The Ecology of Natural Disturbance and Patch Dynamics*, Academic Press, New York.

Rackham, O. (1975) *Hayley Wood: its history and ecology*, Cambridge and Isle of Ely Naturalist's Trust, Cambridge.

Rackham, O. (1976) *Trees and Woodlands in the British Landscape*, Dent, London.

Rackham, O. (1986) *The History of the Countryside*, Dent, London.

Soulé, M. and Lease, G. (eds) *Reinventing Nature: responses to postmodern deconstruction*, Island Press, Washington D.C..

Vincent, P. (1990) *The Biogeography of the British Isles: an introduction*, Routledge, London.

Chapter Seven   Nature and the Wild

Evernden, N. (1992) *The Social Creation of Nature*, Johns Hopkins University Press, Baltimore.

Fowles, F. (1979) *The Tree*, The Sumach Press, St Albans.

Kellert, S.R. and Wilson, E.O. (eds.) (1993) *The Biophilia Hypothesis*, Island Press, Washington D.C..

Mabey, R. (1980) *The Common Ground: a place for nature in Britain's future*, Hutchinson, London, with the Nature Conservancy Council.

McHarg, I. (1969) *Design with Nature*, Natural History Press, Garden City, NY.

McKibben, B. (1990) *The End of Nature*, Penguin Books, Harmondsworth.

Robert E. Goodin (1992) *Green Political Theory*, Polity Press, Oxford.

Nicholson-Lord, D. (1987) *The Greening of the Cities*, Routledge and Kegan Paul.

Norton, B.C. (1991) *Towards Unity Among Environmentalists*, Oxford University Press.

Oeschlager, M. (1991) *The Idea of Wilderness*, Yale University Press, New Haven.

Rolston, H. III (1988) *Environmental Ethics*, Temple, Philadelphia.

Sessions, G. (ed.) (1995) *Deep Ecology for the 21st Century*, Shambhala, Boston and London.

Chapter Eight   The Conservation Landscape

Buckley, G.P. (ed.) (1989) *Biological Habitat Reconstruction*, Belhaven, London.

DiSilvestro, R.L. (1993) *Reclaiming the Last Wild Places: a new agenda for biodiversity*, Wiley, New York.

Forman, R.T.T. and Godron, M. (1986) *Landscape Ecology*, Wiley, Chichester.

IUCN Commission on National Parks and Protected Areas (1994) *Parks for Life: Action for Protected Areas in Europe*, IUCN, Gland, Switzerland.

Love, J.A. (1983) *The Return of the Sea Eagle*, Cambridge University Press, Cambridge.

Potter, C., Burnham, P., Edwards, A., Gasson, R. and Green, B. (1991) *The Diversion of Land: conservation in a period of farming contraction*, Routledge, London.

Spellerberg, I.F., Goldsmith, F.B. and Morris, M.G. (eds) (1991) *The Scientific Management of Temperate Communities for Conservation*, Blackwell, Oxford.

Western, D. and Pratt, M. (eds) (1989) *Conservation for the Twenty-first Century*, Oxford University Press, Oxford.

Whitby, M. (ed) (1994) *Incentives for Countryside Management: the case of ESAs*, CAB International, Wallingford.

Chapter Nine   Nature, Landscapes, Lives

Berry, W. (1977) *The Unsettling of America: culture and agriculture*, Sierra Club, San Francisco.

Dillard, A. (1976) *Pilgrim at Tinker Creek*, Picador, London (first published 1974).

IUCN Commission on National Parks and Protected Areas (1994) *Parks for Life: action for protected areas in Europe*, IUCN, Gland, Switzerland.

Jacobs, M. (1993) *Sense and Sustainability: land use planning and environmentally sustainable development*, Council for the Protection of Rural England, London.

King, A. and Clifford, S. (1985) *Holding Your Ground: an action guide to local conservation*, Maurice Temple Smith, London.

Leopold, A. (1949) *A Sand County Almanac and Sketches Here and There*, Oxford University Press, New York.

McHarg, I. (1969) *Design with Nature*, Natural History Press, Garden City, NY.

Sale, K. (1985) *Dwellers in the Land: the bioregional vision*, Sierra Club, San Francisco.

Timberlake, L. (1993) *Facing the Future: beyond the Earth Summit*, Earthscan/ International Institute for Environment and Development, London.

Western D. and Pratt, M. (eds) (1989) *Conservation for the Twenty-first Century*, Oxford University Press, Oxford.

Boon, P.J., Calow, P. and Petts, G.E. (eds) (1989) *River Conservation and Management,* Wiley, Chichester.

Evernden, N. (1992) *The Social Creation of Nature,* Johns Hopkins University Press, Baltimore.

Feidler, P.L. and Jain, S.K. (eds) (1992) *Conservation Biology: the theory and practice of nature conservation, preservation and management,* Chapman and Hall, London.

Leopold, A. (1949) *A Sand County Almanac,* Oxford University Press, New York.

List of Abbreviations

AONB	Area of Outstanding Natural Beauty
ASI	Area of Scientific Interest
ASSI	Area of Special Scientific Interest
BANC	British Association of Nature Conservationists
BAP	Biodiversity Action Plan
BSE	bovine spongiform encephalopathy
BFSS	British Field Sports Society
CAP	Common Agricultural Policy
CCW	Countryside Council for Wales
CJD	Creutzfeld-Jacob Disease
CPRE	Council for the Protection/Preservation of Rural England
CROW	Countryside and Rights of Way Act
DEFRA	Department of Food, the Environment and Rural Affairs
DoE	Department of the Environment
DoT	Department of Transport
DTI	Department of Trade and Industry
EC	European Commission
ESA	Environmentally Sensitive Area
EU	European Union
FoE	Friends of the Earth
GM	genetically-modified
HAP	Habitat Action Plan
ITE	Institute of Terrestrial Ecology
IPCC	Intergovernmental Panel on Climate Change
IUCN	International Union for the Conservation of Nature and Natural Resources
JNCC	Joint Nature Conservation Committee
LBAP	local biodiversity action plan
MAFF	Ministry of Agriculture, Fisheries and Food

MNR	Marine Nature Reserve
MPA	Marine Protected Area
NERC	Natural Environment Research Council
NCC	Nature Conservancy Council
NCO	Nature Conservation Order
NCR	Nature Conservation Review
NGO	non-governmental organisation
NNR	National Nature Reserve
RSNC	Royal Society for Nature Conservation
RSPB	Royal Society for the Protection of Birds
SNH	Scottish Natural Heritage
SAC	Special Area for Conservation
SAP	Species Action Plan
SPA	Special Protection Area
SPNR	Society for the Promotion of Nature Reserves
SSSI	Site of Special Scientific Interest
TLIO	The Land is Ours
UK	United Kingdom of Great Britain and Northern Ireland
UNEP	United Nations Environment Programme
UNESCO	United Nations Educational, Scientific and Cultural Organisation
WCS	World Conservation Strategy
WTO	World Trade Organisation
WWF	World Wide Fund for Nature

Index

A Better Quality of Life 179
A Park System for Scotland 19
A Sand County Almanac 154
aboriginal peoples and conservation 102, 104, 154
Abruzzo National Park 141, 160
access to the countryside 14, 18, 143, 175
acidification 35, 39
action plans for conservation 48–9, 50
Addison Committee 15
Adventurer's Fen 194
Africa 13, 73, 106, 138, 176
Agenda 21 xiv, 152
agri-food industry 57–9
agriculture
    support 32, 44, 57–9, 83, 132, 135, 147–8
    surplus 132
Agriculture Act 1947 57
Agriculture Act 1985
agriculture and socio-economic change 32, 57–9
Akroyd, John 128
Alexander, Donald 155
alien species 187, 199–200
Alps 84, 160
Amenity Lands (Northern Ireland) Act 1965 22
Ancient Woodland 33, 85–7, 107, 172
Antoinette, Marie 70
Antrim 132
Areas of Outstanding Natural Beauty (AONBs), England and Wales xiii, 6, 18, 78, 117, 139, 142, 148

Areas of Outstanding Natural Beauty (AONBs), Northern Ireland 20
Areas of Scientific Interest (ASIs) 22
Areas of Special Scientific Interest (ASSIs) 22, 39, 40, 44
art, environmental 112–3
Arvill, Robert 65
Association for the Protection of Rural Scotland 15
Attenborough, David 65
Australia 13, 120

Baines, Chris 125
Baldock, David 146
Bangor 139
beaches 1–4
bears, brown 141, 160
Bedford, Earl of xi, 175
Bedfordshire 61, 85, 128
Beinne Eighe 20
Belgium 35
Berg, Peter 155
Berry, Wendell 154
Bilsborough, Simon 108
Biodiversity Challenge 30, 47–50
biodiversity xiv, 30–1, 35, 47–50, 121, 167, 179, 181–186, 194–4, 199, 201, 209
Biodiversity Action Plans ix, xiv, 179–80, 200, 201, 204
Biodiversity Strategy for England 186, 193
Biodiversity: the UK Action Plan 30, 47–9, 100, 106, 152
Biogeographic Areas (Scottish

267

Natural Heritage) 122, 168
biogeography, theory 118–9
Biological Service 17
biomanipulation 168
bioregionalism 153–7
Biosphere Reserves 6, 115, 138
biotechnology 58, 103
Birds Directive (European Community
   Directive on the Conservation of
   Wild Birds) 6, 43–4
Black Mountains 73
Blakeney Point 2, 5, 11, 164
Blueprint for a Green Economy 106
Bonington, Chris 154
Borneo 54
bovine spongiform encephalopathy ix,
   182
British Ecological Society 16, 17, 90
Broads Grazing Marsh Conservation
   Scheme 132
Brown, Robert 40
BSE see bovine spongiform
   encephalopathy
buffer zones 123, 134, 138, 164
Bunce, Michael 71
Bunting, William 28
Burgess, Jacquelin 66–7

Cairns, John 197, 198
Cairngorms 19, 82–3, 107, 181
Caithness 22, 28, 83, 139
Caledonian pine forest x, 82–3, 161,
   162
Cambridge xi, 69, 128, 174, 191, 195
Cambridge and Isle of Ely Naturalists
   Trust 24, 85
Cambridgeshire 24, 61, 73, 85–6, 119
Cambridgeshire Fens x, 193, 204
Cameron, John 207
Canada 13, 155
Cape Cornwall 71
Cape Wrath 71
Cardiff 139
Caring for the Earth 151–2
Carmel Woods 39
cars 4, 53, 55, 57, 60, 63, 64, 69, 71,
   111, 150
Carson, Rachel 108
Catchment Management Plans 149

Caufield, Catherine 28
Chernobyl 95–6
Chippenham Fen xii
children 3,4, 53, 78, 110, 111, 112,
   113, 171
Chilterns 128
Christie, Ian 206
Cider With Rosie 71
CJD see Creutzfeld-Jakob Disease
Clare, John 101
Clark, Julian 146
Clements, F.E. 87
Cley Marshes 11, 167
climatic change x, xiv, 35–7, 93, 152,
   177, 201–4
Coastal Zone Management Plans 167
coasts and coastal conservation 1–6,
   12, 36, 45–6, 75, 143–5, 164,
   165, 167
Coed Eryri 161
Colston, Adrian 194, 200
Common Agricultural Policy xiv, 58–9,
   132, 135–6, 149, 184–5, 187
Common Ground 156
Commons Preservation Society 14
computers 53, 55
Conservation Biology 116
Conservation for the Twenty-First
   Century 116, 153
Conservation of Wild Creatures and
   Wild Plants Act 1975 21
Conservation Service (Northern
   Ireland) 22
conservation and development
   137–143
Conservative government 22
consumption and consumerism 52–5,
   64–5, 150
CORINE 124
corncrake 146–7
Cornwall 179, 201
corridors, ecological 120, 123, 164
Cosgrove, Denis 72
Cotswolds 71, 75
Council for Nature 24
Council for the Preservation of Rural
   Wales 14
Council for the Protection of Rural
   England (formerly Council for

the Preservation of Rural
England) 14, 24, 25, 74, 152
counter-urbanisation 71, 76
Country Landowners Association 64
Countryside Act 1968 18, 32, 38
Countryside Agency 177, 186, 189,
191, 192
Countryside Alliance x, 187–9, 193
Countryside Character Programme
(Countryside Commisssion)
122–3, 168
Countryside Commission 18–19, 22,
23, 62, 78, 117, 122, 132–3,
149, 160, 168, 177
Countryside Commisssion for
Scotland 19
Countryside Council for Wales 21, 22,
38, 62, 134, 139, 177, 185, 186
Countryside and Rights of Way Act
2000 186
Countryside in 1970 Conferences 18,
32
Countryside Stewardship xiv, 19, 59,
133–4, 136, 149, 185, 186
Countryside Survey 1990 34
countryside, ideas and myths 72–8
Cow Green Reservoir 91–2
creative conservation 125–8
Creutzfeld-Jakob Disease 182
Crofting and the Environment 147
crofting and conservation 146–8
cross-compliance 59, 147
Culm Measures 133
cultural and social change in the UK
51–4, 172

Daniels, Stephen 72
Darenth Wood SSSI 127
Dasmann, Raymond 155
Deacon Hill SSSI 128
deep ecology 105
Denmark 166
Department for Trade and Industry 44
Department of the Environment,
England 34, 43, 48, 61, 152
Department of the Environment,
Northern Ireland 20, 23, 40
Department of Food, the Environment
and Rural Affairs 177, 184–5, 186

Department of Transport 44, 78, 126
Design with Nature 104–5, 108,
111–2
Devon 83, 129
Dillard, Annie 104, 155
Dinefwr 134
DiSilvestro, Roger 118, 121
diving and conservation 144
Dorset 33, 71, 125
Dower, John 15, 17, 19, 32, 142
Dower, Michael 62
Downton Gorge SSSI 80
Dutch Nature Policy Plan 123–4
Duxford 51
Dwellers in the Land 155

eagles, golden or sea 82, 94, 130
Earths Survival 148
East Anglia 3, 4, 117, 160, 174, 176,
191, 205
East Anglian Fens xi
Eat the View 189, 191
Ecological Parks Trust 125
ecological footprint 72
ecology, disturbance 88–9, 164, 165
ecology, equilibrial and non-equilibrial
89, 163, 164, 168
economies and conservation 137–142,
145–8, 160, 172
EECONET 123–4
Eigg x, 190
energy use 52–3
engineers 163, 165–6
England Rural Development
Programme 185, 188
English Heritage 78, 133, 192
English Nature 6, 21, 23, 29, 38, 41,
62, 78, 80, 107, 122, 129–30,
133, 143, 145, 149, 167, 168,
177, 189, 192, 194
Environment Act 1995 xiv
Environment Agency xiv, 192, 194
environmental economics 106–9
environmentalism 52, 65–7, 77
Environmentally Sensitive Areas xiii,
19, 59, 132–3, 135, 147, 149, 185
erosion 12, 36, 164165, 166, 167
Essex 72, 182, 185
Essex marshes x,

Essex woman 111
Etterick and Lauderdale District 153
EU Water Framework Directive 203
European Commission 184
European Community 184
eutrophication 29, 168
Evernden, Neil 99, 104, 105, 154, 159, 162
extensification of agriculture 132, 135
extinction 31, 37

Fair Isle 105, 208
Fairbrother Group 112
Fairbrother, Nan 57, 71–2, 112
Fantasy, the Bomb and the Greening of Britain 76
Farming and Wildlife Advisory Group (FWAG) 117
farming and wildlife 31–4, 117
Farne Islands 145
Fens, The xi, xii, 160, 174–6
Fenton, James 182
Fifth Environmental Action Plan (European Community) 152
Findhorn Foundation 161
fishing and conservation 45–6, 144, 168
Fisons Ltd 28
Fitsimmons, Margaret 95, 104
floods 105, 109, 165–6
Flow Country 22, 28, 139
Fontainbleau 70
food 57
Food Standards Agency 188
foot and mouth disease ix, 182, 183, 184, 186–7
footpaths 112
Ford, Henry 55
Fordism 55–6, 58, 64, 76–7
Forest Authority 129
Forest Enterprise 182, 200
Forestry Commision 15, 23, 62, 86, 161
Fowles, John 104
fragmentation of habitat 37, 117–125, 131, 137, 146
France 140–1, 160
Frazier, Charles 205
Friends of Cardigan Bay 145

Friends of the Earth 25, 28, 39, 42, 44, 60, 65–6, 135, 186
Fuller, Robin 29
'Future Care' xvii

Game Conservancy 129
genetic modification 179, 183, 184
Geological Conservation Review 21
Geological Monuments 21
geological conservation 21–22
geomorphological conservation 21–22, 164
Germany 166
glacial period 37, 87–8, 160
Glasgow 78, 111–2
global environmental change *see* climatic change
globalisation 55–7, 63, 65–7
Goode, David 33
Goodin, Robert 101, 103
Goodman, David 58
grassland conservation and loss 29, 117–8, 126–7, 172
Gray, Thomas 73
grazing 83–4
grazing marshes 132, 134
Great Fen Project 194
Great Wood of Caledon 162
great divide, the 23, 139
Green Political Theory 101, 103
greenhouse effect 35–6, 53
Greenpeace 25, 60, 184
Grey, Sir Edward 13
Groundwork Trusts 112
grouse 83
Grzimek, Bernard 65
Gwynedd 72

Johannesburg Summit *see* World Summit on Sustainable Development

Habitat Action Plans 179, 187
habitat creation or re-creation 125–8, 134, 160, 161–2, 174–6
habitat loss 27–30, 37–41
Habitats Directive (European Community Habitats and Species Directive) 6, 43–5, 48, 171, 178

hamburgers 56, 66
Hampshire 107, 129
Haraway, Donna 94–6
Harris 61
Harrison, Carolyn 66–7
Harvey, David 55, 56
Harwicke, Third Earl 70
Hatton, Carol 59
Hayley Wood xvi, 85–7
Hays, Samuel 77
headage payments 83, 135
headlands 120
heathland, conservation and loss 33,
    125, 127, 128
hedgehog, 110, 113
Hedgerow Incentive Scheme 136
Henderson, Norman 162
Heritage Coasts 6, 18, 115, 137, 148
heritage 63–4, 80
Hill Farming Directive, EC 124
Hobbs, Richard 120
Hobhouse Committee 16, 142
Hobhouse, Sir Arthur 16, 19, 142
Hobsbawm, Eric 77
Holland, Alan 69, 108
Holme Fen xii, 174
Hoskins, W.G. 74
house building 51
Hughes, Francine 29
Huxley Committee 204
see also Wild Life Conservation
    Special Committee
Huxley, Julian 17, 90, 93
hydro-electric power generation 113,
    142

Institute of Terrestrial Ecology 21, 36,
    119
international trade 55, 59
Islay 139
Italy 141
IUCN see World Conservation Union

Jefferies, Richard 104
Joint Nature Conservation Committee
    23, 41, 47
Kellert, Stephen 100
Kent 39
Kipling, Rudyard 75

kite, red 130
Knight, Richard Payne 80
Kohák, Erazim 104

Lake District 13, 64, 76, 95, 172,
    179, 201
Land Drainage Act 1930 165
land use change 32–4
landowners and conservation 21, 22,
    64
landscape change 32, 58
landscape ecology 89, 118–121, 149
landscape versus wildlife conservation
    22, 23 (see also great divide)
landscape, making of 72–3
Lankester, E.R. xii
large blue butterfly 36, 129, 131
Larsen, Svend Erik 81
Lee, Laurie 71
leisure 61–4, 69–70, 75
Leopold, Aldo 108, 121, 154
Lewis, C.S. 76
lifestyles 52
Liljelund, Lars-Erik 101
Lindisfarne 45, 139
local distinctiveness 72
Loch Lomond 19, 181
Loch Sween 46, 139, 178
London 4, 53, 71, 78, 109, 113
London Wildlife Trust 112
Lundy Island 46, 178

Mabey, Richard 100, 200
MacEwen, Ann and Malcolm 18
machair 146–7, 172
Magnussen, Magnus 80
Magog Trust 128
managed coastal retreat 167
management agreements on SSSIs 39,
    42
Manifesto for the Highlands 162
Mar Lodge Estate 19, 107
marine conservation 45–7
Marine Consultation Areas 145
Marine Nature Reserves 45–6, 139,
    143–4, 178
Marine Protected Areas 144
Marren, Peter 178, 180, 201, 204
Massingham, Hugh 75–6

271

May, Robert 89
McDaniel, Jay 205
McHarg, Ian 104–5, 108, 111–2, 137, 154
McIntosh, Robert 87
McKibben, Bill 102
McSharry proposals 135
Meirionydd 134
Merchant, Carolyn 103
merger of conservation agencies 22–3
Merseyside 112
migration, birds 2, 30, 105, 175–6
Milton, Kay xv, 72, 73, 204, 207
mineral extraction and conservation 39–40, 45, 61, 125, 142, 164
Ministry of Agriculture, Fisheries and Food xiii, 23, 58, 39, 131–2, 133, 134, 135, 149, 182, 184
Ministry of Town and Country Planning 12, 14, 17
Ministry of Works and Buildings 14
Minsmere 127, 128, 205
Monks Wood NNR 119
Moore, Norman xvi, 32, 33, 93, 99, 178
Moore, Peter, 88
Moray Firth 96, 145
Morecambe Bay 145
Motorways 78
Mountain Flowers 82
Muir, John 108
Mulligan, Martin 207
museums 51
myth 74–9

Naess, Arnie 105
National Audit Office 41, 143
National Farmers' Union 58, 64, 187
National Forest x, 110, 160, 199
National Forest Parks 14, 15
National Nature Reserves (NNRs) xiii, 6, 11, 13, 16–18, 20, 42, 90, 91, 115, 117, 121, 122, 130, 145, 174, 178, 194, 198
National Park Boards 139
National Parks 181
    economic activities 32, 62, 71, 139, 141–2
    establishment 6, 12, 14–16, 76,

117, 142
Northern Ireland 16, 20
outside UK 13, 141, 160
recreation 110
Scotland 15, 16, 19, 142
National Parks and Access to the Countryside Act 1949 6, 16, 18, 22, 90
National Parks Authority 14
National Parks Commission 6, 15–16, 17, 18
National Parks Committees 16, 142
National Parks Scotland Act 2000 181
National Rivers Authority 46, 149, 166, 168
National Scenic Areas 19
National Trust xii, 5, 14, 24, 25, 64, 69, 75, 156, 178, 180, 189, 194–6, 203
National Trust for Scotland 19, 24, 25, 181
National Vegetation Classification 122
national identity 73–4
Natural Areas (English Nature) 122–3, 168
Natural Environment Research Council 21
Natural Heritage (Scotland) Act 1991 153
Natural Heritage Areas (Scottish Natural Heritage) 20
natural capital 106–9
naturalness 3, 72, 81–87, 89
Nature Conservancy (NCC) 6, 18, 20–22, 33, 65, 90, 117, 164, 178
Nature Conservancy Council 20, 21–2, 38–9, 41, 84, 117, 132, 139, 174
Nature Conservation and Agriculture 117
Nature Conservation and Amenity lands Order (Northern Ireland) 1985, 40
Nature Conservation in Great Britain 33
Nature Conservation Order 42
Nature in Cambridgeshire 128
Nature Reserve Agreements 20

Nature Reserves Investigations
    Committee 20, 24
nature, cultural values of 99–103,
    113–4, 153–4, 170
nature, use values 106–9
Neighbours 71
Nelson, Richard 105, 154
Nene Washes 176
Netherlands 35, 123–4, 132
Nevard, Tim 160
New Agricultural Landscapes 32
New Forest 13
New Lives, New Landscapes 112
New Towns 112
New Zealand 13
Newbury Bypass xiv
Nicholson, Max 24, 65, 90, 91
Nicholson-Lord, David 112
Niger Delta 66
NIMBY 71
non-governmental organisations 5,
    23–5, 28, 78, 152
Norfolk 1, 4–6, 11, 12, 64, 106, 167
Norfolk Broads 19, 168
Norfolk Naturalists Trust 11
North America 154–5
North Wales 3
Northern Ireland 73
Norton, Bryan 108–9, 115
Norway 35, 83, 130, 161
nuclear power 76, 95

O'Riordan, Tim 148–9
orchards 133, 141, 156
organic food 183–5, 188–9
Orkney 146, 171
Osprey 130
Our Heritage of Wild Nature 16, 94
Ouse Washes xi, 174–6
Outer Isles, The 146–8
Ozark Area Community Congress
    155

Parcs Régionaux (France) 140–1
Parks for Life 124, 137–8
pastoral ideal 73–4, 77
Patmore, Allan 62
Peak District Integrated Rural
    Development Project 142–3

Pearce, David 106
peatland conservation and destruction
    22, 28–9, 43, 45
Pennines 91
pesticides *see* pollution
Peterken, George 29, 86, 87
Phillips, Hazel 59
picturesque movement 80
Pilgrim at Tinker Creek 155
Pinchot, Gifford 108
pizza 71
place, locality and distinctiveness 63,
    154–5, 156–7
Planet Drum Foundation 155
Planning Acts 13
planning and conservation 107
planning gain 126
Plantlife 35, 179, 200
Platform (arts group) 113
Plymouth Marine Laboratory 35
Policy Commission on the Future of
    Farming and Food 185
pollution 35, 39, 117, 120, 168
Porlock 203
postmodernism 56
Potter, Beatrix 64, 74, 110
Potter, Clive 59
Poundbury 193
Powys 129
Prince of Wales 193
protected areas 116–124, 137–143,
    173 (see also individual cate-
    gories)
Protection of Birds Act 1954 21
protest 77–9
Purseglove, Jeremy 196

Quality of Life Capital 192

Rackham, Oliver 85–7
rainforests 54, 66–7
Rainham Marshes 66–7
Ramblers Association 25
Ramsay Committees 15, 142, 181
Ramsay, Sir J. Douglas 15, 16
Ratcliffe, Derek 31, 35, 44, 109, 117
Rawles, Kate 69, 108
recreation and conservation 40,
    61–64

Red Data Books 31, 36
red deer 82–3
Redclift, Michael 58
Reforesting Scotland 161
Regional Parks (Scotland) 19
Regionally Important
    Geological/Geomorphological
    Sites (RIGS) 22
Reith, Lord 14
renotification of SSSIs 38–9
Research Methods in Ecology 87
Reserves Enhancement Scheme 42
restoration ecology 125–8, 165–8,
    193–9
Rio Conference xiv, 30, 151–2, 179
riparian ecosystems 165, 166
Ritchie, James 17
River Restoration Project 165–6, 197
Rivers
    Cherwell 166
    Cole 166, 197
    Dee 165
    Lyde (Hampshire) 166
    Skerne 166, 197
Rivers and Wildlife Handbook 165
rivers and conservation 41, 165–7, 169
roads and protest 77–9
roads and road transport 60–1, 78–9
    (*see also* cars)
Robertson, James 180
rock climbing 85, 154
romanticism 76, 78
Roosevelt, Theodore 13
Rose, Chris 192–3
Rothschild, Charles xii, 196
Rowell, Terry 40–1
Royal Geographical Society 47
Royal Society for Nature
    Conservation 24, 28
Royal Society for the Protection of
    Birds 5, 16, 24–5, 44, 127, 128,
    135, 146, 150, 167, 175, 180,
    192, 205
RSPB *see* Royal Society for the
    Protection of Birds
Rum 130, 182
Rural Action 156
Rural Development Commisssion 62,
    156, 177

Rural Enterprise Scheme 188

Sale, Kirkpatrick 155
salt marsh 164, 167, 185, 203
sand dunes 163, 164, 203
satellite imagery 34
science
    and conservation 17, 90–3, 104
    and public life 17, 92–3, 94–6
    and landscape beauty 94
Scolt Head 2, 5, 6, 11, 12, 164
Scots Magazine 14
Scott, Lord Justice 15, 31–2
Scott, Peter 199
Scottish Council for National Parks
    15
Scottish Crofters Union 146
Scottish Environmental Protection
    Agency xiv
Scottish Forestry Charter 161
Scottish Green Party 162
Scottish Highlands 181, 200
Scottish Natural Heritage 19, 21, 22,
    38, 62, 80, 122, 145, 153, 177,
    182, 200
Scottish Office 22, 44
Scottish Wildlife and Countryside
    Link 150
sea level rise 36, 167
Seabirds Preservation Act 1869 30
Second World War xiii, 194
Secretary of State for the
    Environment 22, 23, 42, 47, 134
semi-natural vegetation 29, 34
Sessions, George 105
set-aside 59, 134, 135–6
Sharp, Thomas 62, 70
sheep 82–3, 95–6
Shetland 132, 146
Shoard, Marion 33, 77
shopping 52–7, 60
Short, John Rennie 71
Sites of Special Scientific Interest
    (SSSI) xiii, 5, 20–21, 28, 29, 35,
    37–43, 78, 115, 117, 121, 122,
    126, 148, 169–70, 178, 185,
    186, 198, 203
    loss and damage 39–41, 91–2
    selection 93–4

Skomer Island 46, 178
Snowdonia 84, 161–2
Snyder, Gary 155
Society for the Promotion of Nature Conservation 24
Society for the Promotion of Nature Reserves xii, 11, 24
socio-economic change 32, 51–4
soft engineering 167
South Downs Preservation Bill 13
Special Area for Conservation (SAC) xiii, 6, 43–5, 115, 143, 178, 198
Special Protection Areas (SPAs) xiii, 43–4, 115, 198
Species Action Plans 178, 179–80
Species Recovery Programme (English Nature) 129–30
species
   conservation 21, 30–31, 48
   introductions and reintroductions 31, 129–31, 160
Spray, Martin xiv, 113
SSSI see Site of Special Scientific Interest
Standing Committee on National Parks 15
Steers, Alfred 12, 21, 75, 164
Stockholm Conference 1972
storms 89, 105, 165
Strangford Lough 46, 144–5, 178
Suffolk 127, 128, 132
Sussex 75
sustainability xiv, xvi, xvii, 147, 150–3, 161, 190–1, 192–3, 205
Sustainable Development: the UK Strategy 152
sustainable forestry xiv, 150
Swansea 134
Sweden 35

Tansley, Arthur 16, 84, 90, 93, 94, 164, 198
Tassi, Franco141
Taylor, Peter 201
television 13, 53, 54, 56, 65, 71, 81, 110, 172
Thames 66–7
Thatcher, Margaret 19, 54, 63, 66, 106

The Biophilia Hypothesis 100
The British Isles and their Vegetation 84
The Common Ground 100
The Country and the City 71, 73
The Diversity of Life 106
The End of Nature 102
The Greening of the Cities 112
The Land is Ours 190
The Making of the English Landscape 74
The Mountain Areas of Scotland 19
The Theft of the Countryside 33, 77
The Tree 104
Thinking Worm 186
Third World 55, 56, 59, 138, 151, 172
This Common Inheritance 152
Thorne Moors 28
Through the Wilderness 75
Tiggywinkle, Mrs 110
time–space compression 56, 57
Tir Cymen xiv, 234–5, 160, 185
toilet seats 54
Tolkein, J.R.R. 76
Town and Country Planning Act 1947 16
town and country 70–1, 73–7
Trees for Life 161, 181
trees, felling 78–9
trees, planting 110–1, 125–6, 161
Twyford Down 78

Ulster Countryside Committee 22
Ulster Wildlife Trust 24
UNESCO 90, 138
urban conservation 109, 111–3
urbanism and urbanisation 71, 73, 71, 142
USA 13, 77, 87, 102, 108, 115, 142, 155, 159, 160, 163

vegetation 82–3
vegetation history and succession 87–8
Veldman, Meredith 76
Vermuyden, Cornelius xi, 174
Victorian England 73, 75
video 53, 110, 113

Wandle, River 113
Wash, The xi, 145, 160
Watch 24
water meadows 134
Watson, Adam 83, 161
weeds 29
Weiner, Martin 73, 74–5
Welney 175
Welsh Office 44
Western Isles 72
Western, David 116, 153
Wet Fens for the Future 160, 174
Wetlands Centre, London x, 199
Whitehall 15, 21, 59, 152
Whittlesea Mere 174
Wicken Fen xii, 131, 174–5, 194–5,
    200
Widdybank Fell SSSI 91–2
wider countryside 17–8
Wild Life Conservation Special
    Committees 12, 17, 20, 21, 90,
    93
wilderness 101–2, 112, 159, 162–3
Wildfowl and Wetlands Trust 175
Wildlands Project (USA) 159163
Wildlife and Countryside Act 1981
    xiii, 18, 21, 33, 37, 42, 46, 186
Wildlife Link 28, 42, 150
Wildlife Trusts 5, 11, 60–61, 85–6,
    128, 129, 156–7, 168, 175, 178,
    180, 189, 194
wildness 83, 102, 103, 105, 159–163,
    169–70, 173, 174–6
Wildwood 87
Wilkinson, Sir William 41, 42, 43
William Curtis Memorial Park 112,
    125

Williams, Raymond 71, 73, 77
Wilson, Alexander 64, 81
Wilson, Edward O. 47, 100, 106
Wilson, Harold 92
Wimpole Hall 69–70
Winchester 78
wolf 141, 160
Women's Institute 156
Woodland Grant Scheme 136, 185
Woodland Trust 180, 202
Woodwalton Fen xii, 174
Worcestershire 133, 156
Wordsworth 76
World Conservation Strategy 148–9,
    151
World Conservation Union 19, 116,
    124, 137–8, 151
World Heritage Sites 19, 115
World Parks Congress (Fourth,
    Caracas) 138
World Summit on Sustainable
    Development 201
World Trade Organisation 184
World Wide Fund for Nature (World
    Wildlife Fund) vii, 25, 131,
    143–4, 151, 152, 152, 194
Worster, Donald 88, 96, 103
WWF see World Wide Fund for
    Nature
Wynne, Bryan 95

Ynys Môn 132
Yorkshire 72, 112
Young Ornithologists Club 25

Zoest, Johan van 163, 164

AGRI-CULTURE
Reconnecting People, Land and Nature
Jules Pretty

'Filled with successful examples from around the world, Agri-Culture calls for a radical reform of the institutions and policies that control our food'
THE ECOLOGIST

'Refreshingly fluent narrative, brimming full of stories and metaphors.'
TIM O'RIORDAN, UNIVERSITY OF EAST ANGLIA, UK

'A great balance between storytelling and analysis which points to the critical need for gaining control over resources.'
JACQUELINE ASHBY, CIAT, COLOMBIA

'Full of supporting evidence and clear arguments.'
NORMAN UPHOFF, CORNELL UNIVERSITY, USA

'A wonderful manuscript, put together with such vision and passion.'
MARK RITCHIE, INSTITUTE OF AGRICULTURE AND TRADE POLICY, USA

'A superb volume. This is a valuable monograph that all policy makers, scholars and farmers must read to understand their roles and responsibilities.'
VO-TONG XUAN, ANGIANG UNIVERSITY, VIETNAM

'Written in a beautiful style. The implications of the book's ideas are deep and extensive.'
JULIA GUIVANT, UNIVERSITY OF FLORIANOPOLIS, BRAZIL

1-85383-925-6 • Paperback £14.95

To order
www.earthscan.co.uk
Earthscan Freepost • 120 Pentonville Road, London, N1 9BR
Fax +44 (0)1903 828 802 • Email orders@lbsltd.co.uk